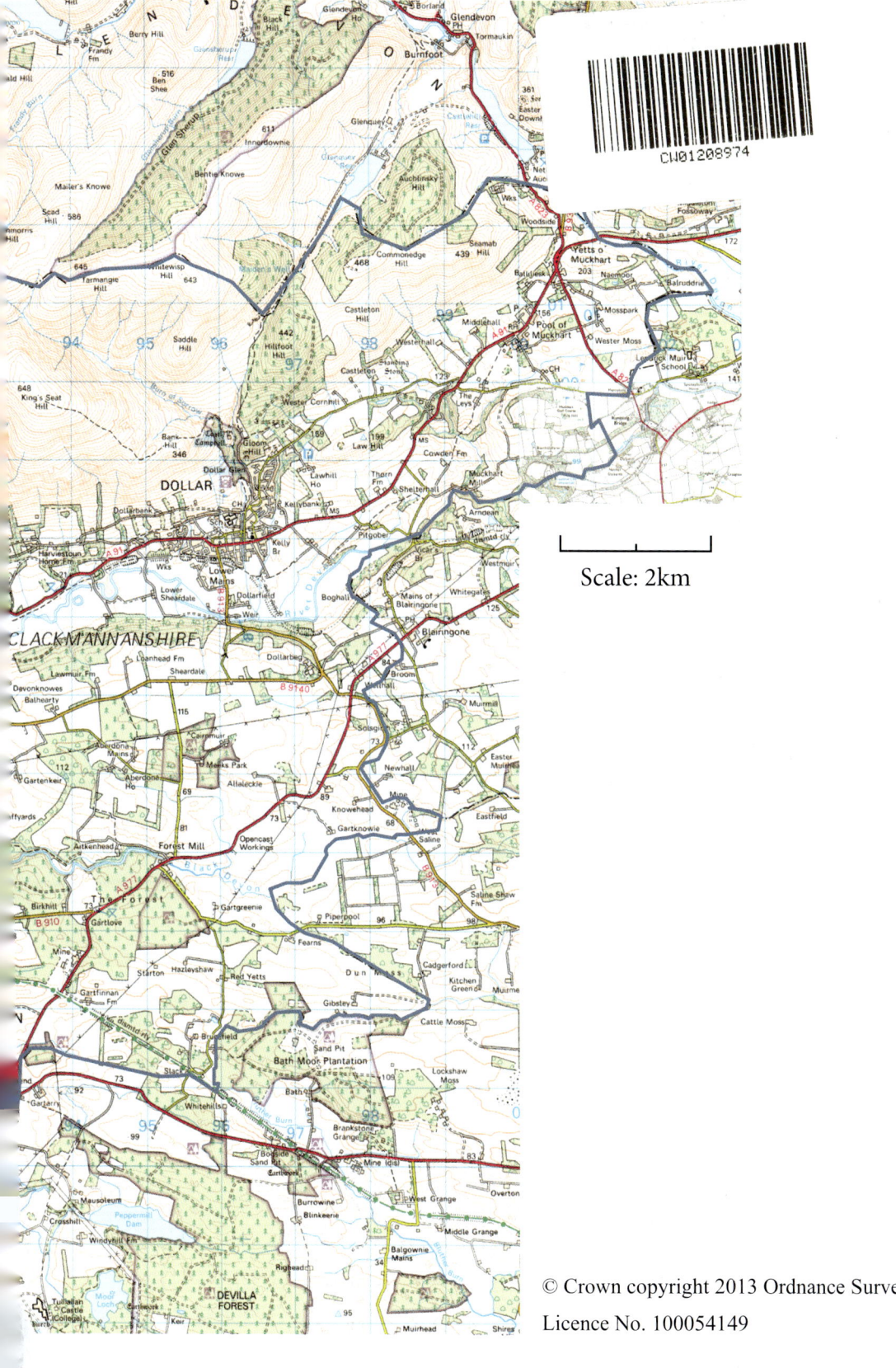
Scale: 2km

© Crown copyright 2013 Ordnance Survey
Licence No. 100054149

The Birds of Clackmannanshire

Neil Bielby, Keith Broomfield
and John Grainger

Published by the Scottish Ornithologists' Club

© 2013 Neil Bielby, Keith Broomfield and John Grainger

All rights reserved. No part of this book may be reproduced, stored in a retrieval system, or transmitted in any form or by any means, electronic, mechanical, photocopying or otherwise without permission of the publisher. However, no reasonable request will be refused (contact n.bielby@sky.com, or keith@catchpr.co.uk).

Designed by Hype Design, Dunfermline.

Printed by Catch PR Ltd.

Published by the Scottish Ornithologists' Club.

First published 2013.

The publication should be cited as Bielby, N., Broomfield, K. and Grainger, G., 2013. The Birds of Clackmannanshire.

ISBN 978-0-9926927-0-4

Any profits from the sale of this book will be held in a specific fund by the Scottish Ornithologists' Club and will be used for future local ornithological projects.

Cover illustration by Darren Rees.

Contents

Foreword
Preface 1
Abbreviations and frequently used references 2
Acknowledgements 3-4
Introduction 5-7
Organisation, methodology and fieldwork 8-14
Geology and landscape 15-16
Habitats and land use 17-26
The climate of Clackmannanshire 27-28
Weather during the survey periods 29-30
Data management and map production 31
A discussion of the Atlas results 32-33
Introduction to the species accounts 34-36
Breeding species 37-135
Non-breeding species 137-158
Other species recorded during the Atlas period 159-186
Species only recorded between 1974-2002 187-190
Species only recorded prior to the start of 'modern recording' in 1974 191-192
Species new to Clackmannanshire in the post Atlas period (2008-2011) 193
Mammals 194-200

Appendices
Appendix 1: KM squares data by habitat 202-206
Appendix 2: Breeding status totals 207-209
Appendix 3: Species list 210-211
Appendix 4: Species ubiquity - breeding 212
Appendix 5: Relative abundancy - breeding 213
Appendix 6: Relative abundancy - winter 214
Appendix 7: Rookeries 215
Appendix 8: Garden BirdWatch 216
Appendix 9: Where to watch birds in Clackmannanshire 217-218
Appendix 10: Useful addresses 219
Appendix 11: Gazetteer 220
Appendix 12: References 221-230
Appendix 13: Artists and drawings 231

Index of species 232-234

Foreword

Clackmannanshire is probably not one of the first names that come to mind when considering the top ornithological counties in Scotland. However, it has a rich history of ornithological endeavour and many of our top 'bird people' live there. This book demonstrates two things if nothing else; the hard work and 'finishing ability' of its birdwatchers and just what an interesting county it is.

The county is the 'basic unit' of bird recording in Scotland and I have the good fortune of being involved in several, most particularly, North East Scotland, Perth & Kinross and Fife. I have a keen understanding of how much work a book like this takes to produce.

Birds of Scotland 3 set a new standard of presentation of ornithological data in Scotland. It was the dream of the editorial team that it should act as a springboard to the production of new county avifaunas. Its production was closely followed by the 2007-2011 BTO Atlas where the observers of Scotland once again showed their tenacity for 'getting the job done'. This important Atlas work became the starting point for new county avifaunas and many Scottish counties are at some stage of producing these new avifaunas. This process often falls on the shoulders of a few dedicated people. It is those people who keep driving ornithology forward in our country and they deserve our congratulations today.

Contribution is the key word here and the observers, recorders, authors and editors who made this book happen should have a keen sense of contribution today and we thank them.

Ken Shaw, President, SOC July 2013.

Preface

This preface attempts to provide a historical background to the present Clackmannanshire Atlas by pointing out some of the ways in which bird records were produced and discussed from the late 18th century and through the Victorian era and the 20th century. Some examples of particular species are mentioned to illustrate where well based comparisons can be made and also when the data are too thin or open to ambiguous interpretations.

The first attempts to provide systematic and locally based accounts of Scottish birds occur in the two Statistical Accounts of Scotland where church ministers produced surveys of their parishes, the first in 1791-1799 (often referred to as the Old SAS) and then a follow up (the New SAS) in 1834-1835. Unfortunately few of the local ministers had a personal interest in natural history or contacts with parishioners who did. For Alloa, in the Old SAS, on the Inches are noted "great quantities of wild ducks, Teal, Wigeon, gulls. Sometimes Cormorants and Goosanders. Stormy Petrels last year", whilst Quail and Landrails (Corncrake) are "abundant in the breeding season" and Bittern had "become very scarce". For Tillicoultry the "Birds as Alloa... Glede (Red Kite) now seldom or never seen" and "in the hills Muirfowls (Black Grouse), plovers (Golden) and Dotterels" – the last two species also mentioned on passage around Alloa. Both these parishes mention Woodlark and Yellow Wagtail, however these species are not known from most other sources and are generally confused with Skylark or Tree Pipit and Grey Wagtail. Dollar records as "very rare" Parus palustris (presumably Willow Tit), Crossbill, Water Rail and Kingfisher. By far the best information for mid-Victorian times can be found in a series of lectures given to the Alloa Society of Natural Science and Archaeology between 1864 and 1870 (and possibly later) by Peter Brotherston, a local doctor. Especially notable is his account of wintering waders on the Forth where his assessments of abundance closely match the numbers counted in the late 20th century. Unfortunately the library archives of both Alloa and Stirling are incomplete and there is no available lecture covering birds of prey.

Birdwatching was not conspicuous in Clackmannanshire in the first half of the 20th century although there are scattered comments in Rintoul and Baxter's Vertebrate Fauna of Forth (1935). When the systematic wildfowl counts started after the Second World War Gartmorn Dam and the Clackmannanshire Forth were admirably covered by the late Tom Paterson of Alloa and many of his records appeared in the annual summaries in Scottish Birds. The organized collection of data on all species was started with the SOC system of local recorders and the eventual publication of an annual report that included Clackmannanshire. Local observers contributed both to BTO surveys of particular species and to the nationwide mapping of all species which eventually led to the high resolution maps of the present publication.

Dr Cliff Henty, Bridge of Allan, March 2013.

(Cliff's modesty has prevented him from mentioning his own remarkable contribution as Local Recorder for the period between 1974 and 2006, and author/co-author of the Forth Area Bird Reports from 1974-2002) Eds.

Abbreviations used in the text

Asl	Above sea level
BAP	Biodiversity Action Plan
BBS	Breeding Bird Survey
BTO	British Trust for Ornithology
CBAP	Clackmannanshire Biodiversity Action Plan
CSRSG	Central Scotland Raptor Study Group
Ha	Hectare
HAP	Habitat Action Plan
JNCC	Joint Nature Conservation Committee
Km	Kilometre
LBAP	Local Biodiversity Action Plan
RSPB	Royal Society for the Protection of Birds
SAP	Species Action Plan
SEPA	Scottish Environmental Protection Agency
SNH	Scottish Natural Heritage
SOC	Scottish Ornithologists' Club
SPA	Special Protection Area
SSSI	Site of Special Scientific Interest
SWT	Scottish Wildlife Trust
The / this *Atlas*	This book
The County	Clackmannanshire
UK BAP	UK Biodiversity Action Plan
WeBS	Wetland Bird Survey (BTO/RSPB/JNCC/WWT)

The following abbreviations used in the text are shortened forms of the authorities cited in full in the References:

1968-72 Atlas	Sharrock, JTR 1976
1988-91 Atlas	Gibbons, D.W., Reid, J.B. & Chapman, R. A. 1993
BBWC	Breeding Birds in the Wider Countryside in *Birdfacts* (q.v.)
BirdFacts	Robinson, R. A. 2005
BS1	Baxter, E.V. & Rintoul, L.J. 1953
BS2	Thom, V.M. 1986
BS3	Forrester *et al* 2007
BWP	Cramp *et al* 1977 - 1994 (qualified by vol. no.)
EBCC Atlas	Hagemeijer, W.J.M & Blair, M.J. 1997
Fife Atlas	Elkins, N *et al* 2003
Historical Atlas	Holloway, S. 1996
Migration Atlas	Wernham, C.V. *et al* 2002
SE Scotland Atlas	Murray, R.D. *et al* 1998
Statistical Accounts	Various Clackmannanshire parish reverends 18th & 19th c.
UFABR	*Upper Forth Bird Reports*. 1974-2008 (published annually in the Forth Naturalist and Historian)
Winter Atlas	Lack, P. 1986

Acknowledgements

A protracted and complex project such as this couldn't have been undertaken or completed without assistance and encouragement from many sources and we are extremely grateful to all the individuals and organisations who helped in whatever way.

Special thanks must go to those individuals whose contributions are acknowledged appropriately within the book; most notably the chapter authors, species account writers and artists; all of whom freely donated considerable time and their abundant talents. In this respect we are greatly indebted to John Grainger and Richard Daly. The former for initially producing comprehensive, yet taut, guidelines for species account writers; then guiding the editing of the species accounts through two incarnations; and the latter for assembling then corralling such an elite group of artists whose works greatly enhance the book. John Calladine compiled a base map of Clackmannanshire on which the breeding and wintering distributions are mapped. Don Matthews collated the records in a suitable format for adding to the maps. Cliff Henty also assisted with both the editing of the ancillary chapters and by providing much sage advice throughout the project. Barbara Bielby contributed valuable and varied IT support throughout the project including scanning 1:10,000 maps for use during fieldwork. Co-ordinating the above were the editors who organised, checked and collated all the submissions and who are wholly responsible for the accuracy of the contents.

Species account writers
Neil Bielby　　Keith Broomfield　　David Bryant　　John Calladine　　Robert Dawson
John Grainger　　Don Matthews　　Duncan Orr-Ewing　　Chris Pendlebury　　Andre Thiel
David Thorogood.

Fieldworkers
The very foundation of the *Atlas* project, and thus this book, are the people who undertook the fieldwork or contributed records by other means. We would like to take this opportunity to express our heartfelt thanks to them all. They are listed below (those who surveyed either breeding or winter squares being in bold). Every effort has been made to make this as accurate and complete a list as possible and we unreservedly apologise to anyone whose name has been omitted or misspelt.

M. Anderson	**R. Daly**	**J. Grainger**	L. McEwan	F. Solomon
P. Ashworth	J. Dawson	D. Gray	S. Mclean	**C. Spray**
N. Bielby	**R. Dawson**	A. Grenfell	G. McLellan	A. Stevens
L. Bond	**A. Downie**	H. Hall	D. Morrison	S. Stewart
K. Broomfield	R. Drysdale	A. Hannah	C. Moyes	**D. Taylor**
A. Cairns	I. Eccles	G. Harewood	**S. Muir**	**A. Thiel**
J. Calladine	G. Edwards	R. Henderson	**B. Osborn**	**D. Thorogood**
L. Campbell	**D. Egerton**	**C Henty**	S. Percival	D. Turnbull
R. Chapman	**A. Everingham**	D. Hodgson	D. Rees	M. Warnock
H. Chillas	**D. Ferguson**	**A. Lavery**	**A. Rogers**	**C. Wernham**
D. Christie	F. Fisher	A. Lyndsay	M. Rooney	**N. Whitelaw**
J. Clifford	**G. Fraser**	G. Lyndsay	N. Rudd	**K. Wilkinson**
J. Coull	C. Gallacher	C. Macadam	**R. Sexton**	A. Wilson
T. Craig	**J. Gallacher**	A. MacCullum	**S. Sexton**	M. Wilson
N. Credland	**R. Gooch**	**D. Matthews**	K. Smith	
T. Credland	S. Gorsky	**P. May**	E. Sneddon	

Artists

We would like to thank Richard Daly and Darren Rees who have shared the art editor role. Together they have brought together a team of eleven of the finest bird illustrators working in Scotland to embellish the text and enhance the visual appeal of the book. The artists are: Paul Bartlett, Keith Brockie, John Busby, Richard Daly, William Neill, Darren Rees, Derek Robertson, Jonathan Sainsbury, John Threlfall, Ian Wallace and Darren Woodhead. All would like to thank Stephen Grala-Wojrezyk at Hype Design for the crisp and sympathetic design and layout.
A full list of artists credits are on page 232.

Thanks are also due to the providers of the photographs, particularly David Jones and Dave Taylor (Wildpix Scotland) who made several dedicated trips for this purpose.

Other Sources of Records

Various sections/people at the BTO provided information. These include:
Andy Musgrove, Mark Collier and Neil Calbrade (WeBS office).
Mike Toms (Garden Birdwatch).
Jacquie Clark (ringing section).
Birdtrack.
British Trust for Ornithology, BirdWatch Ireland and the Scottish Ornithologists' Club for use of data collected during their national Bird Atlas 2007-11 bird surveys.
Other sources included the local Bird Reports which are published annually in the Forth Naturalist and Historian.

Thanks are also due to:

Hugh F. Barron (British Geological Survey) for a map of Clackmannanshire's Bedrock Geology.
Anne Carrington-Cotton for producing a general map of Clackmannanshire.
The benevolence of the Scottish Ornithologists' Club and the Scottish Wildlife Trust (via the Fentons landfill tax fund) with grants during the fieldwork stage of the project.

Sponsors

The Clackmannanshire Bird Atlas Group gratefully acknowledges the following generous support from its major sponsors for The Birds of Clackmannanshire:

The Scottish Ornithologists' Club (SOC) through its publications grant scheme, The Birds of Scotland Fund.
For more information on the Club, visit the SOC website: www.the-soc.org.uk

CEMEX Foundation

RSPB Scotland

Introduction

The name Clackmannan (Scottish Gaelic: *Clach Mhanainn*, translating to 'Stone of Manau'[1]) has ancient roots. The kingdom or territory of Manau stretched on both sides of the middle Forth, and included not only Clackmannan but also Slamannan, Stirlingshire, which also contains the name Manau. The root would appear to be *man-* or *mon-* 'projecting or high land'. In the case of Clackmannanshire's Manau, it would refer to the spectacular ridge of the Ochils, as viewed from the south.[2] The stone, made of whinstone[3], was originally situated on the old tidal shore at the foot of Lookaboutye Brae, and was believed to contain the spirit of the pagan sea god 'Manau'. It now stands in the town square of Clackmannan.

The name 'Clackmannanshire' was resurrected in 1996 for the new unitary authority council area created under the Local Government (Scotland) Act 1994. The current area is identical to that occupied by the preceding 'Clackmannan District', which was comprised of the original county of Clackmannanshire prior to 1971 (which existed from 1889-1975) along with c.1,764 ha. in the Muckhart area which was transferred from Perthshire to Clackmannanshire at this time (c.112 ha. at the Upper Glendevon Reservoir going the other way). The result was an increase in the area of the County by 11%, which at present is c.16,254 ha. which represents only 0.2% of Scotland's land area! So, Clackmannanshire remains as the smallest council area in mainland Scotland with a population, in 2005, of 48,630. Alloa is the main administrative centre having outgrown and replaced the town of Clackmannan in 1822.

Stone of Manau. © *N. Bielby 2012*

Why Clackmannanshire?

Taking the lead from the first UK national atlas [4], the past few decades have seen atlases become a popular and important method of establishing the state of county avifaunas in the UK. Indeed, 42 counties and local areas across the UK and Ireland are taking advantage of the fieldwork for the BTO's third breeding and second wintering atlases to undertake their own. In some cases, these will be their second, or even third atlases. Prior to the start of fieldwork for the Clackmannanshire Atlas, three bird recording areas in Scotland had already published atlases: 'The Birds of North-east Scotland'; [5] 'The Breeding Birds of South-east Scotland' [6] while Fife had produced two: 'The Birds of Fife' [7] and 'The Fife Bird Atlas' [8]. Apart from the first Fife atlas (where the maps are on a 1:10,000 grid) all used the virtually universal tetrad grid. The logical approach locally therefore, would have been to survey our local (SOC) bird recording area – 'The Upper Forth' – at this scale. However, this would have involved surveying around 630 tetrads (over half of which were mountain or moorland) and it was quickly realised that the potential volunteer capacity to do this just wasn't available.

Thus, from this background, the idea of carrying out a breeding bird survey of Clackmannanshire was first muted. The rationale behind this was:
- Being a small area (roughly 160 square kilometres) it was 'achievable'.
- The 'Wee County', with its diversity of landscapes and habitats, is often referred to as 'Scotland in miniature' and would therefore make an interesting study area.
- As far as we were aware, the avifauna of Clackmannanshire had never been surveyed in a systematic manner, nor had any book been written about it.

Organisation and aims

Following initial feasibility discussions between Andre Thiel and Neil Bielby during the 2001/2002 winter, a net was cast among active resident ornithologists, birders and the local representatives of the SOC, BTO, RSPB etc. to see who else would be interested in participating in such a project. This resulted in the formation of a steering group which initially consisted of Andre Thiel, Neil Bielby, John Grainger, Cliff Henty, Angus Smith and David Thorogood. Subsequently, the following were co-opted onto the steering group: Richard Daly (RD, 2005), John Calladine (2005), Don Matthews (2005), Keith Broomfield (2009) and Darren Rees (2010). The current chairs of the local SOC group (Central Scotland) were also invited onto the steering group. They were: A. Smith (2002-2004), R. Daly (2004-2006), A. Mitchell (2006-2008) and G. Fraser (2008-2011).

The steering group first convened in February 2002 when such issues as the type of Atlas (breeding or year round); the size of the survey unit (kilometre square or tetrad); survey methodology etc. were discussed.

The group eventually decided that the Atlas should have the following four primary objectives:
1. *To map the distribution of all bird species occurring in Clackmannanshire.*
2. *To obtain abundance data for common species.*
3. *To link distribution and abundance to habitat distribution.*
4. *To link in with the UK Biodiversity Action Plan (UK BAP) and the Clackmannanshire Local Biodiversity Action Plan (LBAP).*

In the event, objectives one and four were fully met; objective three was partially met while, although objective two wasn't achieved during the survey period due to a lack of manpower; relative frequency data was subsequently obtained during fieldwork for the BTO's UK national Atlas which took place between 2007 and 2011.

Like other atlases', it was also envisaged that the results of the proposed breeding season survey would not only document the distribution of each species occurring in the County during the survey period, and thus act as a baseline for future changes and surveys; they would also suggest where follow-up research/surveys should be directed – both in terms of which species and spatially. Being mapped at the relatively fine scale of a kilometre square, they would also be an essential reference tool for council planners, environmental bodies etc. as well as allowing for precise targeting of conservation action – i.e. through the LBAP or Government funded agri-environment schemes. Above all, the intended subsequent dissemination of the results via a publication would both inform and enthuse people about the birds of Clackmannanshire and hopefully encourage them to take a more active interest in their welfare and conservation.

Initially the steering group was known as 'The Clackmannanshire Breeding Bird Atlas Group' (CBBAG), then, with the adoption of the winter survey 'The Clackmannanshire Bird Atlas Group' (CBAG).

The various office holders on this group were:

Chair: A. Thiel (2002-2003); N. Bielby (2004-2012)
Secretary: A Thiel (2002-2005); N. Bielby (2005-2012)
Minutes Secretary: A Thiel (2002-2005); J. Grainger (2005-2009); N. Bielby (2009-2012)
Treasurer: N. Bielby (2004-2012)

Fieldwork Organiser N. Bielby (2002-2008 (partially aided by A. Thiel 2002))
Newsletter Editor: A. Thiel (2002-2005); D. Thorogood (2005-2009)
Species distribution mapping: N. Bielby (2003-2005); J. Calladine / D. Matthews (2005-2012)
Scientific and statistical advisor: J. Calladine (2005-2011)
Art Editors: R. Daly / D. Rees (2004-2012)
Ordinary members: C. J. Henty (2002-2005)
Editing of species accounts: J. Grainger (2008-2011 (assisted by N. Bielby & K. Broomfield)
Publication, fundraising etc. N. Bielby, K. Broomfield (2011-2013)

Some basic summary Clackmannanshire Atlas facts

Land area: 159 km^2 (61 square miles). (0.2% of Scotland's land area).
Number of kilometre squares covered: 125 full and 73 part.
Total number of species recorded by *Atlas* surveyors 2002-2007 = 147.
Total number of species recorded in Clackmannanshire 2002-2007 = 156.
Detailed breakdown of breeding records (appendix 3):

Confirmed Breeding	90
Probable Breeding	13
Possible Breeding	8
Observed only	23
Total	**134**

Number of observers participating: 37 surveyed at least one square and a further 41 provided supplementary records. (Five surveyors accounted for 61% of the fieldwork).
For the breeding survey, 2080 hours of dedicated fieldwork were recorded with an average of 12.4 hours for those squares with > than 50% of their area in Clackmannanshire. 277.9 hours of dedicated fieldwork were recorded during the winter survey.

Neil Bielby

References:
[1] Website: Mac an Tàilleir, I. 2003 *Placenames* (pdf) Pàrlamaid na-h-Alba.
[2] Taylor, S., 2004, 'Celtic Place-Names of Clackmannanshire', *History Scotland* vol.4 no.4 (July/August, 2004), 13-17.
[3] Website: *Undiscovered Scotland: Clackmannan.*
[4] Sharrock, J.T.R. 1976 *The Atlas of Breeding Birds in Britain and Ireland.* T. & A.D. Poyser, London.
[5] Buckland, S.T., Bell, M.V., and Picozzi, N. 1990. *The Birds of North-east Scotland.* North-east Scotland Bird Club, Aberdeen.
[6] Murray, R.D., Holling, M., Dott, H.E. and Vandrome, P. 1998. *The Breeding Birds of South-east Scotland.* The Scottish Ornithologists Club, Edinburgh.
[7] Smout, A-M. 1986. *The Birds of Fife.* John Donald Publishers Ltd, Edinburgh.
[8] Elkins, N., Reid, J.B., Brown, A.W., Robertson, D.G. and Smout, A-M. 2003 *The Fife Bird Atlas.* Woodlands Studios, Dunfermline.

Organisation, Methodology & Fieldwork

As described in the introduction, the project started life as a breeding bird atlas with the intention of carrying out both winter and abundancy surveys in due course, once surveyor availability and ability could be assessed. Due to manpower restrictions, no abundancy surveys were undertaken during the 2002-2007 survey period and a simple presence survey was conducted in winter instead.

The survey area, survey unit, coverage and time period

The area covered by the survey is that of the Clackmannanshire Unitary Authority as at 2002 and whose boundaries remained unchanged throughout the period of the fieldwork.

As mentioned in the introduction, the kilometre square, uniquely among county atlases as far as we are aware, was chosen as the survey unit for Clackmannanshire. Given the compactness of the County, plus the rapid transition from low to hill ground – notably along the distinctive scarp face – it was decided that a resolution which is four times finer than the normal tetrad unit used by other county surveys, would have real benefits in interpreting the mapped distribution of the County's birds.

Area of a km square within the County	No of squares
100%	125
75-99%	28
50-74%	7
25-49%	18
less than 25%	31
Total	209

All squares that contained a portion of the County above the high water mark of the River Forth, and that could be identified in the field, were visited: this amounted to 198. Surveyors were requested to survey only that portion of a square that fell within Clackmannanshire.

Fieldwork was carried out between 2002 and 2007 inclusively. It was originally estimated that this could be completed within four to five years and indeed, all but one square had received at least one dedicated timed visit by the end of 2006. However, an assessment of all squares with more than 50% of their area in Clackmannanshire after the 2006 breeding season by the steering group (using several methods), identified a number of squares (and species) where it was decided more work was required. This was undertaken during the 2007 breeding season by members of the committee along with a few other experienced surveyors. Special thanks must go to Don Matthews here, who, single-handedly, carried out this 'tidying-up' process in the Ochils.

Definition of 'breeding season'

The following was part of an instruction leaflet distributed to all surveyors:

'This (the breeding season) extends roughly from the beginning of April to the end of July, although breeding records from outwith this period are equally valid. Indeed, several species do breed outwith the main period. They are:-

Grey Heron	March-June	Pigeons & Doves	April-August
Owls (not SE)	Jan-July	Dipper	March-June
Mistle Thrush	March-June	Raven	Feb-July
Siskin	May-July	Crossbill	Feb-May

Late in the season beware of fledged young which may be found some distance from their natal area e.g. Lapwing, Wheatear, Mistle Thrush etc. Record these only if you are sure of the km in which they hatched.'

Recording forms

We adopted the four breeding categories used by the *South-east Scotland Atlas* which are: 'observed', 'possible', 'probable' and 'confirmed'. These categories, along with the types of evidence required to allocate a record, were provided to surveyors on both the front of the km square and supplementary forms; as well as on a laminated aide-memoire (for field use) as shown below. Sections were also provided for registering details of both the surveyor and square, along with visit dates and times. The reverse of the form listed all the species likely to be found breeding in Clackmannanshire with spare boxes for recording both additional species and any mammals encountered.

As noted in the *South-east Scotland Atlas* deciding whether or not a bird was in 'suitable breeding habitat', proved to be very subjective, with quite a number of surveyors seemingly erring on the side of caution by recording birds as 'observed', when 'habitat' would probably have been the more appropriate category. To assist surveyors in deciding which of these habitats to allocate a species to, a detailed clarification was provided in the March 2004 Newsletter. All birds using a square (but not those flying over) whose behaviour didn't correlate to categories 2-4, were classed as 'observed'.

Organisation of fieldwork

Initially, the County was split into two halves with Andre Thiel taking responsibility for the east and Neil Bielby the west. However, after the first season of fieldwork, it was decided that, in order to avoid confusion, there should be a single point of contact for surveyors: as the latter was already printing, distributing and processing all the forms, it was agreed that he should take responsibility for the whole area regarding the organisation and running of the fieldwork.

Throughout the survey, volunteers were able to pick any unallocated square. Their brief was to try and obtain the highest level of breeding for all species nesting or attempting to nest therein. Surveyors were asked to avoid disturbing nests and to try and obtain confirmed breeding using the other categories. They were also reminded about the law regarding Schedule 1 birds with a list of possible species from this list that they might encounter being provided. The instructions also requested that fieldworkers abide by the Countryside Code and that they should not put themselves or others in a position of danger. It was also stressed that the project could take no responsibility, nor incur any liability, for any actions and consequences from the activities of fieldworkers.

It was suggested that 3-4 visits of at least two hours duration would be required, but surveyors could make as many visits as they wished. It was recognized that varying effort would be required according to the type of habitat a square contained and the abilities of the surveyor. It was also recommended that at least one late evening/early night visit be made to search for crepuscular and nocturnal

Bullfinch. © *N. Bielby*

species. Updated km square forms (which included any additional supplementary records) were sent out to the 'trustee' prior to the start of the following field season in case they wished to make more visits. They were also provided to anyone else expressing a particular interest in a square e.g. to those living on a square.

A workshop was held in late April 2002 when surveyors were introduced both to each other and the aims and methodology of the Atlas. A further workshop was held in October to present and discuss the first year's fieldwork. Subsequently, all concerned with the Atlas were kept up to date with progress, and any decisions taken at regular meetings of the steering group, via newsletters which were distributed at the rate of roughly one a year. These were initially written and produced by Andre Thiel, and then from 2005, by David Thorogood.

Volunteers were also encouraged to submit supplementary records for any square in the County. Recording forms with columns to record the km square, year, species seen and level of breeding activity were prepared and distributed to both fieldworkers and anyone else who it was thought may be able to contribute. In the first couple of years an abundance of records in the lowest two breeding categories were received for the most common birds – Wren, Robin, Blackbird *etc.* via this method. Because they greatly added to the time spent on data inputting, and either had been or would be, quickly logged by the designated surveyor for the square, it was advised that only probable or confirmed records should be collected for these particular species.

Goldfinch. © *N. Bielby*

For certain colonial nesting species (Grey Heron, gulls, Sand Martins and Rooks) surveyors were requested to either register 'confirmed' breeding when a breeding colony was located or to use 'observed' for all other records. This allows a distinction to be made between the actual sites where they nest and the wide areas they range over in search of food.

Debate also took place during the survey period as to what constituted 'song' and what could be regarded as 'display'. This was especially critical for Skylark and

Meadow Pipit in the upland squares, where one visit could result in a probable record if the song-flight was regarded as 'display' but would require two records in the same place, a week apart in the same breeding season to achieve that category of breeding if it was classified as 'song'. The steering group decided that there was no black-and-white solution and that the decision should be left to the surveyor in the first instance and the steering group on review. Eventually it was agreed that for Skylark and Meadow Pipit, song-flight should be recorded as display and retrospective action was taken to upgrade any records of 'song' for these species. Later, this interpretation was also applied to the 'roding' of Woodcocks and to the 'drumming' of Great Spotted Woodpeckers.

Common sandpiper on the River Devon. Courtesy of Wildpix Scotland

Fieldworkers were also encouraged to collect mammal records and although not everyone did so, very useful information on their distribution was obtained – especially for the Clackmannanshire LBAP species European Otter and Red Squirrel.

Confidentiality

The instructions to fieldworkers contained a paragraph advising that records of rare, sensitive and vulnerable species, which they thought ought to remain confidential, should be submitted separately to one of the organizers. They were advised that these would not be mapped without their permission and that consultation with the necessary bodies would take place if required.

BAP & LBAP

Great Spotted Woodpecker (Immature). © D. Jones

Surveyors of squares were also issued with a sheet containing a 1:10,000 scale colour habitat map, on which they were asked to recorded any changes since the 1995 Phase One survey which the maps were based on. They were also asked to mark the position of any UK Biodiversity Action Plan (UK BAP) or Clackmannanshire Local Biodiversity Action Plan (LBAP) species encountered and to also record the name and activity code of the bird along with the date. These records were passed on to the Clackmannanshire Biodiversity Officer after each field season so that they could be used in both the writing of the species action plan and inform any decisions regarding implementation of these plans in the field. The UK BAP species recorded were: Grey Partridge, Skylark, Song Thrush, Spotted Flycatcher, Tree Sparrow, Bullfinch and Reed Bunting along with the Clackmannanshire LBAP species: Lapwing, Goldfinch, Linnet and Yellowhammer.

Observer coverage

As mentioned earlier, rather than rely on a 'scatter-gun' approach, km squares were allocated to individual fieldworkers whose remit was to survey the square as comprehensively as possible (i.e. attempt to obtain confirmation for all species suspected of breeding therein). In total, 37 surveyors took up squares although, as would appear to the case with most local Atlases, a much smaller number carried out the bulk of the work with five surveyors executing 61% of the fieldwork.

Grey Heron. © N. Bielby

Fieldworkers were recruited from those already participating in surveys for the BTO along with members from the local RSPB, SOC and SWT groups. A request for volunteers was published in the local paper at the start of the survey which resulted in four responses. However, although instructions and forms were sent out, no records were received. Additionally, a further 41 people submitted supplementary records.

Surveyors of squares were also asked to record the time spent on dedicated fieldwork. This gave us an idea of effort plus the time of day visits were made. This information proved very valuable when assessing whether a square required further work – especially before the final year of fieldwork. Surveyors were also asked to indicate (by circling 'Y' or 'N' at the bottom of the form) whether or not they considered the square required any further visits. However, the value of this decision varied according to the competency of the surveyor. The total number of hours thus logged was 2,080. In general, times were not recorded in those instances where the surveyor lived on the allocated square. The average number of hours for those squares with >50% of their area in Clackmannanshire was 12.4. When broken down to broad geographical areas, the average for squares in the Ochil Hills was 5.3; for scarp squares 13.9 and for lowland squares 14.9 hours.

In total, 111 species were allocated one of the breeding codes with a further 23 being 'observed' only. The average number of species per square with a breeding category record was 31 with the average for 'confirmed' breeding being only 12. As expected, there was a marked geographical variation with an average of only nine species with a breeding record in the Ochil Hill squares compared to 35 on the scarp and 40 on the lowland squares. NS 9597 was the square with the greatest number of species recorded in a breeding category with 56. This square not only had a variety of habitats but benefited from a good number of records sent in by a resident of the square (see appendices 1 & 2).

Completeness of the survey

As noted above, an assessment of each square with over 50% of its area within Clackmannanshire at the end of the 2006 breeding season, highlighted several where more effort would be beneficial (and in some cases essential), to achieve an order of consistency in coverage. To aid this assessment, maps and tables were produced showing both the total number of species on each square and also the numbers and level of breeding for the more common and easily observed species: a low representation of the latter often being a clear indicator that a square required more work. Comparison of squares containing similar habitats was also made – being especially relevant when adjacent.

The number of hours spent on a square was also looked at, although the abilities of the individual surveyor were also an important factor here. In 2006, work on a number of 'completed' lowland squares with a mean of 5.3 hours fieldwork logged, showed that by spending a further 10 hours on each, the number of species recorded rose by an average of 13; along with a significant upgrading of the breeding categories. Some detailed analysis of the correlation between hours spent on a square and the number of species recorded showed a levelling off around the 17 hour mark.

On looking at the provisional maps, several species (especially the crepuscular and nocturnal species – unsurprisingly) appeared to be under-recorded. Targeted visits in 2007 to suitable habitats at specific stages of the breeding cycle notably increased the number of squares with confirmed breeding for selected common species such as Magpie, Carrion Crow and Starling while territorial behaviour was obtained in seven new squares for Woodcock and 14 for Tawny Owl – the latter mostly gleaned from residents in the squares.

A few extra records were obtained from external sources. The local *Bird Reports* were checked for any additional records which could be assigned to a km square as was *Birdtrack* – although the latter only came into existence in the final years of fieldwork. The environmental impact assessment survey for the Burnfoot Hill wind farm yielded a few records, as did a similar exercise for a proposed housing development at Forestmill. Only one BBS square lies fully within the County boundaries and this was adopted for the Atlas by its surveyor. A scheme to monitor and provide nest boxes for Barn Owls commenced during the Atlas fieldwork period and there was a two-way exchange of information between the parties.

Scrutiny of the distribution maps for the most common species shows that for these at least, coverage was virtually complete in the areas where they would be expected to be found.

Winter Atlas

As mentioned in the introduction, a simple presence survey was undertaken using the tetrad as the recording unit. Given that only two winters remained available to carry out the work, a stratified survey was suggested. However, it was felt that the bulk of the effort could be provided by the committee if only those tetrads with more than 50% of their area in Clackmannanshire were surveyed (43 in total – this provided 93% coverage of 'lowland' and 97% coverage of 'upland' areas). This survey was carried out during the 2005/6 and 2006/7 winters ('winter' was defined as November to February inclusive). Fieldworkers were asked to make at least one visit before and one after the New Year; although more visits were encouraged so as to obtain the fullest species list possible for a square. Overall, 113 species were recorded with an average of 45 per tetrad in lowland squares (n=30) and 13 in upland ones (n=13). A total of 277.9 hours were spent in the field with an average of 8.1 on lowland and 4.5 on upland squares. As with the Breeding Survey, supplementary records were encouraged for all except the common species. WeBS counts, the local *Bird Reports* and *Birdtrack* were also scrutinized for additional records.

Relative frequency counts

No counts of birds were made during the Atlas survey period (2002-2007) but use has been made of subsequent one hour counts made within Clackmannanshire for the BTO's 2007-2011 UK Atlas (those tetrads which were not surveyed for the BTO Atlas received one hour visits during the 2011/2012 winter and 2012 breeding seasons). The methodology for the BTO Atlas survey entailed surveyors choosing an available tetrad (2 x 2 km square) and following a route of their own choosing, recording the numbers of all bird species seen and heard which were making use of the tetrad. These counts were of exactly one hour duration. If they wished, surveyors could perambulate for an extra hour following a completely different route within the tetrad. Only counts from those tetrads with > 50 % of their area within the County have been used, so that while the great majority of the birds recorded will be from within Clackmannanshire, a few will have been recorded from just outside. All these separate hourly counts have been used to compile lists of the more common species. In total, 102 counts were undertaken during the breeding season with 104 during the winter period.

Interpretation of these lists must be made with acknowledgement of the following caveats regarding detectability:

1. Size – ability to detect and identify bigger birds at greater distances.
2. Behaviour – whether or not a bird is easily observed (e.g. Carrion Crow) or generally skulking in nature (e.g. Jay) or rarely encountered at all (e.g. Tawny Owl). Species behaviour also varies according to both the stage of the breeding season and the weather.
3. Presence – late returning spring migrants will be missing from early breeding visits while passage migrants will be present for varying periods of time.
4. Flocks – flocks of birds are easier to locate and produce greater numbers than individuals (e.g. Fieldfare v Song Thrush).
5. Observer bias – whilst the great majority of observers would have been competent in identifying most birds by sight and song, some no doubt struggled with calls, especially of the less common species.
6. Habitat – birds in open habitats are easier to observe than those in dense woodland. Bird vocalizations are more difficult to hear close to busy roads.

Hopefully some of the above biases have been mitigated by the design of the survey (e.g. using the period of an hour to standardize effort, having early and late season counts, counting early in the morning – especially in the breeding season, not surveying in poor weather conditions) and some interesting comparisons can be made between species – especially within families and species of similar 'detectability' (appendices 5 and 6).

Neil Bielby

Key

	SCOTTISH COAL MEASURES GROUP - MUDSTONE, SILTSTONE, SANDSTONE, COAL, IRONSTONE AND FERRICRETE	*Cmsc-msci*
	CLACKMANNAN GROUP - SEDIMENTARY ROCK CYCLES, CLACKMANNAN GROUP TYPE	*Ckn-cycc*
	INVERCLYDE GROUP - SANDSTONE, SILTSTONE AND MUDSTONE	*Inv-sdsm*
	ARBUTHNOTT-GARVOCK GROUP - SANDSTONE WITH SUBORDINATE CONGLOMERATE, SILTSTONE AND MUDSTONE	*Atgk-scsm*
	UNNAMED IGNEOUS INTRUSION, LATE SILURIAN TO EARLY DEVONIAN - MAFIC IGNEOUS-ROCK	*Uisd-mfir*
	UNNAMED EXTRUSIVE ROCKS, SILURIAN TO DEVONIAN - MAFIC LAVA AND MAFIC TUFF	*Uexsd-latm*
—	Fault at rockhead	

Key for map on page 16

Geology and Landscape

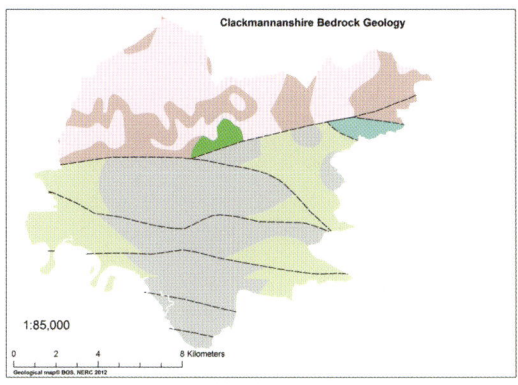

See key to map on page 15

(The following is largely a synopsis of a much more detailed article by M. Browne and D. Grinly which can be found in the *Forth Naturalist and Historian* Volume 19: 3-25. 1996).

Scotland is normally divided into three geological sub-regions: the Highlands, the Midland Valley and the Southern Uplands. Clackmannanshire lies totally within the Midland Valley, being situated in the eastern half and enclosed by the districts of Perth and Kinross to the north, Fife to the east, Falkirk to the south and Stirling to the west.

The volcanic rocks of which the Ochil Hills are composed (Ochil Volcanic Formation) were formed during the Lower Devonian age (410-360 million years ago) when Scotland was located south of the equator and enjoyed a tropical climate. This formation is said to be over 2,000 metres deep and is composed largely of basaltic and andesitic lava flows mixed with conglomerates through which the lava flows had erupted. The southerly dipping limb of the Ochil Anticline is truncated by the Ochil Fault (one of the most dramatic topographical features in Central Scotland), which has a maximum vertical downthrow to the south of about 3,000 metres (at Alva and Harviestoun) of which only c.300 metres is exposed. This brings the Lower Devonian volcanic rocks to the north against the Carboniferous Middle Coal Measures to the south. Although there were undoubtedly many fractures after the initial displacement, there is only one certain record of movement in historical times – the Dollar earthquake of 1736. Occasional tremors still occur to this day along the Hillfoots.

The Clackmannanshire lowlands are basically composed of rocks from the Carboniferous age (360-300 million years ago) when the area was mostly a marine or coastal environment situated around the equator. These very complex formations are the result of repeated fluvial and deltaic sedimentary cycles when sandstones, siltstones, mudstones and limestones were laid down. The decay of the dense, humid tropical forests (which usually covered the coastal plains) formed layers of peat which, over time and under great pressure, subsequently became the (Westphalian) coal measures which have been mined for several centuries (the seams of the Clackmannanshire coalfield form a broad wedge with the base around Alva and Tillicoultry running to the apex near Kincardine–on–Forth). The major earth movements which created the Ochil Fault and marked the end of the Carboniferous period also caused mineralization in the faults and joints of the rocks of the southern Ochils – exploited most notably at the Alva Silver Glen mines in around 1714 which produced the purest silver ore ever found in the UK.

From the Permian (c.290 millions of years ago) onwards, Scotland remained as a landmass, drifting north past the equator into the temperate belt. It is thought that the basic topographic configuration of the Devon and Forth Valleys may have been fashioned by prolonged erosion during the Tertiary period. This steady northward movement eventually brought Scotland under the influence of glaciation around two million years ago. There have been many periods of glaciation and associated inter-glacial periods (known as stades and interstades) during the last two million years but evidence of earlier occurrences is normally eradicated by the later ones.

In Clackmannanshire, these stades and interstades greatly modified the basic landforms and deposited large quantities of varied fluvio-glacial debris, especially in the Devon and Forth valleys. This is most evident in raised beaches (examples of which are at Menstrie, Tullibody, Alloa and Kilbagie), and whale-backed drumlins (on which Clackmannan Tower and Lornshill stand). At times, the ice is estimated to have been a kilometre thick and during one glacial period, over-deepened the Devon valley between Menstrie and Tillicoultry to 100 metres below current sea level (but not, curiously, the Forth valley between Stirling and Kincardine Bridge). However, when the ice melted during the interstades, the sea inundated the Devon valley as far upstream as Dollar with marine sediments being deposited up to 40-45 metres above current sea level in both river valleys.

Forth and carse from Ben Cleuch. Courtesy of Wildpix Scotland

The final glacial invasion of Scotland (the Loch Lomond Readvance) is thought to have ended abruptly about 10,000 years ago. From being 10 metres below current sea level during this last stade, sea-levels again rose as the ice melted, flooding the Forth and Devon valleys up to a maximum of 16 metres and 13 metres above current sea level respectively, around 6,500 years ago. During this period, the shoreline ran along the Hillfoot towns. As the land rose (due to isostatic rebound) and sea-levels fell, the consequent incision of the drainage produced the spectacular Rumbling Bridge gorge on the River Devon. Initially during the latest deglaciation, the upper River Devon flowed east to Loch Leven but the Rumbling Bridge gorge is also a good example of river capture, causing the Devon to flow westwards into the Forth.

The present landscape of Clackmannanshire is the result of complex interactions between geological processes, variations in climate and topography and the development of soils and land cover. It too, can be broadly split into three separate areas: the Ochil Hills and distinctive Ochil Fault scarp; the undulating mid-county 'ridge/plateau' and the low-lying valley floors of the Rivers Forth and Devon.

Although the distribution and quality of soils in the County is primarily influenced by the underlying material, other factors, such as climate and topography, also play a part. These soils range from the blanket peats and leached peaty podzols on the high tops of the Ochils to the fertile alluvial and glacial silts and clays of the Forth carselands with many other types in-between.

The above brief description of the varied geology and landscape of Clackmannanshire illustrates why it is often referred to as 'Scotland in miniature'.

Neil Bielby

References:
Hughes, R., Mackenzie, F. *Clackmannanshire landscape character assessment* SNH report 096. 1998.
Whittow, J.B. *Geology and Scenery in Scotland* Penguin Books 1977.

Habitats and Land Use

Man, as well as natural forces, has also greatly influenced the landscape of Clackmannanshire for thousands of years, whether it be urban and industrial areas or in the wider countryside which is farmed in many different ways – from the rough grazing sheep walk of the Ochils to the intensively farmed, large cereal fields of the carselands. This combination of natural and human influence has resulted in the many varied bird habitats found throughout the County. (Unless accredited otherwise, all the information in this section has been obtained from the Clackmannanshire Biodiversity Action Plan 2003-2008).

Farmland

Figure 1. Farmland and grassland Clackmannanshire Council 2003.

This section is devoted to farming in the 'lowlands' (although the semi-improved and acid grassland/heathland mosaics of the Ochils are technically 'farmland' they will be covered in 'The Uplands' section). The steep gradient of the Ochil scarp, which dissects the County, allows a distinct line to be drawn for the upper limit of actively managed farmland which at no point takes place above the 200 metre contour. Around 40% of Clackmannanshire is devoted to 'lowland' farming with c.17% of this being arable [Macaulay 2008, Clackmannanshire BAP 2012-2017]. During the *Atlas* survey, it had been hoped to separate arable land from permanent improved pasture for analysis purposes of habitat preference and 1:10,000 scale phase one habitat maps were distributed to surveyors of each one kilometre square on which to note any changes. However, this had to be abandoned since field usage often switched from pasture to arable between years. Additionally, birds move between various crops and improved pasture throughout the year, thus further complicating any possible analyses.

Since humans started clearing the forests and draining the marshes during the Neolithic period (4000-2500 BC), the rural lowlands of Scotland have seen constant changes in farming practices and thus landscapes. Nonetheless, until the Second World War, these changes were relatively slow and, although they affected species differently, there was always an ample supply of habitats and food throughout the year to support a rich variety and large number of birds. However, the last 65 years have arguably seen the most rapid ever changes in agricultural practices, with some of the small mixed farms in the County converting (and often amalgamating) to an intensive, mostly monocultural, method of farming which has been supported by an increasing use of herbicides and pesticides, all of which has radically reduced the abundancy and diversity of plant and animal foods for birds.

Tree Sparrow. © D. Jones

The continuing trend towards mechanisation and increased yields has also seen fields enlarged to accommodate today's much larger farm machinery so that, not only are most crops 'deserts' as far as birds are concerned, much vital nesting, foraging and sheltering habitat by way of field boundaries has been lost (c.23,000 km of hedges were removed from Scottish farmland between the 1940s and 1980s). Political policies (notably through the Common Agricultural Policy) have also encouraged higher production for some crops through the availability of subsidies – the aforementioned also being provided for the drainage of any wetland areas that remained. The development of cereal varieties which can be sown in autumn has led to a dramatic reduction in both winter stubbles and spring cultivation, thus further reducing food availability for some bird species during the two most difficult seasons for avian survival. This marked fall-off in spring sowing has also had a profound negative influence on the breeding success of several ground nesting species, notably Lapwing and Skylark. All of this is believed to have had a catastrophic effect on a range of farmland birds across the UK with numbers of Linnet having fallen by 76% between 1967 and 2007; Grey Partridge by 89% and Tree Sparrow by 97% [*BirdFacts*]. Corncrake and Corn Bunting have become extinct in Clackmannanshire and Grey Partridge are now few and localised [*UFABR*]. However, this survey found Tree Sparrows to be more widespread than UK trends, recent bird report records and anecdotal evidence would suggest.

Arable field and Ochils from Dollar. © D. Jones

Arable cropping takes place across the lowlands of Clackmannanshire, but particularly on the flat, fertile carselands adjacent to the River Forth and in the lower Devon valley with the principal crops being Barley (*Hordeum distichon*), wheat (*Triticum aestivum*) and Oilseed Rape (*Brassica napus*) with Oats (*Avena sativa*), making a comeback, largely to feed the increasing number of recreational horses and ponies now occupying many fields adjacent to human settlements. Conversely, fields of root crops are nowadays few and far between.

Permanent improved pasture tends to predominate in the cooler, wetter parts of the UK and in Clackmannanshire occurs along the lower slopes of the Ochil Scarp and to the east of Dollar and more patchily across the rest of the County These grasslands have also undergone radical 'improvement' in the past 65 years, becoming virtual monocultures of fine grasses which are regularly fertilised to allow both intensive grazing and the making of silage, with two crops of the latter being taken from some fields in favourable years. The pre-war herb and flower rich hay meadows/fields are almost a thing of memory – along with much of the fauna which inhabited them. Not all the improved grassland in the County is used for agriculture: some 429 hectares (2.6%) is public open space which includes parks, playing fields and golf courses.

Thankfully, not all is gloom and doom. The past two decades have seen some acknowledgement by political powers in both the UK and Europe of the decline in biodiversity in intensively farmed land and grants for several agri-environmental schemes have been available in Scotland during this period although, due to both under-funding and the competitive nature of allocation, demand often exceeds supply (from 1997-2000, less than half of the 3,000 farmers in Scotland who applied to the Countryside Premium Scheme were funded to implement their biodiversity plans). The continuation and success of these schemes will rely on both political will and adequate funding.

The Local Biodiversity Action Plan (LBAP) for the County includes two plans for arable land: these being for the 'broad habitat' and 'cereal field margins' (as defined in the UK BAP) along with Species Action Plans (SAPs) for the following birds of arable farmland: Grey Partridge, Tree Sparrow, Goldfinch, Linnet and Yellowhammer. A LBAP Wader Action Plan includes Oystercatcher, Lapwing, Snipe, Curlew and Redshank which nest in a variety of farmland habitats.

Permanent pasture 2004. © D. Jones

Additionally, several government and charitable organisations encourage and advise farmers towards environmentally friendly farming (e.g. the RSPB through its Volunteer and Farming Alliance scheme).

A number of farms across Scotland have also become organic, returning to farming practices of yesteryear and thus enjoying a resurgence in avian and other bio-diversity. Currently in the County, only one farm (at Dollarbeg) is pursuing organic status.

A few bird species have benefited from the 'improvements' to pasture, with the recent increases in the wintering Pink-footed Goose and Icelandic-breeding Greylag Goose populations being largely attributed to the availability of this food resource (along with autumn-sown cereals) once the more traditional autumn/early-winter ones of spilt grain in stubbles and root crops have been exhausted [*BS3*].

Yellowhammer. © D. Jones

In recent years, small areas of game-cover crops (which typically contain Millet (*Panicum miliaceum*), Maize (*Zea mays*), Quinoa (*Chenopodium quinoa*), Sorghum (*Sorghum spp*) etc.), have provided winter habitat to flocks of threatened seed-eating passerines such as Tree Sparrows, Linnets, Yellowhammers and Reed Buntings. Despite the intensification of farming as described above, the lowlands of the County (especially in the east) are still composed of relatively small fields, often with hedges as boundaries, and are interspersed with small woods and game coverts, while most farms still have small 'wild' areas of unmanaged/unmanageable land – with many farmers being sympathetic to the wildlife they hold. Additionally, for 20 years many farmers took advantage of the European Union's Common Agricultural Policy's set-aside scheme where they were paid to leave arable fields uncultivated which benefited many farmland bird species. Unfortunately this scheme was suspended in 2008 and abolished the following year, since when most of this farmland has been returned to intensive production.

The uplands

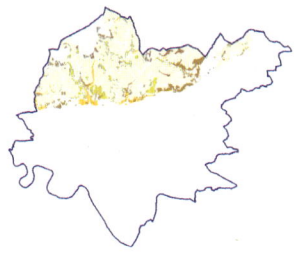

Figure 2. Unimproved grassland - healthland mosaic. Clackmannanshire Council 2003.

The Ochil Hills are the sole representative of upland habitat within Clackmannanshire, occupying c.35% of the County. This compact plateau of rounded tops attains a maximum elevation of 721 metres at Ben Cleuch and is dissected by steep-sided valleys, especially those draining south. All the following references to the 'Ochils' refer to that part lying within the County.

Although upland heath normally occurs over 300 metres and much of the Ochils above the deep valley bottoms exceed that height, this habitat makes up less than 2% of the Ochils. It is concentrated in the north-west corner and is the only place where Red Grouse were found, although it doesn't appear to be currently managed for this species.

Most of the Ochils are covered by a mosaic of acid grassland/heathland – heavily grazed by sheep – and accounts for c.20% of the land area of Clackmannanshire. Meadow Pipit and Skylark are easily the most common species – being virtually ubiquitous. The majority of the other species were found in the valleys and their associated streams. The latter held a few Mallard, Common Sandpipers, Grey Wagtails

Looking west from King's Seat. Courtesy of Wildpix Scotland

and Dippers along with the occasional Pied Wagtail. Wrens and Wheatears were fairly widespread albeit in low numbers (D. Matthews *pers. comm.*), probably utilising the scattered scree slopes and outcrops which lie to the south of the watershed and on the scarp. There were only a few Whinchats, Stonechats, Willow Warblers and the occasional Reed Bunting. On the more open hillsides and tops, a cluster of Curlew were in the Burnfoot Hill area with a few Common Snipe in the wet flushes (both these species are included in the LBAP Waders SAP). Despite thorough coverage, only a single Golden Plover and Short-eared Owl were recorded. Carrion Crows were confirmed as breeding in two kilometre squares (in isolated trees) while Rook and Raven were noted as foraging fairly widely for invertebrates as were Swifts and Swallows. Both Carrion Crow and Raven probably scavenge on any sheep and deer carcasses that may occur. One of the 'target' species before the survey commenced was the Ring Ouzel (there is a SAP for it in the LBAP) but none were found, and this bird must now be considered extinct as a breeding species in the County.

Blanket bogs obtain all of their water from precipitation and there are two main areas in the Ochils – Alva Moss (c.300 ha.) and Menstrie Moss (c.24 ha.). These lie at an elevation of 520-560 metres a.s.l. with the former being located on the flatter ground between Ben Buck and Blairdenon Hill and the latter between Blairdenon Hill and Bengengie Hill. Both mosses form the headwaters of the Alva and Balquharn Burns draining to the south and the Finglen Burn draining to the north. The depth of the peat varies between 30 mm and four metres with c.63% of it considered to be un-degraded by man through drainage, burning, extraction etc. (although they are grazed by sheep) and the remaining 37% is extensively eroded with large areas of bare peat and hags.

Figure 3. Blanket bog. Clackmannanshire Council 2003.

There are also small areas of calcareous grassland (most notably the Craigleith and Myreton Hill SSSI), and an estimated 10 kilometres of exposed, steep linear rock, which is found on the Ochil Scarp and in the more gorge-like parts of the southern glens with the most notable and obvious of these being Craig Leith above Alva. Where inaccessible to sheep, these outcrops support a more varied vegetation and accompanying fauna than the surrounding hillsides. (The LBAP includes Habitat Action Plans (HAPs) for Blanket Bog, the Ochil Glens and the Unimproved Grassland-Heathland Mosaic.)

Skylark. © D. Jones

Water and wetland

Wetland habitats take many forms: from tidal estuaries to small hill streams; from large natural lochs and man-made reservoirs to small lochans and flight ponds, along with a wide variety of reed-beds, marshes, bogs, swamps etc. Wetland habitats in Clackmannanshire currently occupy c.9% of the County.

Clackmannanshire has three main river systems: the Forth, Devon and Black Devon – the Devon especially being supported by several smaller tributaries. The Devon has a catchment area of approximately 210 km^2 and the Black Devon a catchment area of approximately 60 km^2 (CBAP 2011-2017). Rivers and streams form important wildlife habitats with not only the watercourse itself, but also the riparian vegetation, hosting a wide variety of birds. They also act as wildlife corridors, even through the most hostile environments, allowing relatively safe passage and dispersion. All three rivers have been affected by both agricultural and industrial pollution to varying degrees at various times in the past, but the decline of Clackmannanshire's old, 'heavy' industries such as coal mining, allied to increasingly tough anti-pollution legislation (policed and enforced by the Scottish Environment Protection Agency (SEPA), means that their waters are now relatively pure. The main current threat is probably eutrophication due to run-off of artificial fertilisers from farmland. SSSIs cover several stretches and include Mill Glen, Dollar Glen, Devon Gorge and Linn Mill.

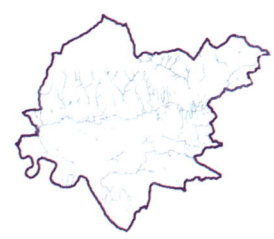

Figure 4. Rivers and streams. Clackmannanshire Council 2003.

The River Forth enters Clackmannanshire at Manor and leaves it at Kennetpans – a distance of approximately 15 kilometres – and forms the southwest boundary of the County, initially with Stirling District, then Falkirk District. The whole of the river within the County is tidal, being roughly 25% the salinity of sea water at Alloa [McLusky 1987]. Excluding the Alloa and Tullibody Inches, the area between the high and low tide lines has been calculated to still cover c.913 ha. (5.4%) of the County; even though it has been estimated that around 49% of the inter-tidal area between Stirling and Kincardine Bridge has been claimed for agriculture and industry over the past 200 years [McLusky et al. 1992].

R. Devon mouth 2004 .© D. Jones

By providing an abundant supply of food, estuaries are one of the most important habitats for waterbirds, especially outwith the breeding season. Although that portion within the County is relatively narrow, with correspondingly limited areas of intertidal habitat (when compared to the vast areas around Grangemouth a little further downstream), it still holds comparatively good numbers of non-breeding Pink-footed Goose, Greylag Goose, Shelduck, Wigeon, Teal, Mallard, Goldeneye, Red-breasted Merganser, Goosander, Cormorant, Grey Heron, Oystercatcher, Lapwing, Curlew and Redshank at various times throughout the year. Also during the survey period, Mute Swan, Whooper Swan, Canada Goose, Little Grebe, Moorhen, Ringed Plover, Golden Plover, Dunlin, Snipe, Black and Bar-tailed Godwit, Common Sandpiper, Sandwich and Common Tern were occasionally recorded in small numbers [WeBS].

The River Forth and its riparian habitats can provide good 'birding' throughout its length in the County and, despite being under-watched compared to the Grangemouth area, occasional semi-rarities and rarities such as Greenland White-fronted Goose, Barnacle Goose, Brent Goose, Red-breasted Goose, Gadwall, Shoveler, Scaup, Red-throated Diver, Little Egret, Spoonbill, Water Rail, Grey Plover, Ruff, Whimbrel, Greenshank, Green Sandpiper, Guillemot all turned up during the survey period [WeBS, *UFABR*]. Notable 'hotspots' include:

Dipper. © D. Jones

- The SWT reserve at Cambus Pools; although this has become less favourable to birds in recent years with reed encroachment and the disappearance of seasonal muddy margins due to a lack of grazing.
- The nearby Cambus Village and Devonmouth Pools.
- The SWT reserves of Tullibody and Alloa Inches which were claimed for agricultural land around 1800 but have since been reclaimed by the Forth, with the former now occupied by a large phragmites reed-bed and the latter reverting to saltmarsh following the breaching of the flood banks in 1983 [Sexton et al, 2005]. Alloa Inch is also an important breeding site for Shelduck.
- The Blackdevon Wetlands sometimes holds reasonable numbers of common waterbirds and the occasional semi-rarity and has great potential as a 'managed retreat' saline lagoon/wetland reserve. A conservation organisation (RSPB) is currently looking into taking over the management of the site.
- The muddy, tidal bay at Kennetpans.

Clackmannanshire has approximately 49 ha of saltmarsh of which c.82% is on Alloa Inch. LBAP HAPs exist for 'Coastal Lagoons', the 'Estuary', and 'Mudflats and Saltmarsh' while several SSSIs cover the area and the whole of the Firth of Forth is designated as a SPA (Special Protection Area).

The c.60 kilometres course of the River Devon describes a 'U' shape. Originating as the Finglen Burn at c.550 m. a.s.l. from Alva Moss, it soon leaves the County and after passing through Glen Devon, re-enters it above Yetts o' Muckhart. After forming part of the boundary of the County for c.2.5 kilometres, it turns abruptly westwards at Crook of Devon, following this course until the final three kilometres, where it flows on a southerly bearing to join the River Forth at Cambus. It again forms part of the County boundary from near Rumbling Bridge to the southeast of Dollar where it is fast flowing with several waterfalls (most notably Cauldron Linn) and many small rapids. After finally entering Clackmannanshire fully downstream from Vicar's Bridge, the current gradually slows as it meanders its way along the Devon Valley. Between 1977 and 1987, the then Stirling Branch of the SOC carried out a series of detailed surveys of the breeding birds of the River Devon (the current avian community is broadly similar now as then and a comprehensive report of these can be found in the Forth Naturalist and Historian volume 14:

River Devon. Courtesy of Wildpix Scotland

Teal.© D. Jones

50-64: 1991). WeBS counts show that the river supports good numbers of Grey Herons, Mute Swans, Teal, Mallards, Goldeneyes and Goosanders between Dollar and Cambus during the winter months. Flooding mainly occurs in the Alva and Tillicoultry area during autumn and early winter and at this time, flocks of Wigeon often congregate alongside the Greylag Geese which graze the flood meadows (or haughs) throughout the winter.

Prior to 1845, the River Devon was known as the 'Dovan' and this older name is thought to be derived from the Gaelic word 'Dobh-an' which translates to 'a swelling or raging water' (CBAP 2003) which, being a spate river, is an apt appellation. In the past it has also been called the South Devon (CBAP 2011-2017).

The Black Devon is c.13 kilometres in length and commences at the confluence of the Saline and Roughcleugh Burns near West Saline in Fife. It flows generally south-westwards, mostly through wooded gorges and narrow valleys, to join the River Forth below Alloa with the final two kilometres being tidal as it twists its way through the Blackdevon Wetlands. It is relatively fast flowing and supports Dippers and Grey Wagtails plus the occasional Kingfisher in its lower reaches. However, only short stretches are fringed by the luxuriant summer vegetation found along the lower River Devon, and so species such as Sedge Warbler and Reed Bunting are found in far fewer numbers than on that river. (There is a local HAP for 'Rivers and Streams').

Gartmorn Dam. 2004 © D. Jones

Gartmorn Dam is easily the largest area of standing water in Clackmannanshire with its 45 ha. forming the centre piece of the Gartmorn Dam Country Park. The oldest man-made reservoir in Scotland, it was constructed in 1713 to provide power (via a large waterwheel) in order to extract water from deep coal mines, and was largely fed by a substantial lade which diverted the water from the Black Devon at Forestmill. From the late 19th century it was used as a source of drinking water for the Alloa area. However, in the mid 2000s, due to contamination from opencast mining, this function ceased and the supply to the lade was cut off at the Forestmill weir. Designated as a SSSI, its nutrient rich waters support locally important numbers of waterbirds throughout the year, but especially wildfowl in winter (it has been monitored by WeBS most winters since 1962), for which it is the most important still water site in the Upper Forth area. The mean of the peak counts during the survey period was 672 birds with a peak of 962 in January 2005. However, these numbers are only a third of relatively recent peak winter counts (2,784 in January 1994) and although not accounting for all of this decline, the dramatic fall in Wigeon numbers from a peak of 1,260 in January 1994, to a mean peak of only 64 during the survey period, is due to the cessation of maintaining an area of grass sward for grazing [M. Callan *pers. comm.*]. Nevertheless, Gartmorn Dam still holds regionally important numbers of Mute Swan, Tufted Duck, Goldeneye, Great Crested Grebe and Coot during the winter period [WeBS] while this survey confirmed Mute Swan, Mallard, Great Crested Grebe, Water Rail, Moorhen and Coot as breeding.

There are a number of small ponds (virtually all of which are scattered throughout the lowlands of the County) which aggregate to approximately 15 ha. of open water [Thiel & Lindsay, 1999]. They have a variety of different origins such as industrial (Delph Pond, Tullibody); ornamental (Inglewood Pond, Alloa); mineral extraction (Kersiepow Ponds); flight ponds (Lawmuir Wood) and ephemeral, natural sink ponds (Cambus Village and Devonmouth Pools). Many of these are monitored by WeBS – some as far back as 1995. The most important of these for wildfowl is the small Kersiepow Pond (NS 899963), whose mean peak monthly count during the survey period was 261 birds made up mostly of Wigeon, Teal and Mallard. (A detailed survey of Clackmannanshire's Ponds was carried out by Craig Macadam in 2004 and subsequently written-up in the *Forth Naturalist and Historian* (vol. 29, 2006; 27-80)). (There is a local HAP for 'Lochs and Ponds').

Woodlands

Broad-leaved woods cover roughly 10% of the land area of the County which is notably higher than that for Scotland (4.5%) or the UK (3.5%). Most of this (c.70%) consists of recently planted broadleaved and mixed areas while only 12.6% is of long-established woodland and a mere 2.4% is classed as ancient woodland. Compared with Scotland as a whole, long established woodland occupies 1.2% of Clackmannanshire (0.7% Scotland) whereas ancient woodland covers only 0.2% of the County (1.1% Scotland). The following key woodland sites have been identified: Upland oakwoods (*Quercus spp*): Dollar Glen and by the Blutherburn in Craigmad Wood SSSIs. Upland mixed ashwoods (*Fraxinus exelsior*): the SSSIs of Back Burn Wood and Meadows; Linn Mill; Dollar Glen; Devon Gorge along with the sloped upland ash/elm (*Ulmus spp*) Menstrie Community Wood and Braewood. Upland birchwoods (*Betula spp*): Back Burn Wood and Meadows SSSI; Brandyhill Wood; Delph Wood; Cowpark Wood and Inglewood. Wet woods: the Gartmorn Dam and Craigmad Wood SSSIs; Devonknowes Bing; Delph Wood and Brucefield Estate. Additionally, the Myreton Wood SSSI is 'a rare Scottish example of wood-pasture' while the Ochil Hills Woodland Park provides way-marked walks through the old policies of the demolished Alva House. The relative abundance and diversity of woodland habitats in the County supports an equally wide range of bird species which favour these habitats.

Figure 5. Broad-leafed woodland. Clackmannanshire Council 2003.

All can be enjoyed as much as anywhere in the lower reaches of the Hillfoot Glens.

There are approximately 822 ha. of planted conifer woodland in Clackmannanshire which equates to c.5.1% of the land area (c.13.4% of Scotland; c.7% in GB). The main areas are The Forest (in the central part of the County) and around Dollar. As well as the ubiquitous Sitka Spruce (*Picea sicthensis*), these plantations contain a variety of conifers including Lodgepole Pine (*Pinus contorta*), Scots Pine (*Pinus Sylvestris*), Norway Spruce (*Picea abies*), larches (*Larix spp*), firs (*Abies spp*) and hemlocks (*Tsuga spp*). Most of these conifer plantations were established after the First World War with the sole intention of replenishing the country's timber stock, which was severely depleted during that conflict. No thought was given to their conservation (or

Deciduous woodland. 2004 © D. Jones

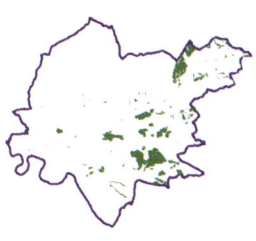

Figure 6. Coniferous woodland. Clackmannanshire Council 2003.

public amenity) value. Indeed, they were often created in important environmental habitats such as raised bogs or native woodland communities. Thankfully, as these stands began to reach maturity, attitudes also changed and forestry managers are now encouraged to consider other values such as nature conservation, scenic quality, access and recreation as well as timber production. This is being achieved by increasing the diversity of tree species, age and structure as well as creating more open spaces and, where possible, returning some areas to their original important environmental habitat e.g., raised bogs and native woodland. The dense, dark and impenetrable mature conifer stands are only utilised by a few conifer specialists such as Goldcrest and Coal Tit and highly adaptable species such as Woodpigeon, Blue Tit and Chaffinch. The more diverse habitats now being created should support a far wider suite of species.

(There are local HAPs for both Broadleaved Woodland and Planted Coniferous Woodland).

Urban and industrial land

Approximately 15% of Clackmannanshire is occupied by housing, industrial and other developments (compared to c.2.4% in Scotland [SNH 1996]) with most of these being located in the western half of the lowlands. Many species of birds make use of the varied habitats to be found within these landscapes; whether it be gulls nesting on the roofs of the otherwise barren expanses of the bonded warehouses to the Red-listed Spotted Flycatcher breeding in the large mature gardens of the older residential properties in Alloa and the Hillfoot towns and villages. Other environments favourable to birds found within these 'concrete jungles' include parks, burial grounds, golf courses, playing fields, wasteland and watercourses.

Crossbill sp's. Courtesy of Wildpix Scotland

River Forth at Alloa 2012. © N. Bielby

Nevertheless, domestic gardens are probably the most important habitat for birds in built – up areas – the total area of gardens in Britain has been calculated to exceed that for all the nature reserves! In the County, they cover about 2% of the land area. The past two decades have seen an increasing number of householders in Scotland providing an ever expanding range of specialist supplementary foods which has undoubtedly assisted the survival of an increased number of birds – especially through the leaner winter and spring periods. However, their value as breeding habitats is not quite as clear-cut, and while urban areas support 62% of Britain's House Sparrows, 54% of the Starlings and 33% of the Blackbirds, studies have shown that species such as Blue and Great Tit (which require large amounts of caterpillars to feed their young) are less productive than their country counterparts [Toms, M. 2008] (some recent data on Clackmannanshire's garden birds can be found online at www.bto.org/gbw under 'Postcode Birds'). Nevertheless, local BBS surveys indicate that, while urban/suburban habitats support less than half the species that are recorded in the combined broad farmland/non-plantation woodland habitat, the number of birds recorded per linear km is 16% higher [Bielby, N. unpubld. data].

(The LBAP contains eight HAPs relative to urban and industrial land).

Neil Bielby

Postscript: a further c.94 ha's (0.6%) of Clackmannanshire was built on subsequent to phase 1 habitat mapping.

Menstrie Maltings 2012. © N. Bielby

Toms, M., Sterry, Dr P. 2008   *Garden Birds and Wildlife*   AA Publishing.
Macaulay Research Consultancy Services   *Land Cover Scotland '88*   2008.
McLusky, D.S. (1987, ed). The Natural Environment of the Estuary and Firth of Forth *Proceedings of the Royal Society of Edinburgh*, 92B, 235-571.
McLusky, D.S., Bryant, D.M., & Elliot, M. (1992). The impact of land-claim on macrobenthos, fish and shorebirds on the Forth Estuary, Eastern Scotland. *Aquatic Conservation: Marine and Freshwater Ecosystems*, 2, 221-222.
Sexton, D., Stewart, E.   Alloa Inch: The Mud Bank that became an Inhabited Island *Forth Naturalist and Historian* Volume 28, 2005, 79-101.
Thiel, A. and Lindsay, H. (1999). Clackmannanshire Local Biodiversity Plan Habitat Audit.
Clackmannanshire Biodiversity Action Plan (CBAP) Campbell, L. et al 2003. Clackmannanshire Biodiversity Partnership.
Clackmannanshire Biodiversity Action Plan (CBAP) Cameron, E. et al 2011. Clackmannanshire Biodiversity Partnership.

Ochil scarp from Cambus. Courtesy of Wildpix Scotland

The climate of Clackmannanshire

Being a small inland county between the Highlands and the Southern Uplands, the weather and climate in Clackmannanshire are largely governed by wind direction. Air-masses affecting the region are modified markedly by topography and by distance from the sea with the Scottish Highlands and Southern Uplands reducing the strength of winds from directions between W and NE and between SSW and SE respectively. However, the Forth and Clyde valleys tend to funnel winds from other directions, especially the prevailing WSW'lies. The strongest winds blow between September and February, the lightest from April to June. During the stormiest winter periods, maximum gusts have reached 80 knots and probably higher over the Ochils. During quiet winter spells, the low ground often receives a cold northerly flow off the Ochils.

The sheltered aspect of the region ensures that the warming (in winter) and cooling (in summer) effects of the sea are reduced except on occasions of strong winds from those directions. In general, average temperatures are lower over the high ground in the north of the region, with an average decrease of 0.7°C per 100 metres of altitude. Mean temperatures rise from a minimum of 3°C in winter to 15°C in summer; likewise, average daily maxima range from 6°C to 19°C. Clackmannanshire's distance from the sea increases the incidence of frost, although even the warmer Forth allows a lower incidence along the river's edge. On the low ground, air frosts (when the air temperature falls below 0°C) occur on 50-60 days in the year, rising to more than 75 over high ground. Ground temperatures fall below 0°C on 120 days in the year rising to 140 over the high ground.

The region's shelter and also proximity to the large conurbations means that fog is common inland in winter, particularly over low ground where it forms overnight. This fog usually clears during the morning except in stagnant winter airmasses, although low cloud can give fog for much longer periods where it sits over the higher ground, especially when east coast 'haar' further down the Forth lifts as it moves westwards.

Rain (or snow) falls from either shower clouds or layer cloud (formed by fronts, i.e. boundaries between air masses). Rainfall is at its minimum in spring and also with wind directions between WNW and NE, reflecting the shelter aspect. Most rain falls during WSW winds and the wettest months are in early winter.

Showery weather in winter is essentially a seaborne type. This means that when showers come from sheltered directions they tend to dissipate over the hills except when driven by strong winds; thus the region remains dry. Showers in Clackmannanshire therefore approach mainly from the southwest, or from the North Sea. In summer, showers are more frequent from landward directions as they develop over the land and move downwind. The heaviest showers are occasionally accompanied by thunderstorms. Although on average six to eight thunderstorms occur over the region during the year, they are most frequent between May and August. Very rarely, the associated hail and rain can be heavy and damaging.

Rain from fronts is more frequent in winter than in summer, as the associated depressions take a more southerly track across the Atlantic, and therefore cross near or over Britain more frequently. Such depressions are also much more active in winter, producing more rain-bearing cloud. For example, over the lower ground there are 16 wet days in an average December, but only 10 in April. The topography of Clackmannanshire is such that the driest parts are in the extreme southeast, south of Clackmannan itself, where the average annual rainfall is 830 mm. The rainfall increases up the Forth, exceeding 900 mm at Cambus and 950 mm along the Hillfoot towns. The higher reaches of the Ochils receive much more rain, exceeding 1,200 mm in places.

Snow is most frequent in January, but varies considerably from winter to winter. Only in the severest winters does enough snow fall to make conditions hazardous. Again, the area most prone to snowfall is the Ochils, where snow may lie for more than 35 days during an average winter, in contrast to the 15 days per winter on the lower ground and even less by the Forth. Recent mild winters will have reduced this frequency. As with rain, the shelter of the Ochils ensures that snow is distributed according to wind direction, so that the Hillfoot towns remain snow-free in a northerly snow-bearing airstream.

Cloudiness is closely associated with the passage of fronts, and therefore is at its greatest in winter. Sunshine averages at around 1,280 hours per year, considerably less than further east, thus reflecting the higher rainfall. Monthly sunshine over the lower ground ranges from 35 hours in December to 170 hours in June. The higher ground has the greatest frequency of cloud.

Norman Elkins

Weather during the Survey Periods

(Data used is from a Dunblane weather station 1995-2011(the 'overall mean'))

Weather events during a relatively short survey period (such as that for this Atlas) can affect the survival, breeding success and detectability of birds such that the long-term trends of species can be mis-represented. A notable recent example is the Stonechat. A run of comparatively mild winters from 1996/1997 to 2008/2009 saw wintering numbers for this species increase; an increase reflected in the winter map. However, the prolonged spell of severe weather during the winter of 2009/2010 decimated the population in Scotland such that numbers on BBS transects fell by 77% between 2009 and 2010.

Below are descriptive summaries and graphs of the weather during the survey periods. It can be seen that the averaged April to July temperatures are close to the overall mean with rainfall during these months being close to the average apart from in 2002 when it was much wetter. Averaged November to February temperatures were at or above the overall mean while precipitation totals were at or below the overall mean apart from 2002/3, when they were quite a bit higher.

Spring/summer 2002

April was warmer and slightly drier than usual whereas May was a little warmer but much wetter than normal with 77% more rainfall than average. The second half of the month was very unsettled. June was wet with rainfall of 54% above the mean while July continued in the same vein with 156.3 mm of rain, which was 90% above the norm, making it the wettest July in 17 years at this station.

Spring/summer 2003

April was a little warmer and drier than normal with only 31.2 mm of rain while May was mostly unsettled with both the temperature and rainfall being slightly above average. June and July were both notably warmer and a little drier than usual with temperatures peaking at 29.1°C (14 July).

Spring/summer 2004

April was slightly warmer and wetter than usual with May being both quite a bit warmer and drier than the norm. The mean temperature in June was just above the average but rainfall was 53% greater than the mean with 26 days of measurable rainfall (> 0.1mm). July was slightly cooler with only 52% of the average rainfall.

Spring/summer 2005

April was cool and wet with 53% more rainfall than the norm. May was also slightly cooler than usual and again much wetter – the 117.4 mm being the highest May total during the data period. June was notably warmer with rainfall just above the norm while July was slightly warmer but much drier than normal with the 21.4 mm of recorded rainfall making it the driest ever month at this station, only 26% of the month's mean.

Winter 2005/6

November was a little colder and quite a bit drier than the norm with 67% of average precipitation and 12 air frosts. December was milder and drier than usual with 65% of average precipitation, 19 air-frosts and a low temperature of -5.8°C. January was also milder but much drier than normal with the 56.5 mm of precipitation being only 47% of the norm. There were 11 air-frosts and a low temperature of -6.5°C. February experienced average temperatures but was again much drier than usual with the recorded 45.3 mm of precipitation being only 44% of the mean. There were 14 air-frosts and a low temperature of -4.7°C. In total, snow lay on the ground on only seven occasions at 09.00 hours.

Spring/summer 2006

April was markedly colder and drier than usual with 65% of average rainfall while the May mean temperatures was close to normal but rainfall was 33% above average. June enjoyed warmer and drier weather than the norm with measurable rainfall on only seven days (mean = 15). July was the hottest ever at this station with the mean temperature of 19.02°C being 3.18°C above the average. A high of 29.5°C was recorded with rainfall being only half the norm.

Winter 2006/7

November, December and January were all much wetter than normal (+ 70%; + 102% and + 60% respectively) with above average temperatures. There were a total of 21 air-frosts. February was milder and drier than usual with 10 air-frosts and recorded the coldest temperature of the winter of -8.1°C. In total, snow lay on the ground on only five occasions at 09.00 hours during these months.

Spring/summer 2007

April 2007 was warmer and much drier than the norm with only 26.5 mm of rainfall, 43% of the mean. May was cooler and wetter while June had normal temperatures but 43% more rain. July was a little cooler and wetter than normal.

Neil Bielby (November 2011).

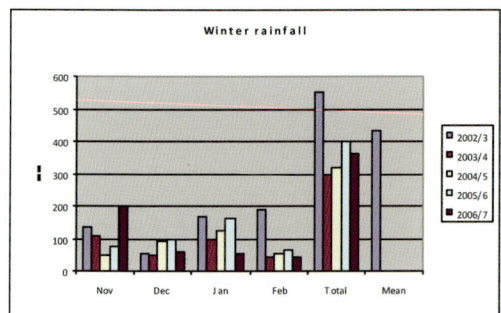
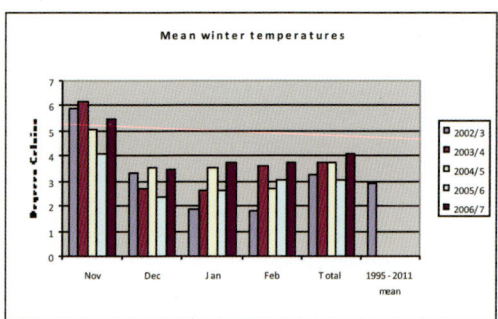
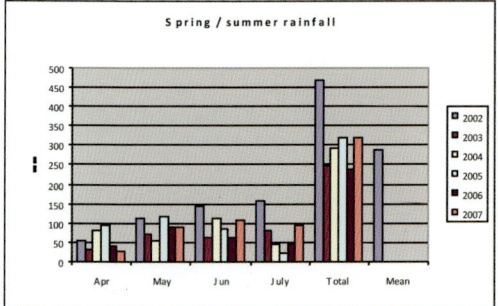
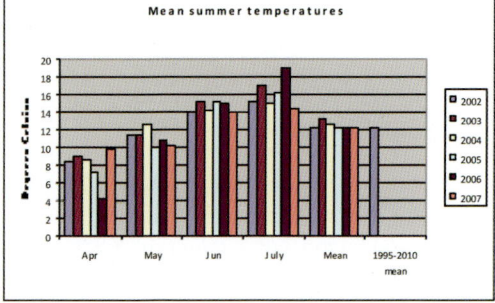

Data Management and Map production

The field recording and supplementary forms were returned to the fieldwork organiser as soon as possible after the end of the relevant season. Their data was then inputted onto master spreadsheets and backed up. Any future printouts of squares were checked against the original archived paper form(s).

Data from the master spreadsheets along with other sources such as the local bird reports, WeBS records and *Birdtrack* (the latter being subjected to critical review before acceptance) were input to a Microsoft Access database where all of the breeding and winter season records were held in a single system. Altogether 6,678 breeding season one kilometre square records and 1,582 winter tetrad records were accumulated, together with 547 mammal records (mostly by 1 km square).

On completion of the fieldwork, an audit was performed which compared all submitted records against their equivalent database records for a randomly generated 10% of squares. Satisfyingly, this threw up very few anomalies, and the computer file data set was deemed fit to be subsequently re-exported as a set of files (each of which contained records for a single species in either the breeding or winter season) for the production of the species maps.

Initial map production for illustrative purposes used DMAP but this was superseded midway through the project by a GIS system (ArcGIS version 9 (ESRI 2006)). Using this, provisional outline species distribution maps for information (and to highlight possible gaps in coverage) were produced. On completion of fieldwork, maps with an added backdrop showing physical features, were sent to species account writers who were asked to note any extra records unearthed during their research. The final distribution maps for publication (incorporating any new records and suggested minor base map changes) were then produced.

Neil Bielby

Reed Bunting. Courtesy of Wildpix Scotland

A discussion of the Atlas results

As mentioned in the introduction, the fundamental reason for undertaking the *Atlas* project was to establish for the first time an accurate baseline for bird distribution in Clackmannanshire. We believe that this has been achieved during the period 2002-2007 by surveying all species systematically, using a uniform methodology during both the breeding and winter seasons.

It is to be hoped that from now on it will be possible to carry out distribution surveys within the County, whether of individual species or complete lists, with confidence that differences found will reflect actual changes that have taken place.

Table 1.   30 Most Widespread Species Breeding in Clackmannanshire.

Rank	Species	No of kms	% of kms	Rank	Species	No of kms	% of kms
1st	Carrion Crow	177	89%	16th	Song Thrush	120	60%
2nd	Wren	169	85%	17th	Rook	119	60%
3rd	Chaffinch	149	75%	18th	Jackdaw	118	59%
4th	Woodpigeon	147	74%	19th	Magpie	113	57%
5th	Blackbird	145	73%	20th	Swift	111	56%
6th	Blue Tit	144	72%	21st	Mallard	109	55%
7th	Swallow	143	72%	22nd=	Coal Tit	108	54%
8th	Buzzard	142	71%	22nd=	Greenfinch	108	54%
9th	Robin	137	69%	24th	Pheasant	106	53%
10th	Great Tit	135	68%	25th	Goldfinch	104	52%
11th	Willow Warbler	133	67%	26th=	Meadow Pipit	103	52%
12th	Skylark	130	65%	26th=	Whitethroat	103	52%
13th	Dunnock	129	65%	28th	House Sparrow	100	50%
14th	Pied Wagtail	123	62%	29th	Kestrel	99	50%
15th	Starling	121	61%	30th	Yellowhammer	96	48%

Despite the habitat of Clackmannanshire differing to varying degrees from the two closest published local breeding bird atlases (SE Scotland and Fife) the five most widespread species are almost identical in all three areas (albeit in different orders) – the exception being that Willow Warbler replaces Blackbird in SE Scotland. With this survey using the one kilometre square as the base unit rather than the tetrad used in the other two atlases, the percentage of squares occupied by a particular species tends to be lower. Additionally, only that part of a square actually falling within the County was surveyed in Clackmannanshire whereas full tetrads were surveyed around the boundaries of the other two atlas areas. Those 'part-squares' with less than half their area in Clackmannanshire also received notably lower surveyor effort than the rest.

It should be noted that the habitat mix in the *SE. Scotland Atlas* area is much closer to that in Clackmannanshire than is that of the *Fife Atlas* area which has much less upland. This explains why the order of the list for Clackmannanshire mirrors that of South-east Scotland more closely than that for Fife.

The most striking difference is probably shown by Buzzard which is the 8th most widespread species in Clackmannanshire but wasn't in the top 30 most widespread species in South-east Scotland or the top 20 in Fife. This is almost certainly due to the time of the survey periods (1988-1994 South-east Scotland and 1991-1999 Fife) and in itself, illustrates the rapid eastward expansion of the species in Scotland during the past two decades. Current fieldwork for a second *South-east Scotland Atlas* will no doubt show the Buzzard to be as ubiquitous there as in Clackmannanshire.

Other differences which stand out are the Magpie, which is the 19th most widespread species in Clackmannanshire but doesn't appear in either Fife's top 20 or South-east Scotland's top 30. Somewhat surprisingly, Blue Tit is only 20th in the ubiquity list for South-east Scotland while being 6th in Clackmannanshire and 7th in Fife. Similarly, the Great Tit (10th) was relatively more ubiquitous in the County than in Fife (15th) or South-east Scotland where it fell just outside the top 30 species. There is also a notable difference in the placing of Meadow Pipit in the lists with it being the 13th most widespread in South-east Scotland, 26th in Clackmannanshire but not appearing in Fife's list – probably as good an indication as any of the relative amount of upland in each area.

Changes in the avifauna of Clackmannanshire

Due to both natural causes and the actions of man, the occurrence and numbers of birds in any area are constantly changing and Clackmannanshire is no exception. Intensive *Atlas* fieldwork has almost certainly established that since at least 2007, Black Grouse, Ring Ouzel, Pied Flycatcher and Corn Bunting no longer breed in the County. These species are added to the likes of Bittern, Corncrake and Nightjar which were considered to have either bred or probably bred in 'historical' times (pre 1935).

On the positive side, Buzzards, Chiffchaffs and Magpies have become widespread established breeders in the County during the past two decades, while Common Gulls were recorded breeding in Clackmannanshire for the first time during fieldwork for the *Atlas*.

The following lists are of species whose breeding populations in Clackmannanshire are considered to have changed between 1974 and 2007 (those marked with a * are species whose Scottish BBS trends are statistically significant between 1995 and 2007 period and which corroborate (or at least do not conflict with) the County lists [Risely et al 2009].

Breeding species increased:
Buzzard*, Little Grebe, Coot, Collared Dove, Great Spotted Woodpecker*, Magpie, Jackdaw, Raven*, Goldcrest*, Great Tit*, Swallow*, House Martin*, Chiffchaff*, Blackcap*, Whitethroat*, Wren*, Blackbird*, Song Thrush*, Mistle Thrush*, Robin*, Stonechat* (numbers since decimated by the prolonged severe winter weather during 2010), Dunnock*, House Sparrow*, Tree Sparrow, Grey Wagtail* (numbers also greatly reduced by the severe winter weather during 2010), Tree Pipit*, Goldfinch*, Siskin and Reed Bunting*.

Breeding species decreased:
Grey Partridge, Kestrel*, Oystercatcher*, Lapwing*, Curlew*, Common Sandpiper, Cuckoo, Swift*, Rook*, Spotted Flycatcher, Whinchat, Meadow Pipit*, Lesser Redpoll and Bullfinch.

The following lists are of species whose wintering populations in Clackmannanshire are considered to have changed between 1974 and the 2007/8 winter (Nov.-Feb.).

Wintering species increased: Pink-footed Goose, Greylag Goose.

Wintering species decreased: Mallard, Pochard, Tufted Duck, Coot, Starling.
Where appropriate, the individual species accounts have further specific information regarding changes in populations.

Neil Bielby

Introduction to Species Accounts

Accounts of the 98 'breeding' species and 21 'non-breeding' species recorded in the course of the *Atlas* surveys (April 2002 to July 2007) are included in the first two parts of this section (species only considered as 'breeding' if there were at least two 'probable' registrations). Part 3 covers 37 other species recorded in the County during the survey period. Brief accounts for those 25 species which were recorded during the period between the first publication of the present *Bird Reports* in 1974 and the beginning of the *Atlas* surveys follow in Part 4. At one stage it had been hoped to use the *Atlas* findings as the basis for a systematic avifauna of Clackmannanshire – something unattempted since a series of lectures on The Birds of Clackmannanshire given by Dr. P. Brotherston to the rather grandly titled Alloa Society of Natural Science and Archaeology between 1865 and 1870, and published in the Society's Transactions. However, it became apparent that the amount of work involved in assessing historical records (with the attendant problems of imprecise locations and later boundary changes) with the limited resources available would have delayed the project even more than the four years that have elapsed since the completion of the field work. That task awaits a dedicated researcher, but in the meantime a list of historical records of 10 species which were attributed to Clackmannanshire by the redoubtable Misses Rintoul & Baxter (1935) has been included as Part 5. Finally, (and notwithstanding the cut-off date referred to below), a list of 3 'new' species for the County recorded between 2008 and 2011 has been appended as Part 6.

Within each section accounts are arranged in the sequence in The British List published by the British Ornithologists' Union in September 2011. Similarly, the names used are those of The British List: the British (English) vernacular name, followed by the IOC International English name where this is different, and finally the scientific name. Within the text British vernacular names are used throughout. Place names within the text are listed in the Gazetteer (appendix 11) with national grid references.

In summary, each species account is intended to provide a brief introduction to the species, followed by a concise description and analysis of the survey findings. These are related to Scottish and UK population trends and relevant data from other surveys, notably those of the *Upper Forth Area Bird Reports*. Anomalies are highlighted, and opportunities for further survey work identified where this would be practicable. As with the overall scope of the publication, the original intention for the individual accounts was more ambitious, and a considerable debt of gratitude is owed to the long-suffering account writers who were asked to make substantial cuts and revisions to material which they had conscientiously prepared in accordance with earlier guidance. The following paragraphs deal with more detailed aspects of the final versions, together with some of the implications of the pruning processes.

Status: Following the title is a brief description of the species's current quantitative and temporal status in Clackmannanshire, together with its latest UK conservation status at the completion of editing. Local status is based on the following broad definitions:

> Common: occurs regularly in fairly large numbers in suitable habitat.

> Fairly common: widely but thinly distributed in suitable habitat.

> Locally common: occurs in good numbers in specific habitats.

> Uncommon: occurs in small numbers, often restricted to specific habitats.

Scarce: occurs annually in very small numbers.

Irregular: recorded less than annually.

Vagrant: less than six records since 1974.

Resident: breeding and recorded throughout the year, but summer and winter populations do not necessarily consist of the same individuals.

Summer visitor: breeds annually but not present in winter.

Introduced breeder: non-native birds often dependent on captive breeding programmes.

Winter visitor: present outside the breeding season.

Visitor: occurs at any time of the year, but does not breed.

Passage migrant: recorded on passage through the area.

Introductory section: Most accounts open with a short description of aspects of the species which affect its distribution, or which have a bearing on the survey data (confusion species, problems of recording certain categories of breeding etc.). It is not intended to duplicate guidance on identification which is readily available in other publications.

Survey findings: Wherever appropriate the essential findings of the surveys are presented graphically using maps and data boxes. The accompanying text is by way of commentary on the data, for example by relating distribution to habitat preferences. Resident birds usually have a separate paragraph dealing with the winter distribution in the County, as well as references to topics such as movements and the possible existence of sub-species.

Discussion: The fluid nature of bird populations, both in distribution and abundance, is now widely recognised, and no local atlas can present its data without attempting to relate them to a broader picture. There is a mass of information now available: atlases range in focus from continents through countries down to local counties or smaller 'patches'; in the UK there is a continuing stream of survey results from the Breeding Bird Survey, the Wetland Bird Survey, Garden BirdWatch (to mention only the better-known); and more recently the ever-shifting spotlight shone by web-sites such as the BTO's formidable BirdTrack and BirdFacts. Contributors were encouraged to be very selective in their use of this material with an emphasis on clear correlations, even though this brings the attendant risk of over-simplification.

One problem facing the producers of a 'paper-based' publication is that of cut-off; after struggling to keep up with an ever-moving target, it was decided in this case to relate the *Atlas* findings to the trends which were apparent at the end of the survey period – for example the BBS data were those available from the 2008 survey. Inevitably this will lead to some raised eyebrows as readers find mention of the mild winters during the survey period with the harsh winter conditions of 2009/10 and 2010/11 still in their minds.

Many recent atlases have included estimates of population for each species. Ideally some form of abundancy survey would have been undertaken to achieve consistency in such estimates, but as mentioned in the Methodology section this proved to be impracticable. After some discussion it was decided that 'guesstimates' would be of limited value, especially as the latest BTO Atlas surveys were about to take place with Timed Tetrad Visits which would provide more accurate and consistent data across the UK. So the only population estimates included in the species accounts are for those species where numbers are small and breeding behaviour allows a reasonably accurate assessment to be made, or where counts are available from other sources as in the case of wintering wildfowl.

Part of the value of local atlases lies in their capacity to identify local anomalies, as in the case of birds failing to be recorded in areas where the habitat seems to be favourable, or conversely seeming to be attracted to areas where they might not be expected. Species account writers were encouraged to draw attention to these instances, and also to suggest where further studies might be fruitful, bearing in mind that some of the more technically advanced (and expensive) approaches such as radio-tracking or isotope analysis were unlikely to be available for use in the County. Most examples highlighted in this *Atlas* are of unexplained gaps in distribution, whether patchy as in the case of Pheasants, Skylarks and Sparrowhawks, or larger areas of absence as for Stock Doves and Magpies. It also became clear that some species such as Buzzard, Water Rail or Long-eared Owl were in need of more intensive study.

References: References form an essential part of any serious study of bird species today, and these have been included for all but the most basic and general observations. As the species accounts are deliberately concise it was felt that to include such references within the text would be a serious distraction, so the decision was taken to use superscript numerals referring to an abbreviated reference within a footnote, with a full listing in Appendix 12. On-line references present a new challenge, partly because they are constantly being updated, and more seriously, because their permanence cannot always be guaranteed. Although generally with references priority is given to primary sources, for on-line material priority has been given to the more 'official' websites such as the BTO's *BirdFacts*, even though these often contain compilations from other on-line sources.

John Grainger, January 2013

BREEDING SPECIES

Mute Swan   *Cygnus olor*

Fairly common resident

Conservation status: Green

A combination of size, the male's vigorous defence of its breeding territory, obvious large nest, limited site options and prolonged occupation of the latter throughout the breeding season mean that few, if any, breeding pairs of Mute Swans should have been missed. The scattered 16 observed, possible and probable records probably refer to immatures and non-breeding adults.

For breeding, Mute Swans will utilise any still or slow moving waterbody which has an adequate supply of food – either in the form of natural aquatic vegetation or that provided by humans. Prior to this Atlas survey, confirmed breeding had been recorded at five still-water sites and at various locations along the lower River Devon downstream of Tillicoultry.[1] The present survey has added another five still-water sites. A maximum of c.20 breeding pairs is thus indicated which is similar to the 15 confirmed breeding pairs found in the County during the Scottish Mute Swan census of 2002.[2]

WeBS winter maxima in the County during the survey period ranged between 29 and 83 birds (a high of 156 were recorded in November 1997), but some winter flocks feeding on field crops may have been missed. Some site maxima (month/year) include: 156 at Gartmorn Dam (November 1997); 46 on the lower Devon (January 1999) and 35 in the Cambus area (February 1975).

Although Mute Swans are largely sedentary, some movement does occur, especially during the moult and winter periods.[3] Birds with Darvic leg rings have been recorded from ringing schemes in Angus, Clyde, Fife & Lothian.[4]

The 2002 Scottish census revealed a 41% increase in numbers over the previous one in 1990 to a new national high of 7,028 birds. However, any future increase in the breeding numbers in Clackmannanshire will depend upon the creation of suitable new sites.

Neil Bielby

[1] UFABR [2] Brown & Brown, 2005 [3] BS3 [4] UFABR

Breeding Distribution

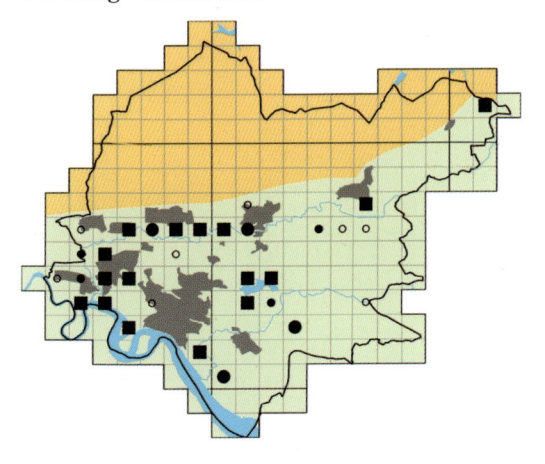

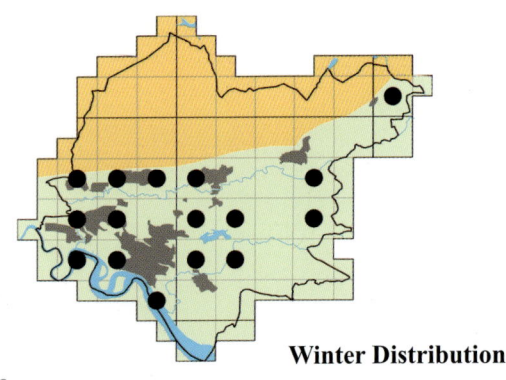

Number of km² in which recorded:	32	(16.2%)
■ Confirmed breeding	16	(50.0%)
● Probable breeding	4	(12.5%)
• Possible breeding	4	(12.5%)
○ Present, breeding unlikely:	8	(25.0%)

Winter Distribution

Shelduck   (Common Shelduck)   *Tadorna tadorna*

Fairly common resident

Conservation status: Amber

Shelducks are mostly located around the British coast wherever suitable habitat of muddy or sandy estuary and foreshore occurs. Typically cited as nesting in rabbit burrows, they will use a wide range of nest sites so long as they are adjacent to good feeding areas and provide the concealment necessary for such a strikingly plumaged duck.

The breeding map shows the main concentration to be in the vicinity of the River Forth while inland there are small clusters in the Devon Valley below Alva, to the east of Gartmorn Dam and on Parklands Moss to the east of Forestmill. Well over half of all registrations were of pairs; the fact that these were not converted to confirmed breeding is probably due to the difficulty in finding nests combined with a low success rate; also, once inland clutches have hatched the parents probably head with their broods straight for the Forth where crèches are formed.[1,2]

Breeding dispersal begins in late winter with birds appearing in the Cambus area from January onwards.[3,4] Although pairs have been recorded on the River Devon by Alva on a regular basis since 1982, breeding has yet to be confirmed here and thus appears to be confined to the Forth and its immediate environs.[5] It is thought that less than half the Shelducks present in spring attempt to breed,[6] and this would account for local records of up to 147 birds on Tullibody Inch and 102 on Alloa Inch in May.[7]

In July and August the nearby Grangemouth area of the Forth is one of the Shelduck's major UK moult sites, and up to 210 birds have been recorded around the Alloa and Tullibody Inches during this period.[8] The winter map shows Shelducks to be virtually confined to the Forth with a December mean of c.50 birds (2004-2006).[9]

Neil Bielby

[1] *BS3* [2] *Pers. obs.* [3] *BS3* [4] *WeBS unpub. data* [5] *UFABR* [6] *Yarker & Atkinson-Willes, 1972* [7] *UFABR* [8] *ibid.* [9] *WeBS unpub. data*

Breeding Distribution

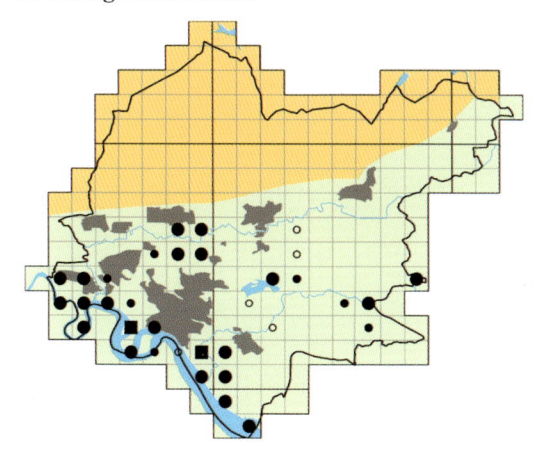

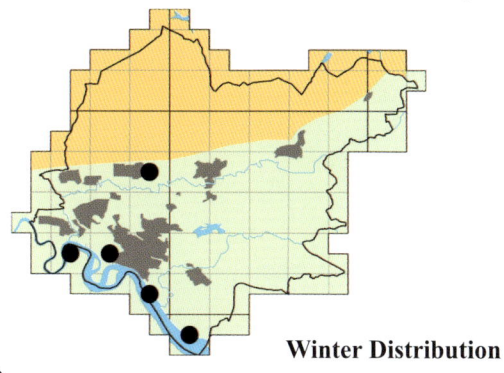

Number of km² in which recorded:	34	(17.2%)
■ Confirmed breeding	2	(5.9%)
● Probable breeding	20	(58.8%)
• Possible breeding	7	(20.6%)
○ Present, breeding unlikely:	5	(14.7%)

Winter Distribution

Gadwall   *Anas strepera*

Scarce passage migrant and summer visitor   Conservation status: Amber

Appearing somewhat dull and grey at a distance, close views reveal the drake Gadwall to be subtly plumaged with exquisite vermicular body markings. From afar, or given a brief or casual glance, the slightly smaller female duck can be mistaken for its Mallard counterpart. Shallow eutrophic waters with dense submerged plant growth suitable for their essentially vegetarian diet are preferred. The nest, normally close to the water's edge, is hidden in long grass or under thick scrub.[1] The species has a scattered, localised distribution in Scotland where the breeding population is put at 100-150 pairs.[2]

Several factors (secretiveness, scarcity, *etc.*) contribute towards the Gadwall being a difficult species to monitor during breeding. Three probable and three possible registrations were returned during *Atlas* fieldwork. Two of the probable records came from adjacent squares in the Cambus area where a maximum of three pairs were recorded at Cambus Village Pool, two at Cambus Pools and one at Devonmouth Pool. The other probable record was of a pair on the Blackdevon Wetlands pools. Single birds were recorded on the two main Gartmorn Dam squares with another in the Tullibody Inch/Longcarse area.

The first County record was of a pair at Marchglen in April 1975. Despite being recorded almost annually during the breeding season at both Gartmorn Dam and various pools in the Cambus area since 1990, there has only been one record of confirmed breeding – a female with six young at Cambus Pools (May 1990).[3]

Local Bird Report records clearly indicate spring and autumn peaks for the occurrence of birds in the County suggesting that many of these are likely to be passage migrants. Occasionally a few overwinter – always on Gartmorn Dam.[4]

Neil Bielby

[1] BWP [2] BS3 [3] UFABR [4] ibid.

Breeding Distribution

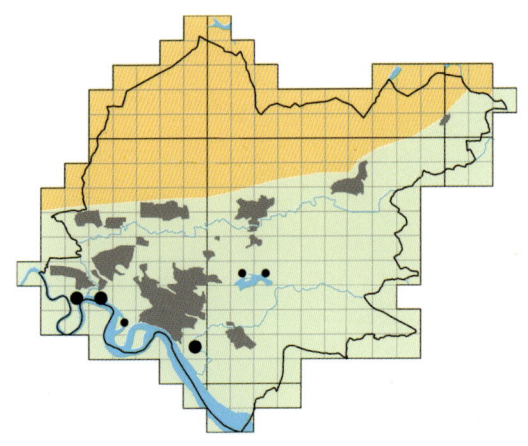

Number of km² in which recorded:	6	(3.0%)
■ Confirmed breeding	0	(0.0%)
● Probable breeding	3	(50.0%)
• Possible breeding	3	(50.0%)
○ Present, breeding unlikely:	0	(0.0%)

Teal (Eurasian Teal) *Anas crecca*

Uncommon resident and common winter visitor

Conservation status: Amber

The Teal is our smallest duck. In the breeding season it occurs on small, often isolated, waterbodies and slow-flowing streams with a dense fringe but it also nests on heathland and under scrub.[1]

Teal were registered in 11% of Atlas squares, making them the second most common duck during the breeding season. They occurred primarily along the River Forth and at its confluence with the Black Devon (mainly probably breeding) and along the River Devon downstream of Dollar (mainly non-breeding). They were virtually absent from the Black Devon and from the upper reaches of the Devon. There are only two confirmed breeding records from Clackmannanshire since 1974 – on the Blackdevon Wetlands in 1998 and 1999 – with suspected breeding at Alva and Menstrie Mosses in 1987 and 1988.[2] Although Teal are elusive during breeding, in the light of these records the small number of squares with probable and possible breeding records still appears high and some if not all of these may refer to non-breeders and/or passage birds.

In winter the UK population is swelled by migrants from northern Europe.[3] In contrast to the general situation noted in the Winter Atlas of the early 1980s, the Teal's winter distribution in Clackmannanshire mirrors that of its breeding distribution. Between 1974 and 2002 the largest concentrations were recorded from Gartmorn Dam 500 (January 1986), the Forth at Cambus 474 (January 1990), Tullibody Inch 466 (January 1979), Kennetpans 164 (January 1995) and, latterly, Kersiepow near Tillicoultry 136 (November 2000).[4] Earlier, in November 1962 (before the discharge of waste grain from the distillery there was stopped) 4,390 Teal were counted at Cambus.[5] WeBS counts during the Atlas period suggest a peak of just under 1,000 birds with around 70% being recorded on the Forth, 19% on the Devon and 11% on still-water inland sites.[6]

Andre Thiel

[1] BWP [2] UFABR [3] Migration Atlas [4] UFABR [5] BS2 [6] WeBS unpub. data

Breeding Distribution

Number of km² in which recorded:	21	(10.6%)
■ Confirmed breeding	0	(0.0%)
● Probable breeding	5	(23.8%)
● Possible breeding	3	(14.3%)
○ Present, breeding unlikely:	13	(61.9%)

Winter Distribution

Mallard   *Anas platyrhynchos*

Common resident and winter visitor   Conservation status: Amber

The Mallard's relatively undemanding habitat requirements, varied omnivorous diet and range of feeding methods allow it to occupy all manner of water features.[1] Familiar to most and conspicuous away from the nest, Mallard provide few survey problems. However, the difficulty of spotting the cryptically plumaged duck when sitting on eggs (often in dense vegetation) may have given rise to some under-recording in squares with sub-optimal habitat from which the young would probably have been led on hatching.

Mallard were registered in over 50% of squares with the breeding map showing a widespread distribution in the lowlands but a more scattered one in the Ochils. In lowland areas, they were absent from urban squares without a water component and from the mid-county ridge to the east of Gartmorn Dam (which also contains few water features). Although there were several probable records, breeding wasn't confirmed in the Ochils.

The most obvious feature of the winter distribution in comparison to the breeding map is the Mallard's absence from the Ochils. The species was also apparently absent between Dollar and Muckhart (an area where this species had also been sparsely recorded during the Breeding Survey). Overall County winter peaks during the *Atlas* period ranged from 312 to 587 birds. The WeBS Scottish Index shows a steady decline with numbers now only a third of those in the mid 1960s.[2] This decline is very evident at Gartmorn Dam where there has been a dramatic drop in numbers since the mid 1980s with the peak count falling from 1,290 (December 1985) to a maximum of 254 (December 2004) during the Atlas years.

Further observation and monitoring at Gartmorn Dam and elsewhere might help to explain the recent declines; whether they result from changes in wintering distribution or from pathogenic or other causes.

Neil Bielby

[1] 1998-91 Atlas   [2] WeBS unpub. data

Breeding Distribution

Number of km² in which recorded:	109	(55.1%)
■ Confirmed breeding	39	(35.8%)
● Probable breeding	44	(40.4%)
• Possible breeding	17	(15.6%)
○ Present, breeding unlikely:	9	(8.3%)

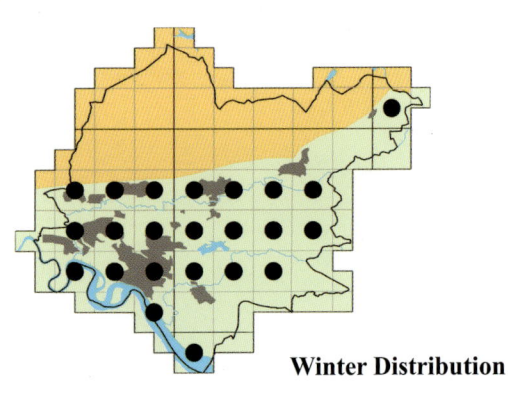

Winter Distribution

Tufted Duck   *Aythya fuligula*

Locally common resident and common winter visitor   Conservation status: Amber

The distinctive pied drake and its more muted mate are probably the second most familiar duck to the general public. The diving Tufted Duck is omnivorous and favours nutrient rich, still waters, preferably no deeper than five metres.[1]

Several pairs were found nesting at Gartmorn Dam in 1934 from where there have been occasional reports of broods since 1974.[2] Current knowledge suggests that there are presently 10-15 breeding pairs in the County.[3] During the *Atlas* survey Tufted Ducks were recorded on most of the few suitable still-water bodies in Clackmannanshire, but breeding was only confirmed on one, although being a late breeder with most broods not hatched until July, some may well have been missed.

The intermittent reports of largish gatherings on Gartmorn Dam during late summer – the highest being 340 (August 1979)[4] – are probably of moulting birds drawn mostly from around central Scotland, with many likely to have come from the large breeding population at Loch Leven (Fife).

Regular counts show that the monthly winter peaks in the County during the Atlas years ranged from 111 to 275 birds with Gartmorn Dam holding 88% of these; other still-water sites held 9% and the River Devon 3%. Numbers at Gartmorn Dam have fallen from a record 807 birds (February 1972) to winter peaks which ranged from 105 to 226 during the *Atlas* period.[5] Since 1982 only the odd bird has been recorded on the River Forth between Cambus and South Alloa but previously there had been the occasional large count – sometimes linked to hard weather e.g. c.750 birds at Tullibody Inch (February1979).[6]

Future observation at Gartmorn Dam during July and August would prove useful, both by monitoring breeding success and by gathering information on the presence and size of any moulting flock.

Neil Bielby

[1] BWP   [2] Rintoul & Baxter, 1935   [3] UFABR   [4] ibid   [5] WeBS unpub.data   [6] UFABR

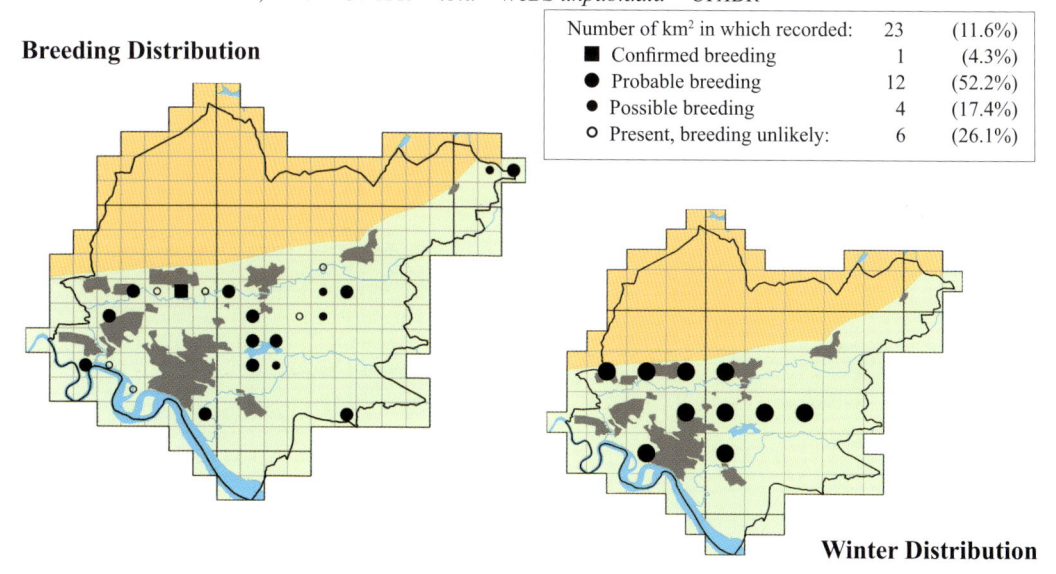

Breeding Distribution

Number of km² in which recorded:	23	(11.6%)
■ Confirmed breeding	1	(4.3%)
● Probable breeding	12	(52.2%)
• Possible breeding	4	(17.4%)
○ Present, breeding unlikely:	6	(26.1%)

Winter Distribution

Goosander (Common Merganser) *Mergus merganser*

Locally common resident and winter visitor   Conservation status: Green

The Goosander nests in tree holes and other cavities adjacent to the upper reaches of rivers and their tributaries as well as by lochs with well wooded shores or islands. The fact that the downy ducklings leave the nest when one to two days old, proceeding first to the nearest waterbody and then fairly quickly downstream on watercourses, makes it difficult to allocate this type of breeding record to any particular location with certainty.[1] Female and juvenile Goosanders can be confused with their Red-breasted Mergansers counterparts if views are poor.

Most breeding *Atlas* records were from the suitable habitat of the upper River Devon and all three confirmed registrations were from this stretch. The probable record at the Blackdevon Wetlands would appear to be in sub-optimal habitat whereas the two 'observed' records on the upper Devon should probably have been listed as possible. There were no registrations from the Black Devon.

The winter map shows Goosanders to be virtually confined to the River Forth and the Devon below Dollar, and with these (and other waterbodies) well monitored by WeBS, there can be some confidence in the calculated winter peak of 30-40 birds. Notable individual counts include 62 at Tullibody Inch (February 1979), 34 at Gartmorn Dam – possibly a roost count (December 1977) and 20 at Cambus Pools (October 1997).[2,3] After a brief doubling of numbers in the early 1980s, the WeBS Scottish index has since reverted to and remained fairly constant around the levels of the early 1970s.[4]

Legal (under licence) and illegal persecution by game fishing interests probably present the main threat to the species.

Neil Bielby

[1] BS3 [2] WeBS unpub. data [3] UFABR [4] WeBS unpub. data

Breeding Distribution

Number of km² in which recorded:	20	(10.1%)
■ Confirmed breeding	3	(15.0%)
● Probable breeding	6	(30.0%)
• Possible breeding	2	(10.0%)
○ Present, breeding unlikely:	9	(45.0%)

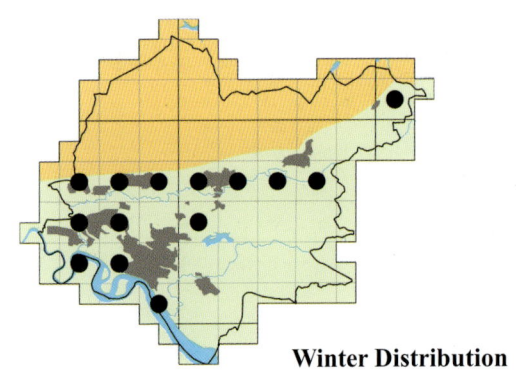

Winter Distribution

Red Grouse   (Willow Ptarmigan)   *Lagopus lagopus*

Scarce Resident

Conservation status: Amber

The Red Grouse (some ornithologists think it should be a separate species – *L. scoticus*)[1] is almost entirely dependent upon heather (*Calluna vulgaris*) for food, shelter and nesting sites. The breeding *Atlas* map shows the species to be restricted to the area around the heather-dominated Alva and Menstrie Mosses in the Ochils.

The Old Statistical Account for Tillicoultry mentions Red Grouse as being on the hills 'but not as frequently as formerly, as the heath is wearing out'.[2] The Bird Reports note it as being 'frequent on heather and heather/grass on Alva & Menstrie Moss' in 1974, whereas there were 'few on the high mosses' two years later – evidence perhaps of the well-documented cyclic nature of Red Grouse populations? They were also found at a relatively low density here during an intensive survey of upland birds during the 1987 breeding season. [3,4]

Unsurprisingly for such a sedentary species, the winter map shows a similar distribution as that for breeding with the addition of an isolated record in the Maddy Moss area.

Although managed grouse moors are viewed as an important economic resource in other areas of Scotland,[5] only occasional rough shooting would appear to take place in the County.[6] Despite several centuries of intensive grazing, during which time heather has become a scarce habitat in the Ochils, Red Grouse appear to be sustaining a small population in Clackmannanshire. However, in order for them to expand, grazing pressure in the Ochils would need to be radically reduced in order to allow the heather to recolonize.

Neil Bielby

[1] *Gutiérrez et al., 2000*   [2] *Rintoul & Baxter, 1935*   [3] UFABR   [4] *Calladine et al., 1990*   [5] BS3
[6] D. Matthews pers. comm.

Breeding Distribution

Number of km² in which recorded:	8	(4.0%)
■ Confirmed breeding	1	(12.5%)
● Probable breeding	3	(37.5%)
● Possible breeding	4	(50.0%)
○ Present, breeding unlikely:	0	(0.0%)

Winter Distribution

Red-legged Partridge *Alectoris rufa*

Scarce introduced resident (sustained by releases)

The Red-legged Partridge is reared and released for recreational shooting purposes in many places in Scotland. These birds are of Mediterranean stock and with only sub-optimal breeding conditions available in this country, it is both unclear and doubtful whether a feral population from these introduced birds is, or could be, self-sustaining.[1]

There are no records in the local Bird Reports of either known releases or breeding,[2] and the provenance of the birds providing the few scattered records on both the breeding and winter maps is unknown.

Neil Bielby

[1] BS3 [2] UFABR

Breeding Distribution

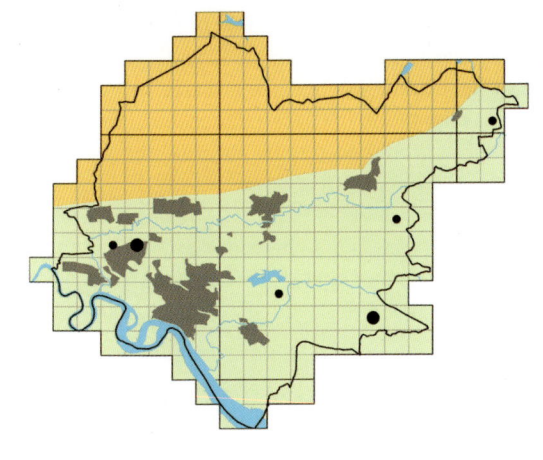

Number of km² in which recorded:	6	(3.0%)
■ Confirmed breeding	0	(0.0%)
● Probable breeding	2	(33.3%)
● Possible breeding	4	(66.7%)
○ Present, breeding unlikely:	0	(0.0%)

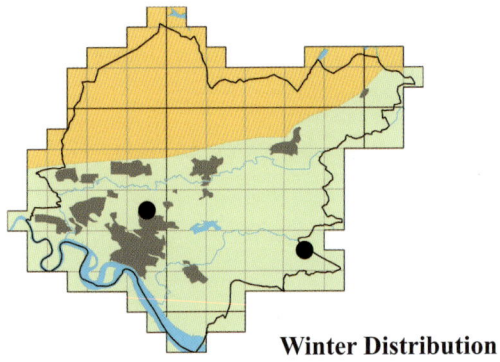

Winter Distribution

Grey Partridge   *Perdix perdix*

Uncommon resident

Conservation status: Red

The Grey Partridge is a resident gamebird that inhabits agricultural land and also some rough grassland in more upland areas. This survey found the current stronghold to be the rich arable land between Clackmannan and the Forth estuary, while a cluster of records in the area around Alva are possibly attributable to captive-reared birds released in that area for sporting purposes. There were no records from the Ochil Hills and scarp where Grey Partridges formerly occurred.[1,2]

Grey Partridge numbers collapsed by 89% in Britain between 1967 and 2007.[3] These declines have been attributed to agricultural intensification: notably the use of herbicides and insecticides that directly and indirectly reduce the availability of invertebrates to chicks,[4,5] and increased levels of predation.[6]

In Clackmannanshire, they were described in 1974 as being 'widespread and frequent on carseland around the River Devon and on the Ochil scarp up to 1,250 feet.'[7] Although the rough semi-natural grasslands of the lower and mid-slopes of the Ochils still appear suitable for the species, corvid and gull predators are now ubiquitous.[8] It is difficult to deduce the extent of the decline in the County's lowlands from the few random records in the Bird Reports. However, this fact in itself could be indicative since, when populations are high and birds breed successfully, the sight of broods in the summer is a frequent occurrence.

The winter distribution appears near-identical to that during the breeding season – as might be expected for a resident and largely sedentary species.[9]

The Grey Partridge's plight in Clackmannanshire is acknowledged by its inclusion as a priority species in the LBAP.

John Calladine

[1] Calladine, J. et al., 1990 [2] UFABR [3] BirdFacts [4] Potts, G.R., 1980 [5] Potts, G.R., 1986
[6] Tapper, S.C. et al., 1996 [7] UFABR [8] Calladine, J. et al., 1990 [9] Migration Atlas

Breeding Distribution

Number of km² in which recorded:	21	(10.6%)
■ Confirmed breeding	0	(0.0%)
● Probable breeding	14	(66.7%)
● Possible breeding	7	(33.3%)
○ Present, breeding unlikely:	0	(0.0%)

Winter Distribution

Pheasant   (Common Pheasant)   *Phasianus colchicus*

Common introduced resident (heavily supported by releases)

The Pheasant, which is an introduced Asian species, is a very familiar country bird. Large numbers are reared and released for game shooting – an estimated 4.5 million being shot in Scotland annually.[1] The male Pheasant is strongly territorial during the breeding season when its conspicuous display, especially in March and April, makes this species one of the easier to record.

The *Atlas* breeding map shows it to be widely distributed throughout the lowlands of the County. The main gaps coincide with urban centres. Other random squares with no registrations may be due to any (or a combination of) the following: the degree of observer effort; low density in areas not supported by releases; the more secretive nature of truly wild birds (especially females) and, in a few locations, a lack of the Pheasant's preferred habitat of woodland edge/farmland. In Clackmannanshire, releases appear to be mainly in the eastern half of the County.[2] Outwith release areas, the density of the self-sustaining population of naturalised birds is very low.[3]

Although Pheasants will breed up to a height of 600 metres they are totally absent from the treeless parts of the Ochils – penetrating only a short distance up the glens. In 1978 they were noted as breeding at 240 metres in the Ochils in a young spruce plantation some 1-2 metres high.[4]

The winter *Atlas* map broadly mimics that for breeding. The absence of a record for the tetrad covering the Aberdona estate is puzzling. Around Alloa, presence for breeding in the east and south and absence in the west and north is reversed in winter. The reasons for this are not clear but are probably the same as those suggested for absences during the breeding season.

Neil Bielby

[1] BS3   [2] Pers. obs.   [3] ibid.   [4] UFABR

Breeding Distribution

Number of km² in which recorded:	106	(53.5%)
■ Confirmed breeding	12	(11.3%)
● Probable breeding	49	(46.2%)
• Possible breeding	42	(39.6%)
○ Present, breeding unlikely:	3	(2.8%)

Winter Distribution

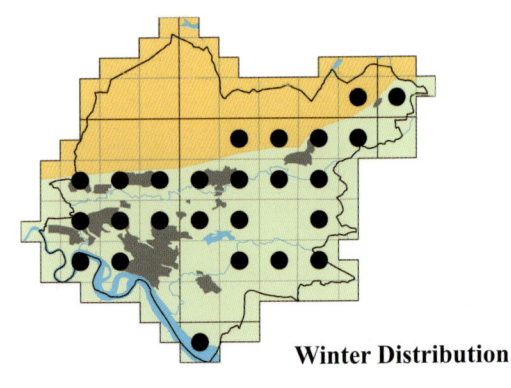

Grey Heron   *Ardea cinerea*

Fairly common resident and winter visitor   Conservation status: Green

The Grey Heron prefers to build its large stick nest colonially in the tops of mature trees – often conifers.[1] Heronries at Sheardale Braes and Gartmornhill Wood were the only ones located during the survey period (small colonies in dense conifer plantations – a favourite location – can be virtually impossible to detect).[2] Surveyors were asked to register birds away from heronries as 'observed' and the *Atlas* breeding distribution map shows how widely the species forages – being logged in 39% of squares. It was absent only from the Ochils, urban centres and an area with extensive coniferous plantations and few water features in the south-east of the County.

The earliest record of breeding in Clackmannanshire was of a 'few pairs' in Alloa Wood in 1793. Subsequently, heronries have also been recorded at Harviestoun, Brucefield, and on the island in Gartmorn Dam.[3,4,5] The mean of recent counts of apparently occupied nests at Sheardale Braes and Gartmornhill Wood indicate a population of c.14 breeding pairs. This gives a breeding density for the County which is almost identical to that recently calculated for Fife and SE Scotland.[6,7]

As the winter survey map shows, the odd bird does venture into the Ochils at this time of year. Just as in the breeding season, there was also, apart from the estuary, an absence of winter records for Grey Heron in the south-east of the County. Migrants from Southern Scandinavia possibly swell the overall winter population,[8] with monthly maxima of up to 32 birds being recorded by WeBS.[9]

With only two known active heronries, annual monitoring of these should be easily achievable.

Neil Bielby

[1] *SE Scotland Atlas* [2] *ibid.* [3] *Rintoul & Baxter, 1935* [4] *BS1* [5] *UFABR* [6] *Fife Atlas* [7] *SE Scotland Atlas* [8] *BS3* [9] *WeBS unpub. data*

Breeding Distribution

Number of km² in which recorded:	67	(33.8%)
■ Confirmed breeding	2	(3.0%)
● Probable breeding	0	(0.0%)
● Possible breeding	0	(0.0%)
○ Present, breeding unlikely:	65	(97.0%)

Winter Distribution

Little Grebe   Tachybaptus ruficollis

Scarce resident and locally common winter visitor   Conservation status: Amber

Although the Little Grebe is frequently shy and skulking during the breeding season, its distinctive courtship calls, combined with the intensive coverage of water bodies in a survey of one-kilometre squares, make it unlikely that any resident birds were missed during fieldwork. Breeding was confirmed in only 33% of the squares in which it was registered, but nests and juveniles on heavily vegetated water bodies may have been difficult to detect. Additionally, any nests/broods after the end of the survey season (31 July) will also have been missed – unfledged young can still be encountered in early September.[1]

The breeding distribution map shows the Little Grebe to be restricted to rural, lowland areas. Three of the occupied squares were on Gartmorn Dam (where they were noted as 'nesting plentifully in 1934'),[2] with the other records coming mainly from small, relatively undisturbed, man-made ponds which typically held only a single bird or pair.[3]

The winter map shows them to be present along the lower River Devon and at Gartmorn Dam. This is backed up by WeBS counts which logged maxima of eight birds along the former and four at the latter during the survey period. Silverhills Pond (Kersiepow) held up to six birds while there was only one record from the River Forth – a single bird at Kennetpans. The maximum monthly WeBS total during the survey period was 20 birds (November 2007),[4] which may well include winter immigrants.[5]

The creation of new habitat in the form of ponds in recent years (e.g. Aberdona) has aided the expansion of the breeding population. More consistent monitoring of the small breeding population would be beneficial and should be relatively straightforward given that potentially suitable sites are few yet easily identified.

Neil Bielby

[1] *Pers. obs.* [2] *Rintoul & Baxter, 1935* [3] *Pers. obs.* [4] *WeBS unpub. data* [5] *Migration Atlas*

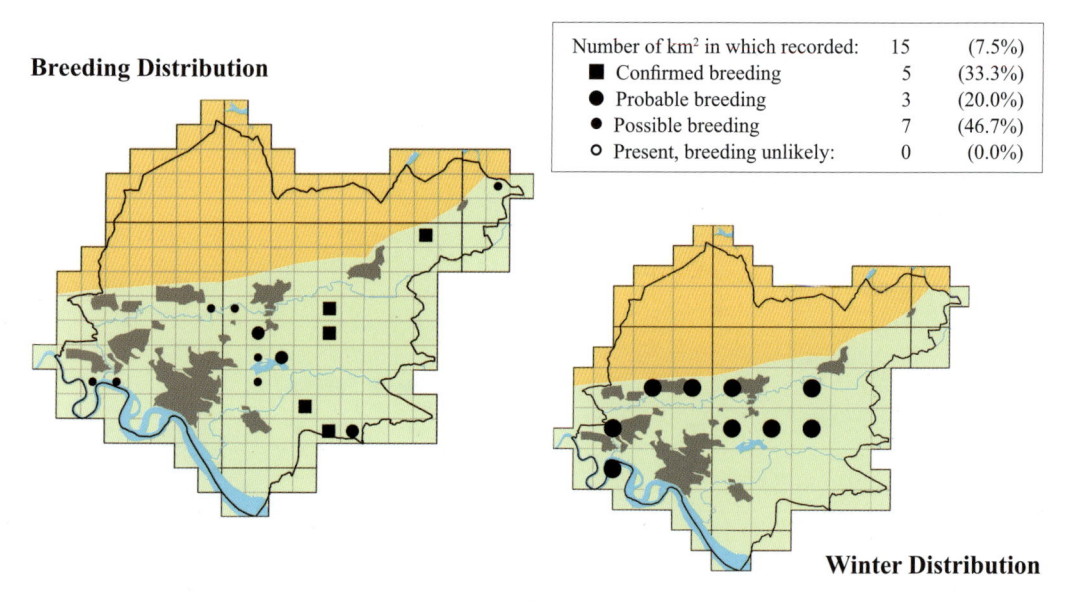

Breeding Distribution

Number of km² in which recorded:	15	(7.5%)
■ Confirmed breeding	5	(33.3%)
● Probable breeding	3	(20.0%)
• Possible breeding	7	(46.7%)
○ Present, breeding unlikely:	0	(0.0%)

Winter Distribution

Great Crested Grebe   *Podiceps cristatus*

Scarce resident, passage migrant and winter visitor   Conservation status: Green

In Clackmannanshire only Gartmorn Dam provides suitable breeding habitat for Great Crested Grebes. Being such large and obvious birds at almost all stages of their reproductive cycle, it is unlikely that any would have been missed. Varying amounts of Gartmorn Dam fall on four different kilometre squares with breeding being confirmed on two and probable on another. Single birds in unsuitable breeding habitat were observed on the River Devon by East Gogar and near Cambus Village.

This species was only regarded as a winter visitor to Scotland before the first proven record of breeding in 1877.[1] A pair was known to be on Gartmorn Dam from 1906-1908 and in 1911, while in 1934 a pair with chicks was observed.[2] Although this species no doubt nests, or attempts to nest, annually at this location, information in the local Bird Reports is patchy, with only 13 entries in 32 years. These suggest that one to three pairs normally attempt to breed with up to five juveniles fledged.[3]

Local records indicate that they are present at Gartmorn Dam throughout most winters with counts of up to 19 birds (November 1997). It is also occasionally recorded on the River Forth between Alloa and Kincardine Bridge with a maximum of six birds in November 2003.[4,5]

Breeding attempts have been thwarted by Coot predation and wave action on occasions,[6] while increasing land-based leisure activity such as dog-walking at Gartmorn Dam could cause undue disturbance. With breeding limited to the one site, monitoring the population on a more consistent basis should be straightforward.

Neil Bielby

[1] BS3   [2] Rintoul & Baxter, 1935   [3] UFABR   [4] ibid.   [5] WeBS unpub. data   [6] UFABR

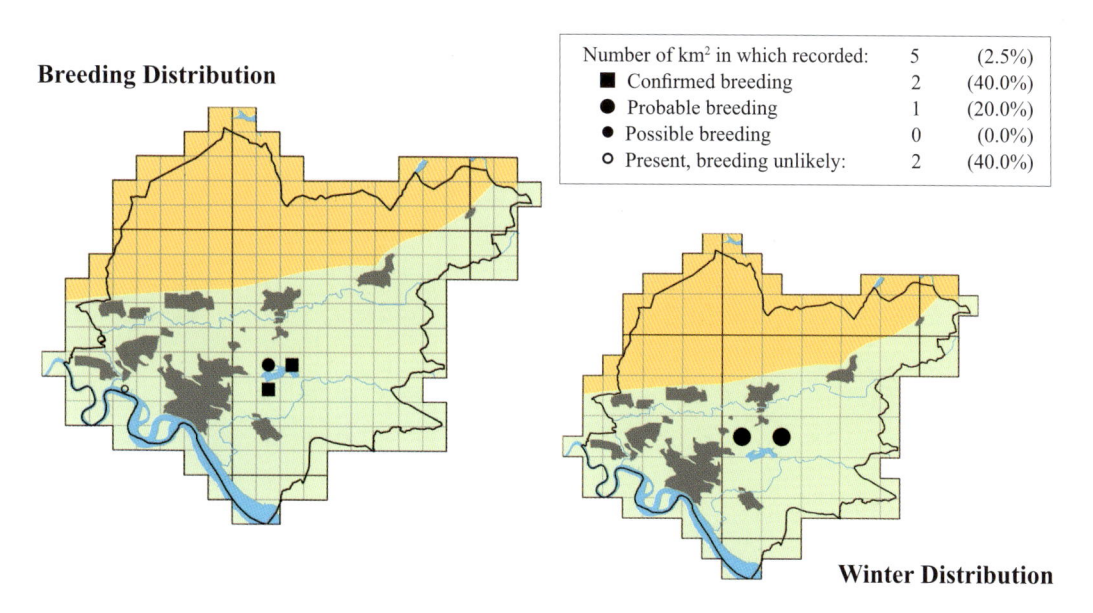

Breeding Distribution

Number of km² in which recorded:	5	(2.5%)
■ Confirmed breeding	2	(40.0%)
● Probable breeding	1	(20.0%)
• Possible breeding	0	(0.0%)
○ Present, breeding unlikely:	2	(40.0%)

Winter Distribution

Sparrowhawk (Eurasian Sparrowhawk) *Accipiter nisus*

Fairly common resident

Conservation status: Green

The Sparrowhawk occurs in a mix of lowland habitats including farmland, woodland and hedgerow, all of which provide a plentiful supply of songbirds – its principal food. Numbers in Scotland appear to have declined since 1989, possibly due to changes in forestry management and falls in farmland bird populations.[1]

The breeding distribution in Clackmannanshire is patchy, perhaps surprisingly so, given the abundance of apparently good habitat. In all, possible, probable or confirmed breeding was obtained from only 27% of squares. It was registered as 'observed' in a further 15 squares – most of which would appear to contain suitable habitat.

This relative scarcity may be due to an element of under-recording. Despite its size the Sparrowhawk is quite secretive when breeding and often hunts at low level, making observation difficult. The nest is also hard to find, usually being concealed high in thick stands of conifers. But even taking these factors into account, the survey does indicate that the Sparrowhawk is a rather sporadic breeder in Clackmannanshire.

The winter distribution broadly reflects that found during the breeding season with the Sparrowhawk being absent from most of the high ground of the Ochils and much of the southern part of the County bordering the River Forth. There is a good spread of records in a broad band to the south of the Ochils including the many woodlands along the southern fringe of the River Devon. Although reasonably regular between Dollar and Alva, Sparrowhawks are rarely recorded further downstream on the River Devon during WeBS counts.[2]

One factor that may influence populations in the future is a general change in conifer management that includes a greater proportion of trees aged 40 years or more,[3] with one study showing that greatest Sparrowhawk breeding success is achieved in plantations of 20-25 years old.[4]

Keith Broomfield

[1] BS3 [2] WeBS unpub. data [3] BBS [4] Newton, I., 1991

Breeding Distribution

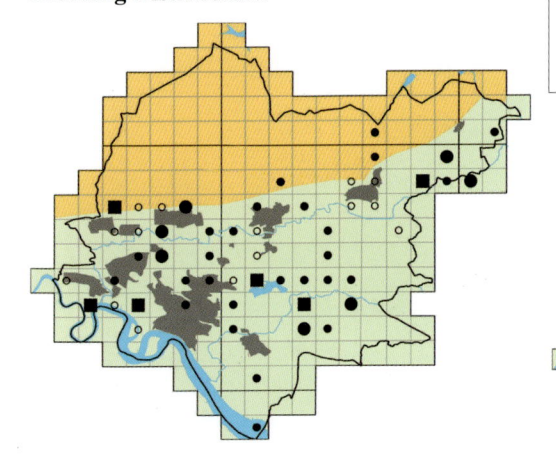

Number of km² in which recorded:	54	(27.3%)
■ Confirmed breeding	6	(11.1%)
● Probable breeding	7	(13.0%)
• Possible breeding	26	(48.1%)
○ Present, breeding unlikely:	15	(27.8%)

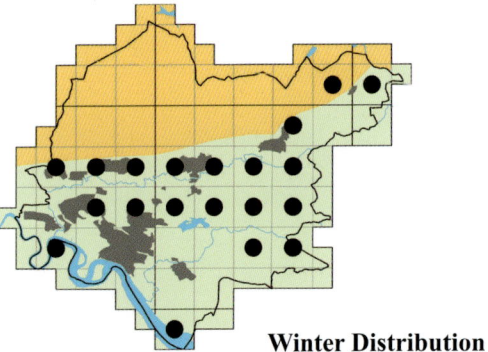

Winter Distribution

Buzzard (Common Buzzard) *Buteo buteo*

Common resident

Conservation status: Green

The Buzzard is a medium sized bird of prey which occurs in a wide range of habitats from hill edge, through to farmland, and increasingly adjacent to urban areas, with most of lowland Clackmannanshire comprising suitable habitat.

Buzzards are conspicuous birds during both the early breeding season, with their aerial displays and defence of territories against intruders, and later when newly-fledged young birds are screaming to be fed. Breeding was confirmed in 33 squares, and was probable in 38 squares. It is likely that fieldwork will have missed a number of breeding attempts, given recent population increases.

The Buzzard has now recolonized most lowland parts of Clackmannanshire consistent with British and Scottish population trends. However, it remains absent as a breeding species from the higher parts of the Ochils where breeding and hunting habitats are probably less productive. It is known that the species has bred in recent years on the edges of large towns in the County such as Alloa and Clackmannan,[1] and this is supported by Atlas data.

Central Scotland Raptor Studies Group (CSRSG) studies of Buzzards in the Stirling Council area have shown that the majority of fledged young will move out of their natal areas by autumn and wander or move into areas that hold few Buzzards.[2] It is possible, therefore, that some juvenile birds will move, for example, to the high ground of the Ochils when weather conditions permit.

The Buzzard has been poorly studied in Clackmannanshire when compared to neighbouring Stirling and Falkirk Council areas. There is certainly room for a local study and accurate census of the species, linked into CSRSG studies in adjacent areas. Such work could help identify areas where illegal persecution of birds of prey may still be occurring in Clackmannanshire.

Duncan Orr-Ewing

[1] *CSRSG data* [2] *ibid.*

Breeding Distribution

Number of km^2 in which recorded:	142	(71.7%)
■ Confirmed breeding	33	(23.2%)
● Probable breeding	38	(26.8%)
• Possible breeding	40	(28.2%)
○ Present, breeding unlikely:	31	(21.8%)

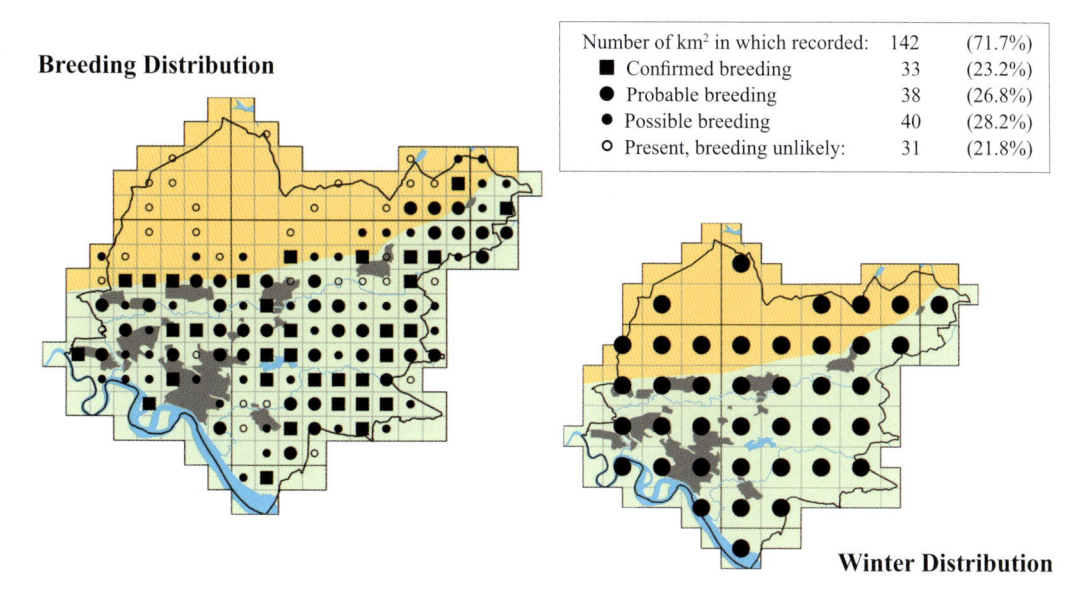

Winter Distribution

Kestrel (Common Kestrel) *Falco tinnunculus*

Fairly common resident   Conservation status: Amber

With its familiar hovering technique when hunting, the Kestrel is a reasonably easy species to record and the breeding map probably provides a true representation of its actual distribution during the *Atlas* survey period. This is somewhat fragmented with the species being recorded in 50% of all squares. Given the variety of nest sites used by Kestrels most of the observed records would have been in suitable habitat.[1]

Confirming breeding proved to be difficult with only 9% of registrations being of this category. Fledging takes place from June onwards with the territorial family staying together for several months making this the easiest time to confirm breeding[2] – but survey effort tended to tail off after June. With the optimum habitat for Kestrels being upland unimproved pasture up to 500 metres the Ochils should be a prime environment,[3] but the records are well scattered here with only one registration of confirmed breeding; whether this is due to food availability, lack of nesting sites or other reasons is unknown. Rintoul & Baxter noted that this was the commonest 'hawk' in the area,[4] but this is no longer the case with this survey showing it to having been superseded by the Buzzard. Scottish BBS data shows a statistically significant 38% decrease in numbers from 1994 to 2007, and it is one of the three species showing the greatest population declines in Scotland since the start of the BBS. However, Scottish BBS data has also highlighted the fluctuation in Kestrel numbers – increasing by 36% between 2007 and 2008 following a smaller increase in the previous year.[5]

Unless driven off by snow cover, home ranges tend to be occupied all year round (at least by the male) [6,7] and the winter distribution map shows a remarkable similarity to that for breeding.

Neil Bielby

[1] BS3 [2] ibid. [3] ibid. [4] Rintoul & Baxter, 1935 [5] Risely et al., 2009 [6] BS3 [7] Migration Atlas

Breeding Distribution

Number of km² in which recorded:	99	(50.0%)
■ Confirmed breeding	9	(9.1%)
● Probable breeding	10	(10.1%)
• Possible breeding	44	(44.4%)
○ Present, breeding unlikely:	36	(36.4%)

Winter Distribution

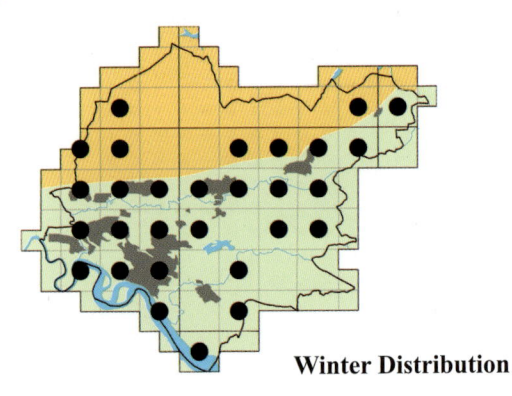

Merlin   *Falco columbarius*

Rare and occasional breeder, scarce passage migrant and winter visitor
Conservation status: Amber

Breeding numbers of Merlins in Britain are considered to be stable or increasing.[1] In Scotland they generally nest amongst long Heather and sometimes in old Crow nests in trees. According to Baxter & Rintoul in 1953 Merlins were 'known to breed in all counties' in the mid-20th century,[2] but Thom, writing in the early 1980s, stated clearly that there were no recent breeding occurrences in Clackmannanshire.[3]

Subsequently there have been some early spring records, notably that involving a pair at Alva Moss in April 1987 and also a number of sightings during March to July from just over the County boundary on Sheriff Muir and at the Upper Glendevon reservoir.[4] These occurrences provide some context to the otherwise exceptional *Atlas* record of breeding on the steep hill-front north-west of Alva in 2007. A male bird was seen on the crags at Craig Leith on 19 May, and then on 6 July a pair was present with three recently fledged young. The nest site was assumed to be on the crags. The observer was familiar with the site and had not sighted Merlins there over the previous six years.[5]

In autumn and winter Merlins frequent any type of open country where they can find avian prey. They are regular visitors, and often temporary residents, along the upper Forth estuary, but surprisingly few of the Clackmannanshire records published in the local Bird Reports come from this part of the County. Perhaps because there are more inland observers the Hillfoots area generally accounts for most autumn and winter sightings. There have been a few occurrences during these seasons in the Ochils.[6] Winter *Atlas* surveyors did not have much luck with the species, the single record being from east of Gartmorn Dam.

David Thorogood

[1] *BS3* [2] *BS1* [3] *BS2* [4] *UFABR* [5] *J. Calladine pers. comm.* [6] *UFABR*

Breeding Distribution

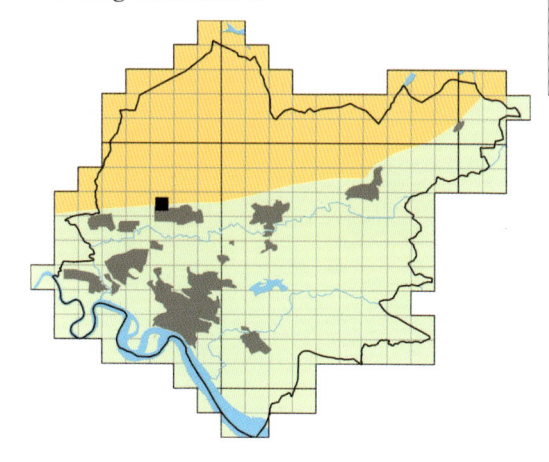

Number of km² in which recorded:	1	(0.5%)
■ Confirmed breeding	1	(100.0%)
● Probable breeding	0	(0.0%)
● Possible breeding	0	(0.0%)
○ Present, breeding unlikely:	0	(0.0%)

Peregrine   (Peregrine Falcon)   *Falco peregrinus*

Scarce resident and passage/winter visitor

Conservation status: Green

The Peregrine's distinctive high-pitched calls during the breeding season and its preference for nesting on cliffs make it an easy bird to survey during spring and summer. It is, therefore, likely that all breeding birds in Clackmannanshire were detected during the survey period with breeding confirmed at two different sites in the Ochils.

The main limiting factor in breeding would appear to be the availability of suitable cliff breeding sites, although in other parts of their Scottish range Peregrines have been recorded nesting on the ground on steeply sloping banks[1] or on man-made structures such as bridges and church towers.[2] The availability of farmland and other open habitat close to nesting sites in the Ochils provides excellent access to a wide variety of prey, especially Woodpigeons.

In winter, the Peregrine can be surprisingly unobtrusive although there were a number of records from along the southern flank of the Ochils, as well as on the River Forth where waders are likely to be an important prey item. In Scotland, Peregrines generally do not move too far from their breeding sites during winter, which means the majority of records from Clackmannanshire are most probably birds from within the County, Fife or Perthshire.[3] Peregrines breed at Longannet Power Station in Fife close to the County border, and it is likely that this is the source of some of the Clackmannanshire birds wintering on the Forth. Generally there is a bias of winter records towards the west of the County, although they do occur in eastern parts, for example near Dollar.[4]

Egg collecting and the removal of chicks by falconers, general persecution by other interest groups, and disturbance by hillwalkers and climbers during the breeding season are constant threats to Clackmannanshire's small breeding population of Peregrines.

Keith Broomfield

[1] *SE Scotland Atlas* [2] BS3 [3] ibid. [4] Pers. obs.

Breeding Distribution

Number of km² in which recorded:	9	(4.5%)
■ Confirmed breeding	2	(22.2%)
● Probable breeding	0	(0.0%)
• Possible breeding	1	(11.1%)
○ Present, breeding unlikely:	6	(66.7%)

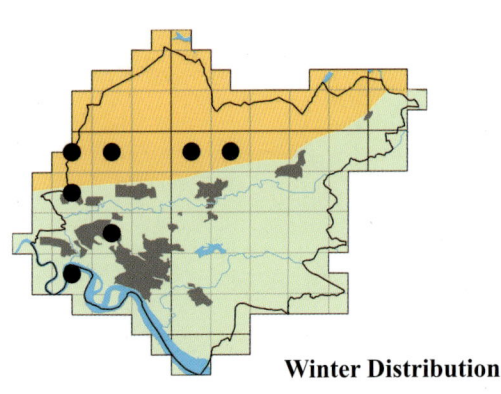

Winter Distribution

Water Rail *Rallus aquaticus*

Scarce resident, passage migrant and winter visitor   Conservation status: Green

The Water Rail's pig-like squeals and grunts (sharming) uttered, along with a range of other vocalisations, from the depths of thickly vegetated wetlands, are usually the only indication of the presence of this elusive and secretive bird. These calls are produced throughout the year, but most frequently during breeding (although less so if few birds are present).[1] The species was registered on only seven squares during breeding Atlas work, five of these along the River Forth.

A calling bird at a flight pond in Lawmuir Wood on 11 April 2007 was possibly a migrant as there was no response to a tape lure on a subsequent visit in mid-May. An adult with two small, downy young at Gartmorn Dam in August 2006 represents the first confirmed breeding record in the County. Undoubtedly there have been others: recent intensive studies in Scotland using tape lures led to an upgrading in the estimate of breeding pairs in the country from between 88-175 to c.1,250-1,400.[2,3] Prior to *Atlas* work, the majority of County records have come from Cambus Pools with a maximum count of four in July 1998.

Records from the local Bird Reports suggest an August/September peak which probably contains a mixture of local birds and early migrants.[4] Water Rails are solitary and less vocal during the winter so that most birds are probably happened on by chance; the winter map shows birds at Gartmorn Dam, Longcarse and the Blackdevon Wetlands.

As well as hard winters and fluctuating water levels, nests are vulnerable to Brown Rats and American Mink.[5] A dedicated census, both during breeding and in winter (especially at dusk and using recorded song and calls as lures), is probably the only way of establishing the true distribution and population level in the County for this covert species.

Neil Bielby

[1] *Fife Atlas* [2] *1988-91 Atlas* [3] *BS3* [4] *UFABR* [5] *Fife Atlas*

Breeding Distribution

Number of km² in which recorded:	7	(3.5%)
■ Confirmed breeding	1	(14.3%)
● Probable breeding	3	(42.9%)
● Possible breeding	2	(28.6%)
○ Present, breeding unlikely:	1	(14.3%)

Winter Distribution

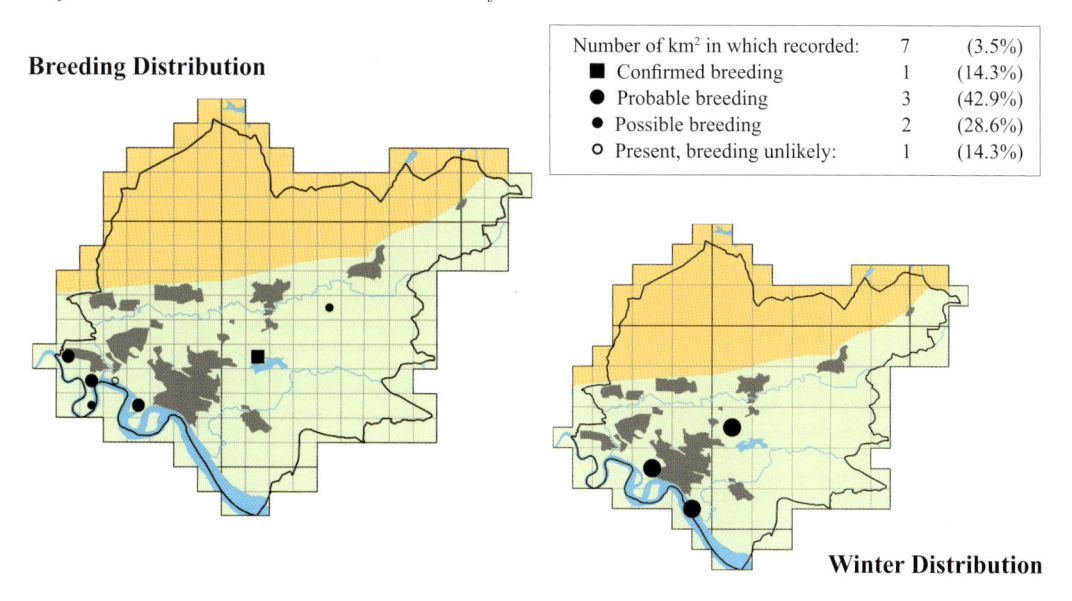

Moorhen   (Common Moorhen)   *Gallinula chloropus*

Fairly common resident   Conservation status: Green

Moorhens are relatively easy to locate because they often betray their presence with loud alarm calls – even if hidden in dense vegetation. Additionally, the fledged young (which remain on their natal territory) retain their juvenile plumage for several months. Nevertheless, birds habituated to humans at urban duck ponds proved easier to observe than their more skittish country cousins.[1] Prior to the commencement of *Atlas* work, there had been only three records of confirmed breeding in the County.[2] With confirmation of breeding in 16 squares plus either probable or possible registrations in a further 19, the breeding map illustrates the value of a comprehensive survey.

Moorhens inhabit a wide range of water features, and the blank areas on the breeding map roughly correspond with the parts of the County where these are largely absent. Although recorded on 11 of the 15 squares along the course of the River Devon between Dollar and Cambus, breeding was confirmed on only one. This could be due to predation or fluctuating water levels, but after late May tall, dense riparian vegetation makes it very difficult to access the river along most of this stretch to confirm breeding.

As would be expected for such a sedentary species, the winter distribution map broadly mirrors that of the breeding one. Much of the suitable habitat in the County is covered by WeBS and winter monthly peaks ranged between 16 and 33 birds during the survey period (although given the bird's often skulking nature this will be an under-representation of the true numbers). Notable individual counts include 15 at Gartmorn Dam (October 2007) and 13 at Inglewood Pond (January 2004).[3,4]

The Moorhen's sedentary nature makes it vulnerable during prolonged periods of frost (as in 1978/9).[5] Furthermore, American Mink (encountered during *Atlas* work) are known to take eggs, young and adults – wiping out whole populations.[6]

Neil Bielby

[1] Pers. obs.   [2] UFABR   [3] WeBS unpub. data   [4] UFABR   [5] Henty,– 1991   [6] 1998-91 Atlas

Breeding Distribution

Number of km^2 in which recorded:	39	(19.7%)
■ Confirmed breeding	16	(41.0%)
● Probable breeding	5	(12.8%)
• Possible breeding	16	(41.0%)
○ Present, breeding unlikely:	2	(5.1%)

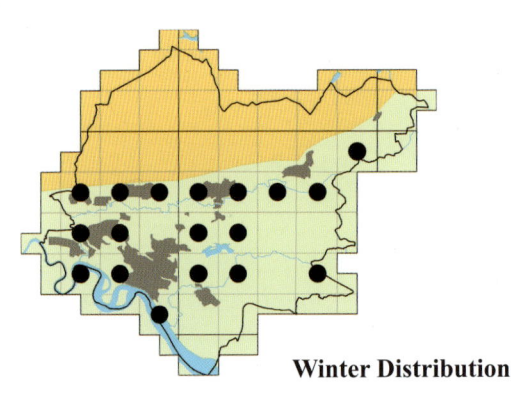

Winter Distribution

Coot (Common Coot) *Fulica atra*

Fairly common resident; common winter visitor   Conservation status: Green

The Coot is normally found on relatively shallow still or slow-moving eutrophic waters where it is able to dive down to six metres to obtain its predominantly vegetarian diet. Additionally, it requires emergent vegetation on which to construct its bulky nest which is often surrounded by water for safety. When these well-defined and limiting habitat requirements are allied to highly visual, noisy and aggressive territorial behaviour during the breeding season, it is unlikely any Coots will have been missed – apart from any breeding after July. Over half of the 15 registrations were in the confirmed category, doubling the number of sites in Clackmannanshire where successful breeding had previously been recorded.[1]

Gartmorn Dam is by far the principal site throughout the year and a maximum of seven broods (plus two birds on nests) were recorded here during the *Atlas* period which, along with observations from other sites, would indicate a current breeding population in the County of c.20 pairs. Recently there has been a marked drop in breeding numbers across southern Scotland in which the reviving Otter population may be implicated.[2]

During the autumn there is a substantial influx of continental immigrants (presumed to be from north-western Europe),[3] with winter peaks at Gartmorn Dam ranging from 131 to 513 birds during the Atlas period (the maximum number of Coot recorded at Gartmorn Dam is 820 in November 1989).[4] WeBS indices indicate a 75% fall in peak numbers for Scotland during the decade since 1996/97 – a trend mirrored locally.[5] Silverhills Pond (Kersiepow) was the only other site to hold over 10 birds (14) during this time with none being recorded on the Rivers Devon and Forth.[6]

The main threats would appear to come from predation by Otter, American Mink and Pike, (*Esox lucius*).[7]

Neil Bielby

[1] *UFABR* [2] *BS3* [3] *Migration Atlas* [4] *WeBS unpub. data* [5] *Austin et al., 2008* [6] *WeBS unpub. data* [7] *BS3*

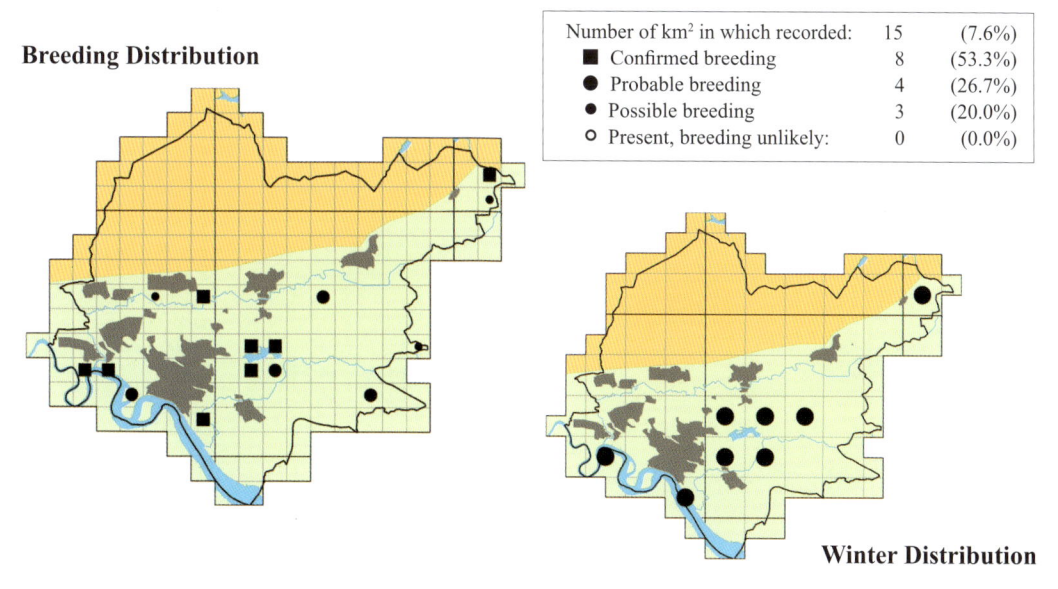

Breeding Distribution

Number of km² in which recorded:	15	(7.6%)
■ Confirmed breeding	8	(53.3%)
● Probable breeding	4	(26.7%)
● Possible breeding	3	(20.0%)
○ Present, breeding unlikely:	0	(0.0%)

Winter Distribution

Oystercatcher (Eurasian Oystercatcher) *Haematopus ostralegus*

Common summer visitor and passage migrant   Conservation status: Amber

Oystercatchers with their pied plumage and large orange/red bills are unmistakeable and unmissable, being particularly noisy and feisty during the breeding season – especially around their nests.

The *Atlas* breeding map shows that they are totally absent in the Ochils and, except for an absence from heavily wooded areas in the Devon valley above Dollar and around Forestmill, the Oystercatcher is widely distributed within the lowlands with breeding confirmed even in the middle of urban areas.

Originally regarded as a coastal breeding bird only, over the last two centuries the Oystercatcher has progressively colonized inland Scottish loch shores, river valleys and, increasingly, arable and pasture farmland.[1,2] It has also been recorded nesting on roofs,[3] and this survey recorded a pair with young on the roof of the now demolished Jaeger knitwear factory in Tullibody in 2002. A Scottish survey of breeding farmland waders in 1997 found that 59% of all one kilometre squares were occupied – a finding with which the results of this *Atlas* roughly corresponds.[4] The first confirmed breeding in Clackmannanshire was in 1977,[5] although it is likely to have bred here for many years previously.

Despite the winter map showing Oystercatchers to be present along the River Forth and up the Devon valley to Dollar, they are rarely seen inland (and only occasionally on the Forth above Kincardine Bridge) from August to January. The earliest record was at Kersiepow, Alva on 14 January (2006) but mid-February is the norm for their return inland in spring. Initially, they gather in flocks prior to breeding dispersal, with Tullibody Inch and the fields around Cambus being favoured locations in Clackmannanshire – up to 120 birds having been recorded at each.[6,7]

Neil Bielby

[1] *BS3* [2] *BS2* [3] *BS3* [4] *O'Brien et al., 2002* [5] *UFABR* [6] *ibid.* [7] *WeBS unpub. data*

Breeding Distribution

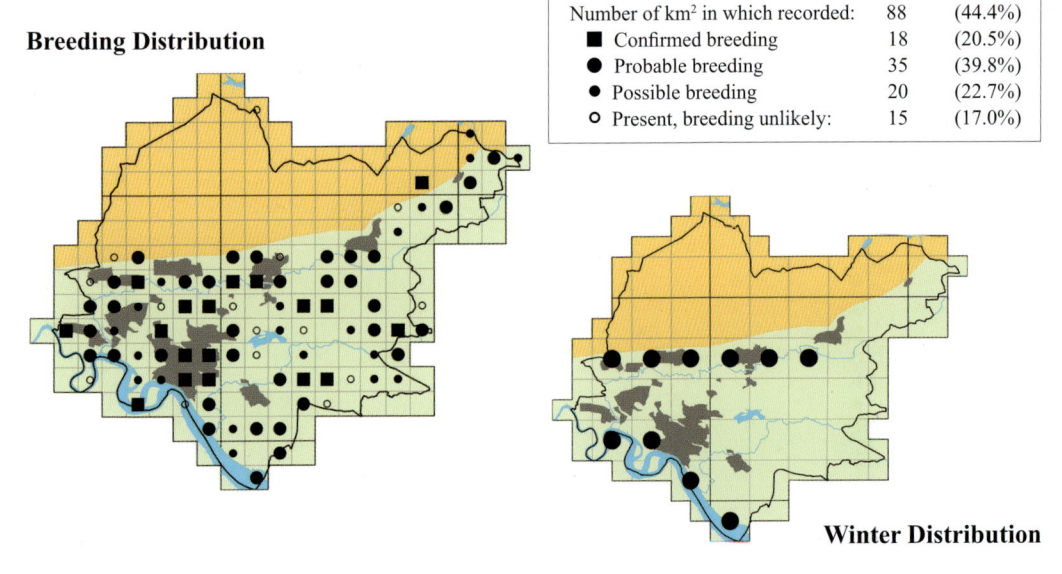

Number of km² in which recorded:	88	(44.4%)
■ Confirmed breeding	18	(20.5%)
● Probable breeding	35	(39.8%)
• Possible breeding	20	(22.7%)
○ Present, breeding unlikely:	15	(17.0%)

Winter Distribution

Ringed Plover   (Common Ringed Plover)   *Charadrius hiaticula*

Scarce resident and passage migrant   Conservation status: Amber

When breeding inland Ringed Plovers nest on the sandy, gravel and pebble banks of streams, rivers and lochs as well as on man-made features – especially areas of small aggregates.[1] With only two confirmed and two probable records, the breeding distribution map probably reflects the dearth of suitable habitat in Clackmannanshire.

A pair with four young discovered during *Atlas* work in late May 2002 by the River Devon at Marchglen was only the second record of confirmed breeding in the County (a pair having reared two young at Gartmorn Dam in 1992). A nest with eggs found on a mixture of crushed glass and gravel at the glassworks in Alloa in July 2006 was probably a replacement clutch – second clutches being rare in Scotland.[2,3] A pair were in the lunar landscape of the demolished Solsgirth mine in late May 2005, while up to seven on newly excavated pools at the Blackdevon Wetlands in spring 2007 were 'giving display calls in March'.[4]

The Ringed Plover's Amber listing is due to significant decreases in the wintering population.[5] It seems that breeding numbers have been similarly affected, as a repeat of the 1984 UK breeding season survey in 2007 revealed that numbers had fallen by 41% in Scotland during the intervening period.[6]

In winter Ringed Plovers were only recorded along the River Forth downstream of Alloa and the few records in the local Bird Reports point to these being early returning spring passage birds. A return passage on the Forth between June and September is also indicated by records from these reports.[7]

Neil Bielby

[1] *BWP*   [2] *T. Craig pers. comm.*   [3] *BS3*   [4] *UFABR*   [5] *Eaton et al., 2009*   [6] *Conway, 2009*   [7] *UFABR*

Breeding Distribution

Number of km² in which recorded:	5	(2.5%)
■ Confirmed breeding	2	(40.0%)
● Probable breeding	2	(40.0%)
• Possible breeding	0	(0.0%)
○ Present, breeding unlikely:	1	(20.0%)

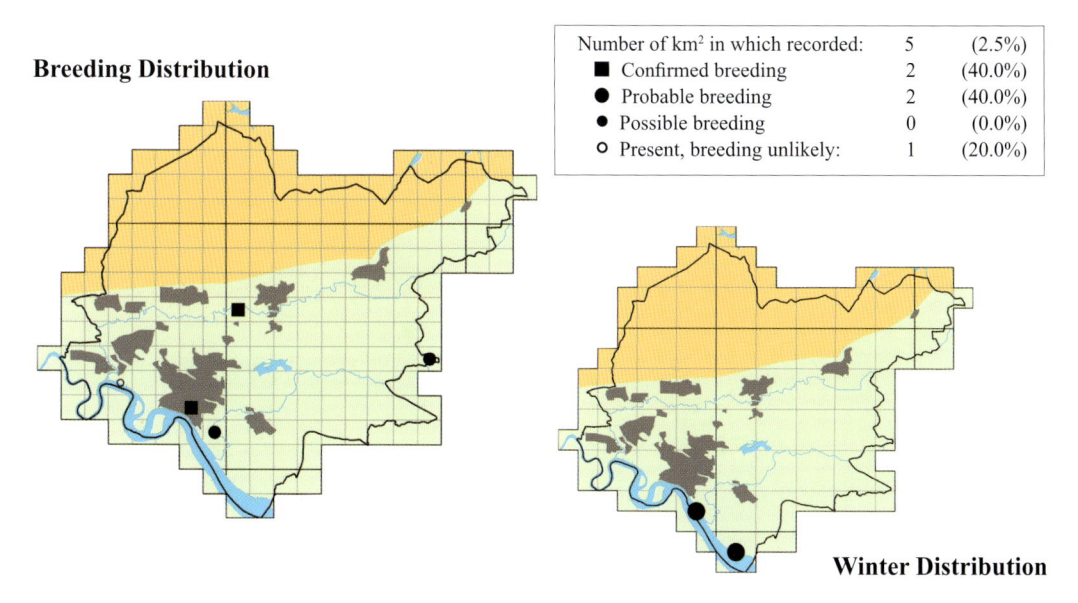

Winter Distribution

Lapwing (Northern Lapwing) *Vanellus vanellus*

Common resident and winter visitor　　　　　　　　　　Conservation status: Red

The Lapwing is a widespread bird in Scotland and is found on both arable and pasture farmland in both lowland and upland areas, although the Scottish population has declined in the latter half of the 20th century.[1]

During the *Atlas* period, breeding Lapwings were widespread in Clackmannanshire, occurring in most areas apart from the uplands of the Ochils, forested areas in the south-east of the County and urban areas. On lowland farmland, Lapwings prefer to nest in short or sparsely vegetated areas that have adjacent suitable vegetation and damp areas for chick rearing.[2] In Clackmannanshire, suitable breeding sites are provided by a mosaic of spring-sown cereal fields (principal nesting areas) with pastures and wet ditches (chick rearing areas). The high proportion of confirmed and probable breeding records reflects the relative ease of detecting such strikingly plumaged birds in open fields, including individuals attending young.

Lapwings can return to the breeding areas as early as February in mild conditions.[3] Given the mild winters experienced during the *Atlas* period, the majority, if not all the winter records away from the estuary represent the first returning birds to their breeding sites. The upper Forth estuary holds quite important wintering populations of Lapwing with the tidal flats between Cambus and Kennetpans being favoured areas.[4]

Although at the time of the *Atlas* the status of Lapwings in the County appeared reasonably healthy, there is some cause for concern. In the latter years covered, there have been losses and declines from at least some parts of western Clackmannanshire.[5] Along with urban encroachment, this is probably the result of the conversion of some spring-sown arable fields to autumn-sown or to pasture, thereby losing potential nesting areas or isolating them from chick-rearing areas.

John Calladine

[1] *BBS*　　[2] *Redfern, 1982*　　[3] *Galbraith, 1989*　　[4] *UFABR*　　[5] *Pers. obs.*

Breeding Distribution

Number of km² in which recorded:	75	(37.9%)
■ Confirmed breeding	31	(41.3%)
● Probable breeding	27	(36.0%)
• Possible breeding	14	(18.7%)
○ Present, breeding unlikely:	3	(4.0%)

Winter Distribution

Snipe (Common Snipe) *Gallinago gallinago*

Uncommon resident, locally common passage migrant and winter visitor
Conservation status: Amber

Snipe are birds of bogs, marshes and damp meadows. They are most often encountered when flushed or when giving their characteristic drumming display during breeding. Snipe breed in any area where drainage is impeded and where they have access to shallow water. They feed mainly on invertebrates but seeds are taken in small quantities.[1]

The methods employed in this *Atlas* survey do not capture Snipe particularly well. Registrations were scattered widely but spread equally between the lowlands, with a cluster south of Dollar (mostly confirmed and probable breeding) and a scattering along the southern County boundary (mostly possible breeding), and the uplands (mostly possible breeding).

In winter the species appeared more widely spread along the Hillfoots and the southern boundary with fewer records from the Ochils. Counts during the survey years include 17 at Tullibody Inch (September 2002) and 13 at Gartmorn Dam (October 2004) while historically, 55 were at Cambus (December 1984); 41 at Kennetpans (October 1993) and 83 were on the Blackdevon Wetlands (August 1998).[2] It should be noted that the numbers of those Snipe remaining in Britain and Ireland during the winter are swollen by up to an estimated million birds from Iceland, Fennoscandia and northern Europe, some being on passage to winter further south in France, Iberia and northern Africa.[3] It is therefore likely that some of the birds wintering in Clackmannanshire are of northern origin.

There was a rapid decline in lowland England as a result of drainage of farmland between the early 1970s and 1984,[4,5] followed by range loss in Wales, Scotland and lowland England in the late 1980s/early 1990s,[6] suggesting that the decrease is widespread. However, current data are unclear, as although WeBS shows a continuing decline in the UK,[7] BBS results show a significant increase of 35% in the UK index between 1995 and 2007, and even greater (48%) in Scotland.[8]

Andre Thiel

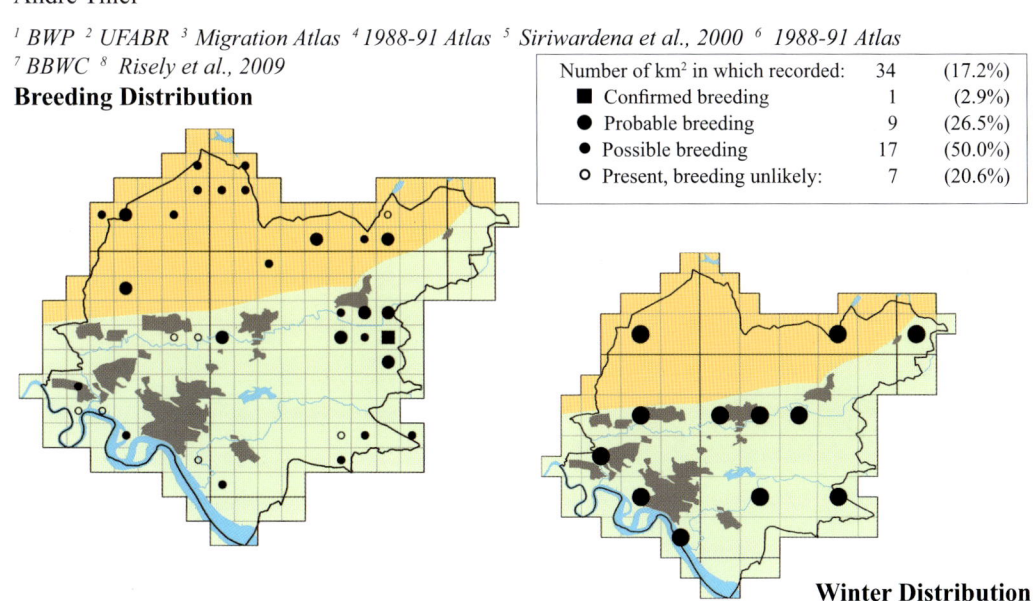

[1] BWP [2] UFABR [3] Migration Atlas [4] 1988-91 Atlas [5] Siriwardena et al., 2000 [6] 1988-91 Atlas
[7] BBWC [8] Risely et al., 2009

Breeding Distribution

Number of km² in which recorded:	34	(17.2%)
■ Confirmed breeding	1	(2.9%)
● Probable breeding	9	(26.5%)
● Possible breeding	17	(50.0%)
○ Present, breeding unlikely:	7	(20.6%)

Winter Distribution

Woodcock (Eurasian Woodcock) *Scolopax rusticola*

Fairly common resident, winter visitor and passage migrant   Conservation status: Amber

The Woodcock occurs in a variety of woodland habitats, particularly favouring moist areas close to muddy ditches and other damp margins such as bogs on the edge of moor and pasture where it can feed at night on worms and other invertebrates.

While the male's 'roding' display fight can be conspicuous in spring, in overall terms, the secretive nocturnal nature of the Woodcock combined with its excellent cryptic camouflage make it a difficult bird to census accurately. In the survey breeding could not be confirmed in any of the squares, with probable and possible breeding registered in 17 squares concentrated in the east and south-east of the County. This part of Clackmannanshire is characterised by numerous patches of woodland interspersed with damp pasture, providing plenty of suitable wet areas for Woodcock to feed in.

Winter records were also scarce, with the eastern part of Clackmannanshire again holding all the records. The first migrants usually arrive in Scotland during the second week of October.[1] Woodcock tend to use a wider variety of wooded habitat during winter.[2] From our knowledge of winter movements, it is reasonable to conclude that many migrant arrivals stay in the County over winter.

The BTO Common Birds Census has reported a rapid decline in Woodcock numbers, but because the survey is biased towards the south of England it is uncertain whether this fall is reflected throughout the whole of Britain. The Woodcock is very susceptible to habitat change, with maturing conifer plantations and the drying out of natural woodlands cited as possible reasons for the decline in overall numbers.[3,4] Other threats include the drainage of pasture and disturbance by dog walkers, especially during egg laying or the early stages of incubation.[5]

Keith Broomfield

[1] BS3 [2] Winter Atlas [3] BBWC [4] 1988-91 Atlas [5] BS3

Breeding Distribution

Number of km² in which recorded:	19	(9.6%)
■ Confirmed breeding	0	(0.0%)
● Probable breeding	14	(73.7%)
• Possible breeding	3	(15.8%)
○ Present, breeding unlikely:	2	(10.5%)

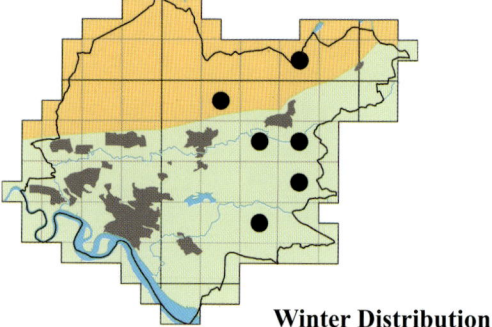

Winter Distribution

Curlew (Eurasian Curlew)   *Numenius arquata*

Fairly common resident, locally common passage migrant and winter visitor
Conservation status: Amber

The bubbling song during display flights along with its haunting calls make the Curlew one of the easier species to record, although the very low number of confirmed breeding registrations illustrates the difficulty in finding both nests and young. The majority of birds spend their winters by the coast and on estuaries with inland return taking place during March, so that by early April almost all birds are on their breeding territories.[1,2]

Conventionally thought of as an upland breeding species, recent Scottish surveys have found that 78% are now located on farmland with the remainder on unenclosed moorlands.[3] This survey would seem to support these findings with a widespread but discontinuous distribution in the lowlands where 65% of all squares containing more than 50% farmland had a breeding registration, and an irregular distribution in the Ochils where only 23% of squares did so. The lowland records are weighted to the east of the County and along the Devon Valley – areas most abundant in the preferred habitat of wet rushy patches, lowland heath and damp grass fields.[4]

In the mid-1970s Curlew were noted as being 'frequent in spring in the Ochils …up to 600 metres' and 'abundant on the Ochils in summer',[5] while a further study found them to be the 'most abundant breeding wader' on the Menstrie and Alva Mosses.[6] In stark contrast the present survey found the only concentration in the Ochils to be in the Ben Buck and Burnfoot Hill area.

Curlew start returning to the coast at the end of June and flocks of up to 300 wintering birds can be found all along the River Forth and its adjacent fields from then on, as shown on the winter map. The few inland registrations were probably early inland returnees in late February.

A UKBAP and Amber listed species, BBS returns suggest a 51% decline in Scotland between 1995 and 2007.[7]

Neil Bielby

[1] *BS3* [2] *Bainbridge & Minton, 1978* [3] *O'Brien et al., 2002* [4] *BS3* [5] *UFABR*
[6] *Calladine et al., 1990* [7] *Risely et al., 2009*

Breeding Distribution

Number of km² in which recorded:	88	(44.4%)
■ Confirmed breeding	4	(4.5%)
● Probable breeding	43	(48.9%)
• Possible breeding	30	(34.1%)
○ Present, breeding unlikely:	11	(12.5%)

Winter Distribution

Common Sandpiper *Actitis hypoleucos*

Locally common summer visitor and passage migrant   Conservation status: Amber

For breeding the Common Sandpiper prefers open riparian habitats of a stony or rocky nature in upland areas.[1] The fact that there was only one confirmed breeding registration is probably due to a combination of a very short breeding season, luxuriant bank-side vegetation along the lower River Devon from mid-May onwards and observer effort.

The first returning birds to the County are usually recorded in mid-April with the earliest on 10 April.[2] The 'observed' registrations (mainly along the River Forth) most probably relate to passage birds both in spring and on post-breeding migration – the latter beginning as early as mid-June with most having left by September.[3,4]

The breeding map shows Common Sandpiper to be present on the River Devon in the Yetts o' Muckhart area and from Dollar down to Menstrie, but missing from the Rumbling Bridge to Dollar stretch where the river runs for the most part through a wooded gorge – although it will apparently tolerate such hemmed-in sites.[5] Surprisingly, it is absent from virtually all of the Ochils, with only a couple of registrations from the Broich Burn. A recent decline in the breeding population led to the Common Sandpiper being placed on the Amber list in 2009.[6] Scotland is estimated to have 80% of the UK breeding population.[7]

Normally solitary during spring return, it is often found in small groups during summer/autumn passage. This feature is well-illustrated in the local Bird Reports with parties of up to nine birds being noted, virtually all on the Forth. The latest record is of a bird at Cambus on 21 December (1987).[8,9]

Neil Bielby

[1] BWP [2] UFABR [3] Migration Atlas [4] BS3 [5] BWP [6] Eaton et al., 2009 [7] BS3 [8] ibid. [9] UFABR

Breeding Distribution

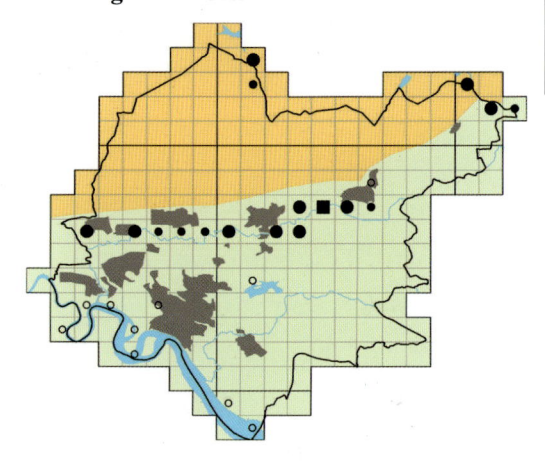

Number of km² in which recorded:	27	(13.6%)
■ Confirmed breeding	1	(3.7%)
● Probable breeding	10	(37.0%)
• Possible breeding	6	(22.2%)
○ Present, breeding unlikely:	10	(37.0%)

Redshank (Common Redshank) *Tringa totanus*

Scarce resident, locally common passage migrant and winter visitor
Conservation status: Amber

Often the first species to raise the alarm, the call of the Redshank is familiar to all who visit our coasts in winter. This habit also quickly reveals the presence of this distinctive wader (with its 'day-glow' orange legs) on its breeding grounds. The spring return of Redshanks to their breeding grounds begins in earnest in March. In Scotland 91% of the breeding population of c.14,700 pairs breed on farmland (typically wet grassland and machair) with only 6% using saltmarsh and 3% damp, rough pasture on the moorland edge.[1,2]

The *Atlas* survey produced breeding registrations in only five squares with the sole confirmation of breeding being in the Cambus Pools area where it has been recorded on a fairly regular basis since the mid-1980s.[3] There are two probable registrations in the Devon Valley where Redshanks have been noted apparently occupying territories since 1979, but breeding has never been confirmed.[4] The other probable record is on the Blackdevon Wetlands where up to four pairs have been noted, but again breeding has yet to be confirmed.[5] The two inland 'observed' registrations in the Devon Valley were presumably attributed to birds considered to be on passage, as were a further three along the River Forth.

Redshanks start to leave the breeding grounds for their wintering quarters around the coast in mid-June.[6] The main wintering concentrations are to be found on the larger estuaries, the Forth Estuary being pre-eminent in Scotland [7] with a mean monthly peak (December) during the 2002/03 to 2006/07 winters of 5,466 birds.[8] As the map shows, this wintering area reaches up the Forth as far as Cambus with up to 120 birds recorded between Cambus and Alloa during the survey period.[9] There are only two winter 'inland' records in the County – both in December on the River Devon below Tillicoultry.[10]

N. Bielby

[1] O'Brien & Whyte, 2004 [2] BS3 [3] UFABR [4] ibid. [5] ibid. [6] BS3 [7] ibid [8] Austin et al., 2008 [9] WeBS unpub. data [10] UFABR

Breeding Distribution

Number of km² in which recorded:	10	(5.1%)
■ Confirmed breeding	1	(10.0%)
● Probable breeding	3	(30.0%)
● Possible breeding	1	(10.0%)
○ Present, breeding unlikely:	5	(50.0%)

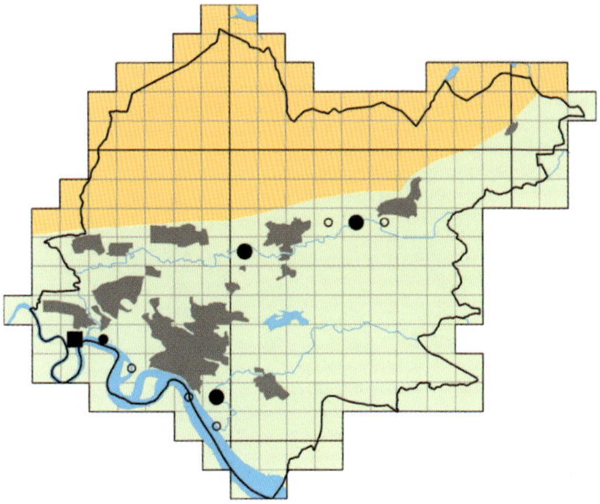

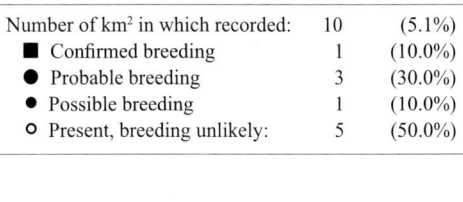

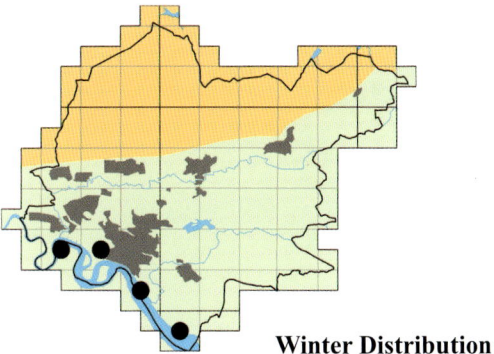

Winter Distribution

Common Gull   (Mew Gull)   *Larus canus*

Scarce breeder, common winter visitor   Conservation status: Amber

Somewhat atypically all the confirmed breeding registrations in Clackmannanshire were associated with man-made features. Breeding Common Gulls forage widely and this behaviour is illustrated in the scattering of 'observed' records.[1]

A colony of 18 nests discovered among the rubble of a demolished mill in the Hallpark area of Alloa in early May 2004 was the first record of confirmed breeding within the current County boundaries (they probably had done so previously, eg. on the bonded warehouse roofs, but this was never recorded). These had produced a minimum of 15 unfledged juveniles by mid-June. The precarious and often transient nature of such colonies was demonstrated the following year, when a visit revealed that all the nests containing eggs had been destroyed (a car park now occupies the site).[2] Other colonies also located in Alloa during the survey period were in the rubble of the demolished Skol brewery (now an Asda supermarket) and on the roof of the glassworks – this latter consisting of c.50 pairs. Small colonies were also located on the roofs of the Menstrie and Blackgrange bonded warehouses.[3]

Local breeding birds undertake a partial migration to the south and south-west, being replaced from August onwards by immigrants from further north in Scotland, and in greater numbers by birds from north-western continental Europe.[4] In winter flocks are often seen in grass fields and following the plough. The distribution map shows them to be ubiquitous in the lowland areas in the western half of the County, sporadic from Tillicoultry to Yetts o' Muckhart, but curiously absent from the farmland areas in the south-east. Continued monitoring of the existing known roof-top breeding colonies would be worthwhile. American Mink have been recorded as decimating ground-breeding colonies in several parts of Scotland.[5]

Neil Bielby

[1] *SE Scotland Atlas* [2] *Pers. obs.* [3] *J. Calladine pers. comm.* [4] *Migration Atlas* [5] *BS3*

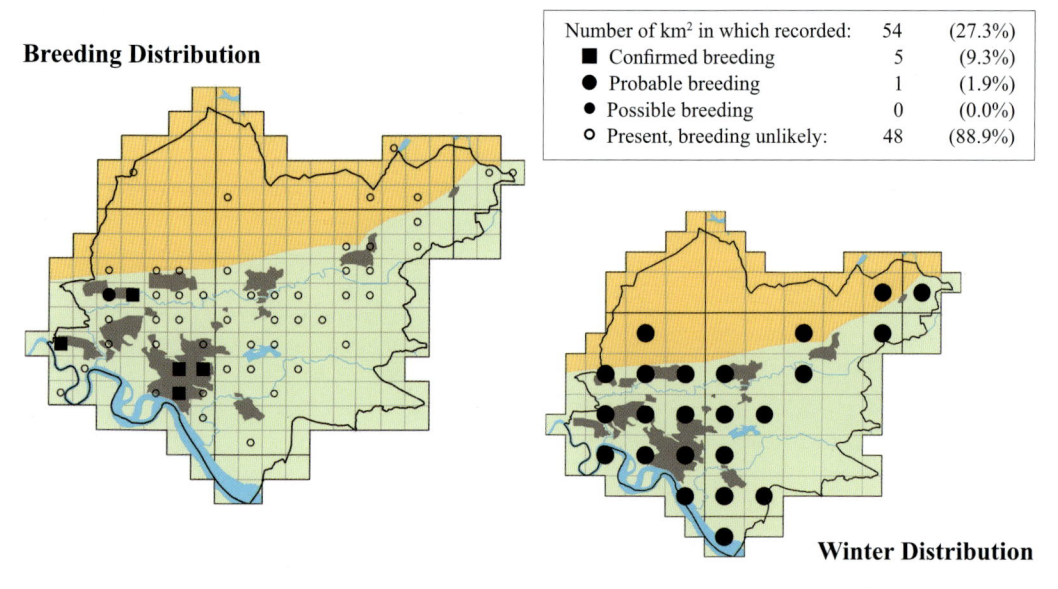

Breeding Distribution

Number of km² in which recorded:	54	(27.3%)
■ Confirmed breeding	5	(9.3%)
● Probable breeding	1	(1.9%)
● Possible breeding	0	(0.0%)
○ Present, breeding unlikely:	48	(88.9%)

Winter Distribution

Lesser Black-backed Gull   *Larus fuscus*

Locally common summer visitor and passage migrant, occasional winter visitor
Conservation status: Amber

The Lesser Black-backed Gull is essentially a summer visitor to Clackmannanshire. Breeding was confirmed in two *Atlas* squares, and was considered probable in a further three. All were roof-nesting sites, principally the large gently sloping roofs of the extensive bonded warehouses by Menstrie, Cambus and Blackgrange. Some of these are difficult to access or examine and breeding was only confirmed for sites where there are convenient places to overlook the roofs (e.g. the hills above the Menstrie warehouses) or where there were fortuitous observations of pre-fledged young running around on the roof edges. Away from the breeding sites Lesser Black-backed Gulls were widespread in the spring and summer months throughout the County. These large gulls generally do not breed until they are four years old,[1,2] and a proportion of the adult population does not breed in any one year.[3] Therefore a considerable proportion of the population might be expected to range widely without necessarily being tied to breeding areas.

In Clackmannanshire between 1998 and 2002 up to 88 apparently occupied nests were counted or estimated.[4] Previously, the warehouse roofs provided predator-free nest sites close to the food sources of the land-fill garbage tips near Fallin and at the mouth of the Black Devon. However, in 2004 these food sources were eliminated with the closure of the tips. In other areas where such rich food sources (garbage or fishery discards) have become unavailable, breeding Lesser Black-backed Gulls resort to feeding principally on terrestrial invertebrates resulting in a subsequent decline in breeding success – and ultimately a reduced breeding population.[5] It might thus be predicted that numbers of these birds breeding in Clackmannanshire may similarly decline.

In winter, Lesser Black-backed Gulls were reported from two tetrads, indicating that the species remains quite scarce in the County during that period.

John Calladine

[1] *Harris, 1964* [2] *Duncan, 1981* [3] *Calladine & Harris, 1997* [4] *Mitchell et al., 2004* [5] *Perrins & Smith, 2000*

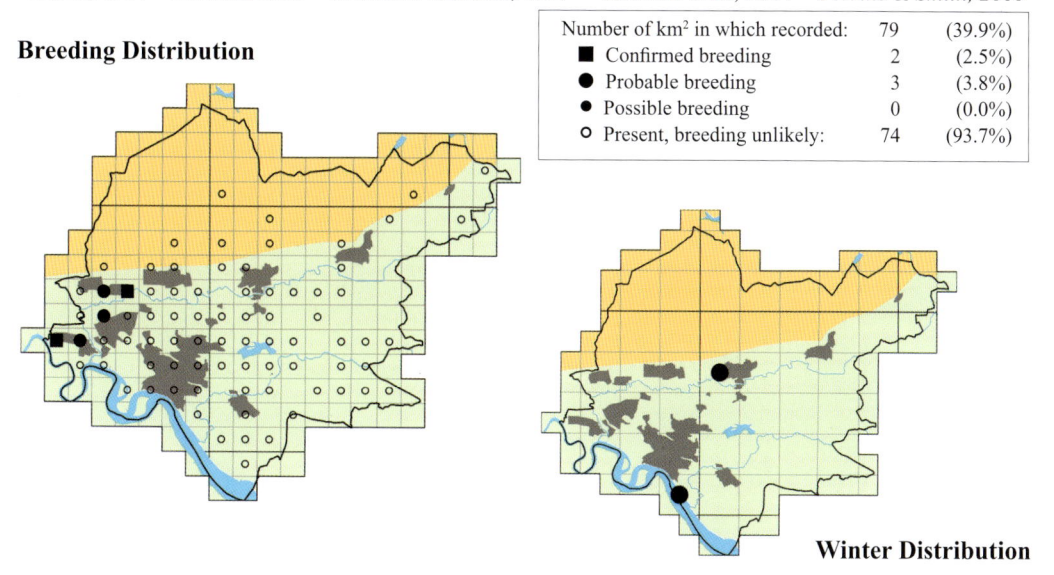

Breeding Distribution

Number of km² in which recorded:	79	(39.9%)
■ Confirmed breeding	2	(2.5%)
● Probable breeding	3	(3.8%)
• Possible breeding	0	(0.0%)
○ Present, breeding unlikely:	74	(93.7%)

Winter Distribution

Herring Gull *Larus argentatus*

Fairly common resident and common winter visitor

Conservation status: Red

The Herring Gull has a near-Holarctic breeding distribution. In 1998-2000 the total breeding population in Scotland was estimated at 72,130 pairs with Clackmannanshire contributing only 35 of these.[1] During the *Atlas* period breeding was considered as probable in two 1km squares – on warehouse rooftops at Blackgrange and on industrial building roofs in central Alloa (both sites were occupied by breeding colonies of either Lesser Black-backed Gulls or Common Gulls). The difficulty in monitoring this type of site probably accounts for the absence of confirmed breeding. Away from the probable (or at least former) nesting sites, Herring Gulls were found quite widely, being noted in 40 squares, all except two of these being in the lowland areas. Many of the widespread 'observed' birds could have been individuals that had not yet started breeding (most do not start breeding until four years of age),[2,3] or those adults which do not breed in any one year.[4]

In winter the resident *L. a. argenteus* race is augmented by birds from Scandinavia of the nominate race *L. a. argentatus*.[5,6] The species is then widespread throughout the lowland parts of the County where they can be seen foraging in fields, on garbage within towns and also feeding more 'naturally' in the inter-tidal areas of the River Forth. Flocks of up to c.3,000 birds can occur at favourable food sources.[7] In Clackmannanshire any decline is likely to be associated with the closure of the Blackdevon landfill refuse site within the County and that at Polmaise, just over the River Forth.

John Calladine

[1] *Mitchell et al., 2004* [2] *Harris, 1964* [3] *Chabrzyk & Coulson, 1976* [4] *Calladine & Harris, 1997* [5] *BWP* [6] *Migration Atlas* [7] *UFABR*

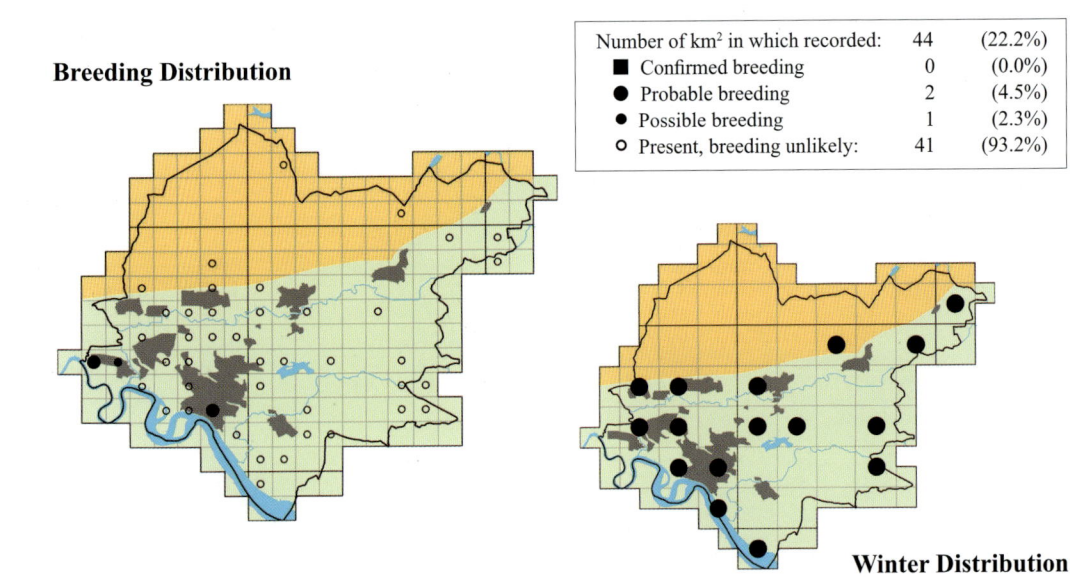

Breeding Distribution

Number of km² in which recorded:	44	(22.2%)
■ Confirmed breeding	0	(0.0%)
● Probable breeding	2	(4.5%)
• Possible breeding	1	(2.3%)
○ Present, breeding unlikely:	41	(93.2%)

Winter Distribution

Feral Pigeon (Common Pigeon) *Columba livia*

Common resident

Conservation status: None

The varied size and plumages of hybrid Feral Pigeons frequently create confusion in identification with other pigeons, especially among juveniles. Some adult birds lack the diagnostic white rump and on a casual sighting can be mistaken for Stock Doves. These difficulties, allied to the birds' extraordinary ability to breed almost continuously throughout the year (and well outside the dates of the breeding survey), have presented the main problems in recording this species for the *Atlas*.

The survey results show a distribution within Clackmannanshire which mirrors that of the UK as a whole.[1] In the breeding season it was almost entirely absent from upland squares and was recorded in some 46% of lowland squares. Across the lowland areas there were notable concentrations in urban areas and a spread around rural farmsteads and old industrial sites (as is to be expected of a species which commonly nests in buildings and other man-made structures), but records are sparse across the carselands in the south-east of the County. Confirmed breeding records were low (17% of all squares with records) probably reflecting the inaccessibility of many nest sites within buildings. BBS data suggest that the breeding population of Feral Pigeons may be declining in Scotland and in the UK as a whole, though the findings have yet to reach a level of significance.[2]

The winter survey shows a similar pattern with even fewer records in the south-east. Local records tend to concentrate on the larger flocks (up to 540 birds), which have been reported in and around Alloa and the Hillfoot towns.[3] The Feral Pigeon is noted as being remarkably sedentary throughout its range[4] so that it is likely that the wintering flocks are made up of local breeding birds.

John Grainger

[1] *1988-91 Atlas.* [2] *Risely et al., 2009* [3] *UFABR* [4] *Migration Atlas*

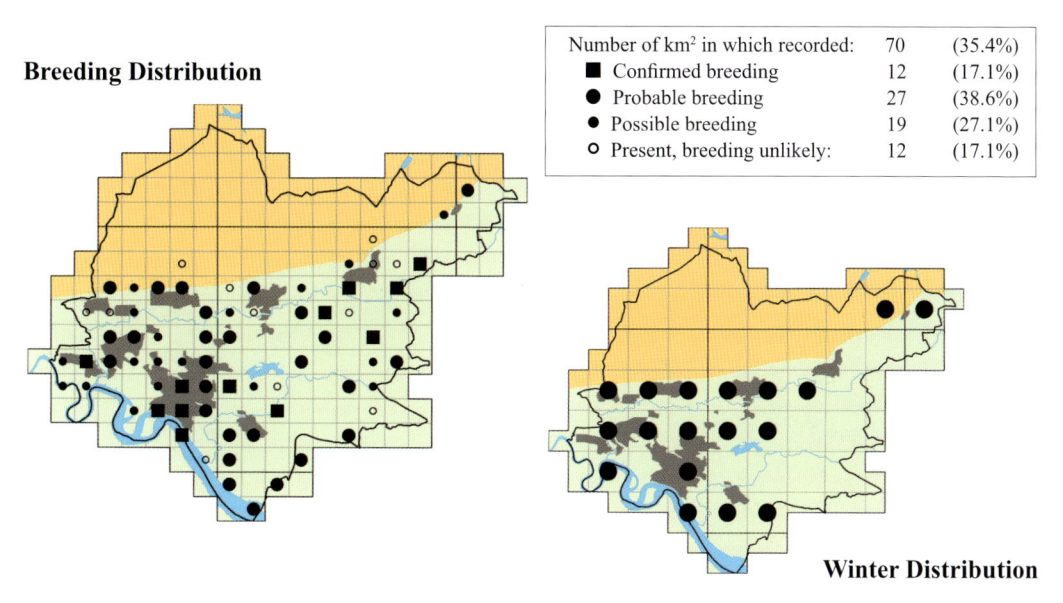

Breeding Distribution

Number of km² in which recorded:	70	(35.4%)
■ Confirmed breeding	12	(17.1%)
● Probable breeding	27	(38.6%)
• Possible breeding	19	(27.1%)
○ Present, breeding unlikely:	12	(17.1%)

Winter Distribution

Stock Dove *Columba oenas*

Fairly common resident   Conservation status: Amber

The Stock Dove flourishes best along the border between forest and open farmland, where there are trees providing holes or hollows for nest-sites and fields with a ready supply of food.[1] It shares this habitat with both of the species with which it is most likely to be confused – the larger and more strikingly patterned Woodpigeon, and the slightly smaller and variably plumaged Feral Pigeon.

The *Atlas* survey confirms the species to be a lowland bird in Clackmannanshire – despite most of the confirmed breeding registrations being from the woodland strip at the foot of the Ochils there were no records from the upland areas immediately to the north. (Indeed, there is only a sparse scattering of this species above the Central Belt).[2] It proved to be difficult to confirm breeding for this species, with only 11% of the squares in which it was registered reaching this category. This is likely to reflect the problems of locating breeding holes and of identifying newly fledged birds. Within the lowland squares there was a notable concentration in the west of the County, which is slightly surprising considering the amount of apparently suitable habitat in the east.

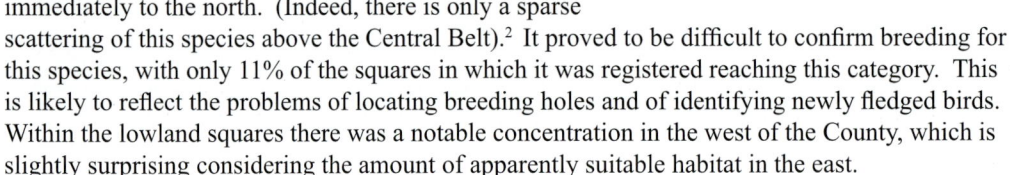

A similar pattern emerges from the winter survey results – records mainly from the Hillfoots areas and the western parts of the County (with a single registration from an upland square). The Stock Dove is noted to be a very sedentary species in Britain,[3] so it seems safe to assume that birds recorded in Clackmannanshire in the winter are of local origin. Local records refer to small flocks, rarely exceeding 20 in number.[4]

John Grainger

[1] BWP [2] 1988-91 Atlas [3] O'Connor & Mead, 1984 [4] UFABR

Breeding Distribution

Number of km² in which recorded:	55	(27.8%)
■ Confirmed breeding	6	(10.9%)
● Probable breeding	26	(47.3%)
• Possible breeding	20	(36.4%)
○ Present, breeding unlikely:	3	(5.5%)

Winter Distribution

Woodpigeon   (Common Wood Pigeon)   *Columba palumbus*

Common resident and winter visitor

Conservation status: Green

Like most other British pigeons, the Woodpigeon is a particularly adaptable species, with a varied diet and a potential to breed almost throughout the year. Although it commonly breeds in woodlands as its name suggests, it is now typically a farmland species and can be a serious pest.[1] Its habitats therefore overlap with those of the species with which it is most easily confused, the Feral Pigeon and the Stock Dove (*q.v.*).

The present *Atlas* survey found the Woodpigeon to be present in virtually all lowland squares in Clackmannanshire, with confirmed breeding in almost half of these. Within the upland areas there was very little penetration beyond the wooded fringes, and most of that was at the eastern end above Dollar. A similar pattern is evident in the winter distribution. Recent local records are of winter flocks, including a count of 2,000 at Menstrie in December 1988, though no flocks with more than 350 birds have been recorded since then.[2] British Woodpigeons are essentially sedentary though there are some coastal movements, and these winter flocks are likely to be made up of local birds.[3]

Within the UK as a whole BBS results indicate an increase in the Woodpigeon population of about 30% between 1995 and 2007,[4] which has been attributed to a spread of arable cultivation (especially Oilseed Rape (*Brassica napus*) which promotes winter survival), and to an increase in autumn-sown cereals.[5,6] However, the smaller Scottish BBS sample shows a more stable population north of the Border,[7] and there is nothing in the limited Clackmannanshire winter data to suggest otherwise.[8]

John Grainger

[1] BS3   [2] UFABR   [3] Migration Atlas   [4] Risely et al., 2009   [5] BBWC   [6] O'Connor & Shrubb, 1986
[7] Risely et al., 2009   [8] UFABR

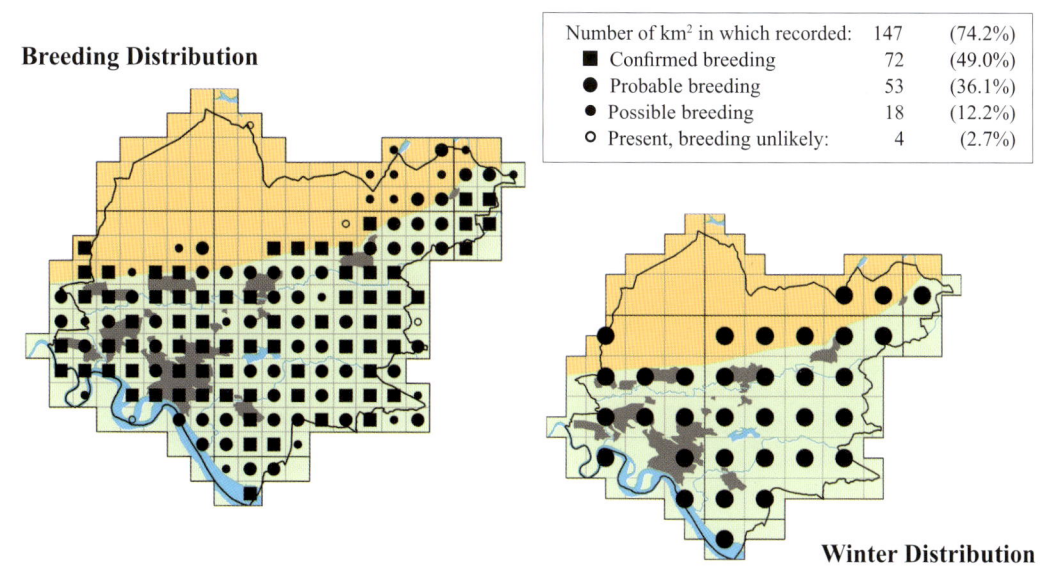

Breeding Distribution

Number of km² in which recorded:	147	(74.2%)
■ Confirmed breeding	72	(49.0%)
● Probable breeding	53	(36.1%)
• Possible breeding	18	(12.2%)
○ Present, breeding unlikely:	4	(2.7%)

Winter Distribution

Collared Dove (Eurasian Collared Dove) *Streptopelia decaocto*

Common resident   Conservation status: Green

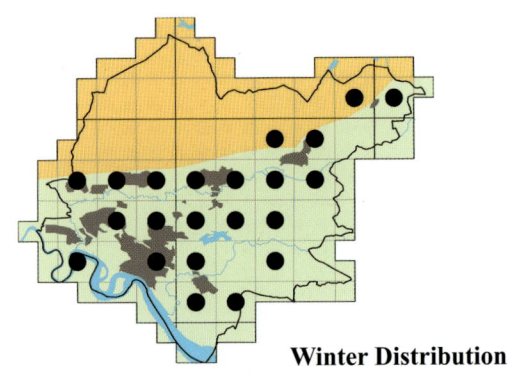

The extraordinary colonization of Britain by Collared Doves from its first recorded appearance in 1952 to a UK population of 15,000-20,000 pairs by 1970 has been described as the avian success story of the twentieth century.[1,2]

Local records show that in 1974 it was still absent from Alva and only 'doubtfully resident' in Tillicoultry, and it seems that the expansion into the area round the Hillfoot towns during the next six years was part of the Collared Dove's final expansion within mainland Britain.[3]

The present survey results show that the species is now present in about half of all lowland squares, with the main concentrations around Alloa, Clackmannan and the Hillfoot towns, as would be expected of a bird which favours mixed habitats such as woodlands, scrub and gardens, and which associates readily with man. It was the ninth most commonly recorded species in Clackmannanshire gardens during the *Atlas* period.[4] Although displaying Collared Doves are conspicuous during the breeding season, they are not easily established as confirmed breeders, as the present survey and other atlases bear out.[5,6]

The results of the winter surveys show a distribution very similar to that for breeding birds, supporting the suggestion from the *Migration Atlas* based on ringing data that Collared Doves do not move far from their breeding areas. The small flocks of between 20 and 46 birds in winter which have featured in local Records since 1982 are likely to be gatherings of local birds at food sources, rather than an indication of dispersal.[7]

John Grainger

[1] *May & Fisher, 1953* [2] *BBWC* [3] *UFABR* [4] *Garden BirdWatch unpub. data* [5] *Fife Atlas* [6] *SE Scotland Atlas* [7] *UFABR*

Breeding Distribution

Number of km² in which recorded:	79	(39.9%)
■ Confirmed breeding	13	(16.5%)
● Probable breeding	41	(51.9%)
• Possible breeding	23	(29.1%)
○ Present, breeding unlikely:	2	(2.5%)

Winter Distribution

Cuckoo *(Common Cuckoo)   Cuculus canorus*

Uncommon summer visitor and passage migrant   Conservation status: Red

Less often seen than heard, the Cuckoo does not readily fit the pattern of the 'breeding pair', which forms the basis of most population surveys. Its very distinctive song can be heard from a considerable distance, but the male and female birds are seldom seen together and the young, as is well-known, are reared by 'foster parents' of a different species. Within the UK Dunnocks, Meadow Pipits and Reed Warblers together comprise 80% of the host species.[1] The territory of a pair of Cuckoos is dependent on the breeding density of hosts and can be extensive.

In the late 19th century the Cuckoo was common throughout the UK, and Clackmannanshire was no exception.[2] Numbers have declined since then (recent BBS results show a significant decline of 37% in the UK between 1995 and 2007 despite a slight increase in Scotland during the same period).[3] The present survey combined with local records since 1974[4] show that the bird is now mainly confined to the fringe upland areas of the Ochil scarp, where its principal host species is likely to be the Meadow Pipit. There was also a probable breeding registration to the south of Dollar, with possible breeding records in two adjoining squares, which are likely to represent one territory. Given the bird's elusive nature, it is not surprising that there was only one confirmed breeding registration during the survey – a juvenile being fed by a Whinchat above Dollar.

Throughout Europe and western Asia the Cuckoo is a summer visitor that winters in Africa. Few Scottish birds have been ringed, which is a reflection of the difficulties of finding chicks in Meadow Pipit nests and the near-impossibility of catching adult birds other than at observatories. All recoveries of Scottish-ringed Cuckoos have been of migrating birds within Europe.[5]

John Grainger

[1] *Glue, 2006*   [2] *Historical Atlas*   [3] *Risely et al., 2009*   [4] *UFABR*   [5] *Migration Atlas*

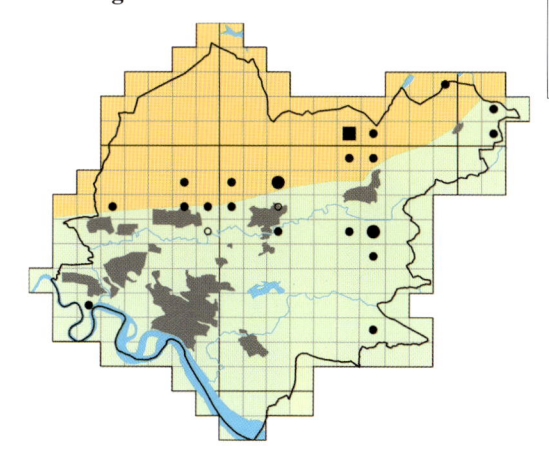

Breeding Distribution

Number of km² in which recorded:	22	(11.1%)
■ Confirmed breeding	1	(4.5%)
● Probable breeding	2	(9.1%)
• Possible breeding	17	(77.3%)
○ Present, breeding unlikely:	2	(9.1%)

Barn Owl *Tyto alba*

Scarce resident   Conservation status: Amber

The Barn Owl is a true bird of farmland where its favoured prey of small mammals (especially voles) is plentiful. It thrives best in warmer climes than those of the UK where the Scottish population is at the limit of its northern range.[1,2] In particular it does not survive cold, wet and windy weather, or long periods of snow cover – conditions which limit the bird's food supply and its ability to hunt and result in reduced productivity in the subsequent breeding season.[3] The Barn Owl's Amber status reflects its declining population during the 20th century (mainly as a result of changing agricultural practices and the loss of traditional breeding and roosting sites in farm-steadings).[4,5]

Atlas surveys inevitably tend to under-record nocturnal species and, although the Barn Owl does hunt more often in twilight than Tawny or Long-eared Owls, it also tends to be less vocal. The breeding survey registered the species in 21 squares, well spread across the lowland farming areas of the County. In four of those breeding was confirmed. Barn Owl territories vary considerably in size and there can be overlapping of adjacent territories,[6] making any estimate of the population within the County highly conjectural. Bearing in mind also the fact that the species tends to be under-recorded, one can assume that the total figure is likely to be between four and ten breeding pairs, though there could quite easily be as many as 20. The erection of nest boxes in many parts of the County is likely to aid breeding success.

Outwith the breeding season adult Barn Owls are largely sedentary though young birds disperse short distances from their natal sites within the first few weeks after fledging.[7] The winter *Atlas* records show a reduced number of observed birds, and a pronounced eastward shift within the County.

John Grainger

[1] Toms, 1999 [2] EBCC Atlas [3] Leech et al., 2009 [4] Percival, 1990 [5] Taylor & Walton, 2003 [6] BWP [7] Migration Atlas

Breeding Distribution

Number of km² in which recorded:	21	(10.6%)
■ Confirmed breeding	4	(19.0%)
● Probable breeding	1	(4.8%)
• Possible breeding	10	(47.6%)
○ Present, breeding unlikely:	6	(28.6%)

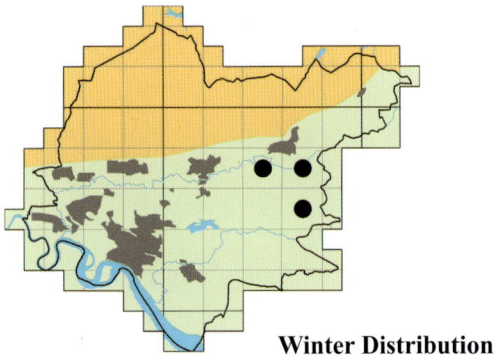

Winter Distribution

Tawny Owl *Strix aluco*

Fairly common resident

Conservation status: Green

The Tawny Owl is the commonest British owl. It is also the one most familiar to the general public, not because it is often seen, but for the hooting calls made by both sexes but especially the males. Following a UK population decline throughout the 18th, 19th and early 20th centuries caused by deforestation and subsequent intense human persecution for game preservation,[1,2] numbers subsequently recovered and are now primarily controlled by the availability of the small mammals which make up its specialised diet – in Scotland Wood Mouse and Bank and Field Voles.[3,4,5] Unfortunately the Scottish Raptor Monitoring Group has few recent data relating to the species in Central Scotland.[6]

Like most nocturnal birds owls tend to be under-recorded in atlas surveys. The Tawny Owl is more vocal than most owl species, but its calls are most often heard early in the breeding season in February and March,[7] too early for the *Atlas* breeding survey. It was nevertheless registered in 77 squares broadly distributed across the lowland areas of the County and reflecting its preferred habitats of broad-leaved and coniferous woodland, scrub, agricultural land and villages.[8] Away from the wooded scarp slopes the bird was absent from the Ochils, and it was also uncommon in the carselands bordering the Forth. Inevitably there were few registrations of confirmed breeding, most (47) falling within the probable category.

The Tawny Owl rarely moves more than a few kilometres from its birthplace throughout the whole of its life.[9] One might therefore expect a similar pattern of distribution from the winter survey. While this is broadly the case, the small number of records is confined to a mere eight tetrads, suggesting that there is scope for a more detailed study.

John Grainger

[1] *Historical Atlas* [2] *BS3* [3] *ibid.* [4] Southern, H. N., 1970 [5] Petty, S. J., 1992 [6] Etheridge et al., 2007 [7] Hansen, L., 1952 [8] *BirdFacts* [9] *Migration Atlas*

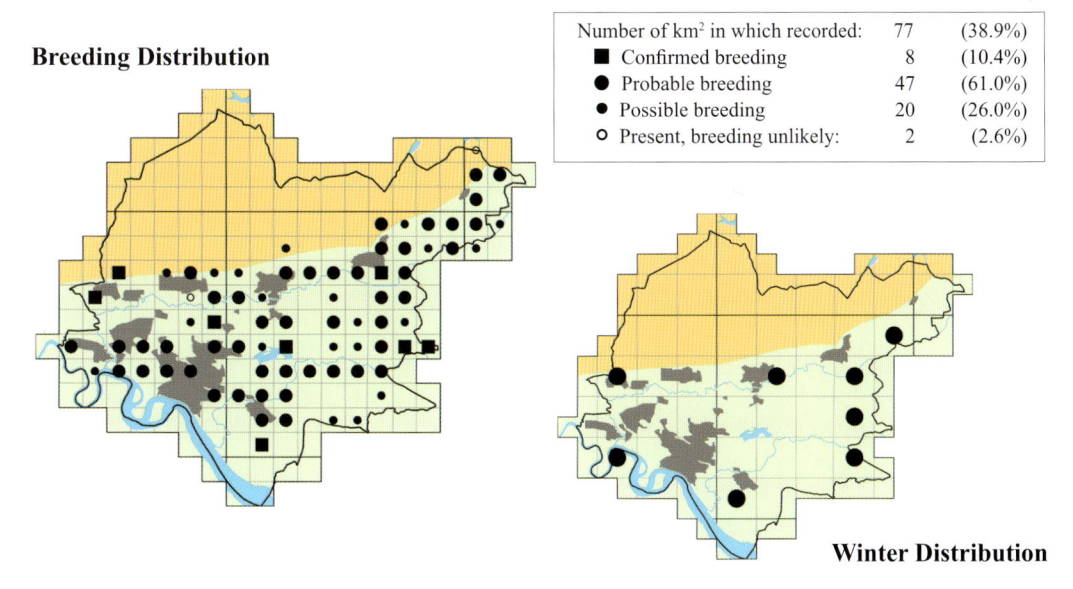

Breeding Distribution

Number of km² in which recorded:	77	(38.9%)
■ Confirmed breeding	8	(10.4%)
● Probable breeding	47	(61.0%)
• Possible breeding	20	(26.0%)
○ Present, breeding unlikely:	2	(2.6%)

Winter Distribution

Long-eared Owl *Asio otus*

Scarce resident and winter visitor   Conservation status: Green

The Long-eared Owl is a nocturnal hunter and spends its daylight hours perched motionless close to the trunk of a tree where its cryptic colouring provides effective camouflage – habits that make it one of the most easily overlooked of British birds. It is traditionally associated with small coniferous woods and shelter belts,[1] and it was the increase in the planting of such features in the mid-19th century linked to the decline in numbers of its competitor, the slightly larger Tawny Owl, that led to the expansion of the species in the UK at about that time.[2] More recently its population has declined in the 20th century as the Tawny Owl population increased.[3]

The *Atlas* results are sparse indeed with one confirmed breeding record in an upland square north-east of Dollar and a possible record to the south of Gartmorn Dam. It is interesting to note that while the former was for a square with no records of Tawny Owls, the lowland square had a probable breeding record for the larger species. It is also notable that no Long-eared Owls were recorded at Cambus as part of the survey, despite their having bred there in 1993 and 1996 and with single birds having been recorded in 1990, 1997, 2001 and 2006 – an indication of the difficulties of recording this elusive bird.[4]

The winter survey recorded a bird in one square close to the County boundary with Fife. Although the Long-eared Owl is one of the few owl species to undertake long-distance movements,[5] the likelihood is that this was a resident bird.

Clearly, a concentrated single-species study would help to establish this bird's real status and even a study limited to a small area such as Clackmannanshire is likely to produce real benefits.

John Grainger

[1] BS3 [2] Mead, 2000 [3] BS3 [4] UFABR [5] Migration Atlas

Breeding Distribution

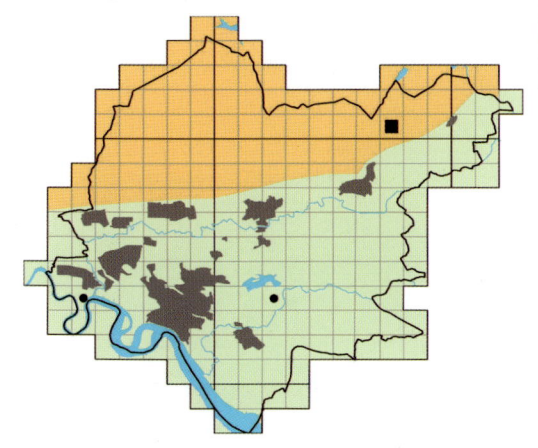

Number of km² in which recorded:	3	(1.5%)
■ Confirmed breeding	1	(33.3%)
● Probable breeding	0	(0.0%)
• Possible breeding	2	(66.7%)
○ Present, breeding unlikely:	0	(0.0%)

Swift   (Common Swift)   *Apus apus*

Common summer visitor and passage migrant   Conservation status: Amber

The Swift's extraordinary aerial lifestyle makes it one of the most difficult common birds to study. It pursues its diet of flying insects and spiders often at a considerable height and occasionally over enormous distances. These long-distance travellers may be breeding birds avoiding wet weather systems as suggested by Koskimies,[1] or they may be non-breeding birds, as Swifts do not normally breed until their fourth year. The Swift is therefore literally non-territorial, and although it nests in buildings in close proximity to man, it is notoriously liable to desert its nest if disturbed.[2] The bird's current Amber conservation status reflects recent BBS population trends which show a decline of some 42% between 1995 and 2007.[3] While this may be due to the aerial plankton on which it feeds becoming less plentiful,[4] other species with similar requirements, such as the House Martin, have not shown a similar decline. The loss of nest sites to modern methods of building construction could well be more significant, highlighting the need for the provision of nest sites in new and restored buildings.[5]

While Swifts were observed in almost all lowland squares in Clackmannanshire (and in several squares in the Ochils), this tends to represent their extensive feeding area rather than their actual breeding distribution. The 16 probable and confirmed squares are concentrated in more urban areas such as Alloa and the Hillfoot towns, where there are suitable buildings to provide nest sites. Other recent records show similar concentrations in urban areas and villages, with feeding parties ranging from Cambus Pools to Ben Cleuch in the Ochils.[6]

The Swift's breeding season is remarkably short, concentrated into the period from mid-May to mid-August. Though it is known that they winter in sub-Saharan Africa, the number of ringed birds recovered is (not surprisingly) very low.[7]

John Grainger

[1] Koskimies, 1950   [2] Lack, D., 1956   [3] Risely et al., 2009   [4] Migration Atlas   [5] BBWC   [6] UFABR
[7] Migration Atlas

Breeding Distribution

Number of km² in which recorded:	111	(56.1%)
■ Confirmed breeding	5	(4.5%)
● Probable breeding	15	(13.5%)
• Possible breeding	6	(5.4%)
○ Present, breeding unlikely:	85	(76.6%)

Kingfisher (Common Kingfisher) *Alcedo atthis*

Uncommon resident					Conservation status: Amber

The Kingfisher is widespread across the Western Palearctic but is a localised breeding species in Scotland, mainly found in the south and west mainland.[1,2]

The prime ecological requirements of Kingfishers are a sufficient supply of small fish, perches for look-out posts and steep banks for nest tunnels. They avoid fast-flowing streams and are very sensitive to pollution. Open, exposed waterbodies are generally avoided. If necessary, they nest up to 250m away from water.[3]

Kingfishers were recorded in 8% or 15 squares during the breeding season. On the River Devon there was one confirmed breeding attempt between Alva and Tillicoultry and two probable attempts to the east of Tillicoultry. Possible attempts were concentrated on the Muckhart to Crook of Devon stretch with smaller numbers between Cambus and Tullibody. On the Black Devon there were two possible breeding attempts, both between its mouth and Clackmannan. During the winter the species was only recorded from four tetrads: one at Cambus, one east of Alva and two between Dollar and Tillicoultry.

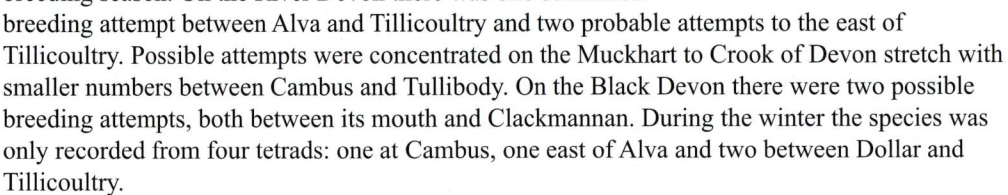

In Britain the species decreased in the 19th century as a result of human persecution. It declined along linear waterways until the mid-1980s but seems to have made a complete recovery and there is no clear long-term trend.[4,5] Kingfishers are prone to severe mortality during harsh winters but being multi-brooded readily recolonize previous areas. It is tempting to speculate that global warming will benefit a species that is vulnerable in harsh winters but accompanying events, such as floods, may adversely affect the species. As a local example, the River Devon is a spate river on which levels can fluctuate dramatically. Given the small number of breeding pairs in Clackmannanshire and the fact that nests are re-used in successive years, it should be possible to build up a comprehensive picture of its breeding distribution.

Andre Thiel

[1] BWP   [2] BS3   [3] BWP   [4] ibid.   [5] Baillie, S. R., et al. 2009

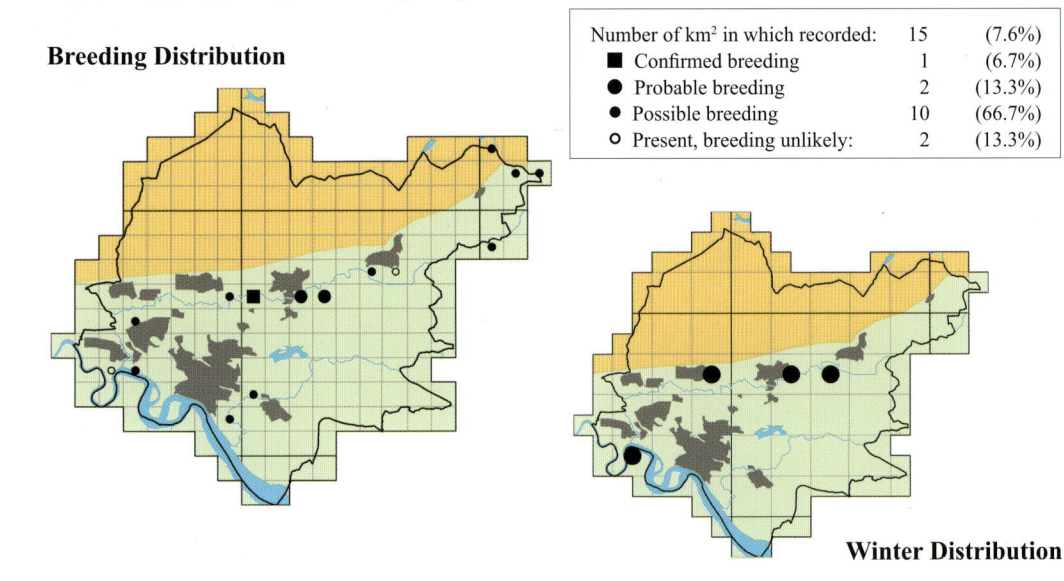

Breeding Distribution

Number of km² in which recorded:	15	(7.6%)
■ Confirmed breeding	1	(6.7%)
● Probable breeding	2	(13.3%)
• Possible breeding	10	(66.7%)
○ Present, breeding unlikely:	2	(13.3%)

Winter Distribution

Green Woodpecker (European Green Woodpecker) *Picus viridis*

Uncommon resident   Conservation status: Amber

The Green Woodpecker is a relatively new bird to Scotland with the first reports of regular breeding occurring in the early 1950s.[1] Its principal habitat requirements are mature trees for nesting and roosting, and foraging areas with a plentiful supply of ants, particularly on south-facing grassy slopes.[2] It is therefore much less tied to woodland than the Great Spotted Woodpecker.

The Green Woodpecker was first recorded breeding in Clackmannanshire in 1963 with increasing records in subsequent years.[3] BBS trends show that it is still expanding its range across most of the UK with a significant increase of 47% from 1995-2007;[4] although it is vulnerable to localised extinctions, which have already happened in several parts of Scotland.[5]

The Clackmannanshire distribution shows a marked preference for the wooded slopes and glens of the Ochils. The mature deciduous woods found here combined with plentiful feeding opportunities on the open grassy south-facing lower slopes with a rich supply of invertebrates (presumably including good concentrations of ants) evidently favour the species' requirements.[6] The distribution is much more patchy away from the Hillfoots, apart from a few records in the south-east close to the Fife border.

There were fewer *Atlas* records during the winter, probably because the Green Woodpecker is not vocal at that time, resulting in birds being missed during the survey period. In the UK it is largely sedentary although there is some random localised post-fledging and winter dispersal.[7]

Although the Green Woodpecker has enjoyed a remarkable extension of range in the UK over the last few decades, there is an underlying fragility in the status of the population, given its dependency on ants and, ultimately, the right amount of grazing by sheep and rabbits.[8]

Keith Broomfield

[1] BS2 [2] BS3 [3] Tewnion, 1966 [4] Ridley et al., 2009 [5] BS3 [6] ibid. [7] Migration Atlas [8] BS3

Breeding Distribution

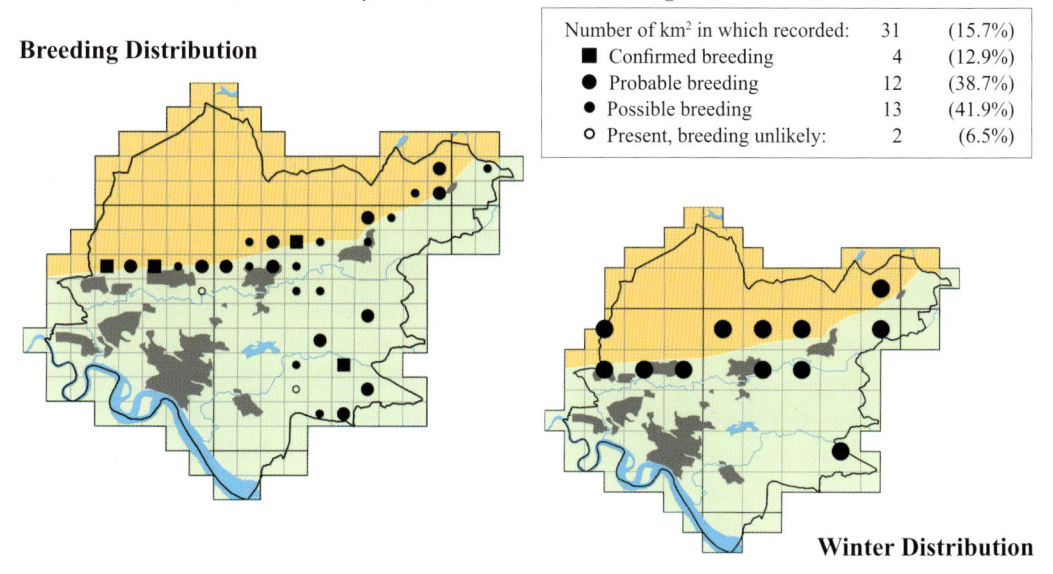

Number of km² in which recorded:	31	(15.7%)
■ Confirmed breeding	4	(12.9%)
● Probable breeding	12	(38.7%)
• Possible breeding	13	(41.9%)
O Present, breeding unlikely:	2	(6.5%)

Winter Distribution

Great Spotted Woodpecker *Dendrocopos major*

Fairly common resident   Conservation status: Green

The Great Spotted Woodpecker favours mature broad-leafed woodland where there is a high proportion of dead wood from which it can source its main food of invertebrate prey.[1] However, it is also widespread in mature conifer woods though at lower densities.[2]

It is widely distributed in Clackmannanshire and is a common breeder in the eastern part of the County. It is frequent in the steep wooded glens of the Hillfoots and in woodland areas on the fringes of towns such as Alloa and Tullibody. Confirmed breeding occurred in 13% of squares and probable and possible breeding in a further 22% of squares.

The Great Spotted Woodpecker is reasonably conspicuous in spring and summer due to its distinctive metallic 'tchick' call and territorial 'drumming'. At other times it can be very secretive with the thick leaf canopy of mid to late summer making detection difficult. Tree nest-holes in particular can be hard to find and it is likely that instances of confirmed breeding have been under-recorded.

The sedentary nature of the species produces summer and winter ranges that tally reasonably closely. In Scotland, Scandinavian immigrants may augment the winter population but even in irruption years the number of birds arriving is not thought to be great.[3]

The general long-term population trend for the species in Scotland since the Second World War has been of conspicuous growth; a significant increase of 111% within Scottish BBS squares from 1995-2007 strongly suggests that this is continuing. [4,5]

The maturing of existing conifer plantations should benefit the Clackmannanshire population. However, the scarcity of dead wood in this habitat will limit numbers, and the eventual felling could lead to localised extinctions as has already happened in some plantations in the Ochils.

Keith Broomfield

[1] BirdFacts [2] BS3 [3] ibid. [4] ibid. [5] Risely et al., 2009

Breeding Distribution

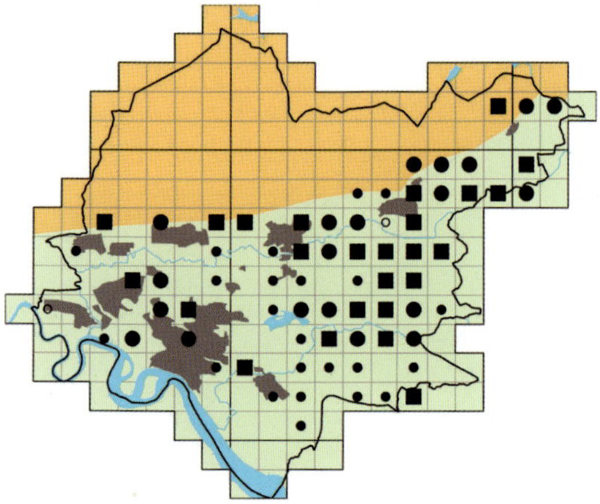

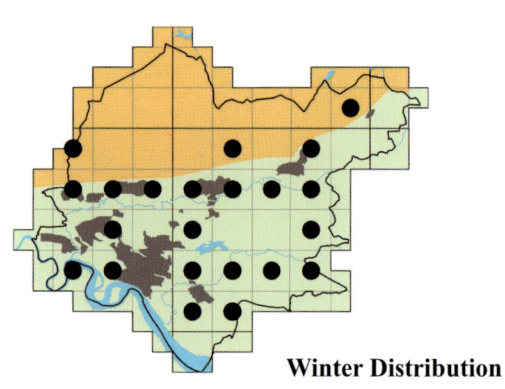

Number of km² in which recorded:	70	(35.4%)
■ Confirmed breeding	25	(35.7%)
● Probable breeding	20	(28.6%)
• Possible breeding	23	(32.9%)
○ Present, breeding unlikely:	2	(2.9%)

Winter Distribution

Magpie   (Eurasian Magpie)   *Pica pica*

Common resident   Conservation status: Green

Historically the Magpie was evidently a familiar breeding bird in Tillicoultry and was often seen but did not breed at Alloa.[1] Rintoul & Baxter noted that it used to be very common but was much reduced by 'game preservation'.[2] Although the first national breeding bird survey showed confirmed breeding records across the County,[3] in reality its distribution then was still patchy. During the 1970s and 1980s the Magpie was expanding and consolidating its distribution, perhaps as rural persecution eased.[4] The available evidence suggests that colonization occurred from west to east. The four SOC surveys of the River Devon (1977-1987) only encountered the species 13 times, mostly below Tillicoultry.[5]

The *Atlas* breeding map for the County confirms that the Magpie is a common and widespread low country bird but the interrupted nature of its rural distribution east of a line from Alloa to Tillicoultry is puzzling. Despite this terrain apparently offering plenty of suitable breeding habitat *Atlas* surveyors did not detect even possible breeding in at least 30 grid squares in this area. Livestock has been mentioned as an attraction because the largely ground-feeding Magpie thrives where there are invertebrate-rich pastures.[6] The Muckhart to Rumbling Bridge area, which has livestock farms and a good deal of 'horsiculture' certainly appears to be a stronghold of breeding Magpies in the east, but an area south of Gartmorn Dam with similar attributes has none. It may be that this is due to control by landowners; it may also be the case that the gaps in its range are attributable to the Magpie still undergoing its natural recolonization of a part of central Scotland which is very close to the northern edge of its continuous breeding range.

David Thorogood

[1] *Statistical Accounts* [2] *Rintoul & Baxter, 1935* [3] *1968-72 Atlas* [4] *BS2* [5] *Henty, 1991* [6] *Birkhead, 1991*

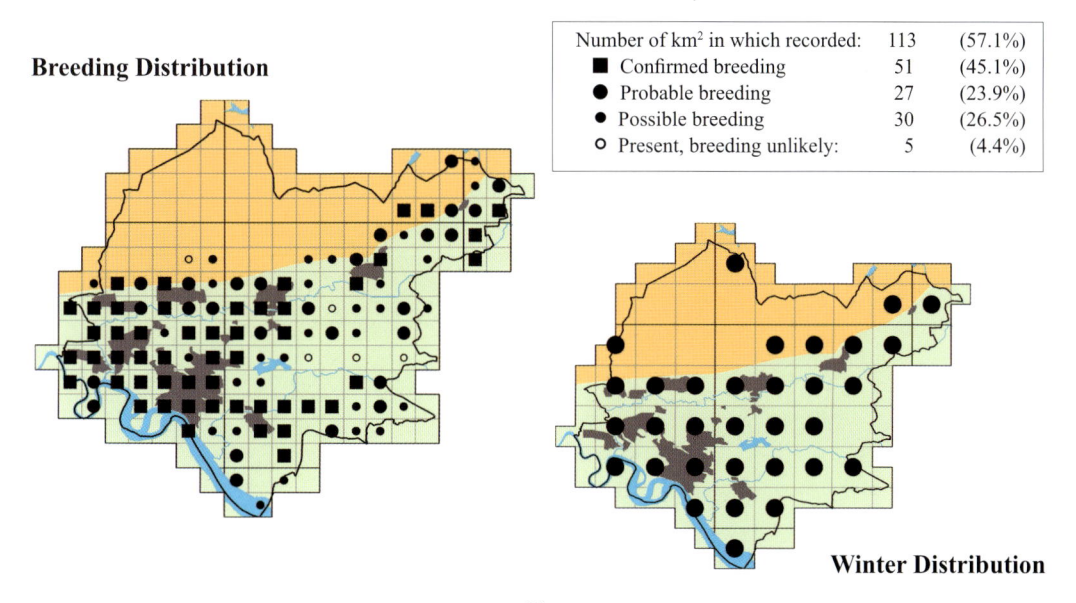

Breeding Distribution

Number of km² in which recorded:	113	(57.1%)
■ Confirmed breeding	51	(45.1%)
● Probable breeding	27	(23.9%)
• Possible breeding	30	(26.5%)
○ Present, breeding unlikely:	5	(4.4%)

Winter Distribution

Jay (Eurasian Jay) *Garrulus glandarius*

Fairly common resident   Conservation status: Green

Jays are widely distributed throughout the Western Palearctic from western Europe to eastern Asia and south to northern Africa. They are strongly arboreal and associate primarily with dense Oak, Beech and Hornbeam woodlands. Locally they have spread into smaller copses and even parks and large gardens.[1]

During *Atlas* fieldwork Jays were recorded from 21% of squares of which the majority referred to possible breeding birds, with few records of probable or confirmed breeding birds. This accords with the findings of other local atlases, and reflects the difficulty of locating this secretive species during the breeding season.[2,3] Records were spread throughout lowland Clackmannanshire with a slight bias towards eastern areas. There is a strong correlation between the distribution of Jays and that of broadleaved, especially ancient, woodlands in the County,[4] although it is also clear that Jays do occur in thinly wooded areas, such as to the south and west of Dollar, between Tillicoultry and Dollar and between Tullibody and Alloa.

The species is sedentary in Britain where the species tends to disperse within 50km of ringing sites.[5] Eruptive movements from north and central Europe are linked to the failure of acorns.[6,7] Within Clackmannanshire the winter tetrad survey shows a distribution which is largely similar to that during the breeding season with a similar eastern bias.

The UK Jay population remained pretty stable in its preferred woodland habitat until the mid-1980s, after which the population declined by about 20% over the next decade, followed by signs of recovery.[8,9] Given its current status there is no immediate urgency to target the species for further survey work.

Andre Thiel

[1] BWP [2] SE Scotland Atlas [3] Fife Atlas [4] Thiel & Lindsay, 1999 [5] Mead & Hudson, 1984 [6] BWP [7] John & Roskell, 1985 [8] Gregory & Marchant, 1996 [9] BBWC

Breeding Distribution

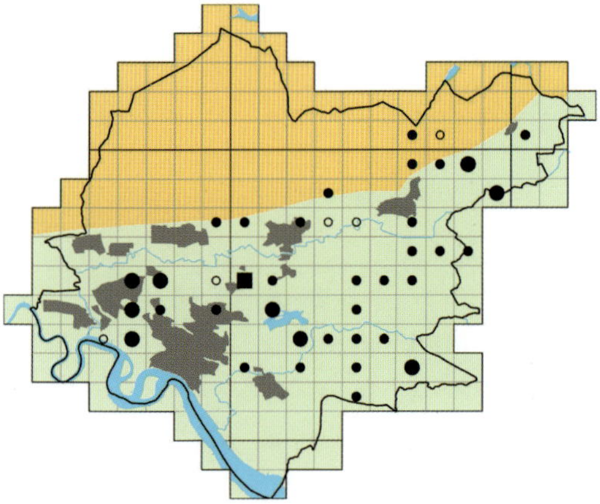

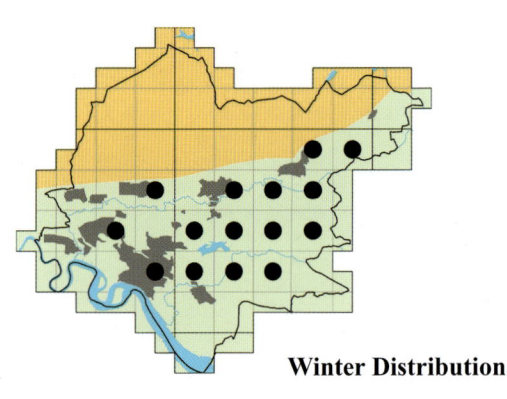

Number of km² in which recorded:	41	(20.7%)
■ Confirmed breeding	1	(2.4%)
● Probable breeding	9	(22.0%)
• Possible breeding	26	(63.4%)
○ Present, breeding unlikely:	5	(12.2%)

Winter Distribution

Jackdaw (Western Jackdaw) *Corvus monedula*

Common resident   Conservation status: Green

Clackmannanshire demonstrates nicely the modern urban nesting habits of the Jackdaw from its original reliance on mature woodlands for nest sites, to rock crevices and holes in man-made structures, notably chimneys.[1] In and around the Hillfoots towns all these habitats are occupied within a few hundred metres of one another. Numbers were reckoned to have increased greatly during the early 20th century,[2] which may have been because of an increase in urban nesting opportunities.

The *Atlas* map confirms the attraction of the Hillfoots towns and their environs for nesting Jackdaws. The Tullibody-Alloa-Clackmannan urban complex is also well tenanted, though there is a lack of confirmed breeding registrations in the western half of that area. Jackdaws are colonial nesters and clearly have an affinity with Rooks, frequently nesting in trees in close proximity to rookeries and flying with the larger birds to shared feeding areas, usually on agricultural land. The breeding distribution also has similarities with that of the Magpie, and as with that species shows some gaps in the south-east and east of the County that are not easy to account for. It may be that both the clearance of mining dereliction and the recent fashion for renovating and converting older rural buildings for residential use have reduced artificial nest sites there.[3]

The species is fairly generally distributed during winter with some birds penetrating into the western Ochils.

Between the first two national breeding Atlas surveys Jackdaws underwent another period of population increase,[4,5] and recent BBS results show a continuing increase in the UK population (31% between 1995 and 2007).[6] The early local Bird Reports give an impression of scarcity but it is more likely that the Jackdaw is one of those familiar birds largely neglected by record-keeping birdwatchers.[7]

David Thorogood

[1] BWP [2] *Rintoul & Baxter, 1935* [3] *1988-91 Atlas* [4] *ibid.* [5] *1968-72 Atlas* [6] *Risely et al., 2009* [7] UFABR

Breeding Distribution

Number of km² in which recorded:	118	(59.6%)
■ Confirmed breeding	34	(28.2%)
● Probable breeding	35	(29.7%)
• Possible breeding	29	(24.6%)
○ Present, breeding unlikely:	20	(16.9%)

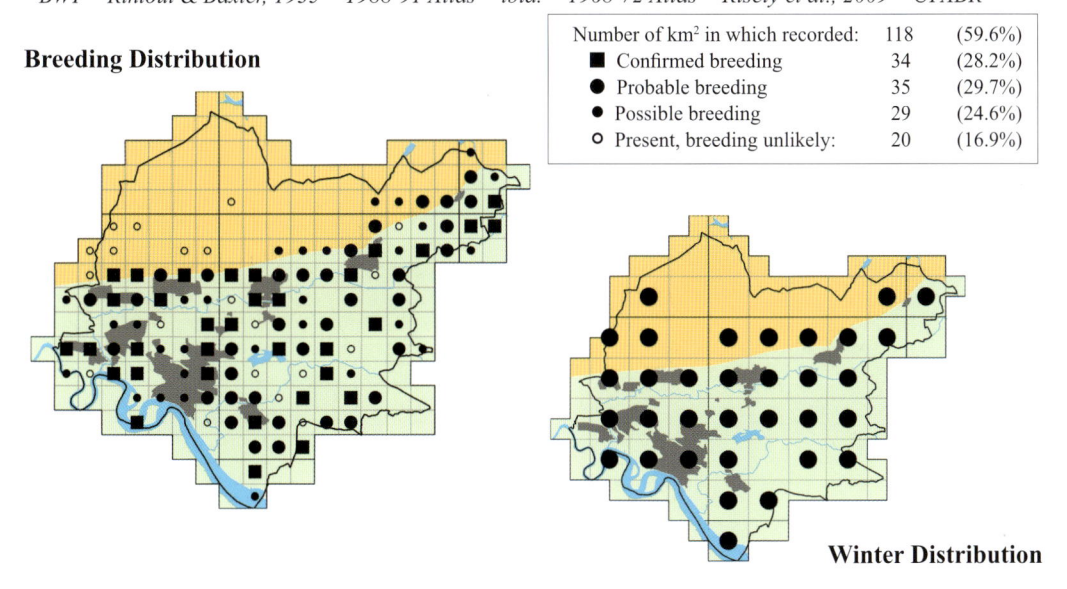

Winter Distribution

Rook *Corvus frugilegus*

Common resident and winter visitor

Conservation status: Green

It seems that the Scottish population of Rooks may still be recovering from a low in the 1960s and 1970s.[1] In Clackmannanshire the *Atlas* surveyors found it certainly nesting in 30 squares and probably in one more. Given the extent of woodland, shelterbelts, hedgerow and parkland trees, and mature gardens across much of the lowland countryside and the hill edges, and the extent of suitable feeding grounds (grassland or agricultural fields) it is perhaps remarkable the degree to which the species nests in built-up areas and urban fringes in the County. All the current existing rookeries are on low ground or in woodlands along the lower parts of the Ochil scarp.

A census of Scotland's Rooks was carried out in the late spring months of 1975 and 1976 when Clackmannanshire was reckoned to harbour 545 nests in 15 locations,[2] but several rookeries seem to have been overlooked or were formed soon afterwards. Regular counts at certain local rookeries show that newly-established colonies may grow or decline rapidly.[3] A further comprehensive local survey was carried out in 1998, when 21 rookeries containing 950 nests were located.[4] The more intensive fieldwork for this *Atlas* revealed a further 12 rookeries with at least 255 nests (nests were counted at only seven rookeries). Some of these rookeries may have been missed in 1998 while others will be new.

A national survey of winter roosts in 1970-1975 found no substantial roosts in the County, suggesting that many local birds were using roosts in neighbouring districts.[5] However, there seems to be no published evidence of such movements, and the fact that roosts have been noted at Gartmorn Dam (5,000 birds in October 1989) and Menstrie suggests that woods with rookeries are probably also used for roosting throughout the year.[6] The winter *Atlas* map shows that Rooks are widespread across lowland areas at this season.

David Thorogood

[1] BS3 [2] Castle, 1977 [3] UFABR [4] N. Bielby unpub. data [5] Munro, 1975 [6] UFABR

Breeding Distribution

Number of km² in which recorded:	119	(60.1%)
■ Confirmed breeding	30	(25.2%)
● Probable breeding	1	(0.8%)
● Possible breeding	0	(0.0%)
○ Present, breeding unlikely:	88	(73.9%)

Winter Distribution

Carrion Crow *Corvus corone*

Common resident

Conservation status: Green

Carrion Crows occur widely throughout the County and their conspicuous nests and breeding behaviour make it unlikely that many birds were missed during the survey. They will nest in a variety of locations including conifer plantations, quite small trees, open ground and on crags,[1] enabling breeding to occur in the hills as well as lowland areas. Three grid squares above the Ochil scarp saw confirmed breeding and another eight or nine had probable or possible breeding registrations. Elsewhere, although a handful of locations had no confirmed breeding, it is possible that Carrion Crows nested in every lowland square during the survey period.

In winter it is similarly ubiquitous, with only some of the higher and more remote hill areas not visited. An apparent absence from near the Forth estuary upstream from Alloa is probably an aberration and unlikely to be significant.

Rintoul & Baxter recorded the Carrion Crow as a much persecuted bird and seemed to suggest that it survived best along the hill margins.[2] Once regarded as a wary species it may also now be encountered sharing urban open spaces with urban pigeons and Magpies, behaving equally boldly as it scavenges across parkland grass and around human litter. The Scottish population is now regarded as probably stable,[3] so there seems little reason to expect it to be anything other than a familiar bird in the County in future.

David Thorogood

[1] BS3 [2] *Rintoul & Baxter, 1935* [3] BS3

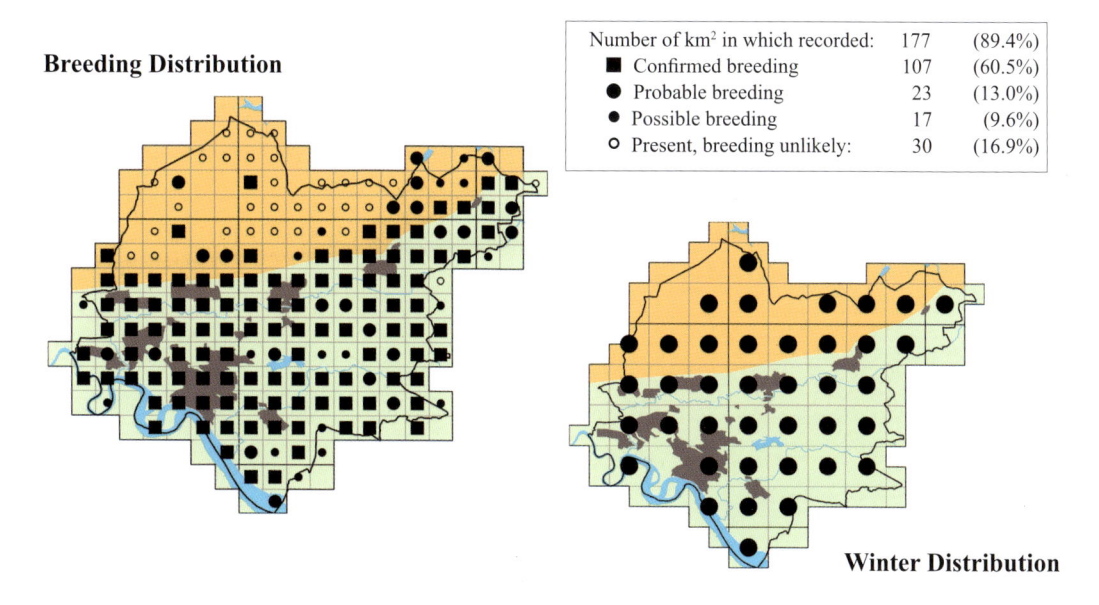

Breeding Distribution

Number of km² in which recorded:	177	(89.4%)
■ Confirmed breeding	107	(60.5%)
● Probable breeding	23	(13.0%)
• Possible breeding	17	(9.6%)
○ Present, breeding unlikely:	30	(16.9%)

Winter Distribution

Raven (Northern Raven) *Corvus corax*

Scarce resident   Conservation status: Green

For much of the latter half of the 20th century the Raven was a scarce bird in central Scotland,[1] but it has enjoyed something of a revival in recent times and is now more widespread,[2] although it still tends to favour areas of high ground for breeding. In Clackmannanshire confirmed and probable breeding was noted at five different sites with many other records of observed birds, principally in the Ochils.

The breeding distribution of Ravens in Clackmannanshire would seem to be mainly restricted by the availability of cliff nest sites on the steep southern slopes of the Ochils where interaction with nearby Peregrines is frequently observed.[3] Breeding was also recorded at one tree nest-site in the hills above Dollar and at an open-cast working in the south-east of the County.

The wide number of observation records in the Ochils during the breeding season reveals that Ravens favour high ground for foraging where there is a high sheep population providing good opportunities for the species to scavenge on carcasses, a favoured food item.[4]

Similarly, the winter distribution is very much tied to the Ochils, although it was recorded in the south-east of the County in areas of rough sheep pasture close to the Black Devon. Ravens are largely sedentary birds and sometimes form communal roosts during winter.[5]

The reduction in persecution combined with an increase in sheep numbers have probably been the main drivers for range expansion in Scotland in recent times.[6] In Clackmannanshire, a fall in sheep mortality caused by mild winters and improved agricultural practices may provide checks on the breeding population of Ravens in the future.

Keith Broomfield

[1] BS2 [2] BS3 [3] Pers. obs. [4] BS3 [5] ibid. [6] ibid.

Breeding Distribution

Number of km² in which recorded:	29	(14.6%)
■ Confirmed breeding	3	(10.3%)
● Probable breeding	2	(6.9%)
● Possible breeding	3	(10.3%)
○ Present, breeding unlikely:	21	(72.4%)

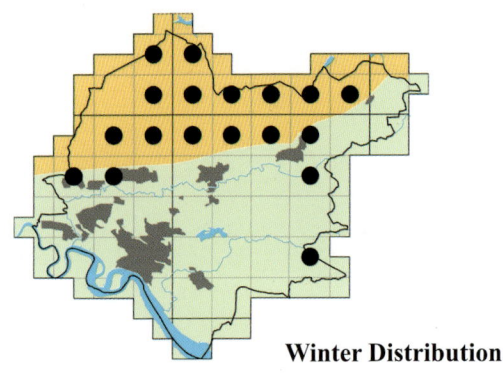

Winter Distribution

Goldcrest *Regulus regulus*

Fairly common resident, passage migrant and winter visitor

Conservation status: Green

The preferred habitat of the Goldcrest – Britain's smallest bird – is coniferous woodland but in winter it may be found in a variety of wooded areas and gardens, often in mixed flocks with tits.[1]

There was a good spread of breeding *Atlas* registrations in Clackmannanshire, which coincides closely with the distribution of coniferous woodland. Overall, there was possible, probable and confirmed breeding from 38% of squares. The conifer plantations in the north-east in the Ochils hold breeding pairs, as do the woodlands along the middle and upper reaches of the River Devon. There was also a good concentration of records in mid and eastern Clackmannanshire where there are many conifer woods of varying sizes, including those at Forestmill and Aberdona. The Goldcrest is scarcer as a breeding bird in the western half of the County and from some areas along the River Forth where woodland of any type is scarce.

The wider winter distribution reflects its broader range of habitat use outside the breeding season when it can often be seen in gardens, parks and birch woods, as well as in alders along the rivers Devon and Black Devon.[2] In autumn, resident Goldcrests in Scotland are joined by immigrants from Scandinavia and in some years there can be quite large falls.[3]

In Clackmannanshire, localised extinctions are likely to occur in areas of tree felling but conversely new areas will be colonized as plantations mature. The biggest population control factor is likely to be the weather with severe winters causing a significant rise in mortality.[4] The trend towards milder winters up to and including the survey period has probably helped to sustain the population at a relatively high level. The BBS in Scotland depicted a significant increase of 54% over the period from 1995 to 2007.[5]

Keith Broomfield

[1] *BWP* [2] *Pers.obs.* [3] *BS3* [4] *ibid.* [5] *Risely et al., 2009*

Breeding Distribution

Number of km² in which recorded:	76	(38.4%)
■ Confirmed breeding	19	(25.0%)
● Probable breeding	16	(21.1%)
• Possible breeding	38	(50.0%)
○ Present, breeding unlikely:	3	(3.9%)

Winter Distribution

Blue Tit *Cyanistes caeruleus*

Common resident

Conservation status: Green

Blue Tits will nest wherever they can find a combination of suitable nest holes and food and the *1988-91 Atlas* found them to be ubiquitous in Britain with the exception of parts of the Scottish Highlands and Islands.[1] The breeding season map for Clackmannanshire matches this broader picture and shows that although the Blue Tit is absent from wholly grass and moorland squares in the Ochil Hills it is found throughout the County elsewhere, both in lowland squares and in wooded areas along the southern scarp of the hills. This reflects the availability of a widespread mix of woodland, hedgerow trees and rural gardens within the agricultural parts of the County, and some mature trees extensively supported by nest-boxes in urban areas. It was the second most commonly recorded species in Clackmannanshire's gardens during the *Atlas* period.[2] The Blue Tit's adaptability and ability to coexist with humans have made it the most common of the County's four species of tit, the encounter rate for Blue Tits on local BBS transects being substantially higher than for any of the other tit species.[3]

Scottish Blue Tits tend to be very sedentary,[4] and the winter map for Clackmannanshire, which is essentially identical to that for the breeding season, would match a pattern of predominantly local movements. Within this generally static picture, however, there will be movements between feeding areas, some degree of juvenile dispersal and certainly an increased use of garden feeders. The *Winter Atlas* noted that woodland Blue Tits often leave the woods in winter, some returning to woodland roosts each evening after forays to feeders in suburban gardens.[5]

Don Matthews

[1] 1988-91 Atlas [2] Garden BirdWatch unpub. data [3] UFABR [4] BS3 [5] Winter Atlas

Breeding Distribution

Number of km² in which recorded:	144	(72.7%)
■ Confirmed breeding	101	(70.1%)
● Probable breeding	25	(17.4%)
• Possible breeding	14	(9.7%)
○ Present, breeding unlikely:	4	(2.8%)

Winter Distribution

Great Tit *Parus major*

Common resident and partial migrant

Conservation status: Green

Historically the Great Tit has not always enjoyed its present widespread distribution, having spread slowly northwards through Scotland during the 19th and 20th centuries.[1,2] Its breeding season distribution within Clackmannanshire is now almost identical to that of the Blue Tit, being absent from the grassland and moorland habitats of the Ochil Hills but almost ubiquitous elsewhere, including wooded areas on the southern scarp of the hills as well as most rural, suburban and urban squares in the lowlands. However, despite the similarity of distribution (135 squares with breeding records compared with 140 for Blue Tit), local BBS transect results give Great Tit encounter rates that are only about half those of Blue Tits.[3] Furthermore, it was the seventh most commonly recorded species in Clackmannanshire's gardens during the *Atlas* period, compared with the Blue Tit's second place.[4] These indications of a smaller local population match the relative sizes of the Scottish breeding populations suggested in *BS3*, where the Blue Tit estimate is almost double that for Great Tit. Nevertheless, the species continues to prosper in Scotland with BBS results indicating a statistically significant increase of 48% from 1995 to 2007.[5]

British Great Tits are largely sedentary but some move greater distances, over 17% of birds ringed in one winter and recovered in a later one having moved more than 20 km.[6] Even for the majority that stay closer to their breeding areas, as winter seed supplies run low woodland birds become more mobile in their search for food, including visits to garden feeders.[7,8] Hence, although the winter distribution map for Clackmannanshire is essentially identical to that for the breeding season, hidden within this picture are likely to be elements of post-breeding juvenile dispersal, local movements between habitats and also some degree of longer distance movement between Clackmannanshire and nearby counties.

Don Matthews

[1] *Historical Atlas* [2] *BS3* [3] *UFABR* [4] *Garden BirdWatch unpub. data* [5] *Risely et al., 2009* [6] *Migration Atlas* [7] *BWP* [8] *Toms, 2003*

Breeding Distribution

Number of km² in which recorded:	135	(68.2%)
■ Confirmed breeding	91	(67.4%)
● Probable breeding	32	(23.7%)
• Possible breeding	12	(8.9%)
○ Present, breeding unlikely:	0	(0.0%)

Winter Distribution

Coal Tit *Periparus ater*

Common resident, possible scarce passage migrant and winter visitor
Conservation status: Green

Of the four species of Tit breeding in Clackmannanshire, only the Coal Tit is more abundant in the north and west of Britain than in the south and east, reflecting the availability of its preferred breeding habitat of coniferous woodland.[1] Its distribution within the County also matches this habitat preference. There is only a patchy presence in the agricultural lower reaches of the River Devon valley and similarly in the farmland by the River Forth, but otherwise the Coal Tit is widely distributed in rural lowland squares reflecting the mosaic of woodland and plantation in much of the County. In the Ochil Hills they are present in wooded areas along the southern margin. Although there are also breeding records for urban and suburban areas, local BBS transects show the Coal Tit to be overwhelmingly a bird of coniferous woodland, with only small numbers recorded in other habitats.[2]

British Coal Tits are largely sedentary but local movements do take place during the winter. The scale of these depends on the availability of seed crops, with birds moving further and more appearing in gardens if seeds are scarce in their normal winter habitats.[3,4] The winter map for Clackmannanshire is essentially identical to that for the breeding season, which would fit in with a pattern of mainly local movements but perhaps augmented by some birds from further afield. While northern European birds are subject to eruptive movements in poor seed years and have been recorded in Scotland,[5] there are no records of such birds in the County.

Don Matthews

[1] 1988-91 Atlas [2] UFABR [3] BS3 [4] Toms, 2003 [5] BS3

Breeding Distribution

Number of km² in which recorded:	108	(54.5%)
■ Confirmed breeding	41	(38.0%)
● Probable breeding	24	(22.2%)
• Possible breeding	41	(38.0%)
○ Present, breeding unlikely:	2	(1.9%)

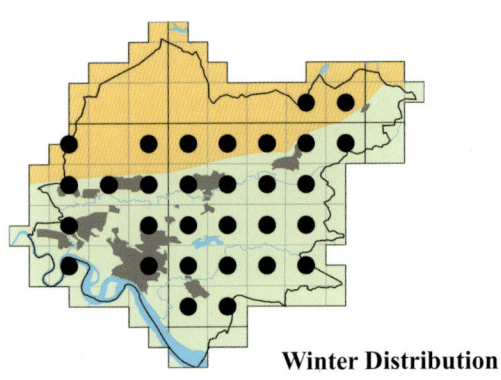

Winter Distribution

Skylark (Sky Lark) *Alauda arvensis*

Common resident   Conservation status: Red

Even though its familiar song is delivered from a great height, the Skylark was one of the easier species to survey. A decision was taken to register all *Atlas* records of song-flight as display; this, combined with the difficulties of confirming breeding compared with many other common passerines, is a major factor in the preponderance (85%) of probable records.

The *Old Statistical Account* notes: 'The Skylark nests throughout our area, in arable parts and grasslands alike, even on the tops of the …Ochils'.[1] The breeding map shows its distribution to be much the same today. It is ubiquitous in the Ochil Hills – despite the intensive grazing regime there – but is largely absent from the scarp, and also from urban areas and mature woodlands as would be expected of a species that only inhabits open spaces. Allowing for these gaps, an initial look at the map would suggest that it is still widespread in the lowlands. However, closer inspection reveals some inexplicable absences in what would appear to be suitable habitat, namely: to the south of Tillicoultry; between Tillicoultry and Dollar; the Pool of Muckhart area; to the east of Solsgirth; and between Cambus and Alloa. Compared to the notable decline in the rest of the UK, recent Scottish breeding numbers have remained relatively stable.[2,3]

The winter map shows Skylarks to be absent from the Ochils (apart from one record – probably of an early spring return) with a patchy distribution in the lowlands that is almost wholly restricted to the western half of the County where winter stubble is more likely to be found. Such farmland habitat is much reduced in recent decades and the winter flocks of up to 500 birds recorded in the 1970s no longer occur – the highest during the *Atlas* period being 45.[4]

Neil Bielby

[1] *Old Statistical Account* [2] BS3 [3] Risely et al. 2009 [4] UFABR

Breeding Distribution

Number of km² in which recorded:	131	(66.2%)
■ Confirmed breeding	14	(10.7%)
● Probable breeding	111	(84.7%)
• Possible breeding	4	(3.1%)
○ Present, breeding unlikely:	2	(1.5%)

Winter Distribution

Sand Martin *Riparia riparia*

Locally common summer visitor

Conservation status: Amber

This small brown and white swallow is among the earliest of the long-distance migrants to reach us and the first Sand Martin over a sheltered loch in March is an eagerly awaited sign of spring. Birds soon move on to their nesting colonies and nearby rivers. A common natural nest site is within the eroding sandy banks flanking some rivers. Equally, however, they will nest away from water if suitable sand cliffs are available, often in man-made sites such as quarries. Sand Martin colonies can contain scores or even hundreds of pairs.[1]

Nationally there were marked declines in abundance after the winters of 1968-69 and 1983-84 probably due to food scarcity from droughts in their winter quarters in the Sahel region of Africa.[2] Fortunately the survey period for the *Atlas* did not follow a population crash, so local numbers and site occupancy are likely to have been at a 'normal' level for the early 21st century. Local breeding numbers are regulated by such colony disasters as tunnel collapses or flooded burrows (e.g. on the River Devon), by natural predators, particularly Sparrowhawks, and by the effect of bad weather on food supplies. Wide annual fluctuations make population trends difficult to establish.[3]

In Clackmannanshire the course and flood plain of the Devon and the higher reaches of the Black Devon provide suitable Sand Martin breeding sites, either along the banks or in exposed deposits nearby.[4] This was borne out by the *Atlas* surveys, which found them breeding along a line to the south of the Ochil scarp. (Birds were registered in a total of 48 squares, but 29 of these were 'observed' only). Away from the rivers there were records associated with workings to the east of Clackmannan, and a quirky nesting site in a small quarry used to win sand for the bunkers on Muckhart Golf Course.

David Bryant

[1] *Jones, 1986* [2] *BBWC* [3] *ibid.* [4] *Jones, 1986*

Breeding Distribution

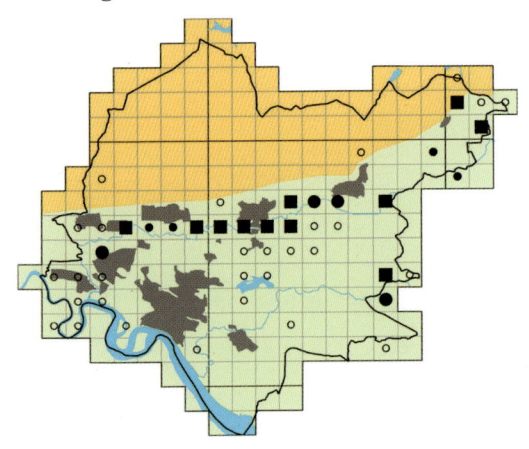

Number of km² in which recorded:	48	(24.2%)
■ Confirmed breeding	11	(22.9%)
● Probable breeding	4	(8.3%)
• Possible breeding	4	(8.3%)
○ Present, breeding unlikely:	29	(60.4%)

Swallow   (Barn Swallow)   *Hirundo rustica*

Common summer and passage visitor

Conservation status: Amber

The Swallow is one of Britain's favourite birds, with its graceful aerial flight heralding the approach of summer. It has close associations with humans (it invariably nests in man-made structures), raising two and occasionally three broods making it one of the easiest birds to confirm breeding.

Population changes among Swallows are affected by variations in rainfall in their southern African wintering zone, and adverse weather during migration or the breeding season probably play a key role as well. Swallows' accessible nest-sites leave them vulnerable to disturbance from humans, and also from such predators as Brown Rats, Cats, Sparrowhawks and Tawny Owls.[1]

The fluctuating UK population showed a marked decline between 1980 and 1985,[2] particularly south of the border. However, following a population recovery during the 1990s Swallows are again widespread, with central Scotland as well-populated as anywhere in the UK.[3]

Swallows are widely distributed in Clackmannanshire, being found in the majority of Atlas squares and with confirmed or probable breeding in 82 of them. They are largely confined to the lowlands, extending to the edges of hill grasslands and moors. Most sites are occupied by one or two pairs but small colonies are often found among the steadings of arable or mixed farms. Any further intensification of agricultural production and modernisation of buildings in the future may reduce the attractiveness of such farms to Swallows.

After breeding, pre-migration gatherings of tens or hundreds of swallows are memorable features in August and September, and at dusk these flocks will focus on a single site to roost, most often in reedbeds as at Tullibody Inch on the River Forth where they can be seen in some years.[4,5] On 31 August 1997 14,000 assembled over the Forth upstream from Cambus before roosting in reedbeds on the opposite bank.[6] Stragglers occur into early November (possibly passage migrants from further north or from overseas).[7]

David Bryant

[1] Turner, 2006 [2] BBWC [3] Turner, 2006 [4] BS3 [5] Pers. obs. [6] UFABR [7] Migration Atlas

Breeding Distribution

Number of km² in which recorded:	143	(72.2%)
■ Confirmed breeding	68	(47.6%)
● Probable breeding	14	(9.8%)
• Possible breeding	19	(13.3%)
○ Present, breeding unlikely:	42	(29.4%)

House Martin   (Common House Martin)   *Delichon urbicum*

Common summer visitor and passage migrant   Conservation status: Amber

The House Martin is notable for its habit (as its name suggests) of nesting on human dwellings. Most nest in small colonies rarely exceeding 20 pairs, usually tucked under the eaves of a favourite building. Not only are these sites relatively inaccessible to predators but the eddies and up-currents from buildings also have the benefit of concentrating supplies of the small insects on which House Martins feed. The recent decline in House Sparrow numbers has reduced the threat of nests being usurped by that species.

Nevertheless House Martin numbers have shown a steep decline within the UK since 2005, leading to its current Amber status.[1,2] However, the Scottish population seems to be less affected as it has been holding its own since 2005.[3,4] In this context it should be noted that the House Martin is less firmly attached to its breeding sites than most species so that local populations can come and go unrecorded; hence it is hard to track wider population changes or determine their causes.[5]

Within Clackmannanshire* the most obvious distributional pattern is the striking division between upland and lowland areas. Even though this species regularly nests within moorland areas elsewhere in Scotland's central belt, the *Atlas* registered no proven breeders in the uplands due to the absence of suitable nest sites. In the lowlands, breeders are widespread and clustered either in built-up areas such as towns and villages or in large farm steadings in more rural areas.

The House Martin is typically the last of our three swallows to arrive, the main arrivals reaching Scotland in early May. Departures begin in late July but can be delayed into October amongst the latest breeders. The species spends the mid-winter months in Africa right down to the southern Cape.

David Bryant

[1] *Eaton et al., 2009* [2] *BBWC* [3] *Risely et al., 2009* [4] *BBWC* [5] *Bryant, 1988 or 1999*
* *Clackmannanshire has the distinction of being the location for the most detailed study of House Martins in the UK which was carried out by David Bryant and colleagues from Stirling University between 1971 and 1988. (Ed.)*

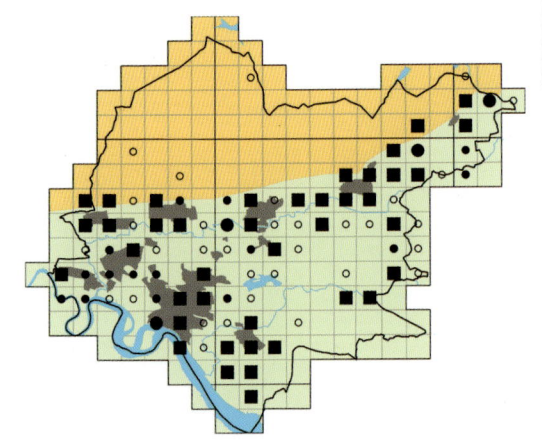

Breeding Distribution

Number of km² in which recorded:	93	(47.0%)
■ Confirmed breeding	41	(44.1%)
● Probable breeding	4	(4.3%)
• Possible breeding	15	(16.1%)
○ Present, breeding unlikely:	33	(35.5%)

Long-tailed Tit   (Long-tailed Bushtit)   *Aegithalos caudatus*

Fairly common resident

Conservation status: Green

Unlike Blue Tits and Great Tits, Long-tailed Tits have remained to a great extent rural rather than urban or suburban birds.[1,2] Their preferred breeding habitat is deciduous woodland and scrub, though they will nest in parks and gardens with suitable vegetation.[3]

The distribution of Long-tailed Tits in Clackmannanshire matches this broader picture. Breeding was registered in just over half of the lowland squares in Clackmannanshire with the main areas of absence being the higher ground of the Ochils, low-lying farmland near the Forth and the urban centre of Alloa. While they can be badly hit by cold winters,[4] no severe winters occurred either during *Atlas* fieldwork or for several years previously and BBS data during the fieldwork period show that a statistically significant rise of 13% occurred in the UK population from 1995 to 2008.[5] Despite this, the number of Long-tailed Tits recorded during local Breeding Bird Survey transects is much lower than for the County's three other Tit species,[6] suggesting a relatively small population.

British Long-tailed Tits are largely sedentary, though some birds move longer distances.[7] After the breeding season they form family-based flocks and establish winter territories, generally in deciduous woodland and scrub though visits to garden feeders have become increasingly common.[8,9] The winter map for Clackmannanshire is essentially identical to that for the breeding season. It is likely that most of the birds present in winter are local breeders but there is probably some interchange with adjacent counties and some wintering birds might have come from further afield.

Don Matthews

[1] BS3 [2] 1988-91 Atlas [3] BWP [4] 1988-91 Atlas [5] Risely et al., 2009 [6] UFABR [7] Migration Atlas [8] BS3 [9] Winter Atlas

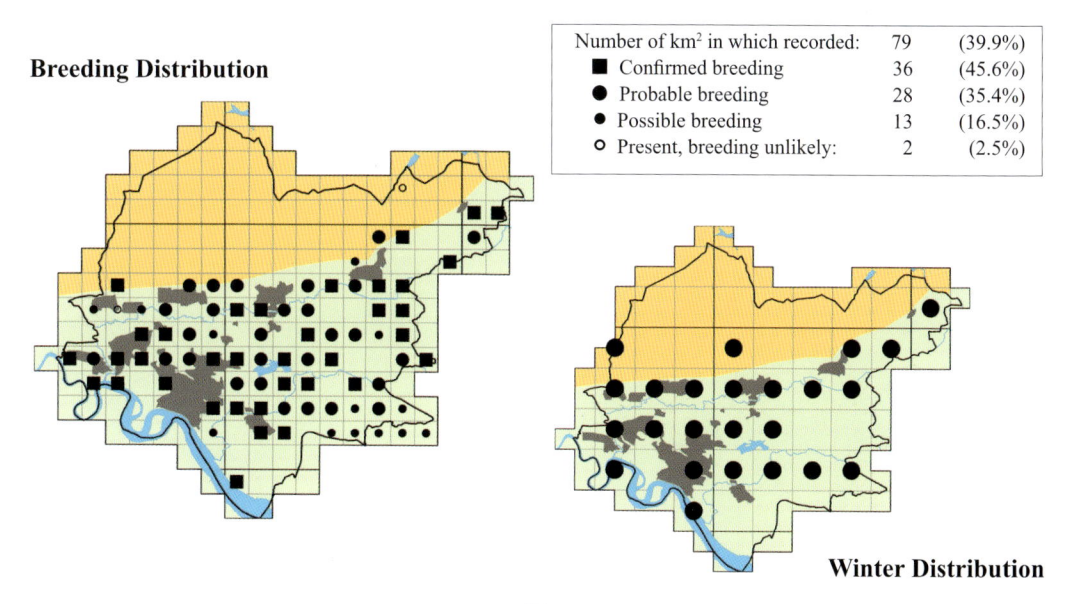

Breeding Distribution

Number of km² in which recorded:	79	(39.9%)
■ Confirmed breeding	36	(45.6%)
● Probable breeding	28	(35.4%)
• Possible breeding	13	(16.5%)
○ Present, breeding unlikely:	2	(2.5%)

Winter Distribution

Chiffchaff (Common Chiffchaff) *Phylloscopus collybita*

Fairly common summer visitor, winter vagrant   Conservation status: Green

The Chiffchaff's distinctive, onomatopoeic song is by far the easiest way to separate it from its very similar, and more numerous congener, the Willow Warbler. It prefers taller deciduous trees than the Willow Warbler and inhabits mixed woodland, parks and large gardens (with trees) which have some dense understorey.[1] The Chiffchaff is the earliest warbler to return to Clackmannanshire in spring with the mean date of the first record over the past decade being 22 March.[2,3]

The *Atlas* survey registered Chiffchaffs in roughly half the lowland squares but there were very few in the confirmed category – probably due to a combination of the difficulty in distinguishing it from Willow Warbler when not singing and that of nest finding. The map shows it to be present along the Devon valley (penetrating a short distance up the Menstrie and Alva Glens) but more patchy to the south, where it is largely absent from the carselands, the less wooded parts of the mid-county ridge and some urban areas. Southern Scotland is towards the northern edge of its range but the *Fife* and *South-east Scotland Atlases* both commented on an expansion of occupied squares since the first BTO Breeding Atlas[4,5], and this would appear to be continuing with BBS indicating a statistically significant increase of 197% in Scotland from 1995 to 2007.[6]

Chiffchaffs begin to depart in late July/early August but migrants from Scandinavia and Russia pass through later and it is thought that the occasional overwintering bird is probably from this latter population.[7] The winter *Atlas* record for Menstrie is the first for the County although both their scarcity and reduction in song as winter progresses will contribute to birds being overlooked.

Neil Bielby

[1] BS3 [2] ibid. [3] UFABR [4] Fife Atlas [5] SE Scotland Atlas [6] Risely et al., 2009 [7] BS3

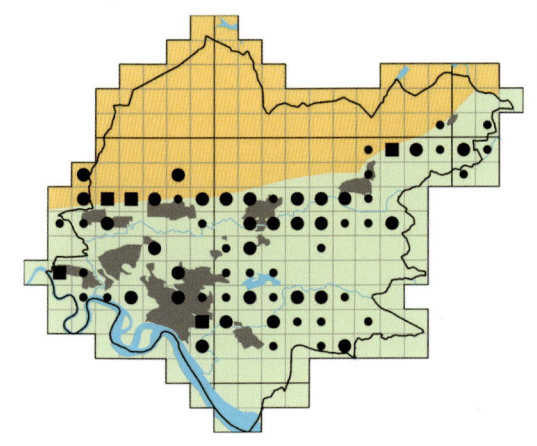

Breeding Distribution

Number of km² in which recorded:	67	(33.8%)
■ Confirmed breeding	5	(7.5%)
● Probable breeding	30	(44.8%)
• Possible breeding	32	(47.8%)
○ Present, breeding unlikely:	0	(0.0%)

Willow Warbler   *Phylloscopus trochilus*

Common summer visitor and passage migrant   Conservation status: Amber

The Willow Warbler's mellow, descending song most easily distinguishes it from its virtually identical close relative, the Chiffchaff. It occupies a range of woodland and scrubby habitats – demonstrating a strong preference for the edges of denser stands of these.[1]

Copious numbers, allied to birds singing throughout the breeding season, made it one of the easier birds to record. The relatively high percentage of confirmed breeding registrations is probably due both to its abundance, and to the ease of identifying young by their yellowish underparts. The breeding map reflects the range of habitats used, with only six lowland squares unoccupied: three of these border the River Forth and contain virtually no suitable habitat while a further two are in urban Alloa. However, apart from the semi-afforested eastern end of the Ochils (where it is found up to c.450 metres), there is, away from the scarp, only a single record in these hills – probably due to the heavy grazing prevalent here. Nevertheless, it was still recorded in 67% of all squares making it the ninth most widespread species.

Since 1980, the median date for the first spring record in the County is 18 April (n=18) with the earliest on 2 April.[2] Usually, the main arrival in Scotland is during the third week in April with males arriving up to 10-14 days before the females.[3] Post-breeding dispersal, followed by a leisurely southerly migration towards the sub-Saharan wintering grounds, begins in the second half of July,[4] although the latest record for the County (14 September) may be of a migrant from further north.[5]

The Willow Warbler's Amber listing is due to marked declines in the south and east of England breeding populations since 1994 whereas numbers in Scotland have remained stable during this period.[6]

Neil Bielby

[1] *Cobb, J.L.S., 2005* [2] *UFABR* [3] *BS3* [4] *ibid.* [5] *UFABR* [6] *Risely et al., 2009*

Breeding Distribution

Number of km² in which recorded:	133	(67.2%)
■ Confirmed breeding	41	(30.8%)
● Probable breeding	67	(50.4%)
• Possible breeding	25	(18.8%)
○ Present, breeding unlikely:	0	(0.0%)

Blackcap (Eurasian Blackcap) *Sylvia atricapilla*

Fairly common summer visitor, scarce winter visitor

Conservation status: Green

The melodic rich song of the male Blackcap is a familiar feature of spring and early summer. A bird of open deciduous woodland with plenty of undergrowth and scrub, it also frequently occurs in mature suburban gardens.[1] The conspicuous song (and its distinctive anxiety call) is clearly a useful aid during survey work, although the neat little nest is difficult to find as it is usually well hidden in scrub, and after fledging, when the leaf cover is at its densest, family parties of Blackcaps are hard to detect.

It is not surprising, therefore, that the bulk of registrations during this survey comprised singing males. Breeding was confirmed in only 10 of the 78 squares in which the Blackcap was recorded. The species is scarce or absent in the southeast where much of the ground is open or woodland is conifer plantation.

There were only two records during the winter surveys (at Alva and Menstrie), indicating that the Blackcap it is a scarce winter visitor. However, there has probably been a degree of under-recording given the difficulty in surveying gardens where the bird is most likely to be found. There are four records of wintering birds in the local Bird Reports with the first being a male at Dollar on 16 November 1974 and the last at Alva on 9 February 2006.[2] Blackcaps seen in October – at Alva in 1997 and Menstrie in 2005 – could have been lingering breeders, migrants or early winter visitors from the central European breeding population.[3]

BBS results indicate that the population in Scotland has undergone significant recent expansion – 168% from 1995-2007 albeit from a small sample.[4] The main constraint in Clackmannanshire is probably the availability of suitable habitat, as Blackcaps have been noted to prefer areas where mixed and deciduous woodland is most abundant.[5]

Keith Broomfield

[1] *BirdFacts* [2] *UFABR* [3] *BS3* [4] *Risely et al., 2009* [5] *SE Scotland Atlas*

Breeding Distribution

Number of km² in which recorded:	78	(39.4%)
■ Confirmed breeding	10	(12.8%)
● Probable breeding	29	(37.2%)
● Possible breeding	39	(50.0%)
○ Present, breeding unlikely:	0	(0.0%)

Winter Distribution

Garden Warbler *Sylvia borin*

Fairly common summer visitor   Conservation status: Green

If it were not for its mellow but vigorous warbling song, the drably plumaged and secretive Garden Warbler would probably be one of the most difficult to detect of our common birds. Possible, probable and confirmed breeding was detected in 39% of all *Atlas* squares in Clackmannanshire, though the vast majority of these registrations were in the first two categories.

There was a good spread of records across low-lying areas of the County, although it is scarce or absent along the River Forth due to lack of suitable habitat. The distribution reveals a marked similarity to that of the Blackcap, although it is present in some eastern parts of the county where the Blackcap was not recorded. This part of the County is at a slightly higher altitude than other parts and has little mature deciduous woodland; the Garden Warbler's presence probably reflects its ability to exploit a greater range of scrubby habitats than the Blackcap.[1]

Despite range increases in Scotland since the first half of the 20th century,[2] CBC and BBS data now indicate that the UK population is in long-term decline with the latter survey recording a significant decrease of 16% from 1995 to 2007.[3] Possible factors are inter-specific competition with the earlier-arriving Blackcap excluding the Garden Warbler from the best territories,[4,5] combined with environmental changes occurring in its sub-Saharan wintering grounds.[6]

Keith Broomfield

[1] BS2 [2] ibid. [3] Risely et al., 2009 [4] BS3 [5] SE Scotland Atlas [6] BBWC

Breeding Distribution

Number of km² in which recorded:	77	(38.9%)
■ Confirmed breeding	8	(10.4%)
● Probable breeding	31	(40.3%)
• Possible breeding	38	(49.4%)
○ Present, breeding unlikely:	0	(0.0%)

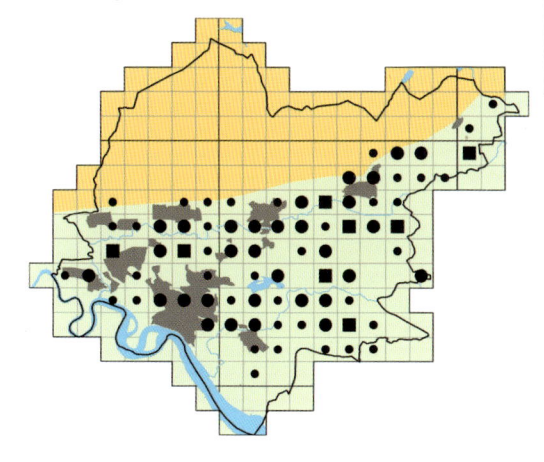

Whitethroat (Common Whitethroat) *Sylvia communis*

Common summer visitor and passage migrant   Conservation status: Amber

The rapid grating warble of the Whitethroat is one of the more distinctive and easily identifiable bird songs of late spring. The species is frequent in hedgerows and other areas with abundant undergrowth, and is widely distributed in most low-lying parts of Clackmannanshire.

Absent from the higher ground of the Ochils, the Whitethroat is also scarce in some south-eastern areas of the County where there is a predominance of sheep pasture and unimproved ground with little undergrowth. While the conspicuous song makes it easy to detect birds on territory, breeding is often hard to confirm given the difficulty in finding nests and the skulking nature of fledged birds. This is reflected in the survey with confirmed breeding in only 14% of squares but suspected breeding in an additional 37%. The Whitethroat can occur at reasonably high densities in some areas of Clackmannanshire, such as scrub habitat along the River Devon.[1]

A steep crash in the UK population occurred in 1969, which was linked to droughts in the Whitethroat's wintering grounds in the Sahel.[2] Since then the Scottish population fluctuated along a relatively low base until fortunes changed in more recent times with a very large increase of over 80% being recorded between 1995 and 2007.[3]

The Whitethroat's susceptibility to climate change in its sub-Saharan wintering quarters is likely to pose the most significant factor in its future abundance in Clackmannanshire. Clearance of its favoured habitat of low scrub, in particular brambles, nettles and hawthorn – for example for house building projects – will also cause localised extinctions.

Keith Broomfield

[1] Pers. obs. [2] Winstanley et al., 1974 [3] Risely et al., 2009

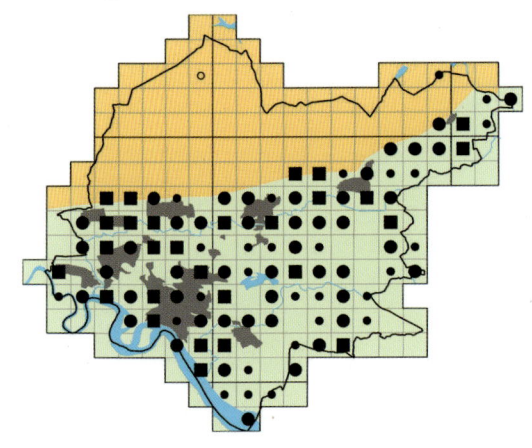

Breeding Distribution

Number of km² in which recorded:	103	(52.0%)
■ Confirmed breeding	28	(27.2%)
● Probable breeding	46	(44.7%)
• Possible breeding	28	(27.2%)
○ Present, breeding unlikely:	1	(1.0%)

Grasshopper Warbler   (Common Grasshopper Warbler)   *Locustella naevia*

Scarce summer visitor and passage migrant.   Conservation status: Red.

Whether skulking in the dense vegetation in which its nest is constructed on or close to the ground, or delivering its reeling song from a low perch (mostly during the anti-social hours from dusk to dawn), the Grasshopper Warbler is one of the more difficult species to survey. The noted fluctuations in annual numbers and irregular occupation of suitable habitat add to these difficulties. Although regular records of singing males means it almost certainly breeds in the County, this has never been confirmed.[1]

The thin scattering of records on the breeding map are almost all in the western half of lowland Clackmannanshire. This correlates with entries in the local Bird Reports where it did not feature until 1980, and has been noted in roughly half the years subsequently. These would suggest that the first birds arrive in late April, with the bulk during the first half of May. There are several July records but none in August, so two records during early September may well refer to passage birds.[2]

The Grasshopper Warbler owes its Red listing to a rapid population decline between the mid-1960s and mid-1980s.[3] Due to a combination of this decline and its aforementioned breeding behaviour, it was only recorded on 3% of BBS squares in the UK in 2008.[4] Given the relative scarcity of the Grasshopper Warbler in the UK, field work to determine confirmation of breeding in Clackmannanshire would prove useful.

Neil Bielby

[1] *1988-91 Atlas*   [2] *UFABR*   [3] *Marchant et al., 1980*   [4] *Risely et al., 2009*

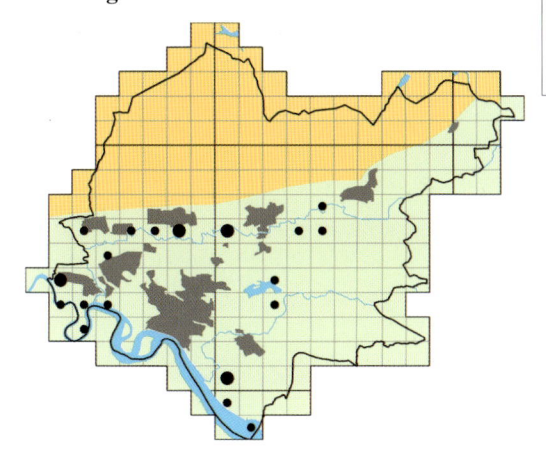

Breeding Distribution

Number of km² in which recorded:	19	(9.6%)
■ Confirmed breeding	0	(0.0%)
● Probable breeding	4	(21.1%)
● Possible breeding	15	(78.9%)
○ Present, breeding unlikely:	0	(0.0%)

Sedge Warbler *Acrocephalus schoenobaenus*

Fairly common summer visitor   Conservation status: Green

The Sedge Warbler is one of the easier warblers to survey due to its loud, explosive, far-reaching song and distinctive cream supercilium. Recorded in just under 50% of all squares, the Sedge Warbler was totally absent from the Ochils. It favours lowland wet or damp areas, but will nest in a variety of scrubby habitats and even in some crops such as Oilseed Rape.[1]

The first males of this sub-Saharan migrant from West Africa are typically recorded in the County towards the end of April (earliest 22 April) with the bulk of both sexes having arrived by mid-May.[2,3] The distribution map shows that they occur throughout the carse areas adjacent to the Rivers Forth and Devon - reaching as far upstream as Tillicoultry on the latter. They are surprisingly uncommon in the rest of the lowlands despite the presence of apparently suitable habitat. Additionally, most of the occupied areas are below 100 metres (in south-east Scotland almost 10% of records were over 300 metres).[4] Local records since 1974 would appear to support this distribution with only one record from outwith the *Atlas* core area.[5] In the carse farmland it typically inhabits reed-filled drainage ditches and can reach quite high densities both here and along the banks of the lower River Devon.[6] A five-year survey of the latter in the late 1990s recorded a mean of 10 apparently occupied territories per kilometre.[7]

August is the usual month for last sightings although six were at Cambus on 14 September 1975.[8,9] Breeding numbers fluctuate annually,[10] together with periodic crashes which have been linked to a lack of rainfall in their wintering quarters.[11] Scottish BBS results suggest a probable rise in numbers during the 1994 to 2007 period.[12]

Neil Bielby

[1] BS3 [2] UFABR [3] BS3 [4] SE Scotland Atlas [5] UFABR [6] Pers. obs. [7] UFABR [8] Migration Atlas [9] UFABR [10] BBWC [11] Peach et al., 1991 [12] Risely et al., 2009

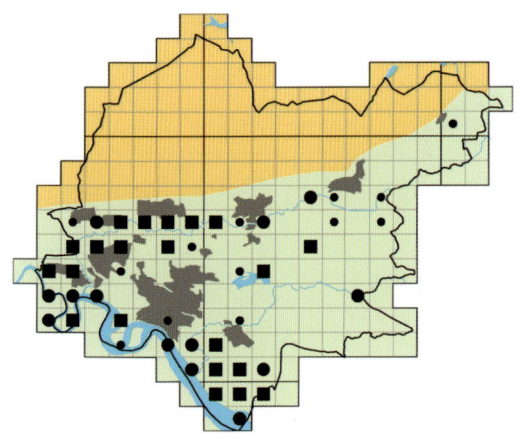

Breeding Distribution

Number of km² in which recorded:	47	(23.7%)
■ Confirmed breeding	21	(44.7%)
● Probable breeding	13	(27.7%)
• Possible breeding	13	(27.7%)
○ Present, breeding unlikely:	0	(0.0%)

Treecreeper   (Eurasian Treecreeper)   *Certhia familiaris*

Fairly common resident

Conservation status: Green

The Treecreeper occurs in mature deciduous and mixed woodland but as a general rule is never abundant, with its small size and cryptic plumage making it one of our more unobtrusive birds.

This difficulty in detection is reflected in the Clackmannanshire survey with breeding confirmed in only 11 of the 75 squares in which it was recorded, while possible breeding occurred in 47 squares. The breeding distribution coincides closely with the availability of suitable tracts of wooded habitat, with a distinct bias towards the east and south-east of the County and in woodlands along the Hillfoots. It is scarce as a breeding bird in the south-west due to a lack of suitable woodland. A lack of registrations in suitable habitat in the far north-east could indicate under-recording, given that it is generally able to cope with small woodland habitats.[1]

The winter distribution corresponds closely to the breeding range. The Treecreeper is a highly sedentary species with ringing studies showing birds being consistently re-trapped in their home areas,[2] although there may be some small scale dispersion of young birds outside the breeding season.[3] There is very little winter immigration from the Continent of the nominate subspecies *familiaris*, usually referred to as the Northern Treecreeper, with only up to eight recorded in Scotland in any single year.[4] However, this is most likely to be an under-estimate of the true level of arrivals. It is likely that small Treecreeper populations in isolated areas of woodland will suffer localised extinctions – for example after a cold winter – followed by repopulation in subsequent years,[5] although it may take some time for more isolated woodlands to become colonized again. Scottish BBS results suggest a probable increase of 20% between 1995 and 2007, most likely due to the relatively mild winters during this period.[6]

Keith Broomfield

[1] SE Scotland Atlas [2] Fife Atlas [3] Migration Atlas [4] BS3 [5] ibid.

Breeding Distribution

Number of km² in which recorded:	75	(37.9%)
■ Confirmed breeding	11	(14.7%)
● Probable breeding	13	(17.3%)
• Possible breeding	47	(62.7%)
○ Present, breeding unlikely:	4	(5.3%)

Winter Distribution

Wren (Winter Wren) *Troglodytes troglodytes*

Common resident

Conservation status: Green

The Wren is the most widespread breeding bird in Clackmannanshire with evidence of breeding in 85% of squares, its favoured habitat of dense undergrowth being present to some extent in all of the lowland squares and in many of the upland ones. Although predominantly a lowland bird Wrens were found at up to 500 metres in the Ochil Hills,[1] a situation that mirrors the findings of other Scottish atlases.[2,3] Territorial presence is easily recorded in good lowland habitat as the density of birds leads to frequent singing but upland birds are more sparsely distributed and most of the possible breeding registrations where birds were heard singing on only one occasion were in upland squares. Wrens are exceptionally vulnerable to extreme cold, and a harsh winter can drastically reduce the population.[4,5] However, no severe winters occurred during the period of *Atlas* fieldwork, nor for several years previously, and BBS data indicate an increase of 76% in the Wren population in Scotland between 1995 and 2007 covering the fieldwork period.[6]

British Wrens are largely sedentary and although there is some post-breeding dispersal most of these birds move only short distances.[7,8] The winter distribution map is very similar to that for the breeding season and any gaps perhaps reflect the greater difficulty of recording Wrens during this period of low song output rather than a lack of birds. The BTO's *Winter Atlas* noted that some breeding territories are vacated in winter for areas with better feeding conditions but no such movement was discernable at the tetrad level during the winter surveys, even on higher ground.

Don Matthews

[1] Pers. obs. [2] BS3 [3] Fife Atlas [4] Winter Atlas [5] BS3 [6] Risely et al., 2009 [7] BS3 [8] Migration Atlas

Breeding Distribution

Number of km² in which recorded:	169	(85.4%)
■ Confirmed breeding	53	(31.4%)
● Probable breeding	88	(52.1%)
• Possible breeding	28	(16.6%)
○ Present, breeding unlikely:	0	(0.0%)

Winter Distribution

Starling (Common Starling) *Sturnus vulgaris*

Common resident and winter visitor

Conservation status: Red

The Starling is one of those ubiquitous species that only seems to attract particular attention when noisily invading a domestic roof space to nest, or when gathering in spectacular winter roosts. It is hard to believe that such a familiar bird is on the UK 'Red List' of species of conservation concern. National monitoring schemes have demonstrated serious declines, matched in much of north-west Europe, so it is pleasing that Scotland seems to be bucking the trend and registering some sustained increase, though populations are still below historic levels.[1]

Rintoul & Baxter concluded that the Starling had been very scarce as a breeding bird in the Forth basin in the early 19th Century but that at least in the Alloa area it was very much on the increase at the time of the *New Statistical Account*.[2] Perhaps, like the Jackdaw (another hole-nesting species) it found increasing nesting opportunities with the expansion of some of the urban settlements from the 1830s and '40s. It was very common as recently as the 1970s.[3] The *Atlas* map shows it still breeding widely across the County, absent only from the Ochils plateau and scattered rural pockets. In winter it is similarly widespread in the lowlands but like some of the pasture-feeding crows is perhaps discouraged from visiting parts of the south-east by the extent of conifer plantations.

The winter population is boosted by large numbers of continental immigrants.[4] There are no especially large winter roosts in the County, but in November 1994 an estimated 20,000 birds occurred in the reeds at Tullibody Inch. Other estuarial reed beds have hosted smaller roosts, but the oldest regularly used local communal roost, recorded from the 1970s, is in the girders of the Kincardine Bridge 1.5 kilometres beyond the County boundary, with 4,000 birds at its high point in November 2000.[5]

David Thorogood

[1] BS3 [2] Rintoul & Baxter, 1935 [3] BS2 [4] Migration Atlas [5] UFABR

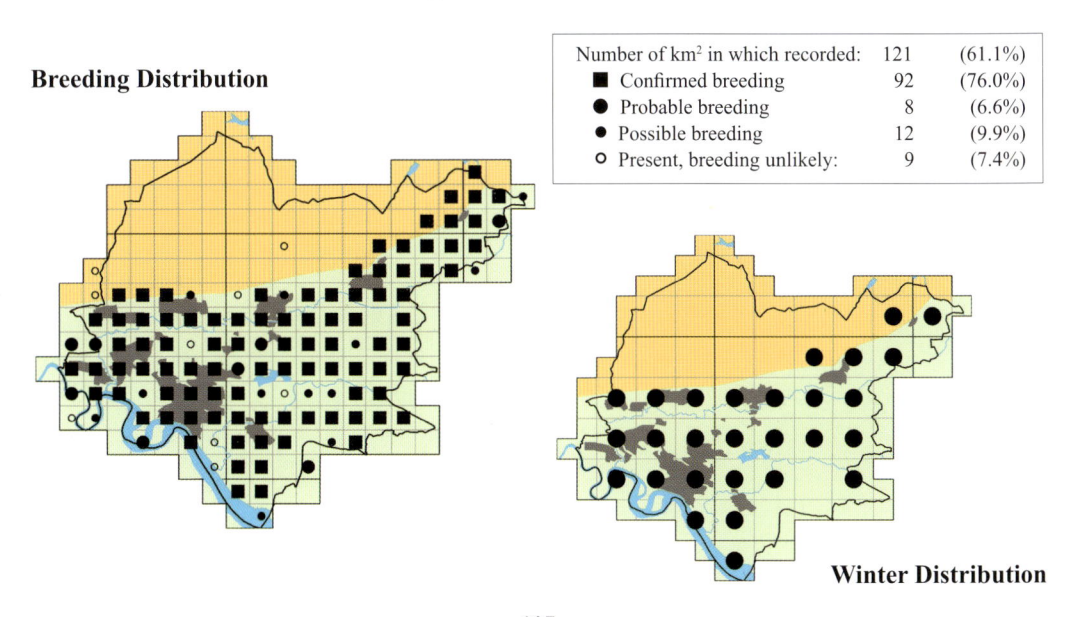

Breeding Distribution

Number of km² in which recorded:	121	(61.1%)
■ Confirmed breeding	92	(76.0%)
● Probable breeding	8	(6.6%)
• Possible breeding	12	(9.9%)
○ Present, breeding unlikely:	9	(7.4%)

Winter Distribution

Dipper (White-throated Dipper) *Cinclus cinclus*

Fairly common resident   Conservation status: Green

Unlike other British waterside passerines the Dipper lives a truly aquatic life. While it will feed at the water's edge it has many other options. These include feeding underwater using a technique sometimes wrongly described as 'walking under water' but actually using its wings in a similar way to puffins or penguins.[1]

The wide variety of freshwater life that thrives in unpolluted water is crucial to the Dipper's survival. This makes it vulnerable not only to spasmodic and short-term pollution from farms or industry but also to less obvious and more persistent causes of degradation such as acid rainfall.

However, while Scottish Dipper densities have been shown to be closely related to acidification, the waters of the River Devon are much less affected because the acid deposited during rain and snow is buffered by the base-rich geology of the Ochil hills. As a result, Dipper densities here were the highest on record in the UK during the late 20th century.[2] Clackmannanshire Dippers can be found along the entire course of the Devon and also along the Black Devon. This is reflected in the *Atlas* results: both the Devon and Black Devon and their tributaries show evidence of birds along their full lengths, though the breeding pattern is patchy. Although some Dippers can be exceptionally elusive (despite commonly held assumptions), and so very hard to prove as breeders, survey work from the late 1990s supports the view that there has been a decline from the high densities recorded by Newton in his 1989 study.[3,4]

The winter *Atlas* shows a similar distribution to the breeding survey. However, a direct correlation cannot be assumed as studies have shown that while Dippers are highly territorial in summer, they are only partially so in winter and can share roosts with immigrants many kilometres from their daytime feeding sites.[5]

David Bryant

[1] *Bryant & Tatner, 1987* [2] *Logie et al., 1996* [3] *WBBS unpub.data* [4] *Newton, S.F., 1989* [5] *Bryant & Tatner, 1987*

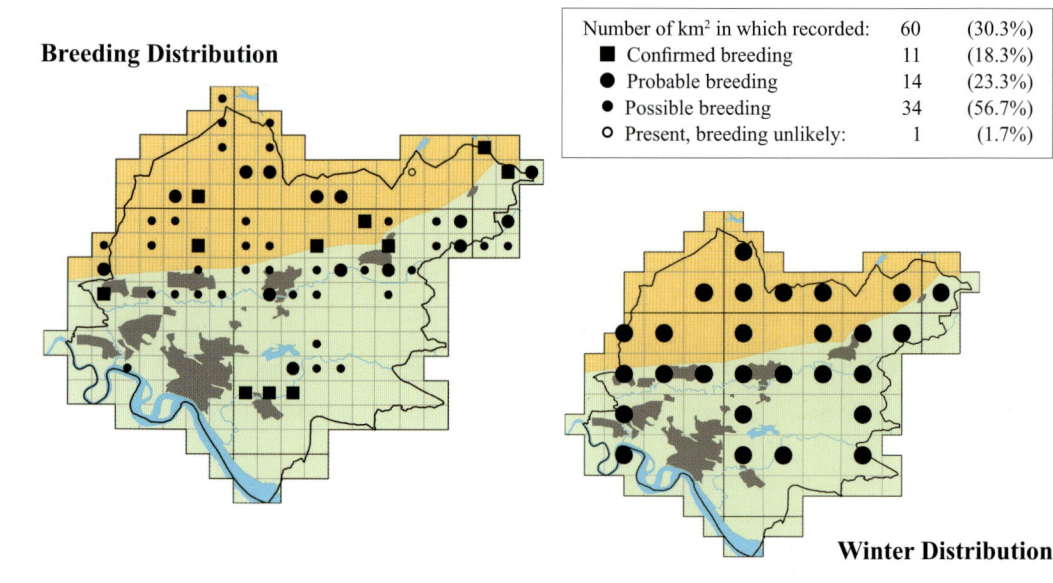

Breeding Distribution

Number of km² in which recorded:		60	(30.3%)
■ Confirmed breeding		11	(18.3%)
● Probable breeding		14	(23.3%)
• Possible breeding		34	(56.7%)
○ Present, breeding unlikely:		1	(1.7%)

Winter Distribution

Blackbird (Common Blackbird) *Turdus merula*

Common resident, passage migrant and winter visitor   Conservation status: Green

The Blackbird is the most adaptable of our native thrushes and has been able to take advantage of the parkland and garden habitats created by the massive growth of our towns and cities, to the point where around a quarter of the British and Irish population now occurs within areas of human habitation.[1,2] Although parks and gardens hold the highest densities, it is also widespread in broadleaved woodland and farmland with hedgerows and trees as well as, to a lesser extent, pinewoods and conifer plantations.[3] The UK population trend shows a steady increase from a low-point in 1995,[4] with a significant matching increase in Scotland of 29% between 1995 and 2007.[5]

The breeding map shows that Blackbirds are ubiquitous in lowland squares within Clackmannanshire and their range extends to suitable habitat in the lower areas of the Ochil Hills. Establishing breeding for this species proved to be relatively straightforward, almost 90% of registrations being in the probable or confirmed categories.

Local BBS results broadly match the national pattern, with a higher density in urban/suburban areas than in farmland,[6] though the much larger area of the latter means that the bulk of the County's Blackbird population breeds in rural habitats. It was the most commonly recorded bird in Clackmannanshire gardens during the survey period.[7]

Blackbirds breeding in Scotland are largely sedentary or, particularly in the case of birds in upland areas, short distance migrants to milder wintering sites, longer distance migration being more uncommon.[8] However, although the winter distribution map for Clackmannanshire is essentially identical to that for the breeding season, Scandinavian and other North European populations are migratory and large numbers pass through Scotland in the autumn, and some of these stay to overwinter (probably within the County) while others continue to migrate further south and west.[9]

Don Matthews

[1] 1988-91 Atlas [2] Toms, 2003 [3] BS3 [4] BBWC [5] Risely et al., 2009 [6] UFABR [7] Garden BirdWatch unpub. data [8] BS3 [9] Migration Atlas

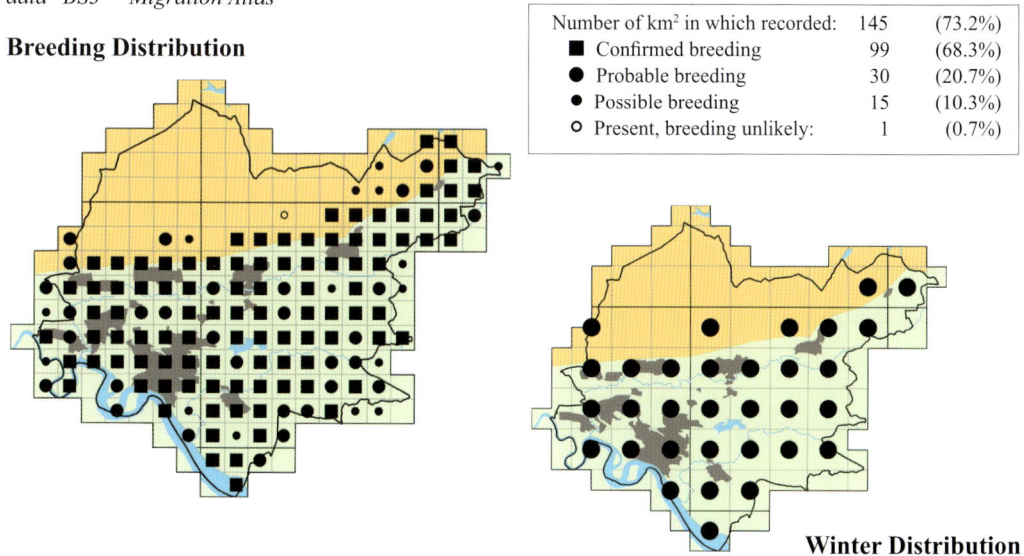

Breeding Distribution

Number of km² in which recorded:	145	(73.2%)
■ Confirmed breeding	99	(68.3%)
● Probable breeding	30	(20.7%)
• Possible breeding	15	(10.3%)
○ Present, breeding unlikely:	1	(0.7%)

Winter Distribution

Song Thrush *Turdus philomelos*

Common resident and passage/winter visitor   Conservation status: Red

The Song Thrush occurs throughout Europe east to central Siberia and south to Iran, Sudan and Eritrea. It is mostly resident but in winter Britain migrants arrive from northern Europe as well as the Netherlands. Many birds breeding in northern Britain winter in Ireland.[1]

The species occurs where there is ample tree cover or shrub understorey and moist ground conditions – snails and earthworms are critical for its survival. Snails (seasonally up to 62% of prey items)[2] are beaten on hard surfaces traditionally known as anvils.[3]

During *Atlas* fieldwork Song Thrush was registered from 60% of squares. The species was widespread throughout lowland Clackmannanshire, being present in almost every square. The winter distribution on tetrads is similar if a little patchier with a noticeable absence in the north-eastern corner of the County.

CBC data show a rapid decline in abundance of about 60% in the UK from the mid-1970s until 1997,[4] since when BBS results show a significant increase of 25%, although population levels remain relatively low.[5] Farming practices, pesticides, drainage of damp ground, disappearance of shrub layers, deer browsing and predators are all listed as possible causes of its decline. [6,7,8]

Milder winters as a result of global warming may mean that larger numbers of birds will forego winter movements, but warmer and drier summers are likely to lead to a deterioration of the Song Thrush's main requirement of damp soil conditions. The maintenance of these conditions together with a dense woodland understorey will present a conservation challenge. Given the vulnerable status of the species, it would be worthwhile monitoring the population in Clackmannanshire more closely.

Andre Thiel

[1] BWP [2] Davies & Snow, 1965 [3] BWP [4] Siriwardena et al., 1998 [5] Risely et al., 2009 [6] Fuller et al., 1995 [7] Robinson et al., 2004 [8] Fuller et al., 2005

Breeding Distribution

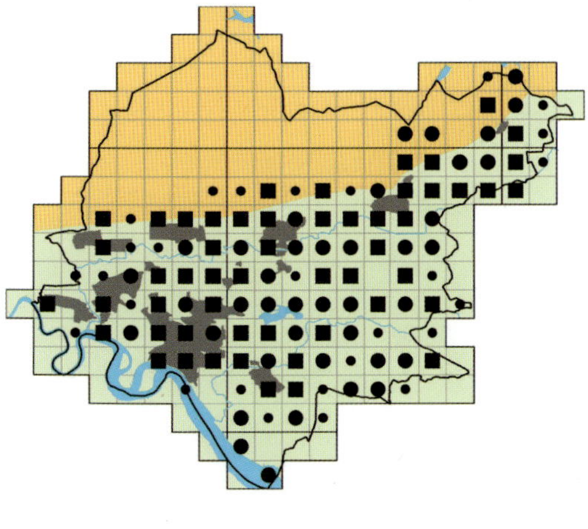

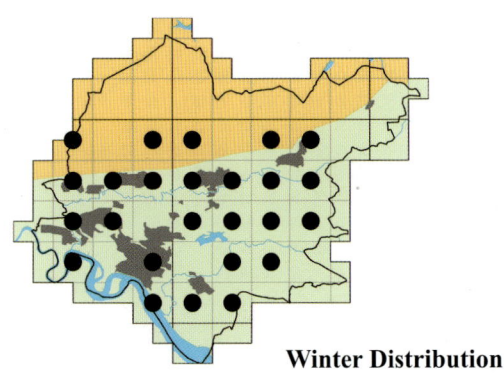

Number of km² in which recorded:	120	(60.6%)
■ Confirmed breeding	53	(44.2%)
● Probable breeding	40	(33.3%)
• Possible breeding	27	(22.5%)
○ Present, breeding unlikely:	0	(0.0%)

Winter Distribution

Mistle Thrush *Turdus viscivorus*

Fairly common resident, passage migrant/winter visitor   Conservation status: Amber

The Mistle Thrush is a bird of open wooded areas and woodland edge covering a range of habitats from moor and hillside to gardens and parks. Widely distributed but never numerous, it is found throughout much of Clackmannanshire but is largely absent as a breeding bird from the higher treeless areas of the Ochils and the fringes of the River Forth.

Breeding was confirmed in only 9% of squares with possible and probable registrations in a further 28%. There was a bias of records towards the eastern half of the County, which is indicative of the suitable habitat here in the form of open sheep and cattle pasture combined with woodland tracts of varying sizes. The Mistle Thrush also breeds along the lower south-facing slopes of the Ochils with a particular concentration in the afforested hills near Dollar. It is an early breeder and some birds may have been missed during the survey because they had stopped singing by April.

The winter distribution corresponds closely with the breeding range. A small number of ringing recoveries in Scotland suggest that migratory movements are largely limited to less than 10km, although some birds move as far as France.[1] Mistle Thrushes begin to flock from July onwards with most winter flocks comprising less than 20 birds. [2]

Despite a significant decline in the English Mistle Thrush population, the Scottish BBS trend has shown a significant increase of 20% from 1995-2007.[3] Little is known about the factors affecting the population and the extent of migratory movements, so further study into the species would be useful in better understanding its requirements. The abundance of suitable habitat in Clackmannanshire would suggest there is little threat to the population on a local scale.

Keith Broomfield

[1] BS3 [2] BS3 [3] Risely et al., 2009

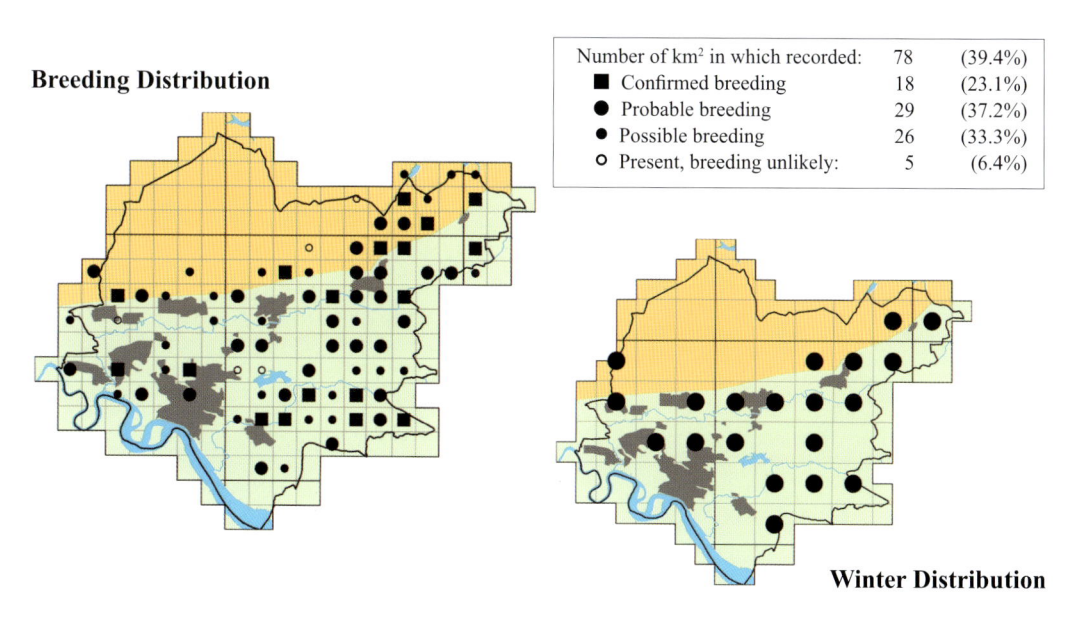

Breeding Distribution

Number of km² in which recorded:	78	(39.4%)
■ Confirmed breeding	18	(23.1%)
● Probable breeding	29	(37.2%)
• Possible breeding	26	(33.3%)
○ Present, breeding unlikely:	5	(6.4%)

Winter Distribution

Spotted Flycatcher   *Muscicapa striata*

Uncommon summer visitor

Conservation status: Red

Having a song that is frequently described as 'insignificant', the Spotted Flycatcher makes itself obvious by its habit of launching forth from a prominent perch in pursuit of its insect prey. It is one of the latest of our summer breeding migrants to arrive; this is typically during the second half of May, with the earliest recorded date in the County during the Atlas period being the 19th.[1,2,3] Mature deciduous or mixed woodlands with open areas are preferred – a habitat replicated in large gardens, parks, cemeteries etc. with the use of these latter areas being aided by the relatively tolerant and confiding nature of the species where humans are concerned.[4]

The distribution map shows a distinct linear pattern along the Hillfoot towns continuing eastwards from Dollar up the narrowing River Devon valley; there are also a couple of short incursions into the Ochils via the steep-sided Alva and Dollar glens. Undoubtedly there is much suitable habitat in this area, but not obviously to a greater extent than in the rest of lowland Clackmannanshire where the bird is scarce or absent.

The Spotted Flycatcher owes its Red-listed status to a dramatic fall in British numbers since the 1960s, the population in 1999 being only a quarter of that in 1974.[5] This decline would appear to be ongoing, with BBS results indicating a significant fall of 38% in the UK between 1995 and 2007 (it is not recorded on enough Scottish BBS squares to allow reliable analysis).[6] The reasons for this pronounced decrease in the UK population are not fully understood but, among other possible factors, appear to be linked to the survival rates of first-year birds on their migration routes to (and in) their wintering grounds down the West African coast from the Gambia to Angola.[7,8]

Neil Bielby

[1] BS3 [2] BWP [3] UFABR [4] BWP [5] Gregory et al., 2002 [6] Risely et al., 2009 [7] BBWC [8] BWP

Breeding Distribution

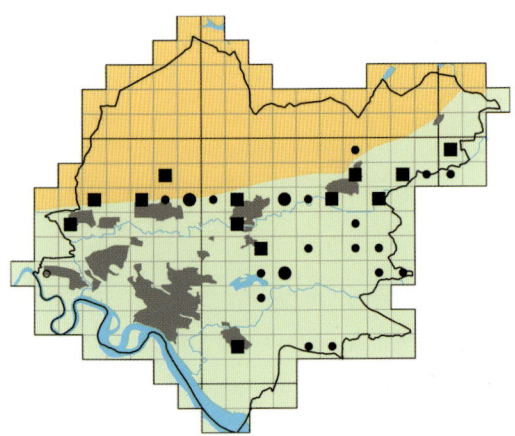

Number of km² in which recorded:	33	(16.7%)
■ Confirmed breeding	13	(39.4%)
● Probable breeding	3	(9.1%)
• Possible breeding	16	(48.5%)
O Present, breeding unlikely:	1	(3.0%)

Robin (European Robin) *Erithacus rubecula*

Common resident, passage and winter visitor

Conservation status: Green

The Robin is a ubiquitous bird in lowland areas of Clackmannanshire and also in areas of suitable habitat on the lower slopes of the Ochil Hills. It is a high-profile bird with a conspicuous song and alarm calls making it unlikely to be overlooked by surveyors. Robins occupy a wide range of wooded and scrubby habitats and are found extensively in gardens, broadleaved and coniferous woodland and in hedgerows as long as these have not been severely trimmed.[1,2]

Whereas some agricultural areas in eastern Scotland have become too intensively farmed to support breeding Robins,[3] almost all of the squares within lowland Clackmannanshire retain some suitable habitat. The distribution map suggests that the situation is most marginal in the reclaimed carse farmland along the shore of the River Forth, where Robins were not recorded in several low-lying squares. In the Ochil Hills, they are restricted to suitable habitat in conifer plantations and in woodland and scrub in the lower reaches of the steep incised glens.

Some British Robins are sedentary while others, particularly females and juveniles, move short distances to winter territories and a few migrate further, though mainly within Britain.[4,5] Post-breeding mobility includes a movement into urban and suburban gardens, garden use peaking during the winter months.[6,7] (During the survey period it was the fourth most commonly recorded bird in Clackmannanshire gardens).[8] The winter distribution map for Clackmannanshire is essentially identical to that for the breeding season. However, short distance dispersion and movements between habitats would not show up at this scale of mapping, nor would any turnover between our breeding and wintering populations due to local breeders heading south and birds from further north moving in.

Don Matthews

[1] *BWP* [2] *BS3* [3] *ibid.* [4] *ibid.* [5] *Migration Atlas* [6] *BS3* [7] *Toms, M., 2003* [8] *Garden BirdWatch unpub. data*

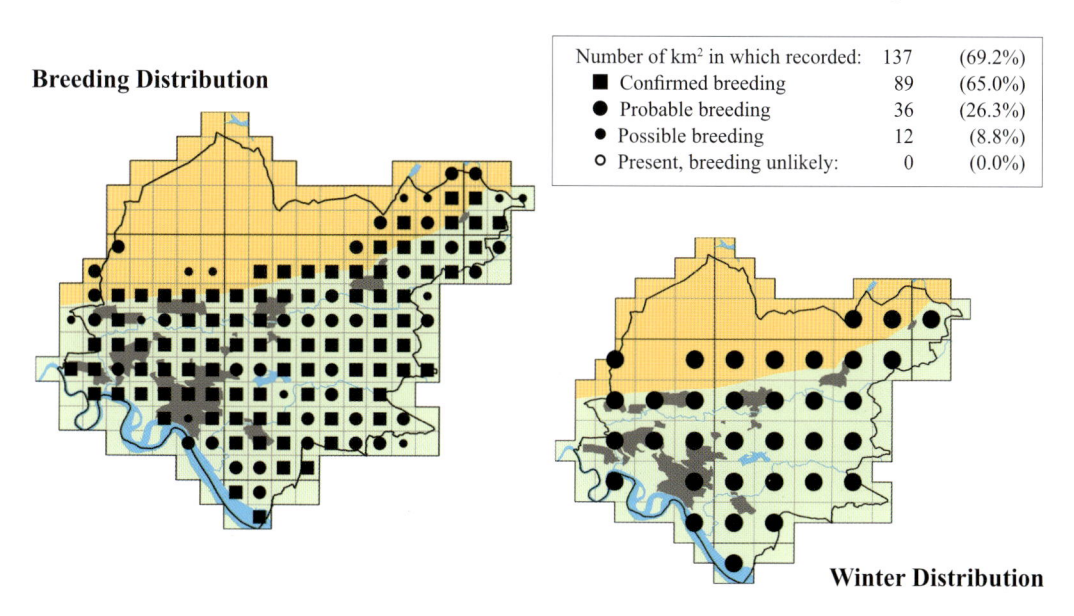

Breeding Distribution

Number of km² in which recorded:	137	(69.2%)
■ Confirmed breeding	89	(65.0%)
● Probable breeding	36	(26.3%)
• Possible breeding	12	(8.8%)
○ Present, breeding unlikely:	0	(0.0%)

Winter Distribution

Redstart   (Common Redstart)   *Phoenicurus phoenicurus*

Scarce summer visitor and passage migrant   Conservation status: Amber

A local but widespread summer visitor to Scotland, the Redstart is typically found in open mature oak and pine woodland, especially in hilly areas. It is an extremely scarce breeder in Clackmannanshire with only one instance of confirmed breeding and two possible records during the survey period.

The confirmed breeding was from mature deciduous woodland on the lower slopes of the Ochils above Tillicoultry with the two possible records from similar habitat in the large woodland park below Wood Hill and also near Menstrie. Suitable habitat exists in other parts of the County, particularly the steep wooded glens that cut into the Ochils, most notably Dollar Glen. It is possible, therefore, that despite the distinctive song of male birds in May and June, a very small number of Redstarts were missed during the survey. However, it is known that Redstart numbers in Scotland fluctuate from year to year.[1] The *Fife Atlas* noted possible and probable breeding at two sites west of Saline very close to the Clackmannanshire border.[2]

Records of Redstarts are sparse before the *Atlas* period, with breeding activity noted in only nine years between 1974 and 2001. All except one were from the Wood Hill area above Alva, the exception coming from Dollar Glen. Additionally, there have been five late summer/autumn (passage) records between 1979 and 1997.[3]

Following a steep decline in numbers and loss of range in the UK in the late 1960s and early 1970s, the population has since undergone a partial recovery,[4] although the long-term trend is still one of shallow decline.[5] The Redstart is always likely to remain a scarce bird in Clackmannanshire due to the lack of appropriate habitat, although more birds could be encouraged to breed through nest box projects in suitable areas, as has happened in the Trossachs.[6]

Keith Broomfield

[1] BS3 [2] *Fife Atlas* [3] UFABR [4] CBC/BBS [5] BirdFacts [6] BS3

Breeding Distribution

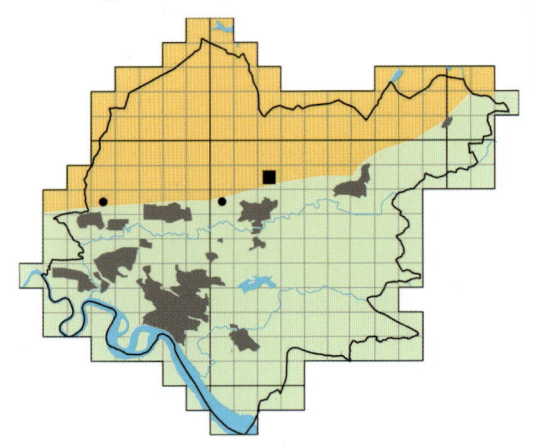

Number of km² in which recorded:	3	(1.5%)
■ Confirmed breeding	1	(33.3%)
● Probable breeding	0	(0.0%)
• Possible breeding	2	(66.7%)
○ Present, breeding unlikely:	0	(0.0%)

Whinchat *Saxicola rubetra*

Uncommon summer visitor

Conservation status: Amber

The Whinchat favours rough ground and open hillsides with a cover of scrub or young conifers and is reasonably widely distributed in the Ochils. Its conspicuous habits make it unlikely that many birds were overlooked during fieldwork.

The main concentration of registrations was on the lower south facing slopes of the Ochils where the abundance of gorse provides good habitat, especially around Myreton Hill to the east of Menstrie Glen. Registrations also occurred further into the Ochils in areas of gorse and young tree habitat. Two 'observed' records – one in central Clackmannanshire and the other on the edge of Alloa – may have been birds on passage, although there are areas of rough ground away from the Ochils that offer breeding potential.

Most breeding birds arrive in Scotland at the end of April and beginning of May and there is a distinct autumn passage between mid-August and early October,[1] although this is likely to be most noticeable in eastern coastal areas rather than more central areas of the country such as Clackmannanshire.

The UK Whinchat population has undergone long-term decline since at least the early 1970s,[2] and which has continued since the 1990s.[3] However, this has been most pronounced in lowland England rather than Scotland, with changes in land use cited as a major cause.[4] The prevalence of gorse in parts of the Ochils and new tree planting projects should help to sustain the Clackmannanshire population, although environmental changes on wintering grounds in sub-Saharan Africa could pose a threat to numbers in the future.[5]

Keith Broomfield

[1] BS3 [2] 1988-91 Atlas [3] BBS [4] 1988-91 Atlas [5] BS3

Breeding Distribution

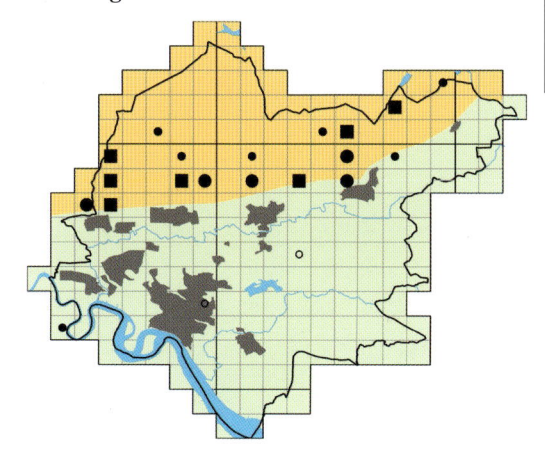

Number of km² in which recorded:	21	(10.6%)
■ Confirmed breeding	7	(33.3%)
● Probable breeding	5	(23.8%)
• Possible breeding	7	(33.3%)
○ Present, breeding unlikely:	2	(9.5%)

Stonechat   (European Stonechat)   *Saxicola torquatus*

Scarce resident and partial migrant

Conservation status: Green

In Scotland, the Stonechat has a very local distribution focusing on areas of rough ground typically with gorse, broom or other shrubs, often on the coast, marshland or on the edge of heather clad higher ground.[1]

According to the survey results, the Stonechat is scarce in Clackmannanshire with only two confirmed breeding registrations and a further 12 probable and possible records. It is almost exclusively confined to the high ground of the Ochils with only four records outside this area.

The Stonechat is a reluctant migrant with inland birds only moving out of their home areas in winter during periods of hard weather and with coastal populations tending to be more sedentary.[2] In overall terms, little is known about the wintering population in Scotland and the number of birds that may leave the country in any given year.[3] The series of relatively mild winters during the Clackmannanshire survey resulted in a spread of records outside the breeding season that correlated reasonably closely with the summer range, indicating limited migratory movements in at least some years of the census period.

Scottish BBS results show a statistically significant increase of 259% from 1995 to 2007 (the highest of any species listed),[4] which underlines the potential for the Stonechat to increase its population in Clackmannanshire, particularly since there are good tracts of suitable gorse habitat on the south-facing slopes of the Ochils. The felling of mature conifer plantations followed by replanting could also aid recovery in some areas, albeit on a temporary basis. But the marked susceptibility of the species to severe winters allied to other factors such as intermittent gorse-burning in spring means that any recovery could be dramatically reversed, signalling an underlying vulnerability in its status.

Keith Broomfield

[1] BS3 [2] SE Scotland Atlas [3] BS3 [4] Risely at al., 2009

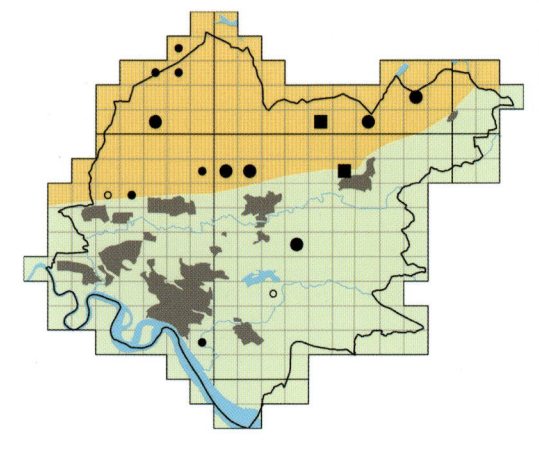

Breeding Distribution

Number of km² in which recorded:	16	(8.1%)
■ Confirmed breeding	2	(12.5%)
● Probable breeding	6	(37.5%)
● Possible breeding	6	(37.5%)
○ Present, breeding unlikely:	2	(12.5%)

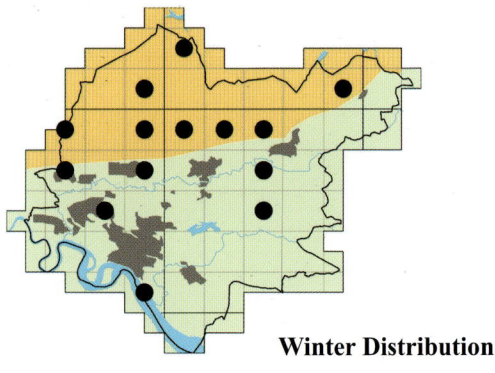

Winter Distribution

Wheatear   (Northern Wheatear)   *Oenanthe oenanthe*

Fairly common summer visitor and passage migrant Conservation status: Amber

The Wheatear is one our earliest spring migrants with the first birds usually first appearing in coastal areas in Scotland from early to mid-March.[1] For breeding, it favours open hillsides and grazed ground that offer a ready food source of small worms, insects, molluscs and caterpillars. It is particularly fond of areas with rocky outcrops, boulders and drystane dykes where it will nest in crevices or beneath rocks.

The Wheatear is widely distributed in the Ochils, with probable or confirmed breeding occurring in most parts. Within its range there will be localised hotspots where boulder scree and other rocky outcrops provide suitable places for nesting. The Wheatear is absent from wooded and forested areas but will temporarily recolonize ground where tree felling has recently occurred, for example in the hills above Dollar.[2]

Away from the Ochils, Wheatears were observed in several parts of the County, including along the upper reaches of the River Forth and also on the open land in the east and south-east of the County. While a proportion of these observations in lower lying areas may have been migrants (probably the Greenland subspecies *O. o leucorhoa*), it is entirely possible that a handful of pairs do breed. The *Fife Atlas* recorded probable breeding close to the Clackmannanshire border, and the remote mosses in this area do offer suitable habitat.

In many parts of its European range numbers are declining.[3] It is thought that the species is vulnerable to severe drought on the wintering grounds of the Sahel.[4] The population declined significantly in lowland areas of Britain between the two BTO Breeding Atlas surveys, probably due to the loss of suitable habitat.[5,6] BBS data show that between 1995 and 2007 the Wheatear declined by 5% in England, 14% in Scotland and a statistically significant 24% in Wales.[7]

Keith Broomfield

[1] *BS3* [2] *Pers. obs.* [3] *BirdFacts* [4] *European Atlas* [5] *1968-72 Atlas* [6] *1988-91 Atlas* [7] *Risely et al., 2009*

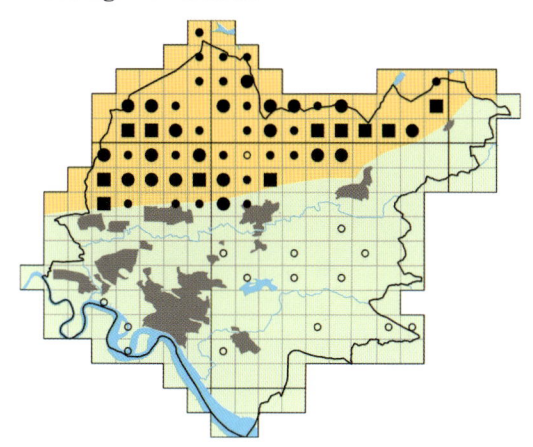

Breeding Distribution

Number of km² in which recorded:	69	(34.8%)
■ Confirmed breeding	11	(15.9%)
● Probable breeding	20	(29.0%)
● Possible breeding	23	(33.3%)
○ Present, breeding unlikely:	15	(21.7%)

Dunnock *Prunella modularis*

Common resident, possible passage migrant and winter visitor   Conservation status: Amber

Ideal Dunnock habitat combines thick scrubby cover for nesting and protection with nearby ground rich in seeds and insects for feeding. It is a bird of habitat edges and linear features such as hedges, inhabiting gardens, woodland margins and agricultural land as long as this is not farmed too intensively.[1,2]

The Dunnock is a widespread breeding bird in Clackmannanshire being present in virtually all lowland squares and to a lesser extent along the southern margin of the Ochil Hills. This broadly matches the wider Scottish picture and although it has been recorded at slightly higher altitudes in other parts of the country it is predominantly a lowland bird.[3,4]

Although densities on local BBS transects are higher in suburban/urban areas than in farmland, (during the survey period it was the sixth most commonly recorded bird in Clackmannanshire gardens),[5,6] its almost ubiquitous presence in the County's lowland squares indicates that suitable habitat remains widely available in rural areas as well as in urban and suburban ones. Despite its Amber listing, Dunnock numbers increased by a statistically significant 45% on Scottish BBS squares from 1995 to 2007.[7]

British Dunnocks are very sedentary, ringing recoveries having generally been within one kilometre,[8,9] and the winter map for Clackmannanshire fits this picture in showing essentially the same distribution as that for the breeding season. Unlike British birds, continental Dunnocks are migratory and some pass through northern and eastern Scotland during the spring and autumn migration periods, though generally in small numbers.[10,11] The plumage of continental birds is virtually indistinguishable from that of our local breeders and there is no evidence of such birds occurring in the County.

Don Matthews

[1] BS3 [2] BWP [3] BS3 [4] 1988-91 Atlas [5] UFABR [6] Garden BirdWatch unpub. data [7] Risely et al., 2009 [8] Winter Atlas [9] Migration Atlas [10] BS3 [11] Migration Atlas

Breeding Distribution

Number of km² in which recorded:	129	(65.2%)
■ Confirmed breeding	48	(37.2%)
● Probable breeding	50	(38.8%)
• Possible breeding	30	(23.3%)
○ Present, breeding unlikely:	1	(0.8%)

Winter Distribution

House Sparrow *Passer domesticus*

Common resident   Conservation status: Red

The House Sparrow owes its familiarity to its close association with man. Its principal habitat is in towns and villages, and in rural areas colonies are often found in farmsteads.[1] Since population estimates began to become available in 1976 a substantial decline has led to the House Sparrow being Red-listed in Britain. Although the UK population appears to have stabilised in the last decade (increases in Scotland, Wales and Northern Ireland off-setting a continuing decline in England),[2] serious concern still remains over the population of this bird that was once so common that it was considered a pest.[3]

House Sparrows are widely distributed in lowland Clackmannanshire, having been registered in all urban/suburban squares and in most, though not all, lowland rural ones. Garden Bird Watch showed that it was the third most commonly recorded bird in Clackmannanshire gardens during the *Atlas* period.[4] The more urbanised western half of the County has few gaps in the distribution and probably also holds the bulk of the breeding population as local BBS results for 2006 and 2007 indicate an urban/suburban density two to three times that on farmland.[5,6] The more agricultural eastern half of the County has more extensive conifer plantations which these birds avoid,[7] and the villages, farms or cottages where the right combination of conditions exists to support breeding are more localised, which probably accounts for their patchier distribution here.

British House Sparrows are extremely sedentary, rarely moving more than two kilometres from their breeding site. Juveniles and non-breeding adults sometimes move further than this but few exceed 20 kilometres.[8,9] The winter map for Clackmannanshire is essentially identical to that for the breeding season and it is likely that our wintering birds are our own local breeders plus a few from nearby areas of adjacent counties.

Don Matthews

[1] *BirdFacts* [2] *BBRC* [3] *Mead, 2000* [4] *Garden BirdWatch unpub. data* [5] *UFABR* [6] *N Bielby unpub. data* [7] *BWP* [8] *Migration Atlas* [9] *BS3*

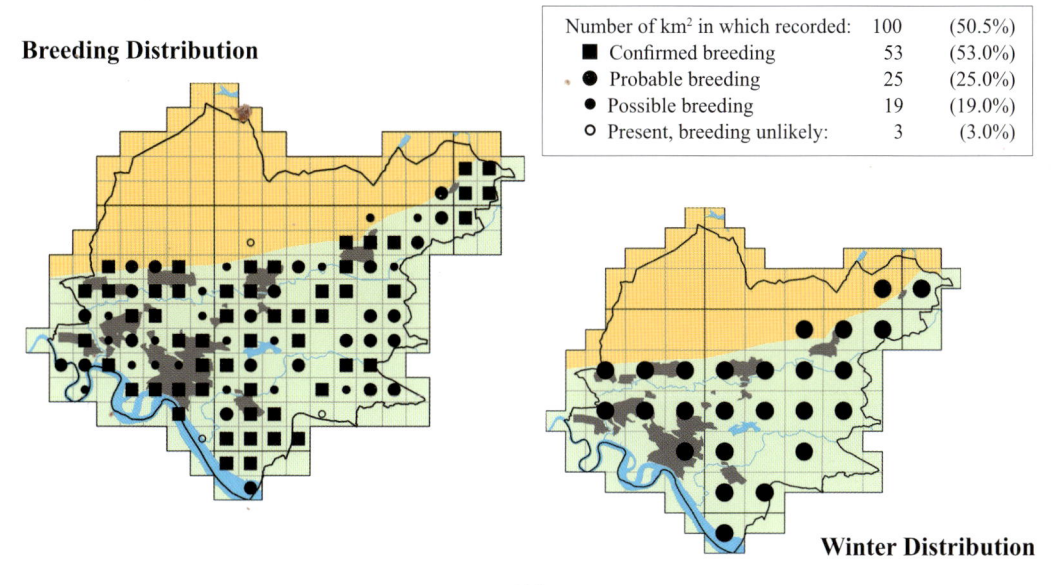

Breeding Distribution

Number of km² in which recorded:	100	(50.5%)
■ Confirmed breeding	53	(53.0%)
● Probable breeding	25	(25.0%)
• Possible breeding	19	(19.0%)
○ Present, breeding unlikely:	3	(3.0%)

Winter Distribution

Tree Sparrow   (Eurasian Tree Sparrow)   *Passer montanus*

Uncommon resident   Conservation status: Red

The Tree Sparrow closely resembles the familiar House Sparrow but differs in having a full red-brown crown, a black patch on its white cheeks and the male and the female being similar in appearance. The species is widespread across Eurasia, breeding in a wide variety of habitats and nesting generally in loose colonies. Suitable habitat is, however, occupied only patchily.[1]

The Tree Sparrow was not confirmed breeding in Clackmannanshire until 1968, following a substantial local increase over the preceding 30 years in the Stirling region.[2] During *Atlas* fieldwork it was recorded from 15% of squares. There was a concentration in the centre of Clackmannanshire, stretching from Alva, Coalsnaughton, Gartmorn, the eastern edge of Alloa, and Clackmannan down to the River Forth. There were also small clusters around Cambus/Tullibody and to the south/south-east of Dollar. The species was largely absent from the Hillfoots, the east of the County and the built-up areas of the west. During the winter the species was scarcer but where it did occur its distribution overlapped with that during the breeding season.

The species undergoes major fluctuations. Following an influx to Britain during 1957-1962, the population increased six-fold, then suffered massive declines between the late 1970s and early 1990s and became locally extinct in the UK in the late 1990s. Agricultural practices (changes from spring to winter sowing and from hay to silage making, and also a reduction in winter stubble) are thought to be causes.[3,4]

There is no obvious reason why the species should be less common in the eastern parts of lowland Clackmannanshire. This is where conservation action should be focused: an assessment of the suitability of the habitat there, which, if appropriate, could be followed by a nest-box scheme.

Andre Thiel

[1] BWP   [2] D.M. Bryant, 1974   [3] BWP   [4] J.D. Summers-Smith, 1998

Breeding Distribution

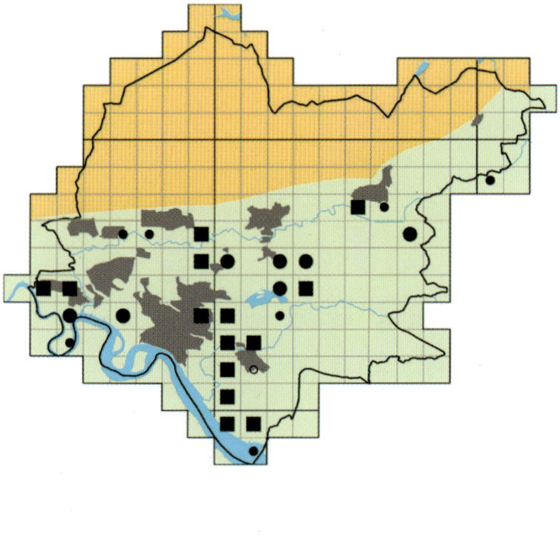

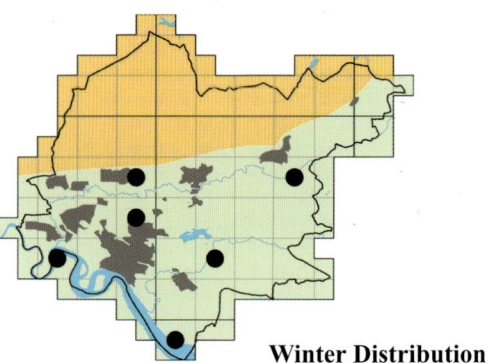

Number of km² in which recorded:	29	(14.6%)
■ Confirmed breeding	14	(48.3%)
● Probable breeding	7	(24.1%)
• Possible breeding	7	(24.1%)
○ Present, breeding unlikely:	1	(3.4%)

Winter Distribution

Grey Wagtail *Motacilla cinerea*

Fairly common resident and passage migrant   Conservation status: Amber

The Grey Wagtail is a colourful bird, which hill-walkers will associate with fast-flowing upland streams and rivers, a habitat it shares with the Dipper. Its insect diet is wider than that of the Dipper, however, and it is to be found in a greater range of riparian habitats, often associated with trees.[1,2] A survey of 673 nests in Britain found that only 3% were more than 30m away from water,[3] so it is very much a 'water wagtail' when compared with its Pied congener. It is a conspicuous bird, both in plumage and behaviour, and is unlikely to have been under-recorded in the course of the surveys.

The species is widely distributed throughout Britain as a whole, though its actual numbers are markedly affected by severe winter weather.[4] BBS data for Scotland are based on too small a sample to deduce trends, but UK data show a significant increase of 38% between 1995 and 2007.[5]

The Grey Wagtail shows a more restricted breeding range in Clackmannanshire than the Pied Wagtail, reflecting its preference for fast-flowing streams and rivers. Most confirmed breeding sites occur in a broad band along the Ochil scarp and the Hillfoot area, and several probable sites have also been found in various locations further into the upland areas.

The results of the winter *Atlas* survey need to be treated with caution. They seem to suggest a pattern of withdrawal from upland areas towards the coast similar to that found in Fife and mentioned as a possibility in the *Migration Atlas*.[6,7] However, local Bird Reports show that Grey Wagtails are scarce throughout the County in winter,[8] and without ringing data it is impossible to tell whether the few wintering birds are displaced local breeders or visitors from further afield.

John Grainger

[1] BS3 [2] Tyler & Ormerod, 1994 [3] Tyler, S.J., 1972 [4] BWP [5] Risely et al., 2009 [6] Fife Atlas
[7] Migration Atlas [8] UFABR

Breeding Distribution

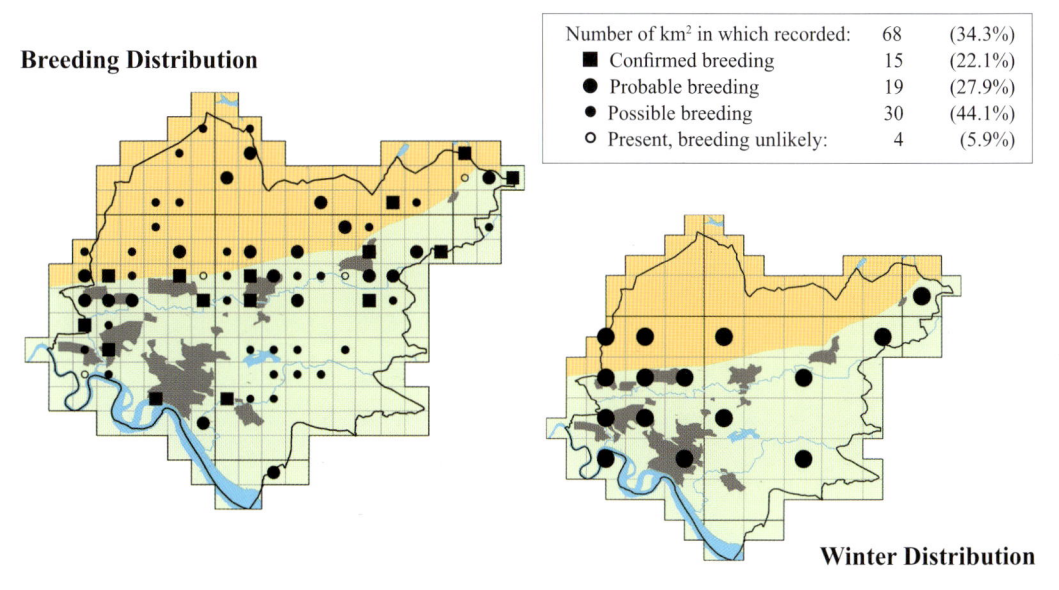

Number of km² in which recorded:	68	(34.3%)
■ Confirmed breeding	15	(22.1%)
● Probable breeding	19	(27.9%)
• Possible breeding	30	(44.1%)
○ Present, breeding unlikely:	4	(5.9%)

Winter Distribution

Pied Wagtail (White Wagtail) *Motacilla alba*

Common summer visitor and resident, passage migrant   Conservation status: Green

The Pied Wagtail is a conspicuous bird with prominent territorial behaviour that shows up readily in atlas surveys. The nest, however, is less easy to detect as it is often hidden in a crevice. It feeds on open ground giving scope to its characteristic 'run-picking' technique, with manicured lawns and tarmac surfaces being attractive places for this 'car-park wagtail'.[1]

The current survey showed it breeding widely across the lowland squares in the County, as would be expected from its preferred breeding habitats of villages and pasture farmland.[2] It is not surprising that distribution was patchy in the more densely built-up areas around Alloa and Tullibody. Isolated registrations of birds in all breeding categories were found in the Ochils, including in some remote squares. Surveyors had not been asked specifically to differentiate between the native *yarrellii* subspecies and the continental White Wagtail *M.a.alba*, but there were two squares in the Cambus area where the White subspecies was recorded in the breeding season. However, these would almost certainly have been passage birds on their way to breeding grounds to the north of Scotland.[3]

Recoveries of ringed birds have shown that northern populations of Pied Wagtails move south in winter, either to southern England or to the Continent,[4] which would account for the dearth of records in the east of the County during the winter survey, an area where it had been found breeding in almost every square. Recorded birds (possibly visitors from further north) were concentrated in the towns and villages. Pied Wagtails can form large winter roosts, but though groups of up to 56 birds have been recorded in the Cambus/Alloa area,[5] roosts of 200 birds or more as recorded in Fife do not appear to have occurred in Clackmannanshire.[6]

John Grainger

[1] BWP [2] BirdFacts [3] BS3 [4] Migration Atlas [5] UFABR [6] Fife Atlas

Breeding Distribution

Number of km² in which recorded:	123	(62.1%)
■ Confirmed breeding	71	(57.7%)
● Probable breeding	17	(13.8%)
● Possible breeding	34	(27.6%)
○ Present, breeding unlikely:	1	(0.8%)

Winter Distribution

Tree Pipit   *Anthus trivialis*

Locally common summer visitor and passage migrant   Conservation status: Red

The Tree Pipit is found in open woodland and scrub, particularly in upland areas, and is most easily detected (and separated from its congener, the Meadow Pipit) when performing its conspicuous song flight. Its rather specialised habitat requirements make it a somewhat local bird in Scotland and this is certainly the case in Clackmannanshire, with possible, probable and confirmed breeding recorded in only 12% of squares.

The breeding map suggests that the Tree Pipit favours areas of unimproved ground in central and south-eastern parts of the County, stretching from Gartmorn Dam in the west across to the Fife border. Two of the confirmed breeding registrations in this part of the range were in damp, birch dominated woodland strips with good ground cover adjacent to sheep pasture.[1] Other breeding registrations occurred along the southern edge of the Ochils, although records were sparse, indicating the lack of suitable habitat.

In England, CBC/BBS data show a continuing severe decrease in the population from 1970 to 2007 resulting in the recent change in its UK conservation status from Amber to Red.[2,3,4] The causes for this decline are unclear but may be linked to the maturation of forest plantations, and reduced management of lowland woods, together with problems during migration and on its sub-Saharan wintering quarters in Africa.[5,6] In Scotland, however, BBS results show that Tree Pipit numbers increased by a significant 47% from 1995-2008.[7]

The production cycle of conifer plantations in Clackmannanshire may also cause localised fluctuations in numbers with the Tree Pipit able to utilise this habitat in the early stages of woodland succession and then again during the clear-fell phase.[8] It is also likely that current natural woodland regeneration schemes using native broadleaved species in the north-east fringes of the County will cause localised increases.

Keith Broomfield

[1] *Pers. obs.* [2] *Eaton, Balmer et al., 2009* [3] *Risely et al., 2009* [4] *Eaton, Brown et al., 2009* [5] *BirdFacts* [6] *Risely et al., 2009* [7] *ibid.* [8] *SE Scotland Atlas*

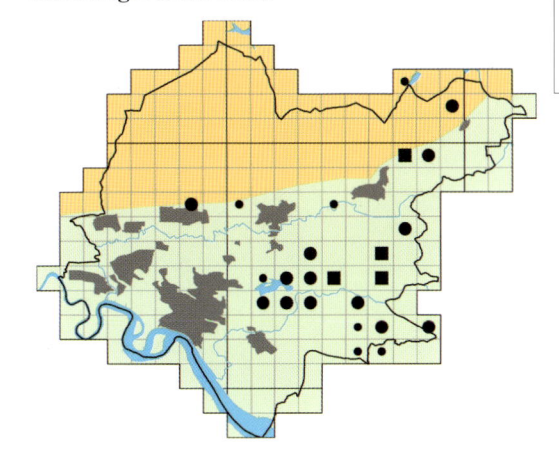

Breeding Distribution

Number of km² in which recorded:	24	(12.1%)
■ Confirmed breeding	4	(16.7%)
● Probable breeding	13	(54.2%)
• Possible breeding	7	(29.2%)
○ Present, breeding unlikely:	0	(0.0%)

Meadow Pipit *Anthus pratensis*

Common summer visitor and passage migrant, scarce in mid-winter
Conservation status: Amber

The Meadow Pipit is an abundant summer visitor and passage migrant to Clackmannanshire where it is most commonly found on hills and rough uncultivated ground, with breeding registrations occurring in virtually every square in the Ochils but more sparsely elsewhere.

Its frequency on open hill ground and ease of observation resulted in a high proportion of confirmed breeding registrations in the areas where it occurs, representing 42% of all breeding registrations for the species. Research has shown that lower densities of Meadow Pipits occur in upland areas dominated by either grass or heather with higher numbers occurring where there is a mixture of the two vegetation types.[1] The dominance of grasses in the Ochils may therefore indicate that Meadow Pipits occur at lower densities here than some other Scottish hills.

The Meadow Pipit is not so frequent as a breeding bird away from the Ochils, although there is a notable small concentration of records in the south-east of Clackmannanshire where remnants of raised mosses and areas of rough grassland provide suitable habitat.

It is much less common in winter with the majority of Scottish breeding birds migrating south to the Continent.[2] Most winter records were on lower lying parts of the Ochils, particularly the slopes along the southern flanks (although some of these birds may have been early arrivals to their breeding areas), as well as open ground areas adjacent to the River Forth.

BBS data indicate that the Meadow Pipit population has experienced a decline of 10% in Scotland between 1994 and 2007.[3] Its importance in upland ecology would make further research into the reasons for this fall desirable.

Keith Broomfield

[1] BS3 [2] ibid. [3] Risely et al., 2009

Breeding Distribution

Number of km² in which recorded:	104	(52.5%)
■ Confirmed breeding	37	(35.6%)
● Probable breeding	48	(46.2%)
• Possible breeding	4	(3.8%)
○ Present, breeding unlikely:	15	(14.4%)

Winter Distribution

Chaffinch   Fringilla coelebs

Common resident, passage/winter visitor   Conservation status: Green

The Chaffinch is one of the most abundant and widespread birds in Scotland with a breeding population that has been estimated at 1,000,000-1,500,000 pairs and winter population that has been estimated at 2,550,000-4,300,000 birds.[1] Trends for Scotland and for the whole of the UK suggest the breeding population was stable between 1995 and 2007.[2]

Chaffinches can utilise almost any scrub, hedgerow, garden shrubs and woodlands for breeding and also have generalist feeding habits, being able to utilise the smallest grass seeds to beech mast, though insects are required for their young.[3,4] It is unsurprising therefore that in Clackmannanshire it was found in all lowland one-kilometre squares in summer and tetrads in winter, and was absent only from the upland squares with no trees or scrub. Breeding was either confirmed or considered probable in 89% of the squares in which they were registered, and indeed it is likely that they bred in at least some of the other squares in which only lesser evidence for breeding was recorded.

In winter, Chaffinches from mainland Europe augment the resident breeding birds, but the number of winter immigrants is thought to be less in northern Britain.[5,6] The proportion of the winter population in central Scotland that is of continental origin remains unknown. A study of the ranging behaviour in winter of a trio of seed-eating passerines (Chaffinch, Yellowhammer and Tree Sparrow) in a west Fife study area just to the east of the Clackmannanshire border found that Chaffinches ranged the least distances of the three species.[7] This is probably related to their ability to utilise a range of habitats and a broad range of seeds. This adaptability and the associated lesser risks of mortality no doubt contribute to the continuing success of this species, which contrasts starkly with some other seed-eating passerines. It was the fifth most commonly recorded bird in Clackmannanshire gardens during the *Atlas* survey period.[8]

John Calladine

[1] BS3 [2] BBS [3] Newton, 1972 [4] Newton, 1967 [5] Swann, 1988 [6] Migration Atlas [7] Calladine et al., 2006. [8] Garden BirdWatch unpub. data

Breeding Distribution

Number of km² in which recorded:	149	(75.3%)
■ Confirmed breeding	63	(42.3%)
● Probable breeding	69	(46.3%)
• Possible breeding	16	(10.7%)
○ Present, breeding unlikely:	1	(0.7%)

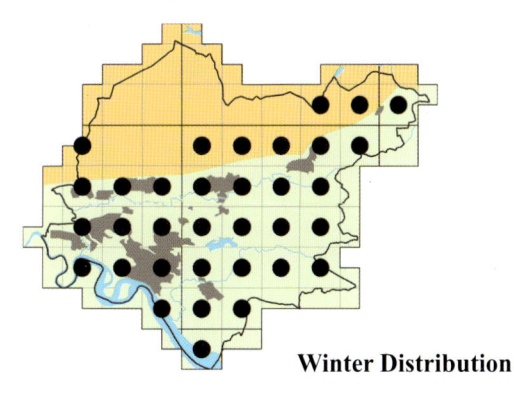

Winter Distribution

Greenfinch   (European Greenfinch)   *Chloris chloris*

Common resident, uncommon winter visitor

Conservation status: Green

A sociable and often vocal bird, the Greenfinch is found in a variety of open areas with scattered trees and bushes such as farmland with hedgerows, parks, gardens, scrub and young conifer plantations.

The UK population of the Greenfinch increased by more than 20% between 1995 and 2007,[1] (despite this including the beginning of the drastic reduction in numbers following the widespread and severe trichomonosis outbreak in 2005)[2,3] and the *Atlas* shows it to be widely distributed throughout most of lowland Clackmannanshire. There has been a trend in the last 50 years or so for the species to move away from farmland and into urban areas[4] and this is well illustrated by the good number of registrations from Alloa, Tullibody, Clackmannan and the Hillfoot villages.

Despite being absent from the high ground of the Ochils, Greenfinches were recorded from some of the lower slopes where there are areas of good habitat comprising gorse, trees and woodland edge.

The winter distribution is not as widespread as that of the breeding range. The lack of arable land in many parts of the County probably accounts for these gaps with the main areas of scarcity coinciding with sheep and cattle pasture in the east and south-east. Ringing recoveries have found that immigrants from Norway arrive in eastern Scotland each autumn with some passage birds moving on to winter further south.[5] The number of Norwegian birds is not thought to be high, probably less than 10% of all Greenfinches present in winter. The good spread of winter records in towns and villages in Clackmannanshire demonstrates the potential benefit of garden bird feeders in sustaining local populations. However, the devastating effect of the recent *trichomonosis* outbreak shows that concentrations of birds at garden feeders can bring attendant risks.[6] Despite this, it was still the eighth most commonly recorded bird in Clackmannanshire gardens during the survey period.[7]

Keith Broomfield

[1] *Risely et al., 2009* [2] *BBWC* [3] *Robinson et al., 2010* [4] *1988-91Atlas* [5] *BS3* [6] *Robinson et al., 2010*
[7] *Garden BirdWatch unpub. data*

Breeding Distribution

Number of km² in which recorded:	108	(54.5%)
■ Confirmed breeding	32	(29.6%)
● Probable breeding	46	(54.6%)
• Possible breeding	27	(25.0%)
○ Present, breeding unlikely:	3	(2.8%)

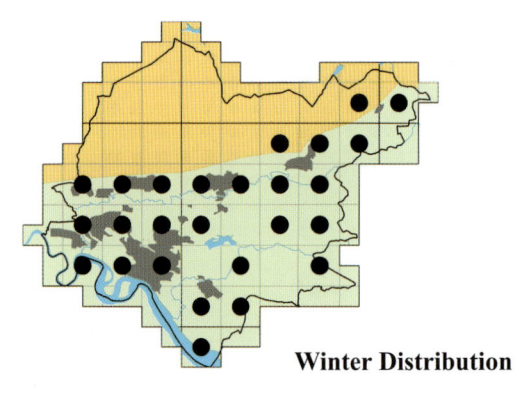

Winter Distribution

Goldfinch (European Goldfinch) *Carduelis carduelis*

Fairly common resident/partial migrant Conservation status: Green

While the Goldfinch is widespread in Clackmannanshire, it is never found at high densities[1] and is most frequent in open wooded areas, gardens, hedgerows and parks where there is a good ground cover of seed plants such as thistles and dandelions. The striking plumage and clear song make it a relatively easy bird to detect in the breeding season.

Confirmed, probable and possible breeding was recorded in 35% of squares, with a particularly strong concentration of registrations in central and western areas as well as in the north-east between Dollar and Muckhart. There is a notable spread of breeding records along the course of the River Devon and Devon Way. The main areas of absence or scarcity are in the Ochils and the eastern fringes of the County adjacent to Fife.

The winter distribution correlates closely with that found in the breeding season, although wandering parties penetrate into the Ochils, possibly seeking out conifer plantations to feed on opening cones. The birches and alders along the River Devon are another favoured habitat at this time of year.[2] Flocking is a feature from late summer, continuing through the winter. Ringing studies in Scotland have shown that, while many birds are largely sedentary, there is also some migratory movement to lower latitudes.[3]

Since the mid 1980s there has been a significant increase in the Goldfinch population[4] – a trend that is still continuing with BBS data for Scotland showing a 76% increase between 1995 and 2007.[5] The increase has been attributed to a variety of factors, including an upsurge in the use of garden bird feeders and the planting of conifers creating a useful alternative food supply during certain periods, as well as birds making good use of set aside fields and unharvested Oilseed Rape fields.[6]

Keith Broomfield

[1] BS2 [2] Pers. obs. [3] BS3 [4] ibid. [5] Risely et al., 2009 [6] BS3

Breeding Distribution

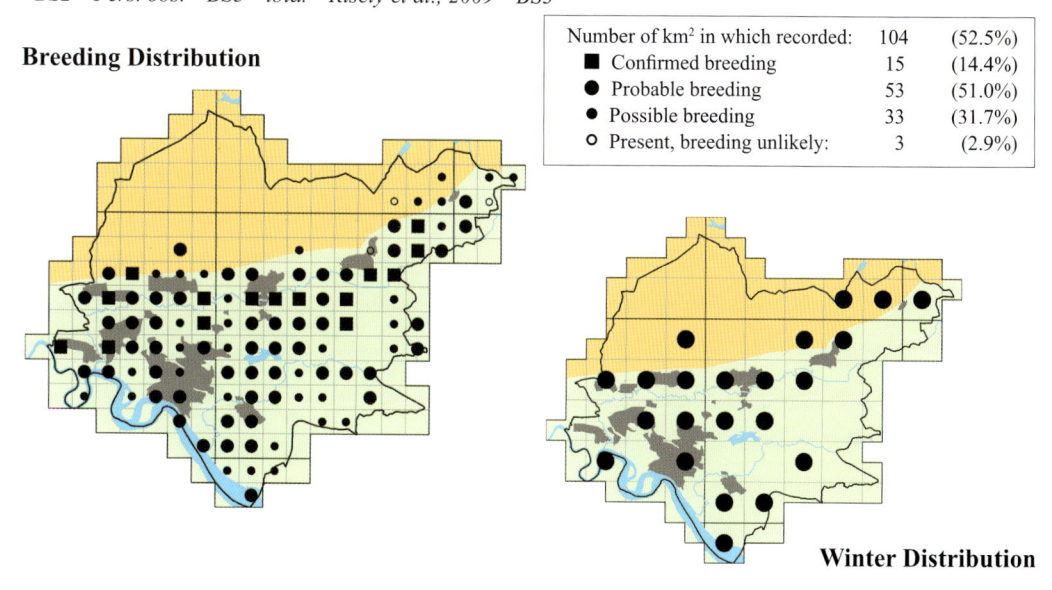

Number of km² in which recorded:	104	(52.5%)
■ Confirmed breeding	15	(14.4%)
● Probable breeding	53	(51.0%)
• Possible breeding	33	(31.7%)
○ Present, breeding unlikely:	3	(2.9%)

Winter Distribution

Siskin   (Eurasian Siskin)   *Carduelis spinus*

Locally common resident, passage/winter visitor in varying numbers.
Conservation status: Green

A conifer specialist, the Siskin has benefited greatly from afforestation and has spread throughout much of Britain into areas from where it was formerly absent.[1] It is a conspicuous bird, its bright plumage and continuous twittering making it an easy bird to detect. Confirmation of breeding, however, is more difficult, given that the small nest is usually well hidden on a horizontal bough at a considerable height above the ground.

These difficulties were highlighted during the Clackmannanshire survey with breeding confirmed in only three squares, all of which related to sightings of fledged young. Possible and probable breeding was recorded in an additional 27 squares.

As recently as 1986 the Siskin had not been recorded as a breeding bird in Clackmannanshire,[2] but since then colonization has been rapid. The breeding distribution in the County is closely tied to its favoured conifer habitat with a distinct concentration in the maturing plantations of the Ochils in the north-east of the County and a further spread of records in the south-east. The breeding population will vary greatly depending on the productivity of the conifer cone crop with birds migrating away from the County in poor years, but with numbers supplemented in other years by Scandinavian immigrants.[3]

The winter range of records is more widespread than summer with birds recorded from most areas apart from the high ground of the Ochils. During autumn and winter Siskins form feeding parties and flocks can spread far and wide feeding on the seeds of alder, birch, spruce and larch. The population is also likely to be sustained by food from garden bird feeders and, without this extra food supply, the annual variation of the winter population in Scotland may be more pronounced.[4]

Keith Broomfield

[1] *1988-91 Atlas*   [2] *BS2*   [3] *BS3*   [4] *ibid.*

Breeding Distribution

Number of km² in which recorded:	38	(19.2%)
■ Confirmed breeding	3	(7.9%)
● Probable breeding	10	(26.3%)
• Possible breeding	17	(44.7%)
○ Present, breeding unlikely:	8	(21.1%)

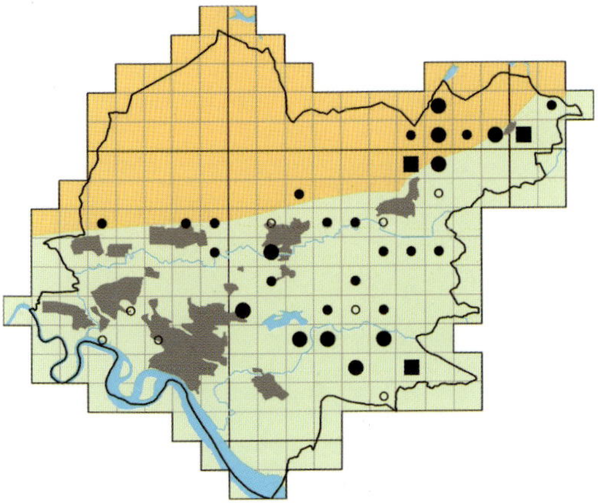

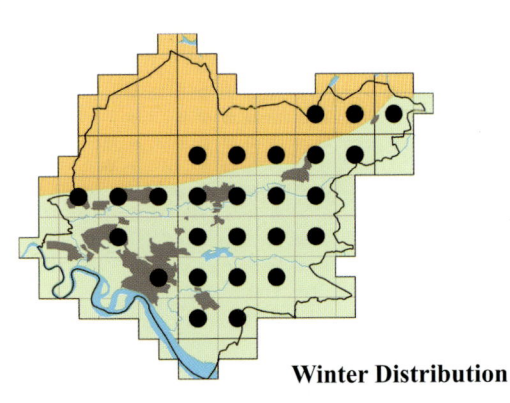

Winter Distribution

Linnet (Common Linnet) *Carduelis cannabina*

Fairly common resident, passage migrant/winter visitor   Conservation status: Red

The Linnet is an avid seed feeder and typical breeding habitat includes coastal areas, arable ground, scrub, and pasture where there are plenty of herbaceous and other seed bearing plants.[1] Areas with low bushes or scrub such as gorse are favoured for nesting and the species often breeds in loose colonies.

The Linnet is relatively easy to record during the breeding season with the constant twittering of courting males being quite conspicuous. However, confirmation of breeding is more difficult. This is reflected in the survey results with confirmed breeding in only eight squares, but probable or possible breeding in a further 35 squares.

The Atlas breeding survey shows a good spread of registrations in Clackmannanshire with it being scarcest in some eastern parts of the County where sheep pasture is predominant. It is absent from most of the high ground of the Ochils but breeds between the 50m and 150m contour lines above the Hillfoot villages, attracted by the numerous patches of gorse for nesting. It is frequent by the edges of towns and villages where open areas of weedy undisturbed ground are often found and is also a regular breeder along the fringes of the River Forth.

In autumn and winter, Linnets congregate into flocks and make mostly local movements in response to changes in food supply.[2] The distribution map shows a bias of records towards the western half of the County, particularly near the edges of towns and villages.

National threats to the future of the Linnet are focused around changes in land-use and agriculture.[3] Its Red conservation status is down to significant declines in England between 1965 and 1990,[4] although BBS data for Scotland show a modest increase between 1994 and 2007, possibly due to increased cultivation of Oilseed Rape.[5]

Keith Broomfield

[1] *BirdFacts* [2] *BS3* [3] *ibid.* [4] *Eaton et al., 2009* [5] *Risely et al., 2009*

Breeding Distribution

Number of km² in which recorded:	78	(39.4%)
■ Confirmed breeding	8	(10.3%)
● Probable breeding	33	(42.3%)
• Possible breeding	32	(41.0%)
○ Present, breeding unlikely:	5	(6.4%)

Winter Distribution

Twite   *Carduelis flavirostris*

Scarce resident and uncommon winter visitor   Conservation status: Red

In Scotland, the Twite's main strongholds are the hills and coasts of the north and west, the Hebrides and the Northern Isles.[1] The Scottish population, estimated at 5,600-13,800 pairs,[2] is thought to have declined markedly but the true extent of the decline is likely to be unclear through poor knowledge of the true status of the species.

This survey found a small number of Twite on the crags around Alva Glen with breeding being confirmed by the sighting of a bird carrying a faecal sac. The Twite is one of the few passerines that feed exclusively on seeds (including the young) and these crags are among the few areas in the Ochils where ericaceous plants are able to grow and readily flower and set seed away from the attentions of grazing sheep. They are also close to the only other confirmed breeding record for the County, on Ben Ever in 1991, when five young fledged from a clutch of six eggs. The scarcity of 'observed' registrations suggests it is unlikely that this small population exceeds five breeding pairs. Otherwise, Twite have only occasionally been recorded in the County during the breeding season.[3]

Twite were not recorded during winter *Atlas* fieldwork (which may have been a result of under-recording as a wintering flock of about 80 birds was in stubble fields near Alva in 2003-04 and a flock of 120 birds was recorded on the Blackdevon Wetlands in November 2007).[4] Winter flocks have been recorded at this latter location several times since 1974 where the juxtaposition of ungrazed or lightly grazed saltmarsh and stubble fields would appear to provide excellent winter feeding as wintering Twite are often associated with these habitats.[5,6]

John Calladine

[1] *BS3* [2] *Langstone et al., 2006* [3] *UFABR* [4] *ibid.* [5] *Brown & Atkinson, 1996* [6] *Clark & Sellers, 1998, 1999*

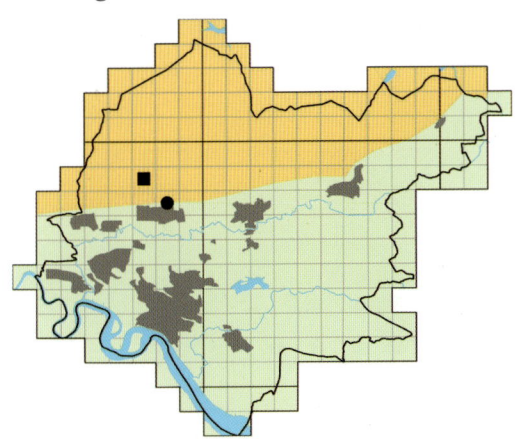

Breeding Distribution

Number of km² in which recorded:	2	(1.0%)
■ Confirmed breeding	1	(50.0%)
● Probable breeding	1	(50.0%)
● Possible breeding	0	(0.0%)
○ Present, breeding unlikely:	0	(0.0%)

Lesser Redpoll *Carduelis cabaret*

Uncommon resident and migrant

Conservation status: Red

The Lesser Redpoll is a lively but unobtrusive little finch that favours young deciduous woodlands – particularly birch and alder – immature conifer plantations and willow scrub which provide a plentiful supply of small seeds to feed on.[1] It is frequently found on the fringes of wooded areas bordering moorland and open hill.

The species is scarce in Clackmannanshire with possible and probable breeding occurring in only 9% of squares, mainly concentrated in the east and south-east of the County, including conifer plantation habitat in the Ochils. Most registrations revolved around individual birds or pairs being sighted in suitable breeding habitat. Breeding is hard to confirm due to the difficulty in finding the small nests or detecting fledged birds feeding high in thick leaf canopy.

The more nomadic nature of the Lesser Redpoll's feeding habits in winter is highlighted by the greater geographical spread in Clackmannanshire compared with summer. The winter distribution correlates closely with the course of the River Devon and the adjacent Devon Way between Dollar and Alloa where there is an abundance of birch, alder and other typical food plants. The wintering population is likely to vary greatly from year to year with many Scottish birds migrating south in some years.[2]

The limiting factor behind the small Clackmannanshire breeding population may not be solely habitat driven, given that there would appear to be a number of suitable breeding areas. This, combined with its Red conservation status arising from the notable decline of the UK breeding population between 1969 and 2006,[3] makes further research into the biology of the Lesser Redpoll a priority.

Keith Broomfield

[1] BS3 [2] ibid. [3] Eaton et al., 2009

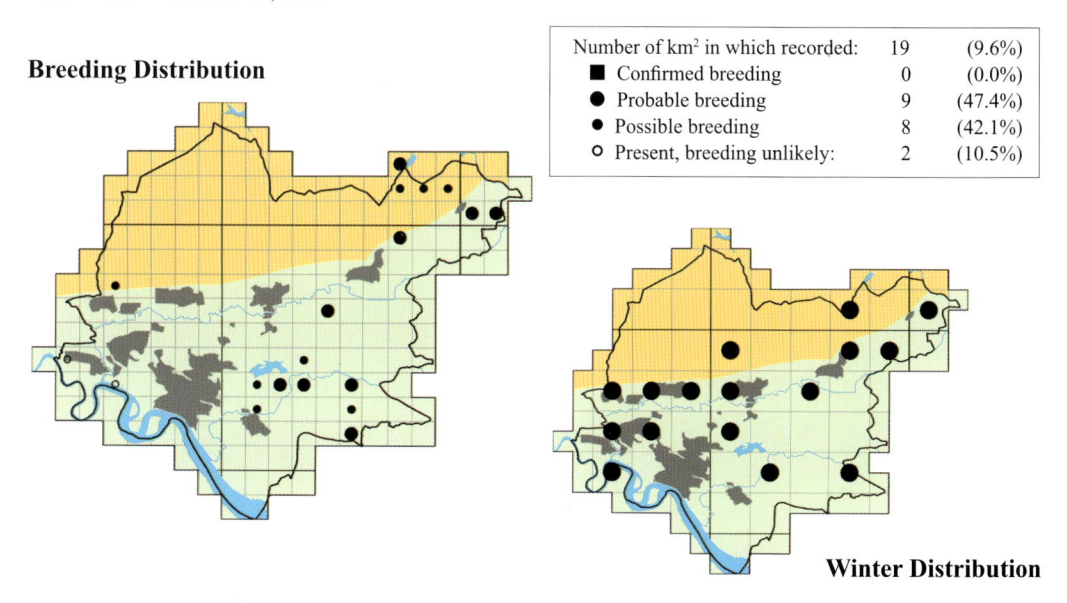

Breeding Distribution

Number of km² in which recorded:	19	(9.6%)
■ Confirmed breeding	0	(0.0%)
● Probable breeding	9	(47.4%)
• Possible breeding	8	(42.1%)
○ Present, breeding unlikely:	2	(10.5%)

Winter Distribution

Common Crossbill   (Red Crossbill)   *Loxia curvirostra*

Uncommon resident breeder and passage visitor   Conservation status: Green

The Common Crossbill is the commonest and most widespread of the three Crossbill species breeding in Scotland. It is a specialist feeder on the seeds of conifers, which it extracts from the cones with its remarkable bill. The irruptive nature of Crossbills is well-described, and in summer and autumn varying numbers arrive in Scotland from Scandinavia and Russia to supplement the resident population, with some of these immigrants staying to breed.[1]

During the *Atlas* survey the Common Crossbill was encountered in only a handful of conifer woods in Clackmannanshire, centred on The Forest at Gartlove and at Hillfoot Hill above Dollar. However, there are many other tracts of suitable woodland that can support foraging birds, such as those in the north-east of the County between Dollar and Muckhart and also in the south-east in areas bordering Devilla Forest and Bathmoor Plantation in Fife. The only confirmed breeding registration was a female bird nest-building in a Scots pine on 3 April 2007 and later found to be incubating (there was a second breeding attempt at the same location in April 2009). The Common Crossbill can be an early or late nester depending on the abundance of the cone crop.[2] As a result some breeding birds may have been missed. The local *Bird Reports* contain few records prior to *Atlas* fieldwork with a group of 34 at Dollar in February 1991 being the most notable.[3]

The main factors affecting breeding numbers of Crossbills are the extent and composition of suitable habitat (mature conifer woodland) and annual variation in cone-cropping.[4] Breeding is probably attempted in all but the most barren of years. Loss of habitat can occur owing to land use change (principally development) and as a consequence of harvesting and restocking patterns. Changes such as these have a significant, potentially permanent impact on the capacity of Clackmannanshire to support breeding Common Crossbills.

Bob Dawson

[1] *BS3*   [2] *BS2*   [3] *UFABR*   [4] *1988-91 Atlas*

Breeding Distribution

Number of km² in which recorded:	10	(5.1%)
■ Confirmed breeding	1	(10.0%)
● Probable breeding	1	(10.0%)
• Possible breeding	5	(50.0%)
○ Present, breeding unlikely:	3	(30.0%)

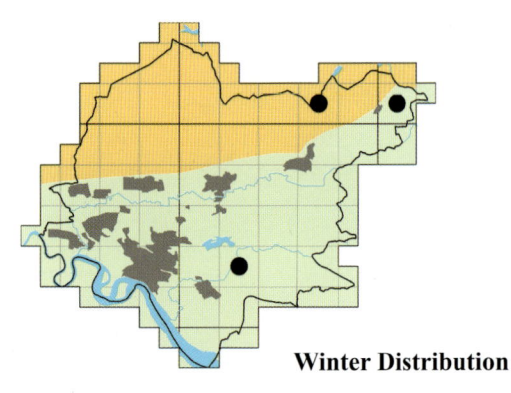

Winter Distribution

Bullfinch   (Eurasian Bullfinch)   *Pyrrhula pyrrhula*

Fairly common resident and possible sporadic visitor

Conservation status: Amber

Although the Bullfinch breeds at low densities in coniferous woodlands over most of its Eurasian range, in Western Europe it also associates with mixed and broadleaved woodlands with a thick understorey. In Britain it prefers scrub over woodland, and it also occurs on pasture.[1,2,3] Although strikingly coloured, the Bullfinch is unobtrusive and, given its rather subdued song, is easily overlooked.

The Bullfinch was recorded from 30% of *Atlas* squares in Clackmannanshire. It shows a rather scattered distribution, with concentrations along the Hillfoots and in south-east and, to a lesser extent, south-west Clackmannanshire. It appears to be largely absent from built-up areas and the Ochils. Its complete absence from southern and parts of central and south-western Clackmannanshire is roughly correlated with the dominance of arable fields there.[4] In Britain the species is mainly sedentary; more than 90% of movements occur over less than 25km, mostly within a 5km radius.[5] The winter distribution in Clackmannanshire is within this small-scale movement pattern. It is possible that a few birds of the northern continental subspecies *P.p.pyrrhula* occasionally occur in the County in late autumn, especially during rare, large scale irruptions.[6]

The Bullfinch spread its range in Britain especially from 1955 onwards, colonizing open farmland with copses of woodland, scrub and hedgerows.[7] Since the mid-1970s there has been a general pattern of decline.[8,9] The probable reasons for this are large-scale hedgerow removal and intensification of farming methods.[10] Clackmannanshire is intensively farmed with many built-up areas, which means the population in the County is likely to have shown a similar trend. One of the principal aims of the *Atlas* has been to establish a baseline against which future changes can be assessed, but given the Bullfinch's unobtrusive habits a more detailed study would be required to obtain a clearer picture of distribution and population for the species.

Andre Thiel

[1] *BWP* [2] *Siriwardena et al., 2001* [3] *BirdFacts* [4] *Thiel & Lindsay, 1999* [5] *BWP* [6] *ibid.*
[7] *Marchant et al., 1990* [8] *CBC* [9] *Gregory et al., 2001* [10] *Mead, 2000*

Breeding Distribution

Number of km² in which recorded:	59	(29.8%)
■ Confirmed breeding	10	(16.9%)
● Probable breeding	26	(44.1%)
• Possible breeding	18	(30.5%)
○ Present, breeding unlikely:	5	(8.5%)

Winter Distribution

Yellowhammer *Emberiza citrinella*

Fairly common breeder, locally common in winter

Conservation status: Red

The Yellowhammer is a bird typically associated with arable land and hedgerows and the male's distinctive repetitive song is a familiar feature of spring and summer. The bird has a broad distribution in Clackmannanshire and is only absent from high ground and some eastern parts of the County. As well as a good supply of weed and grass seed plants to feed on, other important habitat requirements are suitable song posts and bushes and low scrub for nesting.[1]

Confirmed, probable and possible breeding was registered in 48% of squares. Singing males are easy to detect on territory but confirmation of breeding is more difficult and was only achieved in 21% of the squares where nesting was suspected. The Clackmannanshire distribution corresponds closely with areas of suitable arable and open scrub habitat and, as well as the core areas of occurrence in central and western areas, it is also found along the course of the River Devon as far east as Muckhart.

The winter distribution in Clackmannanshire is not so widely spread as summer but because Scottish Yellowhammers are largely sedentary,[2] it is possible that this is indicative of flocks congregating in localised areas where there is an abundance of seeds, with winter stubble being particularly important.

The UK population of the Yellowhammer fell dramatically from 1975 to 1995, leading to a Red listing in 2002, after which the decline slowed.[3] In Scotland there was a less severe fall during the late 1980s and 1990s, after which BBS data show a population increase.[4] The biggest threats to the Yellowhammer population in Clackmannanshire are loss of suitable habitat and more efficient farming practices that result in a reduction of the availability of seeds.

Keith Broomfield

[1] *SE Scotland Atlas* [2] *BS3* [3] *BBWC* [4] *BirdFacts*

Breeding Distribution

Number of km² in which recorded:	96	(48.5%)
■ Confirmed breeding	20	(20.8%)
● Probable breeding	48	(50.0%)
• Possible breeding	27	(28.1%)
○ Present, breeding unlikely:	1	(1.0%)

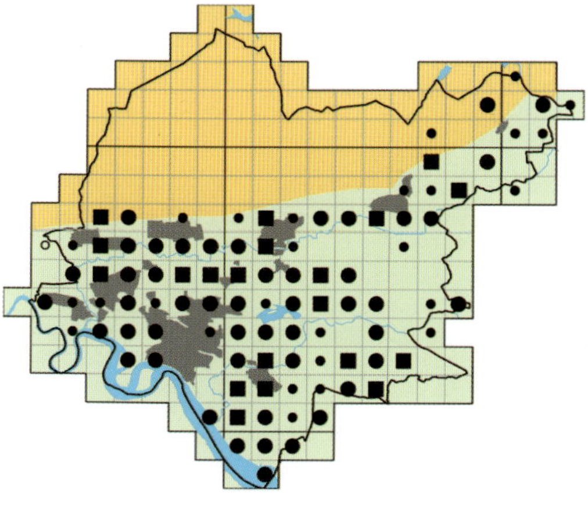

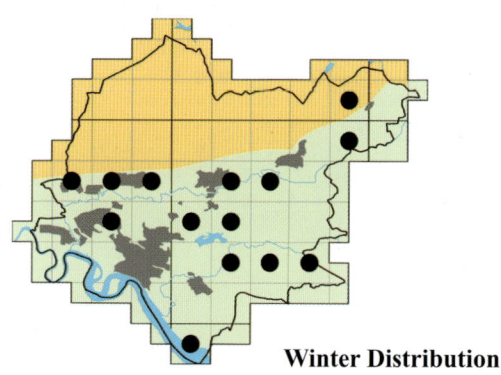

Winter Distribution

Reed Bunting   (Common Reed Bunting)   *Emberiza schoeniclus*

Fairly common resident, passage migrant

Conservation status: Amber

Although best known as a bird of damp margins of rivers, lochs ponds and other areas of marshy ground, the Reed Bunting also occurs in a variety of dryer habitats such as farmland and scrub.[1] This adaptability in habitat use is reflected in Clackmannanshire with confirmed, probable and possible breeding records accounting for 40% of squares.

There was a good spread of breeding registrations along the course of the River Devon and its associated wetland habitats. Other favoured areas include the mosses of central and eastern Clackmannanshire and along the River Forth, including the Blackdevon Wetlands. It is largely absent from the Ochils although it does occur in a handful of lower areas adjacent to water courses and where there is suitable ground cover.

The winter records were more sporadic with the majority concentrated towards the western half of the County, indicating a movement away from the higher reaches of the Devon and areas of high ground. From the very limited ringing recoveries in Scotland it is known that native Reed Buntings tend to show only localised movements in autumn and winter, generally from high ground to lower lying areas.[2] Seeds form an important food source during winter and flocking may occur on arable land.[3]

Changes in land use, in particular land drainage and the removal of rough margins, probably represent the most likely cause of localised extinctions in Clackmannanshire. Conversely, increases in Oilseed Rape production have benefited the Reed Bunting population on a UK scale,[4] as has its ability to exploit young conifer plantations.[5]

The BBS trend (1995-2007) shows a statistically significant increase of 57%, which has resulted in an improvement in the Reed Bunting's conservation status from Red to Amber.[6,7]

Keith Broomfield

[1] BS3 [2] ibid. [3] ibid. [4] BirdFacts [5] BS2 [6] Risely et al., 2009 [7] Eaton et al., 2009

Breeding Distribution

Number of km² in which recorded:	81	(40.9%)
■ Confirmed breeding	14	(17.3%)
● Probable breeding	43	(53.1%)
• Possible breeding	22	(27.2%)
○ Present, breeding unlikely:	2	(2.5%)

Winter Distribution

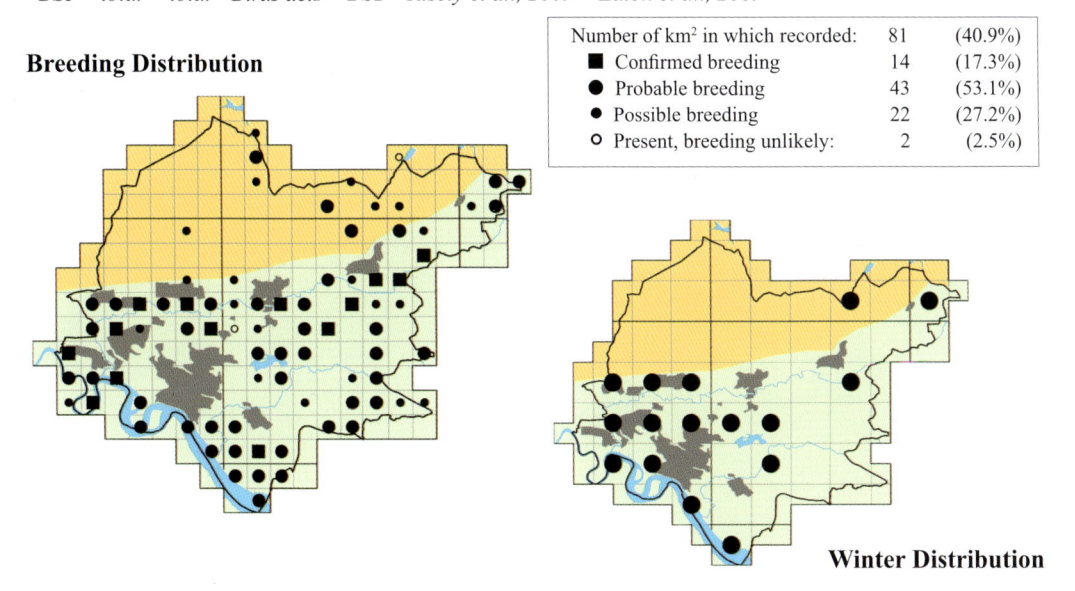

NON-BREEDING SPECIES

Whooper Swan *Cygnus cygnus*

Uncommon winter visitor   Conservation status: Amber

The Whooper Swan is primarily a winter visitor to Scotland with virtually all birds originating from the Icelandic breeding population.[1] The 2005 census recorded 4,142 birds which is 16% of the Icelandic breeding population and represents an increase of 66% over the 1995 census.[2] Although wintering birds occupy a variety of watery habitats where they feed on natural vegetation, increasing numbers are making use of agricultural food sources: typically moving from cereal stubbles to root crops, winter cereals, improved grasslands and increasingly, Oilseed Rape, as autumn progresses to spring.[3]

Since 1974, local Bird Report records indicate that the main daytime feeding areas in the County have been the Devon Valley downstream of Tillicoultry and along the length of the River Forth and its adjacent carselands.[4] The winter *Atlas* map shows them to be restricted to the lowlands with a western bias, which probably reflects suitable food sources during the survey period. Numbers range from single family parties up to herds of 117 (in partly harvested cereal at Cambus, January 2001) and 111 at Menstrie (December 1974). The highest count during the survey period was 32 at Blackdevonmouth Pool (February 2005).[5] Gartmorn Dam and the River Forth would appear to be the main roosts sites for these birds.[6,7]

First arrival dates are typically in mid to late October although small numbers have been recorded as early as 18 September. The latest dated sighting was on 4 April, although a bird summered at Tullibody Inch in 1975.[8]

Neil Bielby

[1] BS3 [2] Warden et al., 2006 [3] BS3 [4] UFABR [5] ibid. [6] Henty, 1977 [7] UFABR [8] ibid.

Winter Distribution

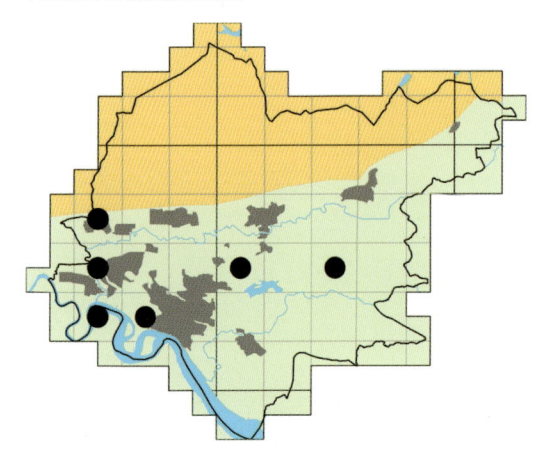

Pink-footed Goose *Anser brachyrhynchus*

Common passage migrant and winter visitor   Conservation status: Amber

From mid-September, Pink-footed Geese from breeding areas in Iceland and Greenland invade agricultural areas of Central Scotland, congregating in tens of thousands at favoured sites such as Strathallan and Loch Leven before fanning out across the country and further south. The Carse of Stirling, from the Lake of Menteith across to Tullibody is the main local wintering area. In late winter and spring the Alloa Inches and Haugh of Blackgrange areas, extending to the fields along from Fallin and down into Falkirk district, are more frequented. The low-lying ground from Clackmannan down to Kennetpans also hosts Pink-feet. With large concentrations around Loch Leven in neighbouring Kinross this goose can be seen and heard, certainly in flight, anywhere in Clackmannanshire. It is currently a very successful species, having significantly increased its total population since the mid-1980s.[1]

The Alloa Inch to Tullibody Inch area regularly hosts a flock of over 1,000 birds in April and some often linger into May. In 1992 there were still 410 at Alloa Inch on 2 May. Occasional Pink-feet seen during the summer are likely to be sick or injured. Four at Cambus on 8 August 1997 probably fell into this category though they could conceivably have been a locally-bred family (from a feral or 'pricked' pair).[2] Not surprisingly given these odd stragglers and the strong late spring migration, the breeding *Atlas* found Pink-feet in five grid squares near the estuary upstream from Alloa and also near Gartmorn Dam.

During the winter *Atlas* period birds were recorded in nine tetrads: six from the Devon valley between Alva and the Forth estuary, Blackgrange, and the Alloa Inches area, so broadly confirming the traditional distribution pattern, and three covering the Blackdevon Wetlands, Kennetpans and Gartarry areas in the south-east of the County.

David Thorogood

[1] BS3 [2] UFABR

Wintering Distribution

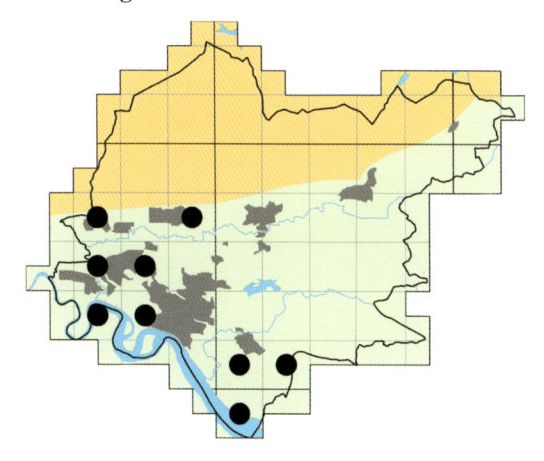

Greylag Goose *Anser anser*

Scarce introduced resident, common passage migrant and winter visitor
Conservation status: Amber

The Greylag Goose is a familiar bird in many parts of Clackmannanshire from autumn to spring. The clear impression from the local Bird Reports is that it is much more regular and numerous in the County than it was 30 years ago, though less numerous overall than the Pink-footed Goose. Coordinated counts suggest that there are now regularly around 1,500 birds in midwinter and spring, with an all-time record 2,000 strong flock at Blackgrange fields to the west of Cambus Pools on 20 March 2006. The Scottish wintering population was increasing until about 1990 but is now declining, possibly due to excessive shooting both in Iceland and Scotland.[1]

Winter distribution in the *Atlas* years was similar to that of Pink-feet in the west but extended somewhat farther up the Devon valley and also included a concentration around Gartmorn Dam and out to the eastern bounds of the County, involving 13 tetrads in all. Gartmorn Dam and the Forth estuary seem to be the most-used roost locations, but the various feeding flocks are not faithful to any one roost.[2]

The migrant Greylags that winter here breed in Iceland, but there is also a resident breeding population in Scotland, including an increasing number of feral birds.[3] It prefers to nest in dense vegetation close to the banks of extensive waters or on small islands in wetlands.[4] A pair was at Gartmorn Dam on 28 May 2007 but there was no suggestion that they were nesting. However, with similar occurrences during the period 2003 to 2005, the *Atlas* has classified the species as a 'probable' breeder. Greylags were noted in nine other grid squares away from Gartmorn during the breeding *Atlas* period, with the distribution broadly mirroring that in the winter. 19 birds at Cambus in August 2004 were probably from the Scottish feral population.

David Thorogood

[1] BS3 [2] UFABR [3] BS3 [4] BWP

Wintering Distribution

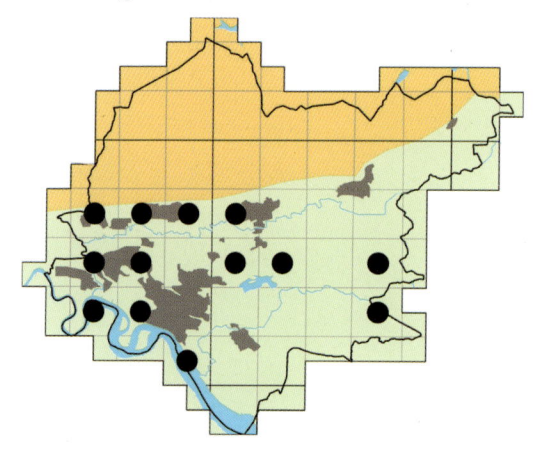

Barnacle Goose   *Branta leucopsis*

Scarce winter visitor and irregular passage migrant – mainly autumn
Conservation status: Amber

The Barnacle Geese seen in winter in the British Isles breed in Greenland and Svalbard. Many of the Svalbard birds, when heading south in autumn to the Solway Firth, track down the east side of Scotland,[1] and sometimes substantial flocks are seen crossing the upper Forth estuary usually during mid-September to mid-October. Greenland stragglers that have travelled south from Iceland with flocks of Pink-footed or Greylag Geese may stay with their host flock through the winter. These birds, sometimes family parties of up to six or seven, can then be seen feeding with the 'grey geese' on agricultural land throughout the local bird recording area. During the winter *Atlas* period single birds accompanying grey geese were found west of Menstrie and at Haugh of Blackgrange.

The occurrence of migrant Barnacle Geese is increasingly confused by the small but growing numbers of feral birds resident in Scotland. Any bird seen during the summer months or acting with an unusual lack of wariness will come under suspicion as being of this origin.

Recently published Clackmannanshire records are not all easy to interpret. Flocks of 150 at Kennetpans in October 1994 and 80 over Alloa Inches in September 1998 were almost certainly Svalbard migrants and most autumn and winter sightings of individuals and small groups with Pink-footed Geese and Greylags have probably also involved wild birds. However, some, especially around Alloa Inches, have lingered well into April and one at Cambus Pools was present on 23 May 2004 and so features on the breeding *Atlas* map. While 'host' grey goose flocks have lingered until May, this bird and one at Tullibody Inch in July 1993 seem likely to have been 'escapees' or of feral stock.[2]

David Thorogood

[1] BS2   [2] UFABR

Wintering Distribution

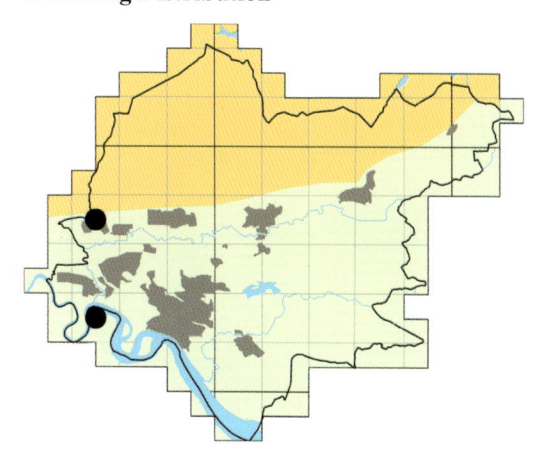

Wigeon (Eurasian Wigeon) *Anas penelope*

Common winter visitor and passage migrant　　　　Conservation status: Amber

At the southern end of its range, the Wigeon is an uncommon and localised breeder in Scotland with an estimated 240 to 400 pairs.[1] There are no records of confirmed breeding in Clackmannanshire. This survey produced just one record of a pair in suitable habitat (Blackdevon Wetlands), along with a smattering of late wintering/summering birds on the River Forth above Alloa and at Gartmorn Dam. Inland, grass sward (for grazing) adjacent to water bodies, appears to be a favoured habitat in the County during winter.[2]

Numbers of this highly migratory duck build steadily from October with the winter peak occurring between December and February.[3] Ringing returns indicate that these birds originate from Iceland, Scandinavia and Siberia.[4] The winter distribution map corresponds with results from local WeBS counts, the Forth, Gartmorn Dam and the Devon Valley around Alva being the main wintering locations.[5] The Forth between Cambus and Alloa currently appears to be the most important site with a maximum count of 1,268 birds in February 2005.[6] The high counts at Gartmorn Dam during the 1990s (with an estimated peak of 1,600 in January 1992), coincided with an adjacent area of grassland being managed for the benefit of grazing wildfowl.[7,8] Since 1999 groups of up to 200 birds have been recorded at Kersiepow Pond and the flooded fields below Alva. A group of 168 was noted on the Blackdevon Wetlands in February 2007, while 120 in January 1994 is the highest count for Kennetpans.[9] Shooting occurs primarily along the Forth but its effect on numbers is unknown.

Neil Bielby

[1] *BS3*　[2] *Pers. obs.*　[3] *WeBS*　[4] *Migration Atlas*　[5] *WeBS unpub. data*　[6] *UFABR*　[7] *ibid.*
[8] *M. Callan, pers.comm.*　[9] *UFABR*

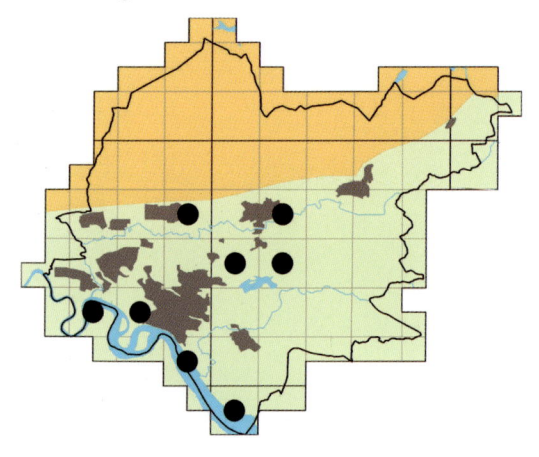

Wintering Distribution

Pochard   (Common Pochard)   *Aythya farina*

Uncommon winter visitor and passage migrant Conservation status: Amber

The Pochard is a scarce and localised breeder in Scotland with an estimated population of 25-50 pairs spread around suitable nutrient rich fresh waterbodies – mostly in the eastern lowlands.[1] No records of confirmed breeding were found for Clackmannanshire prior to the present survey.[2] Rintoul & Baxter mentioned having seen three on Gartmorn Dam in July 1934 but noted there was no proof of nesting.[3] There were only two records during the Atlas breeding survey: single birds at Gartmorn Dam and Cambus Pools, both of which were probably over-summering birds rather than putative breeders.

The Pochard is most familiar in the County as a passage migrant and winter visitor. Rintoul & Baxter note it being seen in "numbers (in winter) on Gartmorn Dam".[4] Ringing recoveries indicate that the bulk of these birds come from breeding grounds around the Baltic Sea and from Russia.[5] There is a marked passage through our area in October with most birds having reached their wintering sites by late November.[6]

Gartmorn Dam is the pre-eminent site for Pochard in Clackmannanshire during winter while small groups sporadically occur on the smaller ponds and, very occasionally, on the lower River Devon. There are only four records of Pochards on the River Forth with a count of 316 in February 1979 at Tullibody Inch being truly exceptional. The highest count in the County was 493 birds on Gartmorn Dam (February 1972)[7] but the peak count at this site during the *Atlas* survey period was only 31 (November 2005).[8] Wintering numbers throughout Britain have declined steadily since 1996/97, a trend mirrored in Clackmannanshire.[9] This decline is thought to be attributable to recent mild winters which have resulted in a north-east shift in the wintering distribution (so-called 'short stopping') with Sweden holding record numbers recently. [10,11]

Neil Bielby

[1] BS3 [2] UFABR [3] Rintoul & Baxter, 1935 [4] ibid. [5] Migration Atlas [6] WeBS unpub. data [7] UFABR [8] WeBS unpub. data [9] Austin et al., 2009 [10] Maclean et al., 2008 [11] Nilsson, 2008

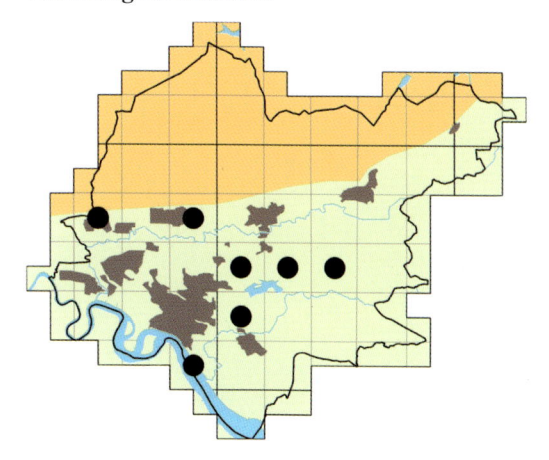

Wintering Distribution

Long-tailed Duck *Clangula hyemalis*

Irregular winter visitor   Conservation status: Green

Breeding on the tundra of the high Arctic, the Long-tailed Duck winters in large numbers at several select locations around the Scottish coast. It occasionally appears on inland fresh waters – mostly in October and November.[1] All three records on the winter map were recorded on the same day (5 November 2005) and could well refer to the same bird – especially as two of the sites (Longcarse Farm Pond and Maggie's Wood Pool) are very small and unlikely to provide much (or any) suitable food. The other site was Cambus Pools where it (or another bird) had been noted a couple of weeks earlier.[2]

Prior to the *Atlas* period, up to two birds had been recorded during the early winter at Gartmorn Dam in 1978, 1979 and 1982 along with single females at Gartmorn Dam and Cambus Pools in 1999.[3]

Neil Bielby

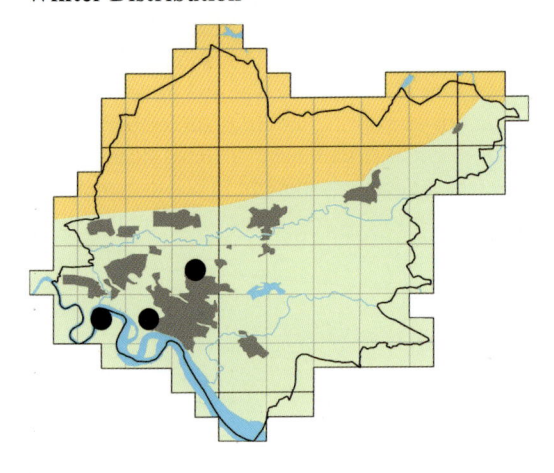

[1] BS3 [2] UFABR [3] ibid.

Winter Distribution

Goldeneye   (Common Goldeneye)   *Bucephala clangula*

Fairly common winter visitor and passage migrant   Conservation status: Amber

The first record of confirmed breeding for Goldeneye in Scotland was as late as 1970 – at Loch an Eilein on Speyside. The current breeding population is put at c.150 pairs with 95% of these being in Badenoch and Strathspey.[1] Although breeding has recently been confirmed in nearby Perth & Kinross, it has yet to be in Clackmannanshire, and the three records on the breeding map are almost certainly of lingering winter visitors or summering birds – a tendency first noted in this area by Rintoul & Baxter.[2]

A notable influx of winter visitors from northern Europe (mostly Scandinavia) occurs with the main arrival in late October.[3] Within the survey period peak counts for Clackmannanshire have ranged from 124 in January 2005 to 187 in February 2007.[4] The winter map hints at the variety of water bodies utilised by these birds the main ones being: the tidal River Forth; the lower River Devon and Gartmorn Dam. Low numbers also occur at several other smaller still-water sites. Considering its relatively narrow width the River Devon from Tillicoultry down to Cambus is surprisingly popular with wintering Goldeneye – a peak of 116 birds being recorded here in December 2002. Other notable counts during the *Atlas* period include 93 at Gartmorn Dam (March 2004) and 55 on the Forth between Cambus and Alloa (February 2005).[5] The highest historical count is of 222 birds on the River Forth at Alloa (December 1974).[6]

Since peaking in 1997/8, numbers of wintering Goldeneye in Scotland had fallen steadily to their lowest ever recorded level by 2006/7.[7] However, this trend has not been apparent in Clackmannanshire.[8]

Neil Bielby

[1] *BS3* [2] *Rintoul & Baxter, 1935* [3] *Migration Atlas* [4] *WeBS unpub. data* [5] *ibid.* [6] *UFABR* [7] *Austin et al., 2008* [8] *WeBS*

Wintering Distribution

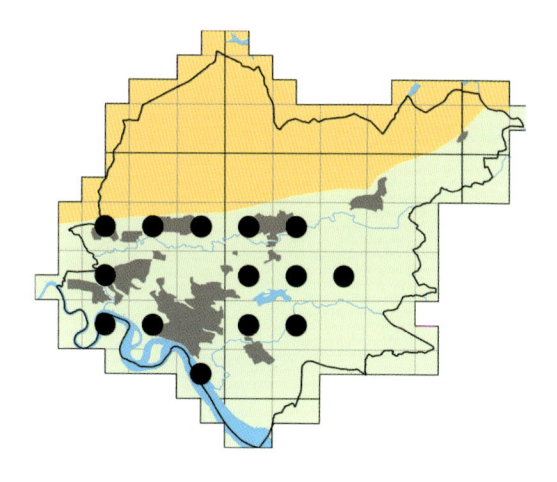

Red-breasted Merganser *Mergus serrator*

Locally common winter visitor and passage migrant   Conservation status: Green

The Red-breasted Merganser is a colourful and demonstrative duck, and while the male should present few identification problems, the female can be confused with its Goosander counterpart when not seen well. Three of the breeding season registrations were along the River Forth from Cambus to Longcarse with the other coming from the River Devon below Dollar – all were probably spring migrant birds.

Red-breasted Merganser has never been recorded as breeding in Clackmannanshire although there are stretches of river that appear to offer very similar habitats to those in the adjacent Stirling and Falkirk districts where it has bred in recent years.[1]

As the map suggests, the species is more or less confined to the tidal River Forth during winter with both numbers and occurrence decreasing markedly as one heads upstream. A maximum of 47 were recorded at Kennetpans during the survey period compared to just the occasional bird around Cambus (on the river and adjacent pools). Mid-winter inland records are rare but now and then birds have turned up at Gartmorn Dam and Delph Pond (Tullibody). Return spring migration appears to begin during the first half of February indicated by an increase in sightings both on the Forth and inland. Normally only a couple of birds are seen (usually a pair) which makes the 13 (seven males) on Delph Pond in February 2002 an exceptional happening.[2,3]

The British winter index has declined by 50% since peaking in the mid-1990s. The Forth Estuary is one of the main wintering sites in the UK but the 2006/7 peak of 347 birds was the lowest here for 15 years.[4]

David Thorogood

[1] *UFABR* [2] *ibid.* [3] *WeBS unpub. data* [4] *Austin et al., 2008*

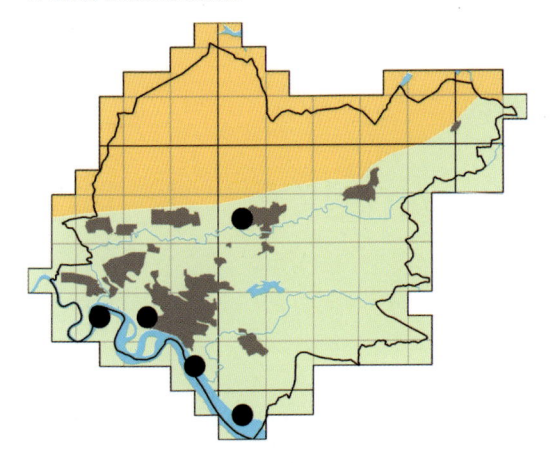

Winter Distribution

Cormorant   (Great Cormorant)   *Phalacrocorax carbo*

Fairly common visitor   Conservation status: Green

The Cormorants occurring in Scotland (subspecies *P.c.carbo*) are for the most part coastal and maritime birds though there are some inland breeding sites.[1] The nearest significant breeding area to Clackmannanshire is on the rocky islands in the outer Firth of Forth.[2] Locally the species is mainly associated with the Forth estuary, where maximum numbers usually occur in December or January. Cormorants were known to visit the Alloa Inches as far back as the late 18th century, when it was noted that the River Forth there supported a variety and profusion of fish.[3]

The Cormorants recorded in the County during the breeding *Atlas* period were exploiting local feeding or roosting opportunities and so feature on the breeding season map only as 'observed'. Their distribution, along much of the estuary, at Gartmorn Dam and in the lower Devon valley, was very similar to that of birds surveyed in winter when they penetrated slightly further up the Devon.

Cormorants will probably be seen in Clackmannanshire most often in flight, for they are great travellers, commuting over considerable distances between salt water and inland feeding waters, and also to find safe roost sites. The Alloa rail bridge, closed in 1968 and partially demolished a few years later, has been adopted as a secure and convenient night-time roosting site. The roost was well established by 1974 and is mainly occupied from September to March, although up to 90 birds have been found there in August and 15 in July. Greatest numbers (there have been two counts of 300 birds) occur any time between September and February. Most of the highest counts were made during the early 1990s, but there were 205 present in November 2004 and 99 in the same month in 2006. Small tree roosts have been observed at Gartmorn Dam.[4]

David Thorogood

[1] *BS2*   [2] *Cramp et al., 1974*   [3] *Statistical Accounts*   [4] *UFABR*

Winter Distribution

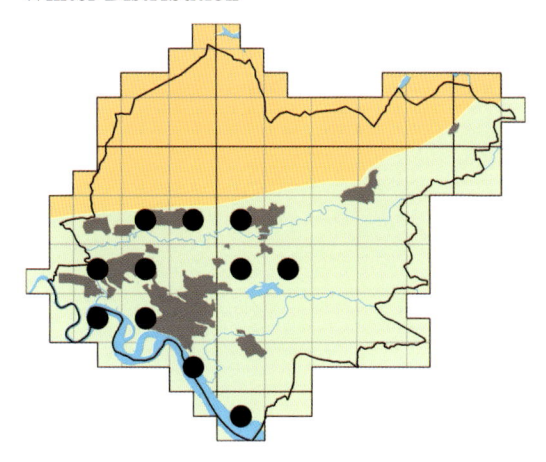

Hen Harrier   (Northern Harrier)   *Circus cyaneus*

Scarce winter visitor   Conservation status: Red

Although broadly sharing both breeding season and winter habitat preferences with the Merlin, the Hen Harrier is a much scarcer bird in Clackmannanshire. Over the period covered by the local *Bird Reports* (1974-2007) there have been no single bird sightings in summer in the Ochils that are definitely within the County.[1]

Thom,[2] summarising the recolonization up to the early 1980s of areas of Scotland from which it is fairly clear that the Harriers had been ousted because of game preservation, mentioned the Ochils as an area where new conifer plantations might attract the species to breed, but the plantations on the Hills are now generally too mature to suit Harriers. The most recent national review unfortunately suggests that Hen Harriers as breeding birds are once again on the decline in east and south Scotland because of continuing persecution on grouse moors.[3] Given reduced recruitment to the population, the generally low quality habitat, the levels of (unintentional) human disturbance on the Hills, and the possible negative effect of wind turbines, the prospects for seeing more of these fine birds on the Ochils are not good.

As an autumn migrant and wintering species the Hen Harrier is occasionally seen over the flatlands flanking the upper Forth estuary but there are very few Clackmannanshire records from this habitat.[4] The County fares a little better inland with a number of occurrences on the Hills, along the Hillfoots and around Gartmorn Dam. (The 2007 *UFABR* adds a male in Glen Devon in October). *Atlas* observers have confirmed this pattern of non-breeding occurrence, with one sighting near the estuary – a female or immature at the Blackdevon Wetlands site – and two inland, east and south-east of Gartmorn Dam.

David Thorogood

[1] *UFABR* [2] *BS2* [3] *BS3* [4] *UFABR*

Winter Distribution

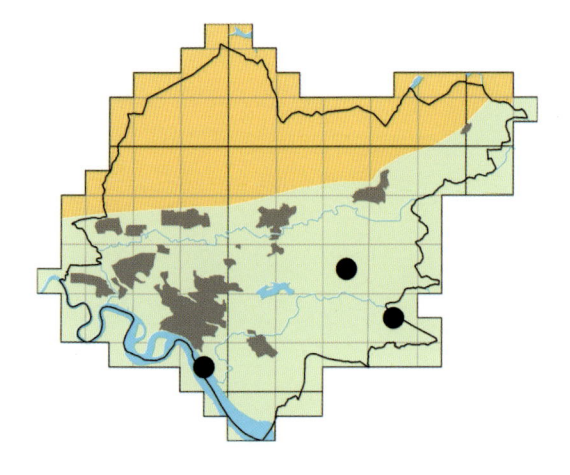

Golden Plover   (European Golden Plover)   *Pluvialis apricaria*

Irregular passage migrant, scarce former resident   Conservation status: Amber

In Britain, the Golden Plover breeds on moorland, peatland and arctic-alpine heath where climate (including exposure) and management (notably grazing and muirburn) maintain short vegetation.[1] Relatively flat terrain, rather than steep slopes, is preferred for nesting.[2,3] In winter they are found on lowland agricultural land and tidal flats,[4] though they can be found visiting some breeding moors in almost any month. The breeding population in Scotland has been estimated at 15,000 pairs.[5]

During the breeding *Atlas* period, a single bird was recorded on the southern edge of Alva Moss. Surveys in 1987 identified a minimum of nine breeding pairs within a 618 hectare study area of Alva Moss and a further two within 671 ha. of Menstrie Moss, most of which lies within the County.[6] Clearly this species has undergone a marked decline in common with some other moorland areas that were also surveyed in the 1980s.[7] The rolling terrain, relatively short vegetation and juxtaposition of blanket bogs and mineral soils on exposed hill tops still appear eminently suitable for breeding Golden Plovers. The only apparent difference with the 1980s is the abundance of predators; in 1987 no Carrion Crows, Rooks, Jackdaws or Lesser Black-backed Gulls were seen around Alva and Menstrie Mosses,[8] which contrasts with the period covered by this *Atlas*. The impact of predators on the ground-nesting birds of the Ochils and causes of the increased densities of predators deserves investigation.

Occasional groups of Golden Plovers have been recorded in the County in late autumn and spring with high counts of 165 at Tullibody Inch (October 1992) and 83 by Menstrie (November 1977). The only spring flock of note was 30 birds at Cambus (March 1980).[9] The sole autumn record during the *Atlas* period was of two birds along the River Forth between Cambus and Alloa (October 2005).[10]

John Calladine

[1] *Ratcliffe, 1976* [2] *Haworth & Thompson, 1990* [3] *Calladine et al., 1990* [4] *Fuller & Lloyd, 1981* [5] *BS3* [6] *Calladine et al., 1990* [7] *Sim et al., 2005* [8] *Calladine et al., 1990* [9] *UFABR* [10] *WeBS unpub. data*

Winter Distribution

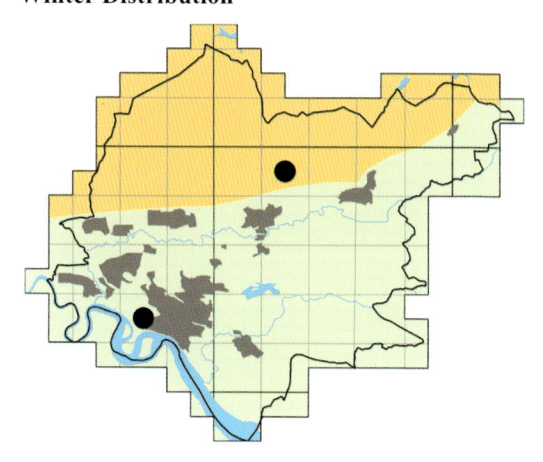

Dunlin   *Calidris alpina*

Scarce passage migrant and winter visitor   Conservation status: Red

The Dunlin breeds in several separate and distinct habitats throughout Scotland, and although limited areas in the Ochils might appear to provide suitable conditions, it has never been recorded as doing so there.[1,2] The two observed records by the River Forth on the breeding Atlas map are almost certainly of passage birds.

Three sub-species (*alpina, schinzii* and *arctica*) occur in Scotland but they all breed and winter in separate areas.[3] Identification of these sub-species in the field post-breeding is very difficult, but the occasional migrants recorded along the Forth in late summer (late June to September) are most likely to be *schinzii* birds which breed in the UK, Iceland, south-east Greenland and southern Fennoscandia.[4,5,6]

However, virtually all the birds which winter on the Upper Forth Estuary (peaking at c.9,700 individuals during the survey period)[7] are of the *alpina* race, which breeds in northern Fennoscandia and north-west Russia.[8] Almost all of these are located downstream of the Kincardine Bridge, but small numbers are found at Kennetpans and on the Cambus to Alloa stretch of the Forth, with up to 82 at the former location and 10 at the latter during the survey period.[9]

The Dunlin owes its Red listing to a decline in the UK non-breeding population of the race *alpina*. Scottish numbers have dropped 90% since peaking in 1995 (most of this fall occurred between the 2001/2 and 2006/7 winters), and by 2006/7 were back to the low levels of the mid 1980s.[10]

Neil Bielby

[1] BS3 [2] UFABR [3] BS3 [4] ibid. [5] Migration Atlas [6] UFABR [7] ibid. [8] Swann & Etheridge, 1996 [9] WeBS unpub. data [10] ibid.

Winter Distribution

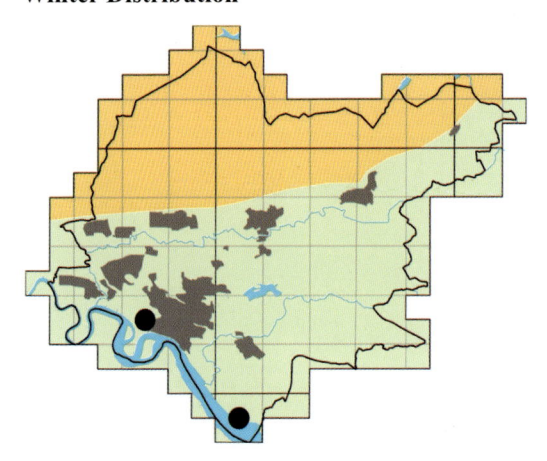

Jack Snipe *Lymnocryptes minimus*

Irregular winter visitor   Conservation status: Amber

The Jack Snipe breeds in Northern Eurasia in taiga, birch and willow-bog habitats.[1] In autumn and winter when it visits Britain it is often regarded as rare simply because it conceals itself so well, utilising a combination of cryptic camouflage plumage and a disinclination to move, even when almost trodden on. It has been encountered in Britain during the breeding season but there has been no proof that it has ever nested. Two remarkable records concern Clackmannanshire. One was found at Alva Moss, high in the Ochils, in spring 1987 by a NCC survey team, and on 22 May 1997 another turned up in the same place.[2] Were these simply late migrants just resting on their way back to Scandinavia or were they looking for somewhere suitable to breed? The habitat hardly seems suitable.

Jack Snipe are reported from Clackmannanshire only about one year in three, with inland sites slightly more frequently tenanted than estuarine ones. The Devon Valley around Alva has long been the most likely place to find the species. Generally only single birds are reported but up to four together have occurred by the Devon and three at Blackdevon Wetlands. A very early migrant turned up at Cambus pools on 21 August 1996.[3]

Three were found during the winter *Atlas* period, one in a fairly open situation on frozen ground at 330 metres on the flank of Dollar Glen on 9 December 2006, one sharing a flooded marsh with Common Snipe in the Muckhart Community Woodland area in February 2007, and the third at Blackgrange in January 2007. Subsequently one was found at Kennetpans in November 2007.[4]

David Thorogood

[1] BWP [2] UFABR [3] ibid. [4] ibid.

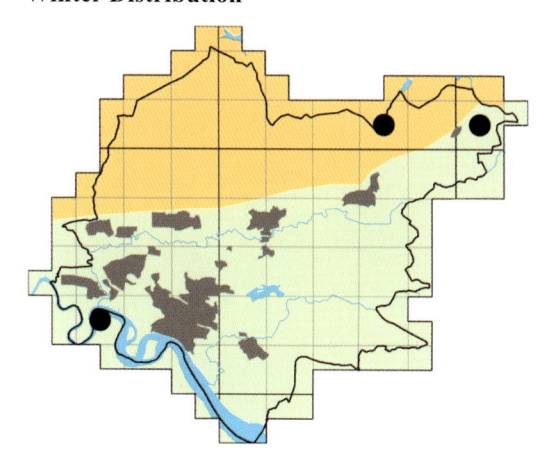

Winter Distribution

Black-Tailed Godwit *Limosa limosa*

Locally common passage migrant and winter visitor

Conservation status: Red

In Iceland the Black-tailed Godwits which visit Clackmannanshire and nearby areas downstream along the River Forth breed in lush vegetation in lowland fields and marshes. During the breeding *Atlas* surveys the species was recorded in three squares containing such habitat, and in one area near the estuary the presence of birds into late spring warranted registration of 'possible breeding'.

Rintoul & Baxter's 1935 account treats this Godwit like a great rarity,[1] and it was very uncommon along the upper Forth estuary into recent times. There was a very small wintering population and a few passage birds, with most reports coming (as now) from the Falkirk shore. From about 1990 however numbers began to grow significantly with a wintering population of over 400, mirroring increases at other east-coast sites such as the Eden estuary in Fife.[2,3]

Overall, County records mainly reflect a spring and autumn passage. In the 2004 *Bird Report* there is reference to a 'good spring passage' at Cambus Village Pools, with at least 74 'bird-days' between 17 April and 1 May. A similar run of records in 2006 did not tail off until 4 June. There were two birds at the site on 28 July, but by that time juveniles are beginning to arrive from Iceland. Sightings further inland in the County are very rare indeed; one at Gartmorn Dam in August 1984 seems to be unique in recent decades. Until 2007 numbers recorded in Clackmannanshire had always been relatively small, with 53 birds at Tullibody Inch in December 2006 being the largest single gathering so far in the County, and apparently among the first midwinter occurrences. However, on 22 April 2007, 200 were recorded at Cambus Village Pool with an astonishing 425 at the adjacent Devonmouth Pool the following day.[4]

David Thorogood

[1] *Rintoul & Baxter, 1935* [2] *UFABR* [3] *Fife Atlas* [4] *UFABR*

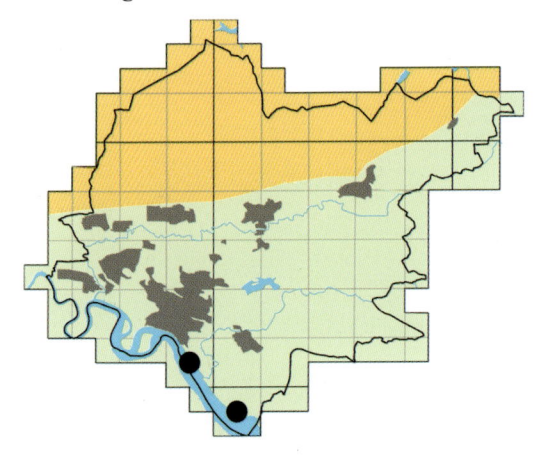

Wintering Distribution

Black-headed Gull   (Common Black-headed Gull)   *Chroicephalus ridibundus*

Common visitor   Conservation status: Amber

Black-headed Gulls forage mostly on lowland grassland and freshly-ploughed arable fields, or over and around muddy estuaries, but also exploit grassed areas (and discarded waste) in urban areas. Clackmannanshire is therefore an attractive area for the species and many people probably assume that it nests locally. However, of all the species recorded during the breeding *Atlas* period this was the most widespread for which no proven breeding occurred. Rintoul & Baxter[1] and Thom[2] also reported no breeding records for the County.

Some birds seen in Clackmannanshire in summer are presumably non-breeders but others may be foraging from colonies in neighbouring districts. Presence was recorded in 53 squares but 'possible breeding' in only one, in the Devon valley near Tillicoultry where the broad flood-plain contains rushy patches and ephemeral pools. Otherwise it was mainly found along the Rivers Devon and Forth, and in or close to many of the urban areas of the west and centre of the County. Strangely it was only reported from one of the four squares containing Gartmorn Dam. Although largely absent from the Ochil Hills it was found by the Glen Quey Reservoir, which looks a possible nesting place, and also near the Upper Glendevon Reservoir. Few were mapped in the more wooded south-eastern parts of the County, but there was a concentration in the north-east, around Muckhart, possibly of birds nesting at Loch Leven.

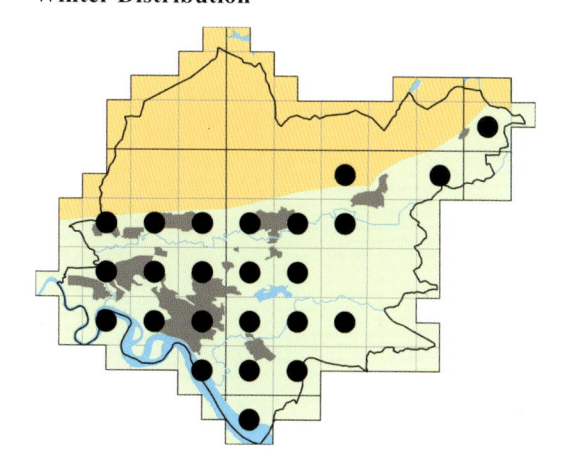

During the winter *Atlas* period the distribution of Black-headed Gulls was very similar to that recorded in the summer. They were found in 24 lowland tetrads with only areas south and south-east of Dollar not visited. Substantial flocks have been noted quite widely, mainly by the Forth estuary, in any month from September to March. 4,000 at Tullibody Inch in December 1996 seems to be the largest modern count.[3]

David Thorogood

[1] Rintoul & Baxter, 1935   [2] BS2   [3] UFABR

Winter Distribution

Great Black-backed Gull *Larus marinus*

Uncommon visitor   Conservation status: Amber

For breeding purposes this is a very maritime bird, in Scotland seeking out offshore islands and inaccessible coastal rock pinnacles. The world population has increased and its range expanded during the 20th century and in Scotland it has spread as a breeder to the north-east.[1] Rintoul & Baxter, considering the whole Forth basin, classed it as a "winter visitor; non-breeding birds remain throughout the summer"[2] This is still a fair description of its status in the Clackmannanshire area.

Birdwatchers, by and large, give less attention to these gulls than they deserve. The local Bird Reports[3] for this species do not include records of less than five birds, so that the value of a concerted Atlas survey effort is well demonstrated for this under-recorded bird. It was found during the breeding season, though obviously only as a casual visitor, in 15 lowland squares, representing much of the middle and lower Devon valley, parts of the Forth estuary, and the vicinity of Gartmorn Dam and the lower Black Devon. During the winter period it was more tied to the estuary but again occurred in the Devon valley and at Gartmorn. There was no evidence of its former habit of visiting the high Ochils.[4]

Generally these birds seem to move up the estuary in late summer and autumn and some stay on through the winter, usually around the Inches. Many are likely to come from more northerly breeding areas such as Norway and perhaps Iceland.[5] There would have been larger numbers when open municipal refuse tips at Kinneil, Alloa and Fallin provided both food and relatively undisturbed loafing and roosting sites. There were 150 Great Black-backed Gulls at Tullibody Inch in August 1990, but a gathering of 47 at Alloa Inch in December 2001 is probably more typical of recent numbers in the County.[6]

David Thorogood

[1] 1968-72 Atlas [2] Rintoul & Baxter, 1935 [3] UFABR [4] ibid. [5] BS2 [6] UFABR

Winter Distribution

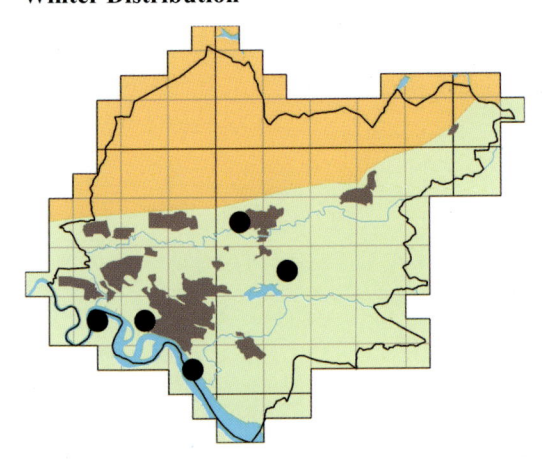

Guillemot   (Common Murre)   *Uria aalge*

Irregular winter visitor

Conservation status: Amber

The Guillemot, nesting on coastal and island cliff ledges and wintering at sea, seems an unlikely species to appear in an account of the birds of Clackmannanshire. County records have, nevertheless, featured in eleven of the local annual *Bird Reports*[1] and the species was encountered in two tetrads along the River Forth upstream of Alloa during the winter *Atlas* period.

Many past occurrences were attributed to bad weather 'wrecks',[2] sometimes only apparent when tide line corpses were discovered. A widespread incident in February 1986 resulted in 40 dead birds being found at Cambus.[3]

There has been an increase in sightings of Guillemots in the upper Forth estuary over the last decade with the regular appearance of healthy birds moving up and down the estuary.[4] This indicates that the area is probably within the normal post-breeding dispersal range of the species, so in autumn it is now less obvious what constitutes a normal influx and what may be part of a 'wreck'. During 19 to 20 November 1988 hundreds were seen moving up-river from Bo'ness to Kincardine Bridge, seven were at Cambus and at least one got as far as Manor Powis. The appearance of two on the River Devon at Alva a few days later suggests that at least some of these birds became disorientated. At Cambus on 22 October 1990 at least 75 were present.[5] In October 2004 the WeBS counters noted 53 Guillemots between Kincardine Bridge and Alloa, and another 124 upstream to Cambus. In the same month the following year that survey reported 48 birds between Alloa and Cambus, and then eight at Alloa Inch in November.[6]

David Thorogood

[1] *UFABR* [2] *Rintoul & Baxter, 1935* [3] *UFABR* [4] *Pers. obs.* [5] *UFABR* [6] *WeBS*

Wintering Distribution

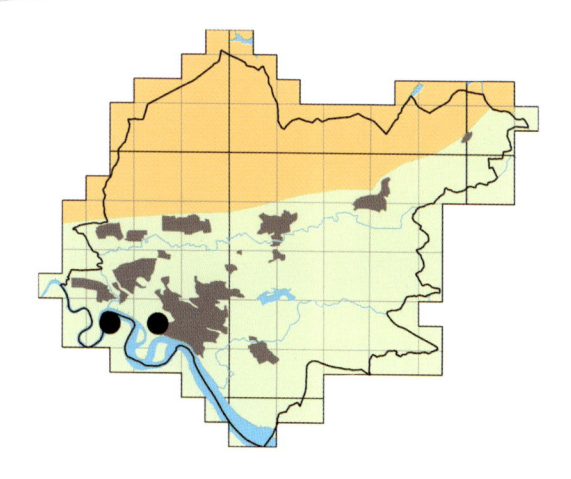

Fieldfare   *Turdus pilaris*

Common passage migrant/winter visitor   Conservation status: Red

Fieldfares are winter visitors to Britain. They are found in most lowland areas in Clackmannanshire, with no records in the upland areas. Distribution is likely to be more widespread in the lowland areas than that shown by the map.[1] The six records during the *Atlas* breeding season refer to birds recorded in April just prior to departure for their breeding grounds.

The Fieldfare is a rare breeder in Britain, limited to less than five pairs per year in 1998-2007,[2] with only two to three in Scotland.[3] In Britain the species is Red-listed due to a long-term breeding population decline between 1973 and 2008.[4,5] There are no breeding records for Clackmannanshire, the nearest records being in Perth & Kinross.[6]

Within the County Fieldfares occupy lowland agricultural land in the winter, feeding in fields, hedgerows, and open wooded areas. They are often found in large groups regularly consisting of several hundred individuals.[7] The largest flock recorded was 7,500 at Cambus during an influx in October 1982. The earliest recorded winter arrival date in Clackmannanshire was 7 October in 1990, and the latest departure 15 May in 2000.[8]

Annual passage and wintering numbers in Clackmannanshire vary annually, as they do elsewhere in Scotland, depending on food supplies in Fennoscandia and the wind direction during migration.[9] More information would be useful on the location and sizes of flocks during the winter to provide further details on habitat use in the County.

Chris Pendlebury

[1] UFABR [2] Holling et al., 2009, Jan 2010 [3] BS3 [4] Holling et al., 2009, 2010a&b [5] Eaton et al., 2009 [6] BS3 [7] BWP [8] UFABR [9] BS3

Winter Distribution

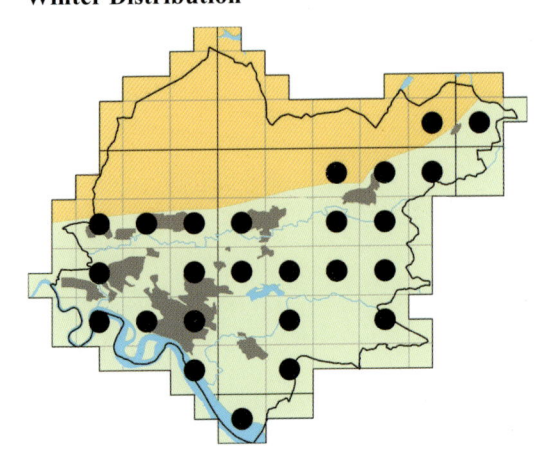

Redwing *Turdus iliacus*

Common passage migrant and winter visitor   Conservation status: Red

Redwings are predominantly winter visitors to Britain. The species is distributed throughout lowland areas of Clackmannanshire, as well as the edges of the Ochil Hills. There were no records during the breeding *Atlas* fieldwork.

In Britain, there is a small breeding population, mainly in Scotland, with less than 40 pairs recorded per year in Scotland between 1995 and 2004.[1] The species is Red-listed due to a long-term breeding population decline between 1973 and 2008.[2,3] Although breeding has occurred between 1970 and 2000 in neighbouring Perth & Kinross and Clyde in four years and two years respectively,[4] it has never been noted in Clackmannanshire.

During the winter Redwings are generally numerous in the Hillfoots glens and slopes when clear of snow. The favoured winter habitat is open fields but they will also use open woodland edges, parks and gardens.[5,6] Redwings are generally gregarious, often found in groups of up to 100-200. Flock sizes of up to 500 have been recorded on several occasions in the County.[7] The earliest recorded winter arrival date in Clackmannanshire was 3 October, and the latest departure date was 29 March, both in 1974.[8]

There is variability in wintering numbers in Scotland, including Clackmannanshire, due to the size of the autumn passage, food supplies and weather conditions.[9] More reports involving the racial identity of birds, perhaps from trapped birds, would provide information on the natal origin of wintering Redwings in the region and the frequency of occurrence of the Icelandic race (*T. i. coburni*) compared with the more common continental race (*iliacus*).

Chris Pendlebury

[1] BS3 [2] Holling et al., 2009, 2010a & b [3] Eaton et al., 2009 [4] BS3 [5] ibid. [6] BWP [7] UFABR [8] ibid. [9] BS3

Wintering Distribution

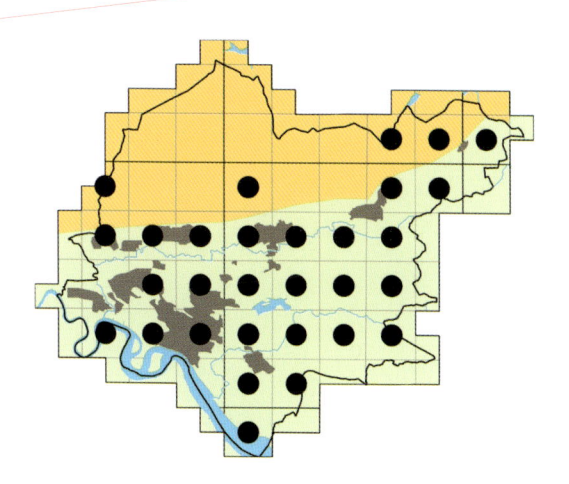

Brambling   *Fringilla montifringilla*

Uncommon and irregular passage migrant and winter visitor   Conservation status: Green

The brindled, tortoiseshell plumage and white rump of the Brambling make it conspicuous among the flocks of Chaffinches with which it normally associates when not feeding on its favourite winter food – beech mast. There have only been around 10 confirmed breeding records in Scotland (all in the northern half). Thus, even though two of the four Clackmannanshire breeding season registrations were of singing birds, as these were on 24 April and 1 May and males are known to pause on migration – singing for up to two weeks – it is very unlikely that these would have been breeding birds.[1]

Several million pairs breed in Northern Europe, but Britain lies on the edge of their wintering range and visiting numbers fluctuate markedly from year to year, according mainly to weather conditions (and thus food availability) on the continent.[2,3] Arrival into Scotland begins in mid-September with the earliest record for Clackmannanshire being 29 September (Muckhart 1984).[4,5] Records from only two tetrads would suggest that the *Atlas* winters were lean ones for Brambling. Indeed, the area Bird Reports have only noted them in the County during a third of the past 34 winters. Normally recorded numbers are in single figures but 175 were observed in Harviestoun Woods (October 1990) and 150 in stubble at Kersiepow (December 2001).[6]

Neil Bielby

[1] BS3   [2] BirdFacts   [3] BS3   [4] Migration Atlas   [5] UFABR   [6] ibid.

Wintering Distribution

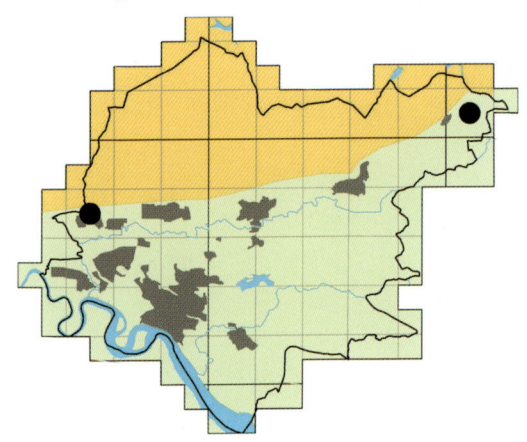

Other species recorded during the Atlas period

Bewick's Swan   (Tundra Swan)   *Cygnus columbianus*

Vagrant   Conservation status: Amber

One of two subspecies, *C.c.bewickii* breeds in northern Russia and winters from western Europe across to Japan. It was a widespread and regular winter visitor to Scotland during the late 19th and early 20th centuries with large flocks recorded on the Outer Hebrides and Tiree.[1] However, by the 1950s Baxter & Rintoul considered that it had virtually disappeared from this country.[2]

Currently, Bewick's Swan is a rare visitor and passage migrant to Scotland with a total of c.100 birds recorded annually – mostly in Fife and south-west Scotland.[3] Relatively large numbers still winter in England, most abundantly on the Ouse and Nene Washes and at Slimbridge, but a recent census in January 2009 (producing 4,153 birds) showed a continuing decline in numbers since a peak in the early 1990s. This decline is mirrored on mainland western Europe and is now being attributed to population decrease on their breeding grounds rather than any impact on their wintering quarters resulting from climatic change.[4]

A single bird (with 10 Whooper Swans) on the Haugh of Blackgrange from 29 October to 2 November 2003 is the only record for the County.[5]

Neil Bielby

[1] *BS3*   [2] *Baxter & Rintoul, 1953*   [3] *BS3*   [4] *Calbrade et al., 2010*   [5] *UFABR*

White-fronted Goose   (Greater White-fronted Goose)   *Anser albifrons*

Vagrant   Conservation status: Red

About 12,500 White-fronted Geese of the Greenland race *flavirostris* migrate south-east from their breeding grounds on the Arctic coastal fringe of west Greenland to winter in around 30 distinct locations spread across the north and west of Scotland, with Islay holding approximately 69% of this population.[1,2]

A total UK-wide ban on shooting in 1981 saw numbers rapidly increase from c.7,000 to a peak of 22,117 in the 1998/9 winter. Since then numbers have steadily fallen to a UK total of 12,506 in March 2009, probably due to low breeding success exacerbated by shooting during their autumn migration through Iceland.[3] A ban on Icelandic hunting introduced in autumn 2006 has slowed the decline. However, breeding success still remains too low to sustain the population which has fallen to its lowest level in 20 years, causing its conservation status to be upgraded to Red.[4,5]

There are only three records for the County: a single bird at Gartmorn Dam in November 1991, 13 at Alloa Inch in February 1993, and three birds on the Haugh of Blackgrange in February 2007. The birds in the latter record were among a large flock of mixed 'grey geese', which often contain vagrant birds. [6,7]

Neil Bielby

[1] *Calbrade et al., 2010*   [2] *BS3*   [3] *Fox et al., 2006*   [4] *ibid.*   [5] *Eaton et al., 2009*   [6] *BS3*   [7] *Fife Atlas*

Canada Goose *Branta canadensis*

Locally common visitor   Conservation status: Not Assessed

The Canada Goose is, by its very name, an 'alien' species, introduced to Britain at various times from as early as the 1660s,[1] but there is no local evidence of occurrence before 1982.[2] There is a well-documented movement of Canada Geese from Northern England to the Beauly Firth and Caithness, mainly during May-July and returning late August-September,[3] and this involves birds regularly flying over east Central Scotland, including Clackmannanshire.

The few records during the 1980s and 1990s generally fit this moult migration pattern but occasional birds visited Gartmorn Dam in winter. Since 2004 both numbers and distribution have expanded more in line with the situation in neighbouring areas, where breeding has occurred since 1985 and there are now regularly large concentrations west of Stirling and at some Perthshire lochs. Most recent County occurrences have been along the Forth estuary and at Cambus pools, with the largest flocks to date being 216 at Tullibody Inch (August 2005) and 70 at Alloa Inch (September 2007).[4,5]

Gartmorn Dam offers an obviously attractive potential breeding location, though Canada Geese will nest by any standing water from secluded ponds to large lakes, and also by rivers. They may also nest on moorland some distance from water. During the breeding *Atlas* period, although birds were found near the estuary between Cambus and the Inches there was still no evidence of breeding having occurred in the County. In winter, rather surprisingly given some of the previous occurrences, Canada Geese were found in only one tetrad, by the estuary near Alloa.

David Thorogood

[1] Lever, C. 1977   [2] UFABR   [3] BS2   [4] McGowan, R.   [5] UFABR

Brent Goose   (Brant Goose)   *Branta bernicla*

Vagrant   Conservation status: Amber

Two subspecies of Brent Goose regularly occur in Scotland: *hrota* (Pale-bellied Brent Goose) and *bernicla* (Dark-bellied Brent Goose).[1]

The main wintering sites of the Svalbard and north-east Greenland breeding populations of *hrota* are in Denmark and at Lindisfarne (Northumberland). They occur as scarce passage migrants down Scotland's east coast – mostly in autumn (September/October) although a small flock of 20-30 birds has recently taken to wintering in the Nairn area. Conversely, the eastern Canadian breeding population of *hrota* which winters in Ireland is observed on autumn and spring passage in both the Inner and Outer Hebrides. Again, small flocks have been noted overwintering around Loch Ryan (Dumfries and Galloway) and on Islay (Inner Hebrides) in recent years.[2]

The subspecies *bernicla* (Dark-bellied Brent Goose) breeds in north-central Siberia and winters around the coasts of north-west Europe. Despite c.72,000 wintering on the south and east coasts of England (February 2009) it remains a 'scarce passage migrant and even scarcer winter visitor' to Scotland with most records coming from the east coast south of Rattray Head.[3,4]

In 1906 the Brent Goose was noted as being 'common …. on the upper reaches of the Firth of Forth and along the Stirlingshire shore' but Rintoul & Baxter recorded it as being only 'occasionally' seen there in 1935.[5] There are only two records for Clackmannanshire: a single bird at Tullibody Inch (4 February 1979) and one at Kennetpans (subspecies *bernicla*) in October 2004.[6]

Neil Bielby

[1] *BS3*   [2] *ibid.*   [3] *ibid.*   [4] *Calbrade et al., 2010*   [5] *Rintoul & Baxter, 1935*   [6] *UFABR*

Red-breasted Goose   *Branta ruficollis*

Vagrant   Conservation status: Not assessed

The Red-breasted Goose breeds around the Taymyr peninsula of Arctic Russia and winters mainly around the Black Sea. Very occasionally individuals attach themselves to flocks of mainly Dark-bellied Brent Geese (*Branta bernicla bernicla*) (or less frequently, of European White-fronted Geese (*Anser albifrons albifrons*)) on the breeding grounds – migrating with them to Western Europe.[1]

Such a bird, discovered on the Haugh of Blackgrange in early February 2007, was the first record for Clackmannanshire and the 15th for Scotland. Although this bird has been accepted by the BBRC, the possibility of it being a free-flying escape or released bird cannot be totally ruled out. The last recorded sighting was on 15 April 2007.[2] Scottish birds have usually been found in flocks of Pink-footed, Greylag or Barnacle Geese, to which it is thought they transfer while in Western Europe.[3] The Blackgrange bird was often observed with up to c.3,000 Pink-footed Geese although its feisty nature ensured it a small oasis of space within the dense ranks.[4]

Neil Bielby

[1] *BS3*   [2] *UFABR*   [3] *BS3*   [4] *Pers. ob.*

Pintail   (Northern Pintail)   *Anas acuta*

Irregular winter visitor   Conservation status: Amber

The Pintail is a very numerous species breeding right across the northern hemisphere from temperate latitudes to the Arctic.[1] In Clackmannanshire it is a winter visitor, arriving in September (rarely August) and generally departing in March. A few are present in April and very occasionally into May.[2]

The exceptional occurrence of a single male at Cambus Village Pools in June 2005 during the breeding *Atlas* period seems to be the only modern mid-summer record. Pintail are only sporadic nesters in Britain, utilising a wide range of open-country waterside and wetland habitats. They have nested in Fife and at Loch Leven, so it is possible that they will breed in the County in the future.[3,4] No birds were found during the winter *Atlas* surveys but there was a male at Gartmorn Dam in December 2004.

Rintoul & Baxter noted a historical report of presence at Alloa.[5] During the 1950s the early Wildfowl Counts for the Forth estuary between Grangemouth and the mouth of the River Devon established a regular winter population figure of 170 birds and a maximum count of 490.[6] The modern local Bird Reports caught the last of these larger upper-estuary gatherings, including 50 at Tullibody Inch in March 1975. Since then five at Alloa Inch at the end of August 1992 has been the most recorded together in the County, and it seems that spectacular flocks of this elegant duck are no longer to be seen here. Numbers downstream have held up rather better, with a winter peak monthly flock, usually at Skinflats in January, ranging between 29 and 150 birds,[7] but these do not seem to venture above Kincardine Bridge.

David Thorogood

[1] *Madge & Burn, 1988* [2] *UFABR* [3] *Fife Atlas* [4] *Allison, Newton & Campbell, 1974* [5] *Rintoul & Baxter, 1935* [6] *Atkinson-Willes, 1963* [7] *UFABR*

Garganey   *Anas querquedula*

Irregular summer migrant   Conservation status: Amber

Scotland lies at the western limit of the Garganey's breeding range and although most records are presumed to be of overshooting birds in spring, it is occasionally recorded as breeding in Scotland and it is thought that up to two pairs nest annually.[1]

During the *Atlas* period single males were recorded at Cambus Pools (13 May 2004) and Cambus Village Pool (21 May 2006). Prior to this there are only two records for the County, both of males at Cambus Pools (in April 1987 and May 1994).[2] The habitat at Cambus Pools, being near the tidal River Forth and with abundant emergent vegetation, would appear to fulfil the breeding requirements for the species. If the climate continues to warm then it may breed here, but proving this for such a secretive bird could prove difficult.[3]

Neil Bielby

[1] *BS3* [2] *UFABR* [3] *BS3*

Shoveler   (Northern Shoveler)   *Anas clypeata*

Scarce passage migrant, may have bred   Conservation status: Amber

While an estimated 260 to 390 pairs breed in Scotland, the Shoveler has never been proved to do so in Clackmannanshire.[1,2,3] The *Atlas* breeding distribution map shows only one probable record – a pair in the Blackdevon Wetlands. The latest date for pairs at this site is 1 May,[4] so these birds could well have been on passage – as was presumed for birds further up the River Forth at Tullibody Inch, Cambus Village Pools and Cambus Pools in April and early May. In the period of modern local Bird Reports (1974 to 2007) there have been 14 records between mid-May and mid-July. Of these, 10 are from the Cambus area and it was noted that 'they may have nested' at Cambus Pools in mid June 1989.[5]

Records from the local Bird Reports are suggestive of an equally strong spring (March-May) and autumn (August-October) passage, peaking in April for the former and August the latter.[6] The peak for autumn passage birds in Scotland is in September and October with an influx of birds from north-west continental Europe and Russia.[7] It is possible that the August peak for sightings in Clackmannanshire comprises local Scottish birds at the start of their passage to their wintering quarters in southern England and western continental Europe. Sightings rarely number more than five birds but there were 24 at Alloa Inch in August 2002.[8]

Winter records are scarce with only four in November, one in December, none in January and two in February. No Shovelers were recorded during the winter *Atlas* period but a bird was present at the Blackdevon Wetlands in December 2007.[9]

Neil Bielby

[1] BS3 [2] *Rintoul & Baxter, 1935* [3] UFABR [4] ibid. [5] ibid. [6] ibid. [7] BS3 [8] UFABR [9] ibid.

Scaup (Greater Scaup) *Aythya marila*

Irregular winter visitor   Conservation status: Red

Although there have been occasional records of Scaup breeding in Scotland, virtually all of the country's wintering population is raised on the arctic or sub-arctic tundra in Iceland, Fennoscandia and northern Russia. Although a few birds can be found around the Scottish coast (especially at their wintering haunts) throughout the summer, the main return from the breeding grounds starts during September, building to a Scottish peak of c.5,000 birds by mid-winter.[1,2]

Essentially a sea-duck (a few do turn up on inland water bodies), Scaup tend to congregate in favourite locations such as the Solway Firth, Loch Ryan, Islay, Orkney and the Inner Moray Firth.[3]

Although Rintoul & Baxter commented that they were known to 'penetrate' up the Forth 'to Stirling and beyond',[4] the first known record for Clackmannanshire is of three males at Gartmorn Dam on 21 July 1974. Subsequently, there have been 12 more records in the County, all except two being from Gartmorn Dam: a bird was at the mouth of the River Devon in September 2006 while a first winter male and female were at Silverhills Pond, Kersiepow in November 2008.[5]

The Scaup owes its recent Red listing to a severe decline (>50%) in the non-breeding population that has occurred over the longer term.[6]

Neil Bielby

[1] *BS3* [2] *WeBS* [3] *BS3* [4] *Rintoul & Baxter, 1935* [5] *UFABR* [6] *Eaton et al., 2009*

Ruddy Duck *Oxyura jamaicensis*

Introduced irregular visitor, possible breeder   Conservation status: Not Assessed

The Ruddy Duck is a recent addition to the British avifauna. A considerable irony, in the light of the recent controversial attempts to eradicate the species, or at least drastically to reduce its numbers, is that it largely owes its presence in the British Isles to escapes and releases from what is now the Wildfowl & Wetlands Trust in Gloucestershire during and after 1952.[1] Trial culls began in 1999 with the ultimate aim of lessening the numbers of birds emigrating to Continental Europe (particularly Spain) – birds which threaten the conservation status of the related White-headed Duck (*O. leucocephala*) through inter-breeding.[2]

In Scotland the species now breeds sparsely across most of the Central Lowlands (perhaps 50 pairs) and sites in Fife were included in the early trial culling.[3,4] In the upper Forth area breeding was first recorded in 1991.[5]

In Clackmannanshire Ruddy Ducks have occurred at Gartmorn Dam occasionally since 1992 but have so far shown no definite signs of breeding. Two males were seen displaying in May-June 1995 and there have been mixed parties or pairs in subsequent years, but usually in the winter half of the year.[6] During the breeding *Atlas* period a male was seen at Cambus Pools in May 2003. Ruddy Ducks breed around relatively shallow still waters, including quite small pools, with fringing emergent vegetation, and nest well on into summer when ducklings will have plenty of opportunity for concealment.[7] The Gartmorn and Cambus records therefore could well presage breeding attempts. The winter *Atlas* period again produced a record from Gartmorn Dam, in February 2006.

David Thorogood

[1] *Hudson, 1976* [2] *Central Science Laboratory (CSL), 2002* [3] *BS3* [4] *CSL, 2002* [5] *UFABR* [6] *ibid.* [7] *Hudson, 1976*

Black Grouse   *Tetrao tetrix*

Irregular visitor   Conservation status: Red

Black Grouse are birds of the moorland fringe, typically where heather moorland merges with farmland or woodland or both. They are a lekking species, where the males display, often communally, and the females visit the lekking males in spring to select the best apparent mating partners. Formerly found on moors and heaths throughout Britain, by the end of the 20th century, the species had become restricted to the uplands and their margins.[1] Sensitive to high levels of grazing,[2] (and other land uses that lead to the degradation and simplification of the habitat mosaics on the moorland fringe) and the maturation of conifer plantations, the population in Scotland was estimated to include 2,580-4,171 lekking males in 2005, representing a 29% decline since 1995.[3]

During the *Atlas* period the only records of Black Grouse in Clackmannanshire were of two near Burnfoot Hill in upper Glen Devon.[4] They were noted as nesting in the County but 'seemed to be decreasing' in 1935.[5] In 1974 38 were recorded on Wood Hill in February and 21 on Alva Moss in November.[6] In 1987 Black Grouse were also reported from Menstrie Moss,[7] and there are anecdotal reports of them from the Ochil hills above Alva and Dollar from around the same time.

Although the future prospects for Black Grouse in Clackmannanshire appear bleak; if suitable conditions could be re-established, including more native-type woodland planting in the hills and the relaxation of grazing intensities, (particularly in winter to permit the development of more extensive cover by ericaceous plants) it is not inconceivable that this charismatic species could return, as in spring 2007, two male and a female Black Grouse were seen in Glen Quey within one kilometre of the Clackmannanshire boundary, in an area that has recently been planted to re-establish extensive native-type upland woodland.[8]

John Calladine

[1] Baines & Hudson, 1995 [2] Calladine, Baines et al., 2002 [3] Simm et al., 2008 [4] Burnfoot Wind Farm EIA
[5] Rintoul & Baxter, 1935 [6] UFABR/C.J. Henty pers.com. [7] Calladine et al., 1990
[8] Calladine, Garner et al., 2008

Quail (Common Quail) *Coturnix coturnix*

Vagrant   Conservation status: Amber

Usually heard rather than seen, the Quail is an 'uncommon and erratic' summer visitor to Scotland with an estimated 20-100 calling males in a typical, non-irruptive year (in 1989 there were c.750!). Normally, the first birds arrive in early May followed by the main influx during the middle of that month.[1]

The *Old Statistical Account* for Alloa mentions it as being abundant in the breeding season with a few sometimes found in autumn. Even though the arable fields of the carse (and elsewhere in the County) would appear to provide suitable habitat, a male seen on NS 9293 (May 2007) during *Atlas* fieldwork is the only recent record for Clackmannanshire.

Neil Bielby

[1] *BS3*

Red-necked Grebe   *Podiceps grisegena*

Vagrant   Conservation status: Amber

The Red-necked Grebe is essentially a non-breeding visitor to Scotland with the largest numbers being found in the outer Firth of Forth – notably Gosford Bay during the late July/August flightless moulting period and off Gullane in spring. Very occasionally, it can turn up anywhere around the Scottish coast (and even less frequently inland), but Scapa Flow and the Moray Firth are the only other locations where it is recorded on a regular basis.[1]

Although birds occasionally over-summer; and have been observed attempting to breed on several occasions in both the Lothians and Borders since 1980, the first confirmed breeding for Britain was only obtained (from a Borders site) in 2001. [2,3]

Scottish Red-necked Grebe are of the nominate subspecies *grisegena* and are believed to originate from the north-west European breeding population.[4]

The sole Clackmannanshire record is of a bird on Gartmorn Dam (1 December 2002) on a day with fresh south-easterly winds.[5]

Neil Bielby

[1] *BS3* [2] *ibid.* [3] *Murray, 2003* [4] *BS3* [5] *UFABR*

Little Egret   *Egretta garzetta*

Vagrant   Conservation status: Amber

Until the early 1990s the Little Egret was recorded only sporadically in Scotland. However, at this time, sharply increasing numbers in southern England led to the first record of confirmed breeding in Britain at Brownsea Island, Dorset in 1996. Since then, the increase in numbers and associated northward breeding expansion of the Little Egret in the UK has continued apace, with the high of count of 3,437 in September 2006 being five times that of a decade earlier.[1] This has had a knock-on effect in Scotland with a marked increase in the subsequent number of records to a peak of 26 birds in 2002.[2]

In the 50 years to 2004, more than 50% of all Scottish records were during May and June,[3] so it comes as no surprise that the first (and so far only) record for Clackmannanshire was on 18 May 2003.[4] This was of an adult in breeding plumage at Cambus Village Pool (during survey work for this *Atlas*).

Assuming a continuation in the amelioration of our climate, it can only be a matter of time before both the second record and breeding occur in the County.

Neil Bielby

[1] Austin, G. et al., 2008 [2] BS3 [3] ibid. [4] UFABR

Spoonbill   (Eurasian Spoonbill)   *Platalea leucorodia*

Vagrant   Conservation status: Amber

The Spoonbill is a regular but very scarce passage migrant to Scotland with most records coming from the east coast. Sightings of several colour-ringed birds since 1975 have established that almost all of these originated from the expanding population in the Netherlands.[1] In 2008 a pair fledged three young in the Kirkcudbright Bay area of south-west Scotland. This is considered to be the first breeding record for the species in Scotland and the third for the UK in modern times.[2]

The first record for Clackmannanshire was of a single bird at Cambus Village Pool on 13 May 2000 while the second was at the same location during the *Atlas* period on 20 December 2006. Subsequently, two birds were seen at Tullibody Inch on 2 July 2010.[3]

Neil Bielby

[1] BS3 [2] Collin, P., 2009 [3] UFABR

Red Kite *Milvus milvus*

Vagrant   Conservation status: Amber.

As part of an ongoing UK-wide reintroduction scheme, 103 young Red Kites from eastern Germany were released near Doune (Stirling District) between 1996 and 2001. The population in central Scotland in 2009 was 55 breeding pairs fledging 74 chicks.[1] Many birds have spread north and west from their original release area into West Perthshire, but there has been no corresponding spread eastwards into Clackmannanshire. There are only two recent records in Clackmannanshire from the local Bird Reports – one was on Ben Buck on 28 August 2004 and another was sighted on Ben Cleuch on 10 May 2008.[2]

Rintoul & Baxter described the Red Kite as 'Formerly resident; now very rare visitor'. They also noted that 'They are mentioned in the *New Statistical Account* for Alloa; while from Tillicoultry, in 1841, comes this record: "Once an everyday object, is never seen in this part of the country". Their final record for the Upper Forth area was of a bird at Loch Ard in 1917.[3]

Despite supposedly living in more enlightened times regarding the persecution of birds of prey, illegal poisoning, whether deliberate or unintentional, is still considered a major limiting factor regarding both the increase in numbers and expansion in range of the Red Kite in Scotland.[4]

Keith Broomfield

[1] *RSPB press release, October 2009* [2] *UFABR* [3] *Rintoul & Baxter, 1935* [4] *BS3*

Marsh Harrier (Western Marsh Harrier) *Circus aeruginosus*

Vagrant   Conservation status: Amber.

The Marsh Harrier is a scarce migrant breeder and passage migrant in Scotland. Although there had been sporadic breeding attempts noted previously from various locations in Scotland between 1937 and 1980, the first recorded confirmation was from the Tay Reedbeds in 1990. Subsequently occasional successful breeding has also been reported from several other sites in the country and from three to nine females were known to have bred each year between 1994 and 2004.[1]

There are two records for Clackmannanshire: a female/immature was quartering the Tullibody Inch reedbeds (2 May 1988); and a radio-tagged juvenile female from the Tay Estuary was logged roosting on Tullibody Inch on 12 September 2006, staying in the general area until at least the 21st. It was last recorded at Poole Harbour (Dorset) on 10 October 2006 after which no further signals were received.[3]

Given that the Tullibody Inch reedbed lies adjacent to rich arable land (a preferred habitat mix for breeding Marsh Harriers)[4] the species may well attempt to breed here, especially if its recent expansion in Scotland continues.

Neil Bielby

[1] *BS3* [2] *ibid.* [3] *UFABR* [4] *BS3*

Goshawk (Northern Goshawk) *Accipiter gentilis*

Vagrant   Conservation status: Green

The Goshawk is a scarce breeding bird in Scotland with 75% of the estimated 130 pairs being located in the Borders, Dumfries & Galloway and north-east Scotland. Having being eradicated from Scotland in the late 19th century by game-shooting interests, the current population stems from birds imported by falconers from Europe, with the majority of these being thought to originate from Fennoscandia. Many of these birds were released deliberately in order to establish a feral breeding population. However, a few also escaped while being flown by their owners.[1]

There are only two records for the County: a single bird at Muckhart (19 September 1984)[2] and a bird during the *Atlas* period near Dollar (21 April 2004). Given the dates both could well be of wandering birds (very small numbers are thought to migrate irregularly from Fennoscandia to Scotland in autumn)[3,4] although the mature coniferous plantations near Forestmill and to the north-east of Dollar would appear to provide suitable nesting habitat.

Monitored Scottish Goshawks show a consistently high breeding success rate and it is considered that illegal persecution is the major factor limiting their spatial and numerical expansion.[5]

Neil Bielby

[1] *BS3* [2] *UFABR* [3] *BS3* [4] *Migration Atlas* [5] *BS3*

Osprey *Pandion haliaetus*

Vagrant   Conservation status: Amber

The Osprey's successful recolonization of Scotland since the 1950s is well known although, contrary to popular belief, it is now known that it did not become totally extinct as a breeding species between 1916 and 1954. It is now considered that some of the occasional breeding attempts during this period were successful, notably at Loch Garten in 1935, 1947 & 1952.[1] In 2007 the number of recorded pairs in Scotland stood at c.220.[2]

The Osprey's catholic taste in both fresh and salt-water fish species as well as in nest sites has undoubtedly aided this expansion, but despite colonizing the Upper Forth to the west of Stirling in some numbers during recent decades – and despite there being apparently suitable habitat in Clackmannanshire – there has been no indication of the Osprey breeding here. Even more surprisingly, there are only two records for the County: a bird at Gartmorn Dam (22 August 1994) and during the *Atlas* period, in Mill Glen, Tillicoultry (12 May 2007).[3]

Neil Bielby

[1] *BS3* [2] *Scottish Osprey Study Group* [3] *UFABR*

Ruff   *Philomachus pugnax*

Scarce passage migrant   Conservation status: Red

The male Ruff present in the Cambus area from 5 to 23 May 2007 was the first record of a spring bird in Clackmannanshire.[1] During its stay it acquired full breeding plumage and was observed displaying to a small group of Icelandic Black-tailed Godwits from 17 to 23 May. As the Ruff is an extremely rare breeder in Scotland, it is difficult to tell if this was a very late passage bird or a putative breeder (males are known to display during spring passage).[2,3] The 'probable' record on NS 8692 during the same period almost certainly concerns the same bird.

Autumn passage through the County is much more pronounced with record dates in the local Bird Reports ranging from 31 July to 22 Oct with a pronounced peak during the second half of August. All the records are from along the River Forth with the Cambus area and Tullibody Inch appearing to be the most favoured locations. The largest count is of 14 birds at Tullibody Inch in late August 1980.[4]

Although there have been occasional records of birds in the Grangemouth area of the Forth Estuary in winter, none have been noted during the November to February period in Clackmannanshire.[5]

The Ruff's move from Amber to Red listing is due to a recent decline in the British breeding population.[6]

Neil Bielby

[1] *UFABR* [2] *BS3* [3] *BWP* [4] *UFABR* [5] *ibid.* [6] *Eaton, M.A. et al., 2009*

Bar-tailed Godwit   *Limosa lapponica*

Irregular winter visitor and passage migrant   Conservation status: Amber

Of the Godwits, the Bar-tailed although common and formerly much the more numerous bird on the upper Forth estuary, seems to attract less attention than its Black-tailed congener, possibly because it is much less often seen in its even more colourful breeding plumage. It is mainly an autumn and winter visitor, with peak numbers usually occurring between December and February and the species favours the wider inter-tidal shores downstream of Clackmannanshire, where it outnumbers the Black-tailed Godwit by about four to one.[1] There has been a significant decline recently in average numbers wintering in Scotland,[2] though WeBS counts suggest that numbers in the Forth estuary as a whole show a less marked decline than elsewhere.[3] The 2004 local Bird Report noted that by then this was the scarcer of the two godwits, and it is now uncommon above Kincardine Bridge.[4]

The local Reports document few Clackmannanshire occurrences. Between 1974 and 2004 there were mentions in only seven years, with Tullibody Inch and Cambus the usual locations, generally for single birds and often during autumn passage rather than in winter. In January 1998 there were four at Kennetpans and in recent years this site has produced more reports; five birds in September and December 2005 and a surprising 31 in January 2006. The 2007 Report adds four at Alloa Inch on 29 August.[5]

The 2005 and 2006 records are the ones shown on the winter *Atlas* map.

David Thorogood

[1] *Austin et al., 2008* [2] *BS3* [3] *Austin et al., 2008* [4] *UFABR* [5] *ibid.*

Whimbrel *Numenius phaeopus*

Irregular passage migrant

Conservation status: Red

The Whimbrel – smaller, darker and neater-looking than the closely-related Curlew – breeds in Shetland, sparingly in the Outer Hebrides, Orkney and northern mainland Scotland, and more commonly across the sub-Arctic from Iceland to western Siberia.[1] Northward spring passage through Scotland is typically concentrated along western coasts, but it may turn up almost anywhere, and the beautiful seven-note whistling call is sometimes heard over land at night during May. Autumn passage is mainly in August with more chance then of the species occurring on eastern coasts including the upper Forth estuary, with birds lingering for a while at suitable feeding sites.

Rintoul & Baxter said there were "many records from both sides of the Firth of Forth" but did not specifically include Clackmannanshire in that summary.[2]

Whimbrels are not common now along the tidal upper Forth. During the 1970s and 1980s very few were seen in Clackmannanshire and most records downstream were during the autumn. Sometimes small parties turn up in the County such as the 11 birds at Cambus in 1998. Birds passing overland have been noticed on three occasions, twice in May and once in September, and always at or near Alva (which may reflect the distribution of local observers rather than the existence of any regular flight-path).[3] Nine birds at The Rhind in April 2006 assured the Whimbrel of a place in this *Atlas*, though only by their presence. (Some Whimbrels do nest in lowland grassland, but breeding so far south in Scotland away from the west coast would be unprecedented).[4]

David Thorogood

[1] BS3 [2] Rintoul & Baxter, 1935 [3] UFABR [4] BS3

Green Sandpiper   *Tringa ochropus*

Scarce passage migrant and irregular winter visitor   Conservation status: Amber

The Green Sandpiper has the most un-wader-like habit of laying its eggs in the discarded tree nests of other species in the Eurasian taiga zone. It has bred rarely in northern England and Scotland (Inverness-shire 1979), and summering birds continue to occur occasionally in the Highlands.[1] Further south in Scotland it is a migrant and an irregular wintering species, generally favouring freshwater or brackish sites more so than the coast or estuaries. Its bold plumage pattern, distinctive call and a tendency to flush as an observer approaches make it unlikely to have been overlooked by *Atlas* surveyors.

During the breeding *Atlas* period one Green Sandpiper was seen at Cambus village pools on 25 June 2004; an unusual date for a migrant but certainly not involving a site where nesting would be suspected.

Records and editorial comments in the area Bird Reports indicate that the species is now more common as a winterer than as a passage migrant in the upper Forth estuary area.[2] In Clackmannanshire there are modern records in most months of the year, with the overwhelming majority coming in August. There is also evidence of a small spring passage in April and May. Despite the statements referred to above, records suggestive of wintering in Clackmannanshire came only in 2000/01 and 2001/02, at Blackdevon Wetlands in each case. Cambus Pools is the location most frequently visited by passage birds, with Blackdevon Wetlands, Devonmouth and Kennetpans also favoured. Surprisingly there are only a couple of inland records – at Craigrie Pond (not far from the Wetlands) in August 1981 and by the River Devon near Alva in March 2000. The latter bird could also have been a winterer rather than an early spring migrant.[3]

David Thorogood

[1] *BS3* [2] *UFABR* [3] *ibid.*

Greenshank   (Common Greenshank)   *Tringa nebularia*

Scarce passage migrant and irregular winter visitor   Conservation status: Green

The Greenshank may be perceived as a quintessentially Scottish bird because the Nethersole-Thompsons' two classic monographs were substantially based on field research on breeding birds in the Spey valley and NW Scotland.[1,2] However, Scotland hosts only a tiny proportion of the overall northern Eurasian breeding population of this moorland, moss and forest-bog nesting wader. Passage and wintering visitors to the upper Forth estuary may include Scottish-bred birds but many are also likely to come from farther afield. The vast bulk of the population winters further south, from Africa east to Australia.[3]

During the breeding *Atlas* surveys it occurred only once; a single bird seen at Cambus pools on 14 July 2003. This may have been an early returning migrant or a bird that had summered, but only the date causes it to appear on the 'breeding' map.

The *New Statistical Account* listed Greenshank among the birds occurring in Alloa parish.[4] Rintoul & Baxter's Forth area characterisation: "A passage migrant; occasional winter visitor"[5] is probably still broadly true for Clackmannanshire, but during the winter *Atlas* period, no Greenshanks were recorded. It is a noisy and conspicuous species and it is unlikely that the monthly WeBS surveys, for instance, will have overlooked any birds present.[6] In earlier years the largest number reported in the County from one site was ten at Alloa Inch on 30 August 1992. Cambus is by far the most regular site in the County with birds also recorded from Alloa and Tullibody Inches, the Blackdevon Wetlands and Kennetpans. There are two inland autumn records from the Devon Valley near Dollar, of single birds on 5 October 1997 and 7 September 1998. Overall, autumn records outnumber spring ones by a factor of ten to one.[7]

David Thorogood

[1] *Nethersole-Thompson, D., 1951* [2] *Nethersole-Thompson, D. & M., 1979* [3] *BWP* [4] *NSA*
[5] *Rintoul & Baxter, 1935* [6] *WeBS* [7] *UFABR*

Arctic Skua   (Parasitic Jaeger)   *Stercorarius parasiticus*

Vagrant   Conservation status: Red

The Arctic Skua is at the southern end of its breeding range in Scotland with the main area for the species in this country being the Northern Isles. In spring most birds pass up the west coast during April and May while, in contrast, return passage during autumn occurs largely down the east coast. Birds tend to stay close to the shore and records in the local Bird Reports show that they occur annually in the Grangemouth area, with the main period being August to October although they have been noted as early as 20 July and as late as 27 November.[1,2]

The only record for Clackmannanshire is of a juvenile flying east at Cambus (4 November 2002) although three birds seen from South Alloa during the previous month may well have been within the County. With several parties observed heading west from Grangemouth over the years, there are three suggested possible reasons for the dearth of records further up-river in Clackmannanshire. Firstly, that stretch of the Forth flowing through the County is under-watched compared to that below Kincardine Bridge; secondly, the birds may be at a greater height as they pass over on their way to the Clyde and thirdly, a direct flight line from Grangemouth to the Clyde Estuary would take them well to the south of the County.

The Arctic Skua's recent dramatic move from the Green to Red list is due to an estimated decline of c.70% in Shetland and c.77% in Orkney during the past 22 years.[3]

Neil Bielby

[1] *BS3*   [2] *UFABR*   [3] *Eaton et al., 2009*

Iceland Gull   *Larus glaucoides*

Vagrant   Conservation status: Amber

Iceland Gulls breed in Greenland and between 50 and 100 birds normally winter in Scotland. The bulk of these are found around the fishing ports of the north and west coasts where discarded fish waste is the attraction. Lerwick, Stornoway, Ullapool, and Mallaig and to a lesser extent, Fraserburgh, Peterhead and Ayr, have been the favoured locations. Occasional aggregations of over 30 birds at the first two ports have been recorded since 1990.[1]

There are three records for the County: first-winter birds were at Cambus (29 March 1993) and the old Alloa tip (1 July 1999) with a bird during the *Atlas* period at the Blackdevon Wetlands (12 February 2006).[2]

Neil Bielby

[1] *BS3*   [2] *UFABR*

Glaucous Gull   *Larus hyperboreus*

Vagrant   Conservation status: Amber

The Glaucous Gull is primarily a winter visitor to Scotland (October to April) with the majority of the estimated annual 50-100 birds being recorded in the Northern and Western Isles. Here, and elsewhere in Scotland, they tend to be found at the major fishing ports – often having followed the boats back in. However, in recent years, a few have been recorded inland, either at landfill sites or at their adjacent roosts or daytime loafing areas.[1]

Very occasionally, large influxes of Glaucous Gulls have been documented. One such was during the winter of 1872-73 when Rintoul & Baxter relate that there was a huge influx during which Gray and his party 'saw as many as two hundred Glaucous Gulls, this including adults and young, between Alloa and Kincardine-on-Forth'.[2] These were apparently with 'thousands' of other gulls following shoals of Herring.[3]

The only modern record for the County is of an adult in winter plumage on the Haugh of Blackgrange (5 November 2002).[4] This bird was with c.3,000 Herring Gulls which had presumably been foraging on the nearby Polmaise refuse tip.[5]

Neil Bielby

[1] *BS3*   [2] *Gray, R., 1873*   [3] *Rintoul & Baxter, 1935*   [4] *UFABR*   [5] *Pers. obs.*

Sandwich Tern *Sterna sandvicensis*

Irregular passage visitor   Conservation status: Amber

Sandwich Terns nest at wide intervals around British coasts and in Scotland are largely confined to a few large colonies, currently including islands in the outer Firth of Forth.[1] Wintering in Britain is by no means rare and is becoming more frequent and has included odd birds in the Firth of Forth. Late summer and autumn gatherings of adults and juveniles extend into the area between Kincardine Bridge and the Forth Bridges. These terns have roosted in very large flocks at places such as Valleyfield ash lagoons.[2,3,4]

During the breeding *Atlas* period Sandwich Terns were seen in spring and summer along the estuary at least as far upriver as Blackgrange. One at Tullibody Inch on 19 June 2005 and two at the same locality on 4 June 2006 were very early for 'autumn' migrants, and could have been failed breeding birds from the outer Forth.[5] This colonial nester is an unlikely candidate for breeding status in Clackmannanshire.

The early Area Bird Reports have only one record of Sandwich Terns in Clackmannanshire, at Alloa in 1975, but from 1990 they are regularly mentioned at sites along the estuary up as far as Cambus, usually in August and September. Improved observer cover rather than any change of status may explain the apparent increase. 60 birds at Tullibody Inch in August 1992 and 120 at Kennetpans in September 1994 are the largest concentrations reported from the County. On a number of occasions in late summer or autumn birds have been noted in circumstances suggesting that there may be an overland passage towards the west coast of Scotland.[5]

David Thorogood

[1] *BS3* [2] *BWP* [3] *BS3* [4] *Fife Atlas* [5] *UFABR*

Common Tern *Sterna hirundo*

Scarce passage migrant   Conservation status: Amber

Although Common Terns will breed in a variety of inland locations near water and formerly often did so in Scotland, nowadays almost all Scottish birds feed and breed at the edge of the sea or by estuaries.[1] Their breeding numbers can fluctuate; indeed Rintoul & Baxter noted this as long ago as 1935 for the River Forth with colonies along the outer Firth and on the islands coming and going.[2] (They, incidentally, did not refer at all to the upper estuary in their account of the Common Tern). The only regular nesting colony now in the Upper Forth Area (over 100 pairs) is to be found on platforms within the security-guarded docks at Grangemouth.[3,4]

Adult Common Terns from Grangemouth may perhaps range far up the estuary, but most of those recorded in the County are probably migrants or post-breeding birds. In September 1975 a "light passage" of Common Terns (with Sandwich Terns) moving westwards up-river was recorded at Alloa and much more recently juveniles have been seen at South Alloa (Falkirk District) in August and September. There are a few spring and early summer records from the Forth at Cambus and the nearby pools, and autumn (mid–August to mid–October) occurrences from the same sites and elsewhere beside the estuary such as Kennetpans.[5] Some of the Cambus occurrences were during the breeding *Atlas* period, when Common Terns were observed in five estuarine squares, extending up as far as Blackgrange. The general paucity of records along the narrowing upper estuary suggests that it is not a particularly good feeding area for the species, otherwise one might expect Common Terns to find a nesting niche somewhere along the less frequented parts of the Clackmannanshire shore.

David Thorogood

[1] *Rintoul & Baxter, 1935* [2] *ibid.* [3] *Cramp et al., 1974* [4] *UFABR* [5] *ibid.*

Short-eared Owl *Asio flammeus*

Scarce winter visitor, has bred sporadically   Conservation status: Amber.

The Short-eared Owl is a bird of moor, grassland and marsh. Despite being the least nocturnal of our owls it is much overlooked in the breeding season, the number of breeding birds varying considerably in response to fluctuations in numbers of Field Voles – its principal prey.[1] Numbers declined substantially between 1970 and 1990, and though they are now stable it is regarded as a depleted species across Europe, the reason for its Amber listing.[2] Apart from vole numbers, distribution and breeding success are also affected by the availability of newly planted conifers – a habitat which has declined in recent years.[3]

The present *Atlas* surveys provided lean pickings: one 'observed' registration at Cambus and one 'possible breeding' in the Ochils above Dollar during the breeding season, and a single record on the carseland south of Alloa in the winter. Despite the small number of records, there does appear to be a pattern: breeding in the Ochils, wintering on the carse. This fits with other recent local records of individual birds around the Cambus/Alloa area, usually in winter or early spring (including five on the foreshore at Blackdevon Wetlands in January 2007),[4] and with records of breeding in the eastern Ochils in 1991 when two pairs raised four and five young each, and again in 1992 though broods were lost to predation by Peregrines.[5]

Recoveries of ringed birds suggest that some British breeding Short-eared Owls winter in Continental Europe, and that there is a substantial influx of Scandinavian birds in late autumn, especially along the east coast.[6] It is therefore possible that the owls found wintering in and around Cambus are Continental breeders.

The BTO is finalizing a methodology for surveying and monitoring these birds,[7] which is likely to fill gaps in our knowledge of this rather elusive raptor in the future.

John Grainger

[1] Etheridge et al., 2008 [2] Eaton et al., 2009 [3] Mead, 2000 [4] UFABR [5] ibid. [6] Migration Atlas
[7] Calladine et al., 2007

Hooded Crow *Corvus cornix*

Vagrant   Conservation status: Green

The Hooded Crow, since 2002 afforded specific status, was reported as having bred at Alloa in 1793.[1] Other comments in the same source suggest it may have continued to breed in the County into the 19th Century, but by the time of the *1968-72 Atlas* it had already retreated to the north and west ahead of the spreading Carrion Crow.[2] There are occasional autumn and winter records in the County, but one by the River Devon at Alva in July 2007 was unusual.[3]

David Thorogood

[1] Rintoul & Baxter, 1935 [2] 1968-72 Atlas [3] UFABR

Wood Warbler *Phylloscopus sibilatrix*

Scarce summer visitor and passage migrant Conservation status: Red

Compared with the Willow Warbler and Chiffchaff, the Wood Warbler is more contrastingly plumaged, presenting a lemon-yellow face and throat above a pure white belly. Although it mainly uses the tree canopy it betrays its presence by its diagnostic song which sounds like a spinning coin on a marble slab.

The Wood Warbler is a migrant from tropical Africa, arriving in its breeding quarters from mid-April onwards. In Britain it favours mature oak woodlands with a dense canopy and avoids coniferous woodland (in Europe conifers are used more regularly). Being ground breeders Wood Warblers need an open understorey.[1]

Its distribution between the two atlases of *1968-72* and *1988-1991* reveals an underlying loss from many central and southern England sites. In line with other trans-Saharan migrants, this trend continued and the species has suffered heavy declines from lowland England since 1994.[2] (Trends for the Scottish population are unavailable).[3]

There are less than 20 records of Wood Warblers in Clackmannanshire since 1974. All, bar passage birds, come from three localities. There were up to six pairs in Dollar Glen/Gloom Hill during the late 1980s to the mid-1990s and up to three pairs each at Wood Hill and Gartmorn during the early to mid-1990s. All of these apparently probable or confirmed breeding birds seem to have been lost.[4] *Atlas* fieldwork identified only possibly breeding birds from four squares (2%): Dollar Glen, Wood Hill, Balquharn and between Dollar and Pool of Muckhart.

Previously breeding in the Ochil glens,[5] Wood Warblers had become rare by the early 1970s[6] due to the scarcity of suitable habitat exacerbated by adverse management and the species has now declined to a level where it may become extinct without intervention. A targeted survey of the above sites to establish its true breeding status is strongly recommended.

Andre Thiel

[1] *BWP* [2] *BirdFacts* [3] *BBRC* [4] *UFABR* [5] *Rintoul & Baxter, 1935* [6] *Bryant et al., (1974)*

Waxwing   (Bohemian Waxwing)   *Bombycilla garrulus*

Irregular winter visitor   Conservation status: Green

The Waxwing is one of a select group of species that is of sufficiently colourful and exotic appearance to attract the attention of non-birdwatchers. It further improves its chances of being seen and reported by frequenting gardens and ornamental plantings in towns and villages. A winter visitor to the area, it is erratic in its occurrence from year to year, depending upon feeding and climatic conditions in its breeding and normal wintering areas on the continent of Europe, but visitations to Scotland are becoming both more frequent and larger.[1]

Rintoul & Baxter mention a "Bohemian Waxwing" that was "shot at Alloa in 1823", suggesting that the species was not noticed much in the County historically.[2] More recently, there is published evidence of 16 'invasions' reaching the Forth Bird Report area, but sightings in Clackmannanshire in only 10 winters. Sometimes when large numbers reach Stirling and Falkirk districts, few or none are seen in Clackmannanshire. Most remarkably this was the case during the largest recorded influx into Scotland in late 2004,[3] when flocks of over 400 spent some time in Stirling, Grangemouth and Dunblane but apparently none at all visited Clackmannanshire, although 11 turned up in Tillicoultry and six in Alva the following January.[4] The only gatherings of 25 or more birds in this period occurred in 1975, 1989, 2001 (41 in Tillicoultry on 7 March – the largest flock ever) and 2006.

The 2006 record, of 27 birds at Cambus Pools on 15 January, fell within the winter *Atlas* period. The great majority of recent County sightings have been in January or later in the winter.

David Thorogood

[1] BS3   [2] Rintoul & Baxter, 1935   [3] BS3   [4] UFABR

Nuthatch   (Eurasian Nuthatch)   *Sitta europaea*

Vagrant; putative breeder   Conservation status: Green

Although the Nuthatch has only recently colonized Scotland with breeding first confirmed in the Borders area in 1989, its subsequent rapid geographical expansion is surprising for such an acknowledged sedentary species.[1] BBS data indicate a statistically significant population increase of 47% in the UK population from 1995-2007.[2] There are only two records for Clackmannanshire – both from the same Alva garden. The first was on the 21 August 1999 with the second during the *Atlas* period on the 22 April 2005.[3]

With the bird's preference for mature deciduous and ancient semi-natural woodlands, Clackmannanshire would appear to offer a range of suitable breeding opportunities with some of the scarp woodlands seemingly especially suitable. As many of these sites are close to supplementary food provided by garden feeders (a factor which is considered to have aided its winter survival and thus the recent northern expansion) [4], it is surely only a matter of time before the Nuthatch is recorded as breeding in the County – especially with the first record of breeding in the Upper Forth area occurring close by at Bridge of Allan in 2009.[5]

Neil Bielby

[1] BS3   [2] Risely et al., 2009   [3] UFABR   [4] BS3   [5] UFABR

Rose-coloured Starling   (Rosy Starling)   *Sturnus roseus*

Vagrant

The Rose-coloured Starling breeds from the Balkans eastwards to Iran. However, it is prone to sporadic irruptions into Central and Western Europe and it is assumed that some of these birds make up the majority of the 319 Scottish records up to 2004. They normally associate with flocks of Common Starlings, but whereas adults and first-summer birds (82% of records) normally arrive during June to August, juveniles typically first appear in September/October.[1]

Since the first Scottish record in 1831, they have been observed in every bird recording area but an adult bird in Sauchie from 'early' to 17 August 2003 is the only record for the County.[2,3]

Neil Bielby

[1] BS3   [2] ibid.   [3] UFABR

Rock Pipit   (Eurasian Rock Pipit)   *Anthus petrosus*

Vagrant   Conservation status: Green

For breeding purposes the Rock Pipit seeks out, as its name suggests, areas with rocky outcrops and boulders, and in Scotland it is confined to such habitats around the coast. In winter, however, it finds suitable niches along almost any type of coastline, rocky or not, and may then be joined by immigrant birds from Scandinavia.[1]

The winter *Atlas* survey resulted in only one report, upstream from Alloa. Its rather dark plumage and the fact that it shares coastal habitats with some of those Meadow Pipits that have not moved out of the County altogether for the winter make it an easy bird to overlook. It is likely that this is as much the explanation of the extreme paucity of recent reports from Clackmannanshire as actual absence. Very small numbers have been found in most years since 1977 along the Falkirk side of the estuary, with a slight increase apparent since 1997.[2]

In Fife Rock Pipits nest as far west as the Burntisland and Kinghorn area. The Fife Atlas also noted a July non-breeding record from Valleyfield and wintering birds at Longannet close to the border with Clackmannanshire.[3] Prior to winter work for this *Atlas* only two Clackmannanshire records had been published since 1974; two birds at the Blackdevon Wetlands on 27 December 1977 and one at Cambus on 26 December 1993.[4]

David Thorogood

[1] *BS2*   [2] *UFABR*   [3] *Fife Atlas*   [4] *UFABR*

Snow Bunting *Plectrophenax nivalis*

Irregular winter visitor   Conservation status: Amber

The presence of breeding Snow Buntings in small numbers on the Cairngorm plateau and sometimes a few other mountains is an indicator of Scotland's remaining ecological toe-hold in the Arctic. In Clackmannanshire only its winter needs are met, when it feeds on small seeds caught up on snow beds on the hills, along tide lines or on lowland farmland. Wintering birds come from Iceland and Scandinavia and perhaps Greenland.[1]

The *Old* and *New Statistical Accounts* both mention 'snow birds' as winter visitors to Alloa,[2] but these buntings are now rarely encountered on low ground or alongside the Forth estuary in Clackmannanshire. The only modern coastal record was of six birds at Alloa in December 1974. Inland, six were seen on stubble near Alva with Skylarks during a blizzard in February 1978.[3]

However, more visit the Ochils. 'Snow Buntings occur on the Ochil Hills ... in moderate to large flocks (30-160), mainly when snow falls in the Grampian mountains 50 km to the north; they frequent broken, boggy ground or wet slopes and small valleys above 400m altitude'.[4] During the period covered by these observations (January 1977), flocks totalling 264 birds were seen and the following November similar numbers occurred. Subsequently such totals were only approached by a flock of 100 on Ben Cleuch in 1983, and 58 birds at Ben Ever in December 2002.[5]

During the winter *Atlas* surveys Snow Buntings were found in only one tetrad in the central Ochils, but later in 2007 three were seen on King's Seat in November and there were 45 above Menstrie Glen in December.[6] The trend towards milder winters (and the two seasons of this survey were generally mild) may already be causing the Snow Bunting to visit the County less often and in smaller numbers.

David Thorogood

[1] *BWP*   [2] *Statistical Accounts*   [3] *UFABR*   [4] *Henty, 1979*   [5] *UFABR*   [6] *ibid.*

Species only recorded between 1974-2002

Species only recorded prior to atlas period (1974-April 2002). Unless credited otherwise, all records are from the local bird reports (*UFABR*).

American Wigeon   *Anas americana*   Vagrant
A male at Gartmorn Dam was first seen on 3 January 1992, with presumably the same bird seen subsequently several times up to March 1993. A male in eclipse (again, probably the same bird) was at Alloa Inch on 23 August 1992.

Red-throated Diver   (Red-throated Loon)   *Gavia stellata*   Vagrant
Three records of single birds: at Alloa Inch in November 1995 and at Kennetpans and Tullibody Inch in January 1996. Conceivably only one bird was involved; it is certainly possible that the same individual accounted for the last two sightings. The species may be less frequent here than in the past. Rintoul & Baxter (1935) reported that in winter "It is … by no means uncommon, and goes well up the Firth, being common as far up as Alloa and being seen more rarely even higher up".

Black-throated Diver   (Black-throated Loon)   *Gavia arctica*   Vagrant
Two records: a single bird at Gartmorn Dam (27 March 1978) and two birds there during February and March 1994. Rintoul and Baxter (1935) noted that "it has frequently occurred on the Forth between Alloa and Stirling".

Slavonian Grebe   (Horned Grebe)   *Podiceps auritus*   Vagrant
Three records: Single birds were at Gartmorn Dam (19 September 1978; 25 August 1984 & 27 December 1999).

Fulmar   (Northern Fulmar)   *Fulmarus glacialis*   Vagrant
Three records: a bird flew north-west over Alloa (15 August 1976) with another flying west by Craig Leith (16 June 1980) while a bird was found dead under pylons at Cambus (21 March 1993).

Gannet   (Northern Gannet)   *Morus bassanus*   Vagrant
Three records: a juvenile flew east over the River Devon at Alva (26 September 1989); a single bird was seen at Cambus (22 September 1991) and a juvenile at the same location (25 September 1997). Rintoul & Baxter (1935) note "one was got near Alloa about 1st October 1931".

Shag   (European Shag)   *Phalacrocorax aristotelis*   Vagrant
The only record is of a single bird on the River Forth at Alloa (2 October 1976).

Golden Eagle   *Aquila chrysaetus*   Vagrant
There is only one record: an immature at Craig Leith (11 October 1975).

Corncrake   *Crex crex*   Extinct summer visitor – now a Vagrant
Rintoul & Baxter (1935) noted that it was "a summer visitor to all the low-lying parts of the area, though not in the numbers it used to be". Also, they quoted the following from the *Old Statistical Account* for Clackmannanshire in 1793: "abundant in breeding season". The only 'modern' record is of a bird at Alva (14 September 1995).

Little Ringed Plover   *Charadrius dubius*   Vagrant
The only record is of a bird at Cambus (17 April 1983).

Dotterel (Eurasian Dotterel) *Charadrius morinellus* Vagrant
Five records: the first was of a pair on Ben Cleuch (24 May 1987) with a single bird at the same location (18 & 21 August 1991) with a pair also on the same hill (10 May 1992) while a single bird was reported from the 'Ochils' (20 June 1993). The Dotterel was mentioned in the *Old Statistical Account* as being "in the hills above Tillicoultry in 1795 and in 1793 at Alloa alights on high ground in spring on way to Ochils (sic)". Also mentioned in the *New Statistical Account* as occurring at Alloa (*Rintoul & Baxter, 1935*).

Grey Plover *Pluvialis squatarola* Vagrant
Three records: 40 were at Blackdevonmouth (2 October 1976) with five at Tullibody Inch (22 September 1996) and seven there (19 October 1996).

Knot (Red Knot) *Calidris canutus* Vagrant
Two records: a bird was at Blackdevonmouth (2 October 1976) with another at Cambus (9 August 1993).

Little Stint *Calidris minuta* Vagrant
Five records: A single bird at Kennetpans (27 July 1975) was followed by a surprising 18 at Blackdevonmouth (2 October 1976) with two at the same location (14 September 1978). A single bird was at Cambus Pool (14 September 1989) with two at Tullibody Inch (22 September 1996) being the most recent record.

Curlew Sandpiper *Calidris ferruginea* Vagrant
Two records: eight birds were at Tullibody Inch (15 September 1991) with a single bird at the same location (1 October 1992).

Spotted Redshank *Tringa erythropus* Irregular passage migrant
There are spasmodic records between 1974 and 1993 from several locations along the River Forth. All are of one or two birds with all except one being in the late summer to early winter period (June-November).

Wood Sandpiper *Tringa glareola* Irregular passage migrant
Six records: the first is of a single bird at Muckhart (25 April 1984) followed by one at Cambus (11 May 1983) then birds at Cambus Pools (10 & 17 May 1990; 31 May 1991 & 2 August 1991).

Grey Phalarope *Phalaropus fulicarius* Vagrant
The only record is of a bird at Tullibody Inch (15 September 1991).

Great Skua *Stercorarius skua* Vagrant
The only record specifically assigned to Clackmannanshire is of a bird flying east at South Alloa (30 August 1992).

Kittiwake (Black-legged Kittiwake) *Rissa tridactyla* Vagrant
Two records: a single bird flying west at Cambus (14 April 1982) and one at Alloa Inch (30 August 1992). During the winter of 1872-73 "Dr Harvie Brown noted that multitudes of Kittiwakes frequented the Forth estuary as far up as Alloa (*Rintoul & Baxter, 1935*).

Mediterranean Gull *Larus melanocephalus* Vagrant
The only record is of an adult in winter plumage floating down the River Forth at Fallin (26 December 2000).

Yellow Wagtail   *Motacilla flava*   Vagrant
The only record is of a female at Cambus Pools (5 May 1996).

Ring Ouzel   *Turdus torquatus*   Vagrant
Four records: five were with Fieldfares in Silver Glen, Alva (30 October 1976) while single birds above Alva (12 September 1988) and at Harviestoun Glen (6 May 1991) with a female in Alva Glen April 2000). Rintoul & Baxter (1935) record it as being a "summer visitor and passage migrant" and noted that "in 1908 it is recorded as a summer visitor to the Ochils".

Great Grey Shrike   *Lanius excubitor*   Vagrant
The only record is of a bird at Menstrie (5 March 1980).

Corn Bunting   *Emberiza calandra*   Once resident, now extinct in the County.
The *New Statistical Account* states that "It breeds sparingly in Clackmannan". In modern times it was recorded at Kennetpans, Cambus and Menstrie (where an albino bird was noted) with the last record being of four birds at Blackgrange (20 January 1988).

Species only recorded prior to the start of 'modern recording' in 1974

Note: these entries are taken from Rintoul & Baxter's *A Vertebrate Fauna of Forth (1935)* and do not include direct reports from earlier sources for the reasons given in the Introduction.

Storm Petrel (European Storm Petrel) *Hydrobates pelagicus* Vagrant

Rintoul & Baxter (1935) record: "In the *Old Statistical Account* we read that Storm Petrels were seen about Alloa Ferry in winter of 1792, and one was killed. In the New Statistical Account they are again recorded from Alloa Ferry". Dr Harvie Brown "killed three at Kincardine-on-Forth on 13th November 1867".

Bittern (Great Bittern) *Botaurus stellaris* Probable historical breeder

Rintoul & Baxter (1935) note "In the *Old Statistical Account* it is said, 'is become very scarce' at Alloa". This suggests that it may have been a former breeder in the County?

Night Heron (Black-crowned Night Heron) *Nycticorax nycticorax* Vagrant

Rintoul & Baxter (1935) note it as a "A very rare visitor" adding, "On the 23rd of May 1879 a Night Heron was shot while perched on a tree on the banks of the Black Devon, adjoining the Alloa Park policies in Clackmannanshire."

Pallas's Sandgrouse *Syrrhaptes paradoxus* Irregular visitor

Rintoul & Baxter (1935) record that it was "An irregular visitor; big immigrations sometimes occur" and that "in the second half of May [in 1888] they arrived in the Carse between Stirling and Alloa, … In Clackmannan there are one or two records of the birds being shot".

Nightjar (European Nightjar) *Caprimulgus europaeus* Summer visitor

Rintoul & Baxter (1935) record that it was "A summer visitor; local" and that "two nests were found near Alloa in 1901, where it is not uncommon".

Hoopoe (Eurasian Hoopoe) *Upupa epops* Vagrant

Rintoul & Baxter (1935) record that it as "An occasional visitor" and that "a late bird was caught on the Menstrie Hills, Clackmannan, on 16th November 1896".

Wryneck (Eurasian Wryneck) *Jynx torquilla* Vagrant

Rintoul & Baxter (1935) record that it as "An occasional passage migrant" and observe that "in the New Statistical Account … it is included in a list of the birds of Alloa. We think this record is probably correct, as the way in which the lists of birds are drawn up in this account, and the footnotes added to it, lead one to think that they were done by one who was interested in natural history".

Golden Oriole (Eurasian Golden Oriole) *Oriolus oriolus* Vagrant

Rintoul & Baxter (1935) recorded it as being "An occasional visitor". A specimen "in the Stirling Museum … [was] found dead at Menstrie, Clackmannan, on 19th May 1899".

Desert Wheatear *Oenanthe deserti*   Vagrant

Rintoul & Baxter (1935) note: "The only record … comes from Alloa, where a male was shot on 26th November 1880. This was the first known occurrence of this bird in Britain". BS3 provides the more detailed information that the bird was discovered on moorland adjacent to Gartmorn Dam. It was shot by the gamekeeper to Lord Balfour of Burleigh, a Mr Watt. The mounted bird subsequently entered the possession of John Taylor of Alloa.

Pied Flycatcher *Ficedula hypoleuca*   Irregular summer visitor and passage migrant

Rintoul & Baxter (1935) noted it as being "A very local summer visitor and passage migrant" and that it was "reported near Alloa in the spring of 1885". A male was reported from Dollar Glen in 1951 with singing males in 1956 and 1959 while breeding was confirmed there in 1957 and 1958.

Species new to Clackmannanshire in the post *Atlas* period (2008-2011)

All records are from the local bird reports (*UFABR*).

White-tailed Eagle *Haliaeetus albicilla*

An immature bird from the Fife reintroduction scheme was at King's Seat, Ochils on 31 October 2010.

Reed Warbler *Acrocephalus scirpacus*

A singing bird at Cambus Pools on 7 May 2011 was followed by three birds at Tullibody Inch on 19 June 2011, one of which was carrying a faecal sac. These are the first confirmed records for both the species and breeding in the Upper Forth Bird Recording Area.

Common Rosefinch *Carpodacus erythrinus*

A bird was at Pool of Muckhart from 21 to 25 June 2010.

Red squirrel near Dollar. Courtesy of Wildpix Scotland

Roe deer at Aberdona Ponds. Courtesy of Wildpix Scotland

Mammals

Mammals

During recording work for the Clackmannanshire Bird Atlas, surveyors were asked to take note of any mammals or their signs observed. Sufficient information was obtained for tetrad mapping to be produced for seven species. Many other mammal species were recorded during the period, although the lower number of individual sightings in these instances did not merit the production of distribution maps.

Mammals with maps

The **Mole** (*Talpa europaea*) is found throughout the County and, although seldom seen, the distinctive mole hills or spoil heaps formed during the excavation of tunnels makes its presence easy to detect. Moles favour habitats where the soil is sufficiently deep for tunnelling such as pasture and other arable land (*Handbook of British Mammals*). However, there are also many records from the high ground of the Ochils, for example Maddy Moss and Ben Cleuch. Moles have been found up to an altitude of 930m on Ben Lawers in Perthshire (*Atlas of Mammals in Britain*).

Also widely spread throughout Clackmannanshire is the **Rabbit** (*Orcytolagus cuniculus*), with the only areas of absence being on the highest parts of the Ochils centred around Ben Cleuch. Rabbit numbers vary greatly from year to year with outbreaks of myxomatosis and rabbit viral haemorragic disease contributing to periodic falls in numbers (*Mammal Society*).

Compared to the Rabbit, the **Brown Hare** (*Lepus europaeus*) is much more localised in its distribution in Clackmannanshire although it was recorded in most low-lying tetrads in the central and western parts of the County. The Brown hare is largely dependent on the open spaces created by farmland and thrive best where there is a good mix of habitats, particularly where there is a patchwork of arable and grass fields and woodland in a relatively small area, so as to provide a continual supply of food and shelter throughout the year (*Handbook of British Mammals*).

Clackmannanshire has a small but important population of **Red Squirrels** (*Sciurus vulgaris*). The main strongholds are in the coniferous woodlands at The Forest between Forestmill and Linn Mill, as well as Brucefield – the latter site lies close to Devilla Forest in Fife, which has a good population of Red Squirrels (*pers. obs.*). Red Squirrels also occur around Dollar and there were sightings during the survey at Gloom Hill and Dollarfield. One Red Squirrel was a daily visitor in the winter 2008/2009 to a garden in Dollar that bordered mixed woodland by the Kelly Burn (*pers. obs.*). During the survey period, there were also records from the Sheardale Ridge area, including near Lower Sheardale and Coalsnaughton. A record was also obtained from woodland near New Sauchie.

The large population of **Grey Squirrels** (*Sciuris carolinis*) in the County may pose a threat to the surviving remnants of Red Squirrels. It is believed that the slightly larger Grey Squirrel can out-compete the Red Squirrel for food, especially in deciduous woodland (*Mammal Society*). The Grey Squirrel is also a carrier of the Squirrel Pox virus, which causes mortality in the Red but not the Grey (*Mammal Society*), although there is no evidence that the virus occurs in Clackmannanshire. Clackmannanshire is at the interface of Grey and Red Squirrel populations and it is therefore important that the Red population is carefully monitored to ensure the species does not become extinct in the County. The Grey is found throughout Clackmannanshire in suitable woodland habitat including many of the Ochil glens. It prefers mature broad-leaved woodlands, but is also found in broad-leaved/conifer mixtures and mature conifer woodland, particularly when broad-leaved trees are nearby (*Handbook of British Mammals*).

The **Fox** (*Vulpes vulpes*) was recorded from throughout the County and the handful of areas with no records are almost certainly due to its field signs being missed by observers. Its droppings are frequently found in the Ochils above the 450m contour line (*pers. obs.*). Hill territories cover a much larger area than those on lower lying ground (*Handbook of British Mammals*). The Fox is highly adaptable and able to utilise a wide variety of habitats, including urban areas.

The **Roe Deer** (*Capreolus capreolus*) is widely spread and occurs virtually anywhere in the County where there is woodland or other cover to provide shelter and adjacent open areas for feeding. As well as low-lying parts of the County, the Roe Deer was recorded on open high ground in the Ochils.

Mammals without maps

The **Hedgehog** (*Erinaceus europaeus*) was widely recorded throughout lowland Clackmannanshire during the survey and is frequent in suburban areas. There were no records from the higher parts of the Ochils.

One interesting omission from the mammal records is the **Mountain Hare** (*Lepus timidus*), which certainly occurred in the Ochils until comparatively recently. The booklet, *The Ochil Hills – Landscape, Wildlife, Heritage, Walks* – published in 1994 states: "On the heather hags above the tree line the Mountain Hare may be seen". Its presence was also noted in the *Atlas of Mammals in Britain* published in 1993.

In 2005, the Clackmannanshire Ranger Service with help from the Ochils Mountain Rescue Team carried out a survey of Mountain Hare in the Ochils but failed to find any signs. This, combined with the absence of confirmed observer records during the Clackmannanshire Atlas survey, suggests that this species is either extinct in the Ochils or is at best present in extremely small numbers.

Another species of particular interest that occurs in the County is the **Otter** (*Lutra lutra*). There was one record during the survey with a sighting on the River Black Devon south-east of Alloa. According to Clackmannanshire Biodiversity records, Otters inhabit almost the entire length of the River Devon and Black Devon, as well as the part of the Forth that sits within the County. It is frequent along the River Devon between Tillicoultry and Rumbling Bridge (*pers. obs.*). The Ranger Service monitor Otter signs twice a year and this has shown an increase in Otter occurrence, which fits with the overall upward trend for the UK. The River Devon has a healthy fish population to help support Otters including Brown and Sea Trout (*Salmo trutta*), Atlantic Salmon (*Salmo salar*), European Eel (*Anguilla anguilla*), River Lamprey (*Lampetra fluviatilis*) and Brook Lamprey (*Lampetra planeri*). Stone Loach (*Barbatula barbatula*), Minnow (*Phoxinus phoxinus*) and Three-spined Stickleback (*Gasterosteus aculeatus*) also occur in the Devon (*Forth Fisheries Trust*). Such a broad fish fauna also helps to support piscivorous birds such as Grey Heron, Kingfisher and Goosander.

There were several records of **American Mink** (*Neovison vison*) during the survey, especially along the River Devon between Alva and Vicar's Bridge. The American Mink is an undesirable alien predator that may impact upon the breeding success of ground nesting riparian birds such as Common Sandpiper and Mallard along the River Devon. The occurrence of Mink may also be responsible for there being no records of **Water Vole** (*Arvicola amphibius* (formerly *A. terrestris*)) during the survey. However, the Devon is a spate river prone to extreme flooding and much of its length may not form entirely suitable habitat for Water Voles due to the flooding out of burrows. Water Voles do occur in some large ponds in the central part of the County (*Clackmannanshire Ranger Service*), possibly because of the absence of American Mink in these areas.

Brown Hare

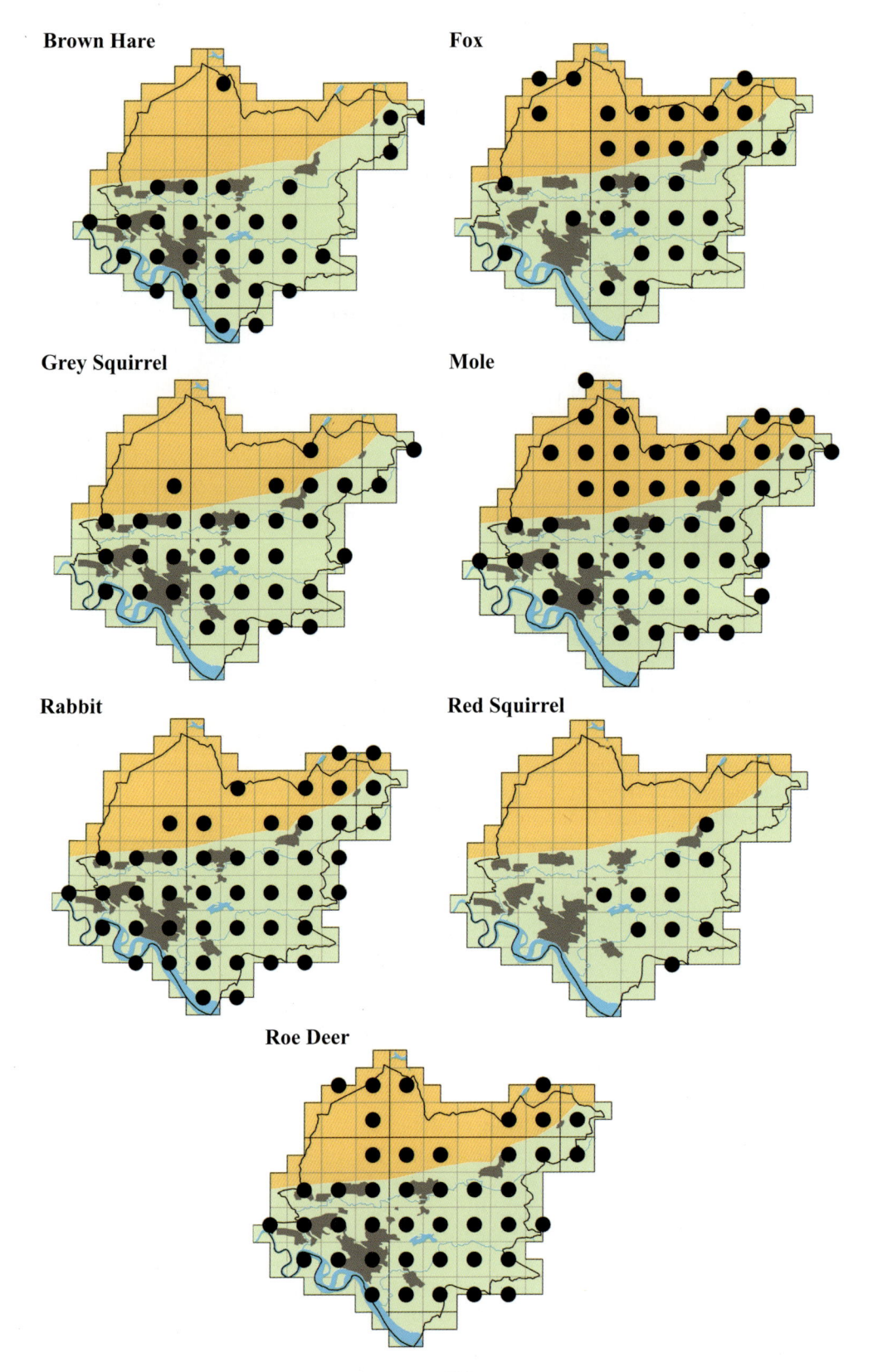

Fox

Grey Squirrel

Mole

Rabbit

Red Squirrel

Roe Deer

The **Badger** (*Meles meles*) would appear scarce within Clackmannanshire although it is likely that there has been a degree of under-recording, given the secretive nocturnal habits of the animal. One sett was recorded during the survey in woodland on the slopes of the Ochils. The representative organisation for Scottish Badger Groups, Scottish Badgers, has records of two setts – one in the north-east of the County and the other south of Tillicoultry (*pers. comm.*). Road kill badgers have been recorded at Alva and Yetts o' Muckhart.

There were several records of **Stoat** (*Mustela erminea*) including from the coastal fringes of the River Forth and along the Hillfoots further inland. There were no records from the high ground of the Ochils.

There were two records of **Polecat** (*Mustela putorius*) or **Feral Ferret** (*Mustela furo*) type species during the survey, which were most likely to be the latter, the darkest forms of which are virtually indistinguishable from the Polecat. As far as it is known, the Polecat is extinct in Scotland (*Handbook of British Mammals*). It seems likely, therefore, that the animals recorded were Feral Ferret escapes, given that the animals are widely kept. It is also possible there is a small breeding population of Feral Ferrets in Clackmannanshire that has resulted from such escapes. Although not recorded during the survey period, there have been recent records of **Pine Marten** (*Martes martes*) in Clackmannanshire as the animal continues its expansion into lowland Scotland (*pers. comm.*).

There were a number of bat sightings during the survey although exact identification of species was impossible. However, the Clackmannanshire Biodiversity Group has recorded several species in the County. **Common Pipistrelle** (*Pipistrellus pipistrellus*) and **Soprano Pipistrelle** (*Pipistrellus pygmaeus*) are the most widespread. **Brown Long-eared Bat** (*Plecotus auritus*) also occur and the **Daubenton's Bat** (*Myotis daubentonii*) can be seen hawking for insects over some parts of the River Devon and other water bodies. **Natterer's Bat** (*Myotis natterreri*) has also been recorded.

The **Grey Seal** (*Halichoerus grypus*) was recorded in the River Forth at Cambus and Tullibody Inch during the survey. The muddy bottom of this part of the River Forth is likely to hold good numbers of Flounder (*Platichthys flesus*), which would form an important food source for seals, and in late summer and autumn the seals will also be predating upon migrating Salmon moving upstream. Surprisingly, perhaps, for so far up the Forth, there were two records for **Harbour Porpoise** (*Phocoena phocoena*).

Other mammals recorded by field workers were **Bank Vole** (*Myodes glareolus*), **Brown Rat** (*Rattus norvegicus*), **Common Shrew** (*Sorex araneus*), **Wood Mouse** (*Apodemus sylvaticus*) **House Mouse** (*Mus domesticus*) and **Field Vole** (*Microtus agrestis*).

Keith Broomfield

References:

Gordon B. Corbet and Stephen Harris, 1991, The Handbook of British Mammals, Blackwell Science.

H. R, Arnold, 1993, Atlas of Mammals in Britain, ITE Research Publication no. 6, HMSO.

L. Corbett et al, 1994, Ochil Hills – Landscape, Wildlife, Heritage, Walks – Clackmannanshire Field Studies Society.

Mammal Society Website, www.mammal.org.uk

P. Fothringham, A Fisheries Management Plan for the Forth Catchment, 2009, Forth District Salmon Fishery Board & River Forth Fisheries Trust.

Badger, Photo courtesy of Wildpix Scotland

Brown Hare, Photo courtesy of Wildpix Scotland

Appendices

Appendix 1: KM squares data by habitat

(p) = less than 50% of the km square falls in Clackmannanshire
Hours = number of logged hours surveying on square
Sp's = toatal number of species
Ob = species observed only (not deemed to be using the square for breeding)
Poss = species deemed to be possibly breeding in the square
Prob = Species deemed to be probably breeding in the square
Conf = species confirmed as breeding in the square
% conf = number of species confirmed breeding in the square as a percentage of the total possible, probable and confirmed records

Square	Hours	Sp's	Ob	Poss	Prob	Conf	% conf
Hill Squares							
NS 8498 (p)	3.5	21	5	3	11	2	13%
NS 8598	7	13	5	1	3	4	50%
NS 8599	6	9	3	0	3	3	50%
NS 8698	2	10	2	2	5	1	13%
NS 8699	9.1	14	9	2	3	0	0%
NS 8798	3	4	0	0	2	2	50%
NS 8799	3	8	1	2	3	2	29%
NS 8898	8.2	23	2	6	10	5	24%
NS 8899	3.4	9	2	4	1	2	29%
NS 8998	8.3	23	3	11	6	3	15%
NS 8999	3	4	1	0	2	1	33%
NS 9099	5.2	8	2	3	3	0	0%
NS 9199	1.9	7	2	3	2	0	0%
NS 9299	18.1	13	8	3	0	2	40%
NS 9399	1.7	6	2	2	2	0	0%
NS 9499	5.7	8	3	1	3	1	20%
NN 8500 (p)	1.7	4	1	1	1	1	33%
NN 8501 (p)	1.4	3	0	2	1	0	0%
NN 8600	1	4	1	0	1	2	67%
NN 8601	8.5	10	4	1	4	1	17%
NN 8700	5.5	15	4	3	5	3	27%
NN 8701	5	8	3	0	2	3	60%
NN 8702 (p)	5.4	8	3	3	2	0	0%
NN 8800	4.4	12	3	3	5	1	11%
NN 8801	8.6	7	0	3	4	0	0%
NN 8802	6.4	8	2	2	4	0	0%
NN 8803 (p)	1.7	4	2	2	2	0	0%
NN 8900	2.9	4	0	2	2	0	0%
NN 8901	3.4	4	1	0	3	0	0%
NN 8902	5.9	11	4	5	2	0	0%
NN 8903	6.3	11	2	5	4	0	0%
NN 8904 (p)	1.3	6	1	5	1	0	0%
NN 9000	2	8	6	0	2	0	0%
NN 9001	17.4	10	0	3	6	1	10%
NN 9002	7.1	7	1	4	0	2	33%
NN 9003	6.7	7	2	2	3	0	0%
NN 9100	1.1	4	1	1	2	0	0%
NN 9101	0.4	9	0	3	3	1	14%
NN 9102	10.9	17	6	4	6	1	9%
NN 9103 (p)	6.3	18	6	8	3	1	8%
NN 9200	1.6	5	1	1	3	0	0%
NN 9201 (p)	0.7	3	0	0	3	0	0%
NN 9300	3.3	7	2	1	4	0	0%
NN 9301 (p)	1.6	3	1	0	2	0	0%
NN 9400	4.4	13	1	1	8	3	25%
NN 9401 (p)	1.2	6	3	1	2	0	0%
NN 9500	3.3	6	2	1	1	2	50%
NN 9501	1.1	6	2	1	2	1	25%

Square	Hours	Sp's	Ob	Poss	Prob	Conf	% conf
Hill & Forestry							
NN 9600	7.6	34	7	14	10	3	11%
NN 9601 (p)	1.1	5	2	3	0	0	0%
NN 9700	6.8	30	4	11	8	7	27%
NN 9701	2.5	23	7	10	2	4	25%
NN 9702 (p)	0.9	14	6	6	2	0	0%
NN 9801	3.9	16	5	7	3	1	9%
NN 9901	13	29	4	8	6	11	44%
NN 9902 (p)	8.4	25	2	12	8	3	13%
Scarp Squares							
NS 9198	12.5	21	1	7	10	3	15%
NS 9298	16.5	32	3	11	2	16	55%
NS 9599	8.4	28	6	6	11	5	23%
Scarp & Suburban							
NS 8497 (p)	8	25	6	0	15	4	21%
NS 8597	?	64	10	6	6	42	78%
NS 8797	8.9	47	6	6	15	20	49%
NS 8897	15.8	47	3	13	13	18	41%
NS 9197	23.8	52	6	7	18	21	46%
Scarp & Farmland							
NS 8697	14.5	46	4	14	11	17	40%
NS 9498	24	31	3	12	1	15	54%
NN 9800	5.9	40	6	6	18	10	29%
Scarp, Woodland, Suburban & Farmland							
NS 8997	10.4	44	4	16	16	8	20%
NS 9598	13.7	44	5	9	12	18	46%
Scarp, Woodland, & Farmland							
NS 9097	10.2	63	8	25	20	10	18%
NS 9398	24	39	6	10	2	21	64%
NS 9699	16.7	51	2	17	15	17	37%
Scarp & Woodland							
NS 9098	3.3	18	1	10	3	4	24%
Farmland							
NS 8395 (p)	0.5	6	1	2	2	1	20%
NS 8693	16.8	42	3	12	15	12	31%
NS 8895	10	38	8	4	8	18	60%
NS 8995	24.5	52	10	10	8	24	57%
NS 9093	17	46	8	9	13	16	42%
NS 9189	5.2	37	5	6	14	12	38%
NS 9190	8.3	43	5	13	13	12	32%
NS 9289 (p)	4.1	24	1	6	14	3	13%
NS 9290	7	36	2	12	12	10	29%
NS 9291	6.4	32	2	8	9	13	43%
NS 9292	15.2	49	8	7	18	16	39%
NS 9390 (p)	3.9	26	3	5	14	4	17%
NS 9391	6	25	5	6	10	4	20%
NS 9395	22.2	50	11	9	15	15	38%
NS 9594	15.5	45	10	11	14	10	29%
NS 9693	22.8	45	7	6	23	9	24%

Square	Hours	Sp's	Ob	Poss	Prob	Conf	% conf
	Farmland Cont.						
NS 9694	11.6	35	3	6	12	14	44%
NS 9791 (p)	3.7	14	2	8	3	1	8%
NS 9792	15.7	33	4	11	9	9	31%
NS 9793 (p)	2.5	20	2	8	9	1	6%
NS 9794	12.9	47	4	10	14	19	44%
NS 9795	18.3	33	1	10	12	10	31%
NS 9798	4.3	39	4	13	10	12	34%
NS 9891 (p)	2.1	8	2	4	2	0	0%
NS 9892 (p)	4.7	17	3	9	5	0	0%
NS 9895 (p)	0.7	11	5	2	2	2	33%
NS 9896 (p)	3	16	3	6	3	4	31%
NS 9897 (p)	1	9	2	6	1	0	0%
NS 9898	21.9	49	4	8	15	22	49%
NT 0099	15.5	45	5	4	10	26	65%
NT 0198 (p)	0.2	2	0	2	0	0	0%
NT 0199 (p)	3.2	23	2	12	7	2	10%
NO 0100	15.1	48	5	17	9	17	40%
	Farmland & Suburban						
NS 8496	3.5	57	7	17	13	20	40%
NS 8593	13.8	88	35	14	14	25	47%
NS 8595	14.5	50	8	11	14	17	40%
NS 8596	?	51	9	7	11	24	57%
NS 8694	15.6	43	6	9	12	16	43%
NS 8695	12.1	43	6	6	14	17	46%
NS 8794	12.1	42	6	12	10	14	39%
NS 8894	16.1	36	4	7	10	15	47%
NS 8992	16.3	45	6	7	9	23	59%
NS 8994	14.8	38	3	8	12	16	44%
NS 9095	11.3	45	12	5	10	18	55%
NS 9191	14.9	37	3	7	6	21	62%
NS 9295	17.3	41	5	8	8	20	56%
NS 9297	6.4	41	7	9	15	10	29%
NS 9698	8.4	51	11	9	10	21	53%
NO 0000	19.6	42	1	11	10	20	49%
	Farmland with Water Feature						
NS 8392 (p)	1.1	15	10	3	2	0	0%
NS 8393 (p)	2.4	31	6	12	11	2	8%
NS 8492	5.1	32	8	12	6	6	25%
NS 8493	12.5	77	29	9	23	16	33%
NS 8495 (p)	8.1	39	9	9	13	8	27%
NS 8691(p)	1.2	26	11	6	5	4	27%
NS 8692	8.9	61	21	13	15	12	30%
NS 8696	16.2	61	10	17	16	17	34%
NS 8990 (p)	6.8	36	15	2	14	5	24%
NS 8991	6.5	58	14	14	22	8	18%
NS 8996	24.3	56	8	11	15	22	46%
NS 9089	6.3	36	4	8	11	13	41%
NS 9090	7.6	44	4	9	21	10	25%
NS 9096	18.3	60	8	12	18	22	42%
NS 9188 (p)	4.9	42	5	11	20	6	16%
NS 9193	17.2	57	10	15	19	13	28%
NS 9497	13.4	61	8	10	25	18	34%
NS 9797	20.7	47	3	7	12	25	57%
NS 9894 (p)	13.6	42	7	5	16	14	40%
NO 0101	19.6	55	9	16	15	15	33%
NO 0201 (p)	5.9	38	13	12	8	5	20%

	Square	Hours	Sp's	Ob	Poss	Prob	Conf % conf
	Farmland with >25% Woodland						
NS 8795	17.7	44	11	5	17	11	33%
NS 9394	24.8	54	7	10	21	16	34%
NS 9491	37.7	48	7	16	13	12	29%
NS 9494	22.1	39	2	11	12	14	38%
NS 9592	32.8	44	4	12	16	12	30%
NS 9596	6.8	60	13	17	11	19	40%
NS 9695	14.6	41	3	9	6	23	61%
NS 9799	10.8	48	6	8	16	18	43%
NS 9998	16.1	38	3	7	13	16	44%
NS 9999	9.4	37	5	4	23	5	16%
NO 0001	15.8	36	2	10	13	11	32%
	Farmland with >50% Woodland						
NS 8396 (p)	1	21	4	8	7	2	12%
NS 9392	8.4	43	4	16	9	14	36%
NS 9492	21.5	45	4	14	13	14	34%
NS 9591	47.8	49	4	13	19	13	29%
NS 9593	20.6	59	6	12	19	22	42%
NS 9692	24.3	58	8	14	20	16	32%
NS 9899	9.9	46	5	7	24	10	24%
	Farmland with >75% Woodland						
NS 9393	30.5	49	3	13	15	18	39%
NS 9493	21.3	38	0	12	15	11	29%
NS 9691 (p)	16.6	22	1	11	4	6	29%
	Farmland, Water & Woodland						
NS 9194	8.7	59	13	18	13	15	33%
NS 9293	18.4	60	7	19	26	8	15%
NS 9294	26.4	63	9	12	21	21	39%
NS 9396	10	50	8	6	31	5	12%
NS 9397	13.9	57	6	11	26	14	27%
NS 9495	18.2	56	7	12	15	22	45%
NS 9496	13.3	53	7	16	15	15	33%
NS 9595	6.5	31	0	9	9	13	42%
NS 9696	17.4	52	7	16	16	13	29%
NS 9796	22.3	54	2	14	15	23	44%
NT 0098 (p)	5.3	36	3	14	10	9	27%
NO 0002 (p)	17.3	36	6	12	12	6	20%
	Suburban / Farmland / Water						
NS 8796	15.2	59	11	17	14	17	35%
NS 8896	13.2	56	10	9	19	18	39%
NS 9091	16.3	43	7	6	16	14	39%
NS 9092	17.4	44	6	9	10	19	50%
NS 9192	17.8	42	5	6	11	20	54%
NS 9196	11	60	9	6	17	28	55%
NS 9296	9.8	50	9	9	17	15	37%
NS 9597	13.9	68	12	8	20	28	50%
NS 9697	4	60	9	12	13	26	51%

Square	Hours	Sp's	Ob	Poss	Prob	Conf	% conf
Suburban / Farmland / Woodland							
NS 9195	8.3	50	9	8	28	5	12%
NN 9900	17.2	35	2	6	18	9	27%
Suburban & Woodland							
NS 9094	8.6	42	10	10	16	6	19%
Industrial / Farmland							
NS 8394	10.9	64	12	4	13	35	67%
NS 8494	12.4	45	3	11	15	16	38%
Suburban / Urban							
NS 8793	13.7	42	7	8	12	15	43%
NS 8893	10.4	35	1	6	15	13	38%
NS 8993	13.9	34	4	4	5	19	68%
Water							
NS 8791 (p)		6	2	3	1	0	0%
Urban / Ind. / Water							
NS 8594	12	45	5	13	14	13	33%
NS 8792	16.1	39	9	3	9	18	60%
NS 8891	10.1	33	7	5	11	10	38%
NS 8892	12.2	34	3	8	6	17	55%

Appendix 2: Breeding status totals

Species	Squares w/Records		Confirmed		Probable		Possible		Observed only	
	Number	%	Number	%	Number	%	Number	%	Number	%
Mute Swan	32	16.2	16	50.0	4	12.5	4	12.5	8	25.0
Whooper Swan	1	0.5	0	0.0	0	0.0	0	0.0	1	100.0
Pink-footed Goose	6	3.0	0	0.0	0	0.0	0	0.0	6	100.0
Greylag Goose	12	6.1	0	0.0	1	8.3	0	0.0	11	91.7
Canada Goose	2	1.0	0	0.0	0	0.0	0	0.0	2	100.0
Barnacle Goose	1	0.5	0	0.0	0	0.0	0	0.0	1	100.0
Wigeon	7	3.5	0	0.0	1	14.3	0	0.0	6	85.7
Gadwall	6	3.0	0	0.0	3	50.0	3	50.0	0	0.0
Teal	21	10.6	0	0.0	5	23.8	3	14.3	13	61.9
Mallard	109	55.1	39	35.8	44	40.4	17	15.6	9	8.3
Pintail	1	0.5	0	0.0	0	0.0	0	0.0	1	100.0
Garganey	2	1.0	0	0.0	0	0.0	0	0.0	2	100.0
Shoveler	4	2.0	0	0.0	1	25.0	0	0.0	3	75.0
Pochard	2	1.0	0	0.0	0	0.0	2	100.0	0	0.0
Tufted Duck	23	11.6	1	4.3	12	52.2	4	17.4	6	26.1
Goldeneye	3	1.5	0	0.0	0	0.0	0	0.0	3	100.0
Red-breasted Merganser	4	2.0	0	0.0	0	0.0	0	0.0	4	100.0
Goosander	20	10.1	3	15.0	6	30.0	2	10.0	9	45.0
Ruddy Duck	1	0.5	0	0.0	0	0.0	0	0.0	1	100.0
Red Grouse	8	4.0	1	12.5	3	37.5	4	50.0	0	0.0
Black Grouse	1	0.5	0	0.0	0	0.0	0	0.0	1	100.0
Red-legged Partridge	6	3.0	0	0.0	2	33.3	4	66.7	0	0.0
Grey Partridge	21	10.6	0	0.0	14	66.7	7	33.3	0	0.0
Quail	1	0.5	0	0.0	0	0.0	1	100.0	0	0.0
Pheasant	106	53.5	12	11.3	49	46.2	42	39.6	3	2.8
Cormorant	9	4.5	0	0.0	0	0.0	0	0.0	9	100.0
Little Egret	1	0.5	0	0.0	0	0.0	0	0.0	1	100.0
Grey Heron	67	33.8	2	3.0	0	0.0	0	0.0	65	97.0
Little Grebe	15	7.6	5	33.3	3	20.0	7	46.7	0	0.0
Great Crested Grebe	5	2.5	2	40.0	1	20.0	0	0.0	2	40.0
Red Kite	1	0.5	0	0.0	0	0.0	0	0.0	1	100.0
Goshawk	1	0.5	0	0.0	0	0.0	1	100.0	0	0.0
Sparrowhawk	54	27.3	6	11.1	7	13.0	26	48.1	15	27.8
Buzzard	142	71.7	33	23.2	38	26.8	40	28.2	31	21.8
Osprey	1	0.5	0	0.0	0	0.0	0	0.0	1	100.0
Kestrel	99	50.0	9	9.1	10	10.1	44	44.4	36	36.4
Merlin	1	0.5	1	100.0	0	0.0	0	0.0	0	0.0
Peregrine	9	4.5	2	22.2	0	0.0	1	11.1	6	66.7
Water Rail	7	3.5	1	14.3	3	42.9	2	28.6	1	14.3
Moorhen	39	19.7	16	41.0	5	12.8	16	41.0	2	5.1
Coot	15	7.6	8	53.3	4	26.7	3	20.0	0	0.0
Oystercatcher	88	44.4	18	20.5	35	39.8	20	22.7	15	17.0
Ringed Plover	5	2.5	2	40.0	2	40.0	0	0.0	1	20.0
Golden Plover	1	0.5	0	0.0	0	0.0	1	100.0	0	0.0
Lapwing	75	37.9	31	41.3	27	36.0	14	18.7	3	4.0
Dunlin	2	1.0	0	0.0	0	0.0	0	0.0	2	100.0

Species										
Ruff	2	1.0	0	0.0	1	50.0	0	0.0	1	50.0
Snipe	34	17.2	1	2.9	9	26.5	17	50.0	7	20.6
Woodcock	19	9.6	0	0.0	14	73.7	3	15.8	2	10.5
Black-tailed Godwit	3	1.5	0	0.0	0	0.0	0	0.0	3	100.0
Whimbrel	1	0.5	0	0.0	0	0.0	0	0.0	1	100.0
Curlew	88	44.4	4	4.5	43	48.9	30	34.1	11	12.5
Common Sandpiper	27	13.6	1	3.7	10	37.0	6	22.2	10	37.0
Green Sandpiper	1	0.5	0	0.0	0	0.0	0	0.0	1	100.0
Greenshank	1	0.5	0	0.0	0	0.0	0	0.0	1	100.0
Redshank	10	5.1	1	10.0	3	30.0	1	10.0	5	50.0
Black-headed Gull	53	26.8	0	0.0	1	1.9	0	0.0	52	98.1
Common Gull	54	27.3	5	9.3	1	1.9	0	0.0	48	88.9
Lesser Black-backed Gull	79	39.9	2	2.5	3	3.8	0	0.0	74	93.7
Herring Gull	44	22.2	0	0.0	2	4.5	1	2.3	41	93.2
Great Black-backed Gull	15	7.6	0	0.0	0	0.0	0	0.0	15	100.0
Sandwich Tern	4	2.0	0	0.0	0	0.0	0	0.0	4	100.0
Common Tern	5	2.5	0	0.0	0	0.0	0	0.0	5	100.0
Feral Pigeon	70	35.4	12	17.1	27	38.6	19	27.1	12	17.1
Stock Dove	55	27.8	6	10.9	26	47.3	20	36.4	3	5.5
Woodpigeon	147	74.2	72	49.0	53	36.1	18	12.2	4	2.7
Collared Dove	79	39.9	13	16.5	41	51.9	23	29.1	2	2.5
Cuckoo	22	11.1	1	4.5	2	9.1	17	77.3	2	9.1
Barn Owl	21	10.6	4	19.0	1	4.8	10	47.6	6	28.6
Tawny Owl	77	38.9	8	10.4	47	61.0	20	26.0	2	2.6
Long-eared Owl	3	1.5	1	33.3	0	0.0	2	66.7	0	0.0
Short-eared Owl	2	1.0	0	0.0	0	0.0	1	50.0	1	50.0
Swift	111	56.1	5	4.5	15	13.5	6	5.4	85	76.6
Kingfisher	15	7.6	1	6.7	2	13.3	10	66.7	2	13.3
Green Woodpecker	31	15.7	4	12.9	12	38.7	13	41.9	2	6.5
Great Spotted Woodpecker	70	35.4	25	35.7	20	28.6	23	32.9	2	2.9
Magpie	113	57.1	51	45.1	27	23.9	30	26.5	5	4.4
Jay	41	20.7	1	2.4	9	22.0	26	63.4	5	12.2
Jackdaw	118	59.6	34	28.8	35	29.7	29	24.6	20	16.9
Rook	119	60.1	30	25.2	1	0.8	0	0.0	88	73.9
Carrion Crow	177	89.4	107	60.5	23	13.0	17	9.6	30	16.9
Raven	29	14.6	3	10.3	2	6.9	3	10.3	21	72.4
Goldcrest	76	38.4	19	25.0	16	21.1	38	50.0	3	3.9
Blue Tit	144	72.7	101	70.1	25	17.4	14	9.7	4	2.8
Great Tit	135	68.2	91	67.4	32	23.7	12	8.9	0	0.0
Coal Tit	108	54.5	41	38.0	24	22.2	41	38.0	2	1.9
Skylark	131	66.2	14	10.7	111	84.7	4	3.1	2	1.5
Sand Martin	48	24.2	11	22.9	4	8.3	4	8.3	29	60.4
Swallow	143	72.2	68	47.6	14	9.8	19	13.3	42	29.4
House Martin	93	47.0	41	44.1	4	4.3	15	16.1	33	35.5
Long-tailed Tit	79	39.9	36	45.6	28	35.4	13	16.5	2	2.5
Wood Warbler	4	2.0	0	0.0	0	0.0	4	100.0	0	0.0
Chiffchaff	67	33.8	5	7.5	30	44.8	32	47.8	0	0.0
Willow Warbler	133	67.2	41	30.8	67	50.4	25	18.8	0	0.0
Blackcap	78	39.4	10	12.8	29	37.2	39	50.0	0	0.0
Garden Warbler	77	38.9	8	10.4	31	40.3	38	49.4	0	0.0

Species										
Whitethroat	103	52.0	28	27.2	46	44.7	28	27.2	1	1.0
Grasshopper Warbler	19	9.6	0	0.0	4	21.1	15	78.9	0	0.0
Sedge Warbler	47	23.7	21	44.7	13	27.7	13	27.7	0	0.0
Nuthatch	1	0.5	0	0.0	0	0.0	1	100.0	0	0.0
Treecreeper	75	37.9	11	14.7	13	17.3	47	62.7	4	5.3
Wren	169	85.4	53	31.4	88	52.1	28	16.6	0	0.0
Starling	121	61.1	92	76.0	8	6.6	12	9.9	9	7.4
Dipper	60	30.3	11	18.3	14	23.3	34	56.7	1	1.7
Blackbird	145	73.2	99	68.3	30	20.7	15	10.3	1	0.7
Fieldfare	6	3.0	0	0.0	0	0.0	0	0.0	6	100.0
Song Thrush	120	60.6	53	44.2	40	33.3	27	22.5	0	0.0
Mistle Thrush	78	39.4	18	23.1	29	37.2	26	33.3	5	6.4
Spotted Flycatcher	33	16.7	13	39.4	3	9.1	16	48.5	1	3.0
Robin	137	69.2	89	65.0	36	26.3	12	8.8	0	0.0
Redstart	3	1.5	1	33.3	0	0.0	2	66.7	0	0.0
Whinchat	21	10.6	7	33.3	5	23.8	7	33.3	2	9.5
Stonechat	16	8.1	2	12.5	6	37.5	6	37.5	2	12.5
Wheatear	69	34.8	11	15.9	20	29.0	23	33.3	15	21.7
Dunnock	129	65.2	48	37.2	50	38.8	30	23.3	1	0.8
House Sparrow	100	50.5	53	53.0	25	25.0	19	19.0	3	3.0
Tree Sparrow	29	14.6	14	48.3	7	24.1	7	24.1	1	3.4
Grey Wagtail	68	34.3	15	22.1	19	27.9	30	44.1	4	5.9
White Wagtail	2	1.0	0	0.0	0	0.0	0	0.0	2	100.0
Pied Wagtail	123	62.1	71	57.7	17	13.8	34	27.6	1	0.8
Tree Pipit	24	12.1	4	16.7	13	54.2	7	29.2	0	0.0
Meadow Pipit	104	52.5	37	35.6	48	46.2	4	3.8	15	14.4
Chaffinch	149	75.3	63	42.3	69	46.3	16	10.7	1	0.7
Brambling	4	2.0	0	0.0	0	0.0	2	50.0	2	50.0
Greenfinch	108	54.5	32	29.6	46	42.6	27	25.0	3	2.8
Goldfinch	104	52.5	15	14.4	53	51.0	33	31.7	3	2.9
Siskin	38	19.2	3	7.9	10	26.3	17	44.7	8	21.1
Linnet	78	39.4	8	10.3	33	42.3	32	41.0	5	6.4
Twite	2	1.0	1	50.0	1	50.0	0	0.0	0	0.0
Lesser Redpoll	19	9.6	0	0.0	9	47.4	8	42.1	2	10.5
Common Crossbill	10	5.1	1	10.0	1	10.0	5	50.0	3	30.0
Bullfinch	59	29.8	10	16.9	26	44.1	18	30.5	5	8.5
Yellowhammer	96	48.5	20	20.8	48	50.0	27	28.1	1	1.0
Reed Bunting	81	40.9	14	17.3	43	53.1	22	27.2	2	2.5

Appendix 3: Species list

Species for which breeding evidence was obtained in Clackmannanshire during 2002 - 2007	Highest Breeding Status	Recorded in Winter	Species for which breeding evidence was obtained in Clackmannanshire during 2002 - 2007	Highest Breeding Status	Recorded in Winter
Breeding Species	**111**	records	Woodpigeon	4	Y
Mute Swan	4	Y	Collared Dove	4	Y
Greylag Goose	3	Y	Cuckoo	4	
Shelduck	4	Y	Barn Owl	4	Y
Wigeon	3	Y	Tawny Owl	4	Y
Gadwall	3		Long-eared Owl	4	Y
Teal	3	Y	Short-eared Owl	2	Y
Mallard	4	Y	Swift	4	
Shoveler	3		Kingfisher	4	Y
Pochard	2	Y	Green Woodpecker	4	Y
Tufted Duck	4	Y	Great Spotted Woodpecker	4	Y
Goosander	4	Y	Magpie	4	Y
Red Grouse	4	Y	Jay	4	Y
Red-legged Partridge	3	Y	Jackdaw	4	Y
Grey Partridge	3	Y	Rook	4	Y
Quail	2		Carrion Crow	4	Y
Pheasant	4	Y	Raven	4	Y
Grey Heron	4	Y	Goldcrest	4	Y
Little Grebe	4	Y	Blue Tit	4	Y
Great Crested Grebe	4	Y	Great Tit	4	Y
Goshawk	2		Coal Tit	4	Y
Sparrowhawk	4	Y	Skylark	4	Y
Buzzard	4	Y	Sand Martin	4	
Kestrel	4	Y	Swallow	4	
Merlin	4	Y	House Martin	4	
Peregrine	4	Y	Long-tailed Tit	4	Y
Water Rail	4	Y	Wood Warbler	2	
Moorhen	4	Y	Chiffchaff	4	Y
Coot	4	Y	Willow Warbler	4	
Oystercatcher	4	Y	Blackcap	4	Y
Ringed Plover	4	Y	Garden Warbler	4	
Golden Plover	2	Y	Whitethroat	4	
Lapwing	4	Y	Grasshopper Warbler	3	
Ruff	3		Sedge Warbler	4	
Snipe	4	Y	Nuthatch	2	
Woodcock	3	Y	Treecreeper	4	Y
Curlew	4	Y	Wren	4	Y
Common Sandpiper	4		Starling	4	Y
Redshank	4	Y	Dipper	4	Y
Black-headed Gull	3	Y	Blackbird	4	Y
Common Gull	4	Y	Song Thrush	4	Y
Lesser Black-backed Gull	4	Y	Mistle Thrush	4	Y
Herring Gull	3	Y	Spotted Flycatcher	4	
Feral Pigeon	4	Y	Robin	4	Y
Stock Dove	4	Y	Redstart	4	

Species for which breeding evidence was obtained in Clackmannanshire during 2002 - 2007	Highest Breeding Status	Recorded in Winter
Whinchat	4	
Stonechat	4	Y
Wheatear	4	
Dunnock	4	Y
House Sparrow	4	Y
Tree Sparrow	4	Y
Grey Wagtail	4	Y
Pied Wagtail	4	Y
Tree Pipit	4	
Meadow Pipit	4	Y
Chaffinch	4	Y
Brambling	2	Y
Greenfinch	4	Y
Goldfinch	4	Y
Siskin	4	Y
Linnet	4	Y
Twite	4	
Lesser Redpoll	3	Y
Crossbill	4	Y
Bullfinch	4	Y
Yellowhammer	4	Y
Reed Bunting	4	Y

Breeding Status Key

1	Observed only
2	Possible breeding
3	Probable breeding
4	Confirmed breeding

Species which were recorded in Clackmannanshire during 2002 - 2007 but which exhibited no evidence of breeding.	Highest Breeding Status	Recorded in Winter
Non-breeding Species	**36**	**records**
Whooper Swan	1	Y
Pink-footed Goose	1	Y
White-fronted Goose		Y
Canada Goose	1	Y
Barnacle Goose	1	Y
Red-breasted Goose		Y
Pintail	1	
Garganey	1	
Long-tailed Duck		Y
Goldeneye	1	Y
Red-breasted Merganser	1	Y
Ruddy Duck	1	Y
Black Grouse	1	
Cormorant	1	Y
Little Egret	1	
Spoonbill		Y
Red Kite	1	
Hen Harrier		Y
Osprey	1	
Dunlin	1	Y
Jack Snipe		Y
Black-tailed Godwit	1	Y
Bar-tailed Godwit		Y
Whimbrel	1	
Green Sandpiper	1	
Greenshank	1	Y
Iceland Gull		Y
Great Black-backed Gull	1	Y
Sandwich Tern	1	
Common Tern	1	
Guillemot		Y
Waxwing		Y
Fieldfare	1	Y
Redwing		Y
Rock Pipit		Y
Snow Bunting		Y

Appendix 4: Species ubiquity - breeding

Rank	Species	No of kms	% of kms	Rank	Species	No of kms	% of kms
1st	Carrion Crow	177	89%	46th=	Great Spotted Woodpecker	70	35%
2nd	Wren	169	85%				
3rd	Chaffinch	149	75%	48th	Wheatear	69	35%
4th	Woodpigeon	147	74%	49th	Grey Wagtail	68	34%
5th	Blackbird	145	73%	50th=	Grey Heron	67	34%
6th	Blue Tit	144	72%	50th=	Chiffchaff	67	34%
7th	Swallow	143	72%	52nd	Dipper	60	30%
8th	Buzzard	142	71%	53rd	Bullfinch	59	30%
9th	Robin	137	69%	54th	Stock Dove	55	28%
10th	Great Tit	135	68%	55th=	Sparrowhawk	54	27%
11th	Willow Warbler	133	67%	55th=	Common Gull	54	27%
12th	Skylark	130	65%	57th=	Black-headed Gull	53	27%
13th	Dunnock	129	65%	57th=	Herring Gull	53	27%
14th	Pied Wagtail	123	62%	59th	Sand Martin	48	24%
15th	Starling	121	61%	60th	Sedge Warbler	47	24%
16th	Song Thrush	120	60%	61st	Jay	41	21%
17th	Rook	119	60%	62nd	Moorhen	39	20%
18th	Jackdaw	118	59%	63rd	Siskin	38	19%
19th	Magpie	113	57%	64th=	Shelduck	34	17%
20th	Swift	111	56%	64th=	Snipe	34	17%
21st	Mallard	109	55%	66th	Spotted Flycatcher	33	17%
22nd=	Coal Tit	108	54%	67th	Mute Swan	32	16%
22nd=	Greenfinch	108	54%	68th	Green Woodpecker	31	16%
24th	Pheasant	106	53%	69th=	Raven	29	15%
25th	Goldfinch	104	52%	69th=	Tree Sparrow	29	15%
26th=	Meadow Pipit	103	52%	71st	Common Sandpiper	27	14%
26th=	Whitethroat	103	52%	72nd	Tree Pipit	24	12%
28th	House Sparrow	100	50%	73rd	Tufted Duck	23	12%
29th	Kestrel	99	50%	74th=	Teal	21	11%
30th	Yellowhammer	96	48%	74th=	Grey Partridge	21	11%
31st	House Martin	93	47%	74th=	Cuckoo	21	11%
32nd=	Oystercatcher	88	44%	74th=	Barn Owl	21	11%
32nd=	Curlew	88	44%	74th=	Whinchat	21	11%
34th	Reed Bunting	81	41%	79th	Goosander	20	10%
35th=	Lesser Black-backed Gull	79	40%	80th=	Grasshopper Warbler	19	10%
				80th=	Lesser Redpoll	19	10%
35th=	Collared Dove	79	40%	82nd	Stonechat	16	9%
35th=	Long-tailed Tit	79	40%	83rd=	Little Grebe	15	8%
38th=	Mistle Thrush	78	39%	83rd=	Coot	15	8%
38th=	Blackcap	78	39%	83rd=	Great Black-backed Gull	15	8%
38th=	Linnet	78	39%				
41st=	Tawny Owl	77	39%	83rd=	Kingfisher	15	8%
41st=	Garden Warbler	77	39%	87th=	Peregrine	10	5%
43rd	Goldcrest	76	38%	87th=	Redshank	10	5%
44th=	Lapwing	75	38%	87th=	Crossbill sp's.	10	5%
44th=	Treecreeper	75	38%	90th	Red Grouse	8	5%
46th=	Feral Pigeon	70	35%				

Total number of squares & part squares surveyed = 198. No of km's = all registrations.

Appendix 5: Relative abundancy - breeding

Wildfowl & allies

Mallard	190
Shelduck	90
Teal	66
Mute Swan	57
Tufted Duck	43
Grey Heron	28
Little Grebe	22
Coot	19
Goosander	17
Moorhen	14
Cormorant	6
Gadwall	6
Red-br'd Merganser	6
Wigeon	5
Greylag Goose	4
Goldeneye	4
Water Rail	3

Waders

Lapwing	92
Oystercatcher	78
Curlew	36
Redshank	13
Snipe	9
Black-tailed Godwit	6
Common Sandpiper	5

Gulls

Lesser-Black-b Gull	159
Black-headed Gull	76
Herring Gull	55
Common Gull	33
Great Black-b Gull	13

Raptors & Owls

Buzzard	79
Kestrel	13
Sparrowhawk	4
Peregrine	2
Barn Owl	2
Tawny Owl	1

Game Birds

Pheasant	62
Grey Partridge	2
Red-legged Partridge	2
Red Grouse	1

Pigeons & Doves

Wood Pigeon	908
Feral Pigeon	180
Stock Dove	67
Collared Dove	60

Woodpeckers etc.

G't Spotted Woodpecker	22
Green Woodpecker	9
Kingfisher	4
Cuckoo	1

Hirundines etc.

Swallow	379
House Martin	152
Swift	106
Sand Martin	89

Larks, Pipits & Wagtails

Meadow Pipit	389
Skylark	281
Pied Wagtail	52
Grey Wagtail	19
Tree Pipit	16

Chats, Thrushes etc.

Blackbird	557
Wren	407
Robin	238
Dunnock	159
Song Thrush	64
Wheatear	22
Mistle Thrush	21
Dipper	11
Whinchat	11
Stonechat	3
Redstart	2

Warblers etc.

Willow Warbler	328
Sedge Warbler	77
Blackcap	60
Whitethroat	56
Chiffchaff	26
Garden Warbler	18
Grasshopper Warbler	7

Tits etc.

Blue Tit	316
Great Tit	234
Long-tailed Tit	53
Coal Tit	33
Goldcrest	25
Treecreeper	13
Spotted Flycatcher	11

Corvids & Starling

Starling	913
Rook	662
Jackdaw	548
Carrion Crow	505
Magpie	144
Raven	14
Jay	8

Sparrows, Finches & Buntings

Chaffinch	640
House Sparrow	453
Goldfinch	148
Greenfinch	88
Yellowhammer	80
Tree Sparrow	72
Reed Bunting	58
Siskin	36
Linnet	21
Crossbill (sp's)	12
Bullfinch	7
Lesser Redpoll	7

Surveyors selected an available tetrad (2 x 2 km square) and followed a route of their own choosing, recording the numbers of all bird species seen & heard which were making use of the tetrad. These counts were of exactly one hour duration. If they wished, surveyors could perambulate for an extra hour following a completely different route within the tetrad. Only counts from those tetrads with > 50 % of their area within the County have been used, so that while the great majority of the birds recorded will be from within Clackmannanshire, a few will have been recorded from just outside. These surveys were undertaken between 2008 - 2012.

Appendix 6: Relative abundancy - winter

Wildfowl & allies

Pink-footed Goose	3563
Greylag Goose	615
Teal	606
Mallard	369
Shelduck	125
Cormorant	79
Tufted duck	74
Mute Swan	71
Goldeneye	66
Grey Heron	58
Goosander	53
Wigeon	51
Coot	47
Moorhen	25
Canada Goose	17
Water Rail	4
Whooper Swan	2
Barnacle Goose	2
Gadwall	2
Shoveler	2
Scaup	2
Guillemot	1
Red-throated Diver	1
Little Grebe	1
Great Crested Grebe	1
White-fronted Goose	1
Pintail	1
Red-br'd Merganser	1

Waders

Curlew	631
Lapwing	291
Redshank	25
Golden Plover	14
Oystercatcher	12
Snipe	12
Woodcock	5
Dunlin	4
Jack Snipe	1

Gulls

Black-headed Gull	1573
Common Gull	210
Herring Gull	141
Great Black-b Gull	14
Lesser-Black-b Gull	5

Raptors

Buzzard	114
Kestrel	18
Sparrowhawk	4
Peregrine	3

Game Birds

Pheasant	36
Grey Partridge	8
Red Grouse	7
Red-legged Partridge	2

Pigeons & Doves

Wood Pigeon	2160
Feral Pigeon	517
Collared Dove	79
Stock Dove	24

Woodpeckers etc.

G't Spotted. Woodpecker	15
Green Woodpecker	6
Kingfisher	1

Larks, Pipits & Wagtails

Pied Wagtail	38
Meadow Pipit	34
Skylark	18
Grey Wagtail	13
Rock Pipit	1

Chats, Thrushes etc.

Blackbird	557
Fieldfare	491
Robin	262
Redwing	208
Wren	153
Dunnock	108
Mistle Thrush	41
Song Thrush	38
Dipper	26
Stonechat	10
Blackcap	1

Tits etc.

Blue Tit	470
Great Tit	240
Long-tailed Tit	125
Coal Tit	71
Goldcrest	48
Treecreeper	27

Corvids & Starling

Rook	1864
Jackdaw	1210
Starling	1033
Carrion Crow	827
Magpie	221
Raven	19
Jay	6

Sparrows, Finches & Buntings

Chaffinch	944
House Sparrow	445
Linnet	238
Yellowhammer	177
Goldfinch	131
Siskin	111
Greenfinch	85
Bullfinch	70
Reed Bunting	65
Tree Sparrow	45
Lesser Redpoll	27
Crossbill (sp's)	12
Brambling	6
Snow Bunting	1

Surveyors selected an available tetrad (2 x 2 km square) and followed a route of their own choosing, recording the numbers of all bird species seen & heard which were making use of the tetrad. These counts were of exactly one hour duration. If they wished, surveyors could perambulate for an extra hour following a completely different route within the tetrad. Only counts from those tetrads with > 50 % of their area within the County have been used, so that while the great majority of the birds recorded will be from within Clackmannanshire, a few will have been recorded from just outside. These surveys were undertaken between 2007 - 2012.

Appendix 7: Rookeries

Location	Grid Ref	Date	Nests	Rookery nest trees
Easter Cornhill	NN 978000	01.04.12	33	Beech.
Windsor St., Menstrie	NS 845968	04.04.12	3	
Main St W., Menstrie	NS 845970	04.04.12	159	Mature deciduous woodland.
A 907 at Cambus.	NS 858941	01.04.12	69	
Menstrie maltings.	NS 858965	04.04.12	16	
Myreton	NS 858974	04.04.12	25	Mature open woodland on scarp slope.
Orchard Farm	NS 860933	01.04.12	78	Copse of Ash, Horse Chestnut, Oak and Sycamore.
Alloa W.	NS 874930	01.04.12	73	
Gean House (a), Alloa	NS 875938	01.04.12	30	Pine and deciduous.
Gean House (b), Alloa	NS 875941	06.04.12	6	
Cochrane Park, Alva	NS 876970	01.04.12	37	
Comely Bank, Alloa	NS 892927	01.04.12	46	Pine and deciduous.
Keilarsbrae, Alloa	NS 894938	01.04.12	2	Sycamore.
Mary Br., Clackmannan Town	NS 909923	01.04.12	13	Sycamore and Willow.
Chapelhill, Clackmannan Town	NS 913914	01.04.12	15	Sycamore and Pine.
Riccarton, Clackmannan	NS 913921	01.04.12	34	
Devonside	NS 923960	04.04.12	11	Mature deciduous copse.
Cunninghar, Tillicoultry	NS 924977	01.04.12	36	
Dollarbank	NS 944982	01.04.12	20	
Aberdona House	NS 945950	04.04.12	2	Mature mixed woodland.
Belmont, Dollar W.	NS 947976	01.04.12	19	
Kellybank	NS 970984	01.04.12	9	Scots Pine and deciduous.
Woodside Farm	NS 975948	01.04.12	7	Scots Pine and deciduous.
Shelterhall	NS 985984	01.04.12	13	
Muckhart Mill	NS 988986	15.03.05	2	Pine.
Total			**758**	

Appendix 8: Garden BirdWatch

	rate		rate
Blackbird	95.67	Swallow	3.24
Blue Tit	90.43	Fieldfare	3.14
House Sparrow	83.4	Brambling	1.89
Robin	82.8	House Martin	1.68
Chaffinch	82.21	Kestrel	1.62
Dunnock	74.69	Chiffchaff	1.51
Great Tit	72.69	Swift	1.3
Greenfinch	72.63	Green Woodpecker	1.19
Collared Dove	68.09	Pheasant	1.14
Starling	67.77	Tree Sparrow	1.03
Woodpigeon	66.79	Grey Wagtail	0.76
Coal Tit	57	Redpoll (Lesser / Common)	0.54
Jackdaw	44.13	Black-headed Gull	0.32
Magpie	40.45	Buzzard	0.22
Wren	39.86	Spotted Flycatcher	0.16
Carrion Crow	39.7	Jay	0.11
Goldfinch	37.16	Garden Warbler	0.11
Siskin	22.82	Lesser Redpoll	0.11
Song Thrush	20.71	Lesser Black-backed Gull	0.05
Goldcrest	15.95	Reed Bunting	0.05
Sparrowhawk	13.9	Nuthatch	0.05
Long-tailed Tit	10.01	Grey Heron	0.05
Pied Wagtail	8.76	Linnet	0.05
Mistle Thrush	8.17		
Feral Pigeon	7.46		
Rook	7.08		
Great Spotted Woodpecker	6.06		
Bullfinch	6		
Treecreeper	5.25		
Redwing	5.03		
Blackcap	5.03		
Tawny Owl	4.22		
Willow Warbler	4.16		
Yellowhammer	3.24		

Garden BirdWatch is a survey organised by the BTO in which c.15,000 participants around the UK record the highest number of each species seen at one time each week. The reporting rates depicted are from the 18 gardens in Clackmannanshire which returned data during the *Atlas* period (2002-2007) and show the number of weeks in which a species was recorded expressed as a percentage of the total number of weeks (n=312).

Appendix 9: Where to watch birds in Clackmannanshire

Haugh of Blackgrange (NS 843925)

Habitat: low lying farmland peninsula bordered by the tidal R. Forth.

Access: park at NS 840935. Access on foot only down the continuation of the unmetalled road. Good views can also be obtained from the south bank of the Forth at Fallin (NS 840919). Also from the upstream corner of Cambus Pools at NS 846935.

Species: principally large flocks of Pink-footed and Greylag Geese in winter/spring which regularly hold small numbers of Barnacle and White-fronted Goose as well as the occasional rarer goose eg. a Red-breasted Goose was present in February 2007. Also common waders in the fields and wildfowl on the river.

Cambus Pools (NS 847937)

Habitat: reed choked freshwater/brackish pools.

Access: on footpaths from Cambus via a bridge over the R. Devon (NS 853940) or from Blackgrange bonds (NS 844943). A SWT reserve.

Species: passage migrants especially wildfowl and waders. Occasional scarce species such as Garganey (spring) and Greenshank.

Cambus Village Pool and Devonmouth Pool (NS 853936)

Habitat: subsidence pools in grazed fields adjacent to the R. Forth.

Access: by path from Cambus Village. Park at NS 854937.

Species: wildfowl and passage waders including scarce species such as Gadwall, Shoveler, Ruff, Black-tailed Godwit, Green Sandpiper and Greenshank.

Tullibody Inch (NS 863923)

Habitat: reed covered island in the R. Forth. The R. Forth (incl. Tullibody and Alloa Inches) is designated as a SPA from Cambus to Alloa.

Access: path along the north shore of the R. Forth.

Species: wildfowl on the river and waders on exposed mud including scarce species such as Gadwall, Shoveler, Water Rail, Curlew Sandpiper, Ruff, Whimbrel, Greenshank or even rarities like Little Ringed Plover (July 2009) or Pectoral Sandpiper (Sep 2008).

Blackdevon Wetlands (NS 893911)

Habitat: ungrazed, marshy area with freshwater pools by the R. Forth.

Access: park at NS 888920. Path to Clackmannan runs through the area from here. Also a track alongside the R. Forth is accessed through the recycling centre at NS 887918 (permission for vehicular access required).

Species: currently the two pools by the R. Forth are of most interest. These are especially good for scarce passage wildfowl and waders. Occasionally there are rarities like Spoonbill (July 2009) or Marsh Harrier (May 2009). Wintering Hen Harriers and Short-eared Owls have also been seen.

Kennetpans (NS 916887)

Habitat: area of mudflats exposed just below high water.

Access: from minor road at NS 920891. (Sun glare can be a problem).

Species: wildfowl and waders. Recent passage waders have included Ringed Plover, Bar-tailed Godwit and Turnstone.

Where to Watch Birds in Clackmannanshire cont.

Gartmorn Dam (NS 910940)
Habitat: this man-made lake is the central component of a country park (LNR) managed by Clackmannanshire Council. A SSSI.
Access: a well made path circumnavigates the lake. There is a hide on the north shore.
Species: the premier inland site in the County for breeding and wintering wildfowl. Scarcer wildfowl such as Gadwall occasionally occur and a Little Egret visited in Oct. 2010. The wooded fringes of the lake are home to a variety of woodland birds throughout the year.

Dollar Glen (NS 961990)
Habitat: a gorge of semi-natural woodland. A SSSI.
Access: car parks at NS 964989 and NS 963993. A path runs up the glen from Dollar.
Species: home to a variety of woodland species. Best in spring. Dipper and Grey Wagtail on the burn.

Tillicoultry Glen (NS 913976)
Habitat: a gorge of semi-natural woodland. A SSSI.
Access: car parking at NS 914975. A made path runs up the gorge exiting onto the open hill.
Species: home to a variety of woodland species. Best in spring. Dipper and Grey Wagtail on the burn.

Alva Glen (NS 886975)
Habitat: a gorge of semi-natural woodland. A SSSI.
Access: car park at NS 884975. A made path runs up the gorge exiting onto the open hill.
Species: home to a variety of woodland species. Best in spring. Dipper and Grey Wagtail on the burn.

Ochil Hills Woodland Park (NS 901976)
Habitat: a wooded hillside – mostly deciduous.
Access: car park at NS 898974. Made paths in the lower part of the wood.
Species: home to a variety of woodland species. Best in spring.

The Devon Valley (NS 8594 - NS 9897)
Habitat: a river valley and floodplain.
Access: by a number of public roads and footpaths.
Species: all common woodland, farmland and river species. Regular flocks of Whooper Swan, Pink-footed and Greylag Geese in winter.

Appendix 10: Useful addresses

Organisation	Postal address	Phone / e-mail / website
British Trust for Ornithology	The Nunnery, Thetford, Norfolk IP24 2PU	Tel: 01842 750050 E-mail: info@bto.org Website: http://www.bto.org
British Trust for Ornithology (Scotland)	School of Biological and Environmental Sciences, Cottrell Building, University of Stirling, Stirling FK9 4LA	Tel: 01786 466560 E-mail: scot.info@bto.org Website: http://www.bto.org/regional/btoscotland.htm
Royal Society for the Protection of Birds	The Lodge, Sandy, Bedfordshire. SG19 2DL	Tel: 01767 680551 Website: http://www.rspb.org.uk
Royal Society for the Protection of Birds (Scotland)	2 Lochside View, Edinburgh Park, Edinburgh, EH12 9DH	Tel: 0131 317 4100 E-mail: rspb.scotland@rspb.org.uk Website: http://www.rspb.org.uk/Scotland/
Royal Society for the Protection of Birds: South & West Scotland Regional Office	10 Park Quadrant, Glasgow G3 6BS	Tel: 0141 331 0993 E-mail: glasgow@rspb.org.uk Website: http://www.rspb.org.uk/Scotland/southandwest/
Royal Society for the Protection of Birds: Forth Valley Local Group		Website: http://www.rspb.org.uk/groups/forthvalley
Scottish Natural Heritage (office covering Clackmannanshire)	Battleby, Redgorton, Perth PE1 3EW	Tel: 01738 444177 E-mail: enquiries@snh.gov.uk Website: http://www.snh.gov.uk
Scottish Ornithologists' Club	Waterston House, Aberlady, East Lothian EH32 0PY	Tel: 01875 871 330 E-mail: mail@the-soc.org.uk Website: http://www.the-soc.org.uk/
Scottish Wildlife Trust	Harbourside House, 110 Commercial Street, Edinburgh EH6 6NF	Tel: 0131 312 7765 E-mail: enquiries@swt.org.uk Website: http://www.swt.org.uk
Scottish Wildlife Trust: Stirling Members Centre	Secretary: Sue Sexton, 22 Alexander Drive, Br of Allan FK9 4QB	Tel: 01786 833409 E-mail: sextonsp@aol.com
Clackmannanshire Ranger Service	Kilncraigs, Greenside St, Alloa FK10 1EB	Tel: 01259 452478 / 450000 E-mail: rangers@clacks.gov.uk Website: http://www.clacksweb.org.uk/environment/countrysiderangerservice

Appendix 11: Gazetteer

(Place names used in the text with one kilometre square location. Large geographical features such as the Ochil Hills and the River Forth have not been listed.)

Aberdona	NS 9495	Haugh of Blackgrange	NS 8492
Alloa	NS 8892	Hillfoot Hill	NN 9600
Alloa Inch	NS 8791	Inglewood Pond	NS 8793
Alva	NS 8897	Kennetpans	NS 9188
Alva Glen	NS 8898	Kersiepow Pond	NS 8896
Alva Moss	NN 8801	Kilbagie	NS 9289
Balquharn	NS 8697	King's Seat Hill	NS 9399
Balquharn Burn	NS 8698	Lawmuir Wood	NS 9496
Ben Buck	NN 8901	Linn Mill	NS 9292
Ben Cleuch	NN 9000	Longcarse	NS 8892
Ben Ever	NN 8900	Longcarse Pond	NS 8692
Bengengie Hill	NN 8600	Lookaboutye	NS 9191
Blackdevon Wetlands	NS 8991	Lornshill	NS 8794
Blackgrange	NS 8494	Maggie's Wood Pool	NS 8995
Blairdenon Hill	NN 8601	Manor Powis	NS 8295
Broich Burn	NN 9102	Maddy Moss	NN 9201
Brucefield	NS 9591	Marchglen	NS 9096
Burnfoot Hill	NN 9003	Menstrie	NS 8496
Cambus	NS 8593	Menstrie Glen	NS 8497
Cambus Pools	NS 8493	Menstrie Moss	NN 8600
Cambus Village Pool	NS 8593	Mill Glen	NS 9198
Clackmannan	NS 9191	Myreton Hill	NS 8598
Coalsnaughton	NS 9295	Parklands Muir	NS 9693
Craig Leith	NS 8797	Pool of Muckhart	NO 0000
Craigrie Pond	NS 8991	Rumbling Bridge	NT 0199
Crook of Devon	NO 0300	Delph Pond	NS 8694
Dollar	NS 9698	Silverhills Pond	NS 9096
Dollar Glen	NS 9699	Solsgirth	NS 9895
Dollarbeg	NS 9796	Solsgirth Mine	NS 9894
Devonmouth Pool	NS 8693	South Alloa	NS 8791
Finglen Burn	NN 8801	The Rhind	NS 8691
Forestmill	NS 9593	Tillicoultry	NS 9297
Gartlove	NS 9493	Tullibody	NS 8594
Gartarry	NS 9390	Tullibody Inch	NS 8692
Gartmorn Dam	NS 9194	Upper Glendevon Resr.	NN 9104
Gartmornhill Wood	NS 9194	Vicar's Bridge	NS 9898
Glen Quey	NN 9702	Wood Hill	NS 8998
Gloom Hill	NS 9699	Yetts o' Muckhart	NO 0001
Harviestoun	NS 9397		

Appendix 12: References

Within the species accounts frequently-used references appear in italic type. Within the List of References these references are signified in bold type.

1968-72 Atlas	Sharrock, J.T.R. 1976
1988-91 Atlas	Gibbons, D.W., Reid, J.B. & Chapman, R.A. 1993.
BBWC	Breeding Birds in the Wider Countryside in *BirdFacts* (q.v.)
BirdFacts	Robinson, R.A. 2005.
BS1	Baxter, E.V. & Rintoul, L.J. 1953.
BS2	Thom, V.M. 1986.
BS3	Forrester, R.W., Andrews, I.J., McInerny, C.J., Murray, R.D., McGowan, R.Y., Zonfrillo, B., Betts, M.W., Jardine, D.C. & Grundy, D.S. (eds.). 2007.
BWP	Cramp, S. & Simmons, K.E.L. (eds). 1977.
	Cramp, S. & Simmons, K.E.L. (eds). 1980.
	Cramp, S. & Simmons, K.E.L. (eds). 1983.
	Cramp, S. (ed). 1985.
	Cramp, S. (ed). 1988.
	Cramp, S. (ed). 1992.
	Cramp, S.& Perrins, C.M. (eds). 1993.
	Cramp, S.& Perrins, C.M. (eds). 1994.
	Cramp, S.& Perrins, C.M. (eds). 1994a.
EBCC Atlas	Hagemeijer, W.J.M. & Blair, M.J.(eds.). 1997.
Fife Atlas	Elkins, N., Reid, J.B., Brown, A.W., Robertson, D.G.& Smout, A-M. 2003.
Historical Atlas	Holloway, S. 1996.
Migration Atlas	Wernham, C.V., Toms, M.P., Marchant, J.H., Clark, J.A., Siriwardena, G.M. & Baillie, S.R. (eds.) 2002.
SE Scotland Atlas	Murray, R.D., Holling, M., Dott, H.E.M. & Vandome, P. 1998.
Statistical Accounts	
UFABR	(Upper) Forth Area Bird Reports – various dates and editors (principally C. J. Henty), published in the Forth Naturalist and Historian.
WeBS	The Wetland Bird Survey Reports – various dates and editors.
Winter Atlas	Lack, P. 1986.

REFERENCES

Allison, A., Newton, I. & Campbell, C. 1974. *Loch Leven National Nature Reserve; A Study in Waterfowl Biology*. WAGBI, Chester.

Atkinson-Willes, G. L. 1963. *Wildfowl in Great Britain*. HMSO London.

Austin, G.E, Collier, M.P., Calbrade, N.A., Hall, C. & Musgrave, A.J. 2008. *Waterbirds in the UK 2006/07: The Wetland Bird Survey*. BTO/WWT/RSPB/JNCC, Thetford.

Baillie, S.R., Crick, H.Q.P., Balmer, D.E., Bashford, R.I., Beaven, L.P., Freeman, S.N., Marchant, J.H., Noble, D.G., Raven, M.J., Siriwardena, G.M., Thewlis, R., & Wernham, C.V. 2001. *Breeding Birds in the Wider Countryside: their conservation status 2000*. BTO Research Report No.252. British Trust for Ornithology, Thetford.

Baillie, S.R., Marchant, J.H., Crick, H.Q.P., Noble, D.G., Balmer, D.E., Barimore, C., Coombes, R.H., Downie, I.S., Freeman, S.N., Joys, A.C., Leech, D.I., Raven, M.J., Robinson, R.A. & Thewlis, R.M.. 2007. *Breeding Birds in the Wider Countryside: their conservation status 2007*. BTO Research Report No.487. British Trust for Ornithology, Thetford.

Baillie, S.R., Marchant, J.H., Leech, D.I., Joys, A.C., Noble, D.G., Barimore, C., Grantham, M.J., Risely, K., & Robinson, R.A. 2009. *Breeding Birds in the Wider Countryside: their conservation status 2008*. BTO Research Report No.516. British Trust for Ornithology, Thetford. (http://www.bto.org/birdtrends),

Bainbridge, I.P. & Minton, C.D.T. 1978. The migration and mortality of the curlew in Britain and Ireland. Bird Study 25: 36-50.

Baines, D. & Hudson, P.J. 1995. The decline of the black grouse in Scotland and northern England. *Bird Study* 42: 122-131.

Baxter, E.V. & Rintoul, L.J. 1953. The Birds of Scotland. Two volumes. Oliver & Boyd, Edinburgh & London.

Birkhead, T. 1991. *The Magpies*. T & A D Poyser, London.

Brown, A.F. & Atkinson, P.W. 1996. Habitat associations of coastal wintering passerines. Bird Study 43, 188-200.

Brown, AW. & Brown, LM. 2005. The 2002 census of the Mute Swan in Scotland. *Scottish Birds* Vol 25: 1-16

Bryant, D. M. 1974. Birds of the Stirling Region. In: Timms, D. (ed.) *The Stirling Region*, 123-146. Stirling University: Stirling.

Bryant, D.M. 1988. Lifetime reproductive success of House Martins. In Clutton-Brock, T.H. (ed.) *Reproductive Success: Studies of individual variation in contrasting breeding systems,* 173-188. Chicago University Press, London.

Bryant D.M. 1999. House Martin. In Newton, I (ed.) *Lifetime Reproduction in Birds*, 89-106. Academic Press, London.

Bryant, D.M. & Tatner, P. 1987. Energetics of the annual cycle of Dippers Cinclus cinclus. Ibis 130: 17-38.

Burnfoot Wind Farm EIA

Calbrade, N.A., Holt, C.A., Austin, G.E., Mellan, H.J., Hearn, R.D., Stroud, D.A.,Wotton, S.R. & Musgrove, A.J. 2010. *Waterbirds in the UK 2008/09: The Wetland Bird Survey.* BTO/RSPB/JNCC in association with WWT, Thetford.

Calladine, J., Baines, D. & Warren, P. 2002. effects of reduced grazing on population density and breeding success of black grouse in northern England. *Journal of Applied Ecology* 39: 772-780.

Calladine, J., Dougill, S., Harding, N. & Stroud, D.D. 1990. Moorland birds on the Campsie Fells, Touch Hills and west Ochil Hills, Stirling: Habitats, distribution and numbers. *Forth Naturalist and Historia*n 13: 53-69.

Calladine, J., Garner, G. & Humphreys, L. 2008. *A sample survey of the breeding birds at woodland expansion sites of the Scottish Forest Alliance in 2007.* BTO Research Report No. 493, BTO Scotland, Stirling.

Calladine, J., Garner, G. & Wernham, C. 2007. *Developing methods for the field survey and monitoring of breeding Short-eared Owls* (Asio flammeus) *in the UK: an interim report from pilot fieldwork in 2006.* BTO Research Report No. 472. BTO Scotland, Stirling.

Calladine, J. & Harris, M.P. 1997. Intermittent breeding in the Herring Gull *Larus argentatus* and the Lesser Black-backed Gull *Larus fuscus.* Ibis 139: 259-263.

Calladine, J.R., Park, K.J., Thompson, K. & Wernham, C.V. 2006. *Review of urban gulls and their management in Scotland. Report to the Scottish Executive.* BTO and Stirling University, Stirling.

Calladine, J., Robertson, D. & Wernham, C. 2006. The ranging behaviour of some granivorous passerines on farmland in winter determined by mark-recapture ringing and by radiotelemetry. *Ibis* 148: 169-173.

Castle, M. E. 1977. Rookeries in Scotland – 1975. *Scottish Birds* 9: 32-334.

Central Science Laboratory. 2002. *UK Ruddy Duck control trial final report.* Report to Department for Environment, Food and Rural Affairs. Chabrzyl, G. & Coulson, J.C. 1976. Survival and recruitment in the Herring Gull *Larus argentatus. Journal of Animal Ecology* 45: 187-203.

Clark, H. & Sellers, R.H. 1998. Winter habitats of Twites in Scotland. *Scottish Birds,* 19, 262-269.

Clark H & Sellers R M 1999. A further survey of Twites wintering in Caithness. *Scottish Birds,* 20, 35-37.

Cobb, J.L.S. 2005. The biology of a population of Willow Warblers in East Fife. *Scottish Birds* 25: 41-49

Collin, P, N. 2009. First breeding of Eurasian Spoonbills in Scotland. *Scottish Birds* 29(1):40-41.

Conway, G. & Burton, N. 2009. Changing Fortunes for Breeding Plovers. *BTO News* 280: 10-11.

Cramp, S., Bourne, W. R. P. & Saunders, D. 1974. *The Seabirds of Britain and Ireland.* Collins. London

Cramp, S. (ed). 1985. *The Birds of the Western Palearctic.* Volume 4. Oxford University Press, Oxford.

Cramp, S. (ed). 1988. *The Birds of the Western Palearctic.* Volume 5. Oxford University Press, Oxford.

Cramp, S. (ed). 1992. *The Birds of the Western Palearctic.* Volume 6. Oxford University Press, Oxford.

Cramp, S.& Perrins, C.M. (eds). 1993. *The Birds of the Western Palearctic.* Volume 7. Oxford University Press, Oxford.

Cramp, S.& Perrins, C.M. (eds). 1994. The Birds of the Western Palearctic. Volume 8. Oxford University Press, Oxford.

Cramp, S.& Perrins, C.M. (eds). 1994a. The Birds of the Western Palearctic. Volume 9. Oxford University Press, Oxford.

Cramp, S. & Simmons, K.E.L. (eds). 1977. The Birds of the Western Palearctic. Volume 1. Oxford University Press, Oxford.

Cramp, S. & Simmons, K.E.L. (eds). 1980. The Birds of the Western Palearctic. Volume 2. Oxford University Press, Oxford.

Cramp, S. & Simmons, K.E.L. (eds). 1983. The Birds of the Western Palearctic. Volume 3. Oxford University Press, Oxford.

Davies, P.W. & Snow, D. W. 1965. Territory and Food of the Song Thrush. *British Birds,* 58: 161-175.

Duncan, N. 1981. The Lesser Black-backed Gull on the Isle of May. *Scottish Birds* 11: 180-188.

Eaton, M.A., Balmer, D.E., Conway, G.J., Gillings, S., Grice, P.V., Hall, C, Hearn, R.D., Musgrove, A.J., Risely, K. and Wotton, S. 2009. *The State of the UK's Birds 2008.* RSPB, BTO, WWT, CCW, NIEA, JNCC, NE and SNH, Sandy, Bedfordshire.

Eaton, M.A., Brown, A.F., Noble, D.G., Musgrove, A.J., Hearn, R.D., Aebischer, N.J., Gibbons, D.W., Evans, A. & Gregory, R.D. 2009. Birds of Conservation Concern 3. *British Birds* 102: 296-341

Elkins, N., Reid, J.B., Brown, A.W., Robertson, D.G.& Smout, A-M. 2003. *The Fife Bird Atlas. Woodlands Studios, Dunfermline.*

Etheridge, B., Holling, M., Riley, H.T., Wernham, C.V. & Thompson, D.B.A. 2007. *Scottish Raptor Monitoring Scheme Report 2005.* SOC, Aberlady.

Etheridge, B., Holling, M., Riley, H.T., Wernham, C.V. & Thompson, D.B.A. 2008. *Scottish Raptor Monitoring Scheme Report 2006.* SOC, Aberlady.

Forrester, R.W., Andrews, I.J., McInerny, C.J., Murray, R.D., McGowan, R.Y., Zonfrillo, B., Betts, M.W., Jardine, D.C. & Grundy, D.S. (eds.). 2007. The *Birds of Scotland.* The Scottish Ornithologists' Club, Aberlady.

Fox, A.D., Francis, I.S. & Walsh, A.J. 2009. *Report of 2008/09 international census of Greenland White-fronted Geese.* Greenland White-fronted Goose Study, Kalo & National Parks and Wildlife Service, Wexford.

Fox, A.D., Stroud, D.A., Walsh, A.J., Wilson, H.J., Norriss, D.W. & Francis, I.S. 2006. The rise and fall of the Greenland White-fronted Goose: a case studying international conservation. *British Birds* 99: 242 – 261.

Fuller, R.J., Gregory, R.D., Gibbons, D.W., Marchant, J.H., Wilson, J.D., Baillie, S.R. & Carter, N. 1995. Population declines and range contractions among lowland farmland birds in Britain. *Conservation Biology* 9: 1425–1441.

Fuller, R.J. & Lloyd, D. 1981. The distribution and habitats of wintering Golden Plovers in Britain, 1977-1978. *Bird Study* 28: 169-185.

Fuller, R.J., Noble, D.G., Smith, K.W. & Vanhinsbergh, D. 2005. Recent declines in populations of woodland birds in Britain: a review of possible causes. *British Birds*, 98: 116-143.

Galbraith, H. 1989. Arrival and habitat use by Lapwings *Vanellus vanellus* in the early breeding season. Ibis 131: 377-388.

Gibbons, D.W., Reid, J.B. & Chapman, R.A. 1993. *The New Atlas of Breeding Birds in Britain and Ireland: 1988-1991.* T.& A.D. Poyser, London.

Glue, D. 2006. Cuckoos in crisis? *BTO News* 263: 22-23.

Gray, R. 1873. On the sea-gulls at present frequenting the estuary of the Forth. *Proceedings of the Natural History Society of Glasgow 2*: 198-208.

Gregory, R.D. & Marchant, J.H. 1996. Population trends of Jays, Magpies, Jackdaws and Carrion Crows in the United Kingdom. *Bird Study* 43: 28-37.

Gregory, R.D., Noble, D.G., Cranswick, P.A., Campbell, L.H., Rehfish, M.M. & Baillie, S. R. 2001. *The State of the UK's Birds 2000.* RSPB, BTO and WWT: Sandy.

Gregory, R.D, Wilkinson, N.I., Noble, D.G., Robinson, J.A., Brown, A.F., Hughes, J., Procter D., Gibbons, D.W., & Galbraith, C. A., 2002. The population status of birds in the United Kingdom, Channel Islands and Isle of Man: an analysis of conservation concern 2002-2007. *British Birds* 95: 410-448.

Gutiérrez, R.J., Barrowclough, G.F. & Groth, J.G. 2000. A classification of the grouse (Aves: Tetraoninae) based on Mitochondrial DNA sequences. *Wildlife Biology 6:* 205-11.

Hagemeijer, W.J.M. & Blair, M.J.(eds.). 1997. *The EBCC Atlas of European Birds: their distribution and abundance.* T.& A.D. Poyser, London.

Hansen, L. 1952. The diurnal and annual rhythms of the tawny owl (*Strix a. aluco L.*). *Dansk Ornithologisk Fovenings Tidsscrift* 46: 158-172.

Harris, M.P. 1964. Aspects of the breeding biology of the gulls *Larus argentatus, L. fuscus* and *L. marinus. Ibis* 106: 432-456.

Haworth, P.F. & Thompson D.B.A. 1990. Factors associated with the breeding distribution of upland birds in the south Pennines, England. *Journal of Applied Ecology* 27: 562-577.

Henty, C. J. 1979. The foraging activity of Snow Buntings wintering inland in Scotland. *Bird Study* 26: 192 – 194.

Henty, C. J. 1991. Birds of the River Devon Surveyed over Ten Years. *Forth Naturalist and Historian* 14: 51 – 64.

Henty C.J. 1977. The Roost-flights of Whooper Swans in the Devon Valley (Central Scotland). *The Forth Naturalist & Historian* 2: 31-35.

Holling, M., and the Rare Birds Breeding Panel. 2009. Rare breeding birds in the United Kingdom in 2006. *British Birds* 102:158-202.

Holling, M., and the Rare Birds Breeding Panel. 2010a. Rare breeding birds in the United Kingdom in 2007. *British Birds* 103:2-52.

Holling, M., and the Rare Birds Breeding Panel. 2010b. Rare breeding birds in the United Kingdom in 2008. *British Birds* 103:482-538.

Holloway, S. 1996. *The Historical Atlas of Breeding Birds in Britain and Ireland 1975-1900.* T.& A.D. Poyser, London.

Hudson, R. 1976. Ruddy Ducks in Britain. *British Birds* 69:132-143.

John, A.W.G. & Roskell, J. 1985. Jay movements in autumn 1983. *British Birds,* 78:611-637.

Koskimies, J. 1950. The Life of the Swift, *Micropus apus* (L.) in relation to the weather. *Annales Academiae Scientiarum Fennicae Series A, IV Biologica* 15: 1-151.

Lack, D. 1956. *Swifts in a Tower.* Methuen, London.

Lack, P. 1986. *The Atlas of Wintering Birds in Britain and Ireland.* T.& A.D. Poyser, Calton.

Langstone, R.H.W., Smith, T., Brown, A.F. & Gregory, R.D. 2006. The status of breeding Twite *Carduelis flavirostris* in the UK. *Bird Study* 53: 55-63.

Leech, D., Shawyer, C.R. & Barimore, C. 2009. Are Barn Owls bouncing back? *BTO News* 280: 16-17.

Lever, C. 1977 *The Naturalized Animals of the British Isles*. Hutchinson, London.

Logie, J.W., Bryant, D.M., Howell, D.C. & Vickery, J.A. (1996) Biological significance if UK Critical load exceeds estimates for flowing waters: assessments of Dipper *Cinclus cinclus* populations in Scotland. Journal of Applied Ecology 33: 1065-1076.

McGowan, R. *Perth & Kinross Bird Reports*. Privately published.

Maclean, I.M.D. & Austin, G.E., Rehfisch, M.M., Blew, J., Crowe, O., Delaney, S., Devos, K. Deceuninck, B., Gunther, K., Laursen, K., van Roomen, M. & Wahl, J. 2008. Climate change causes rapid changes in the distribution and site abundance of birds in winter. *Global Change Biology* 14: 2849-2500.

Madge, S. & Burn, H. 1988. *Wildfowl. An identification guide to the ducks, geese and swans of the world*. Helm (A. & C. Black). London.

Marchant, J.H., Hudson, R., Carter, S.P. & Whittington, P. 1990. *Population Trends in British Breeding Birds*. British Trust for Ornithology, Tring.

May, R. & Fisher, J. 1953. A Collared Turtle Dove in England. *British Birds* 46: 51-55.

Mead, C. 2000. *The State of the Nation's Birds*. Whittet Books, Stowmarket.

Mead, C.J. & Hudson, R. 1984. Report on bird-ringing for 1983. *Ringing & Migration*, 5: 153-192.

Mitchell, P.I., Newton, S.F., Ratcliffe, N. & Dunn, T.E. (Eds) 2004. *Seabird Populations of Britain and Ireland*. T. & A.D. Poyser, London.

Munro, J. H. B. 1975. Scottish winter Rook roost survey – central and northern Scotland. Scottish Birds 8: 309 – 314 & map.

Murray, R.D. 2003. The first successful breeding of Red-necked Grebe for Britain. *Borders Bird Report* 21: 123-126.

Murray, R.D., Holling, M., Dott, H.E.M. & Vandome, P. 1998. *The Breeding Birds of South-east Scotland: 1988-1994*. Scottish Ornithologists' Club, Edinburgh.

Nethersole-Thompson, D. 1951. *The Greenshank*. Collins (New Naturalist), London.

Nethersole-Thompson, D. & M. 1979. *Greenshanks*, T & AD Poyser, Calton.

Newton, I. 1967. The adaptive radiation and feeding ecology of some British finches. *Ibis* 109: 33-98.

Newton, I. 1972. *Finches.* Collins, London.

Newton, I. 1991. Habitat variation and population variation in Sparrowhawks. *Ibis* 133 (supplement 1): 76-88.

Newton, S.F. (1989) Recruitment dynamics of a resident passerine: Dippers *Cinclus cinclus* in central Scotland. Unpubl. PhD thesis, University of Stirling.

Nilsson, L. 2008. Changes in numbers and distribution of wintering waterfowl in Sweden during forty years, 1967-2006. *Ornis Svecica* 18; 135-226.

O' Brien, M., Tharme, A. & Jackson D. 2002. Changes in breeding wader numbers on Scottish farmland during the 1990's. *Scottish Birds* 23: 10-21.

O' Brien, M., & Whyte, C.S. 2004. Estimating the breeding wader population of Scottish uplands and salt marshes. *Scottish Birds* 24 (2): 17-28.

O'Connor, R.J. & Mead, C.J. 1984. The Stock Dove in Britain, 1930-80. *British Birds* 77: 181-201.

O'Connor, R.J. & Shrubb, M. 1986. *Farming and Bird*s. Cambridge University Press, Cambridge.

Peach, W.J., Baillie, S.R. & Underhill, L. 1991. Survival of British Sedge Warblers *Acrocephalus schoenobaenus* in relation to west African rainfall. *Ibis* 133: 300-305

Percival, S.M. 1990. *Population trends in British Barn Owls* Tyto alba, *and Tawny Owls* Strix aluco *in relation to environmental change.* BTO Research Report 57. BTO Tring.

Perrins, C.M. & Smith, S.B. 2000. The breeding *Larus* gulls on Skomer Island National Nature Reserve, Pembrokeshire. *Atlantic Seabirds* 2: 195-210.

Petty, S.J. 1992. *Ecology of the Tawny Owl* Strix aluco *in the Spruce forests of Northumberland and Argyll.* Unpublished PhD thesis, The Open University.

Potts, G.R. 1980. The effects of modern agriculture, nest predation and game management on the population ecology of partridges (*Perdix perdix and Alectoris rufa*). *Advances in Ecological Research* 11: 1-82.

Potts, G.R. 1986. The Partridge: *pesticides, predation and conservation*. Collins, London.

Ratcliffe, D.A. 1976. Observations on the breeding of the Golden Plover in Great Britain. *Bird Study* 23: 63-116.

Raven, M.J., Noble, D.G. & Baillie, S.R. 2004 *The Breeding Bird Survey 2003.* BTO Research Report 363. BTO, Thetford.

Redfern, C.P.F. 1982. Lapwing nests sites and chick mobility in relation to habitat. *Bird Study* 29: 201-208.

L J Rintoul & E V Baxter. 1935. *A Vertebrate Fauna of Forth*. Oliver & Boyd, Edinburgh & London.

Risely, K., Baillie, S.R., Eaton, M.A., Joys, A.C., Musgrove, A.J., Noble, D.G., Renwick, A.R. & Wright, L.J. 2010. The Breeding bird Survey 2009. *BTO Research Report 559*. British Trust for Ornithology, Thetford.

Risely, K., Noble, D.G. & Baillie, S.R. 2009. *The Breeding Bird Survey 2008*. BTO Research Report No.537. British Trust for Ornithology, Thetford.

Robinson, R.A. 2005. *BirdFacts: profiles of birds occurring in Britain & Ireland.* (Various versions). BTO Research Report 407. BTO, Thetford. (http://www.bto.org/birdfacts).

Robinson, R.A., Green, R.E., Baillie, S.R., Peach, W.J. & Thomson, D.L. 2004. Demographic mechanisms of the population decline of the song thrush *Turdus philomelos* in Britain. *Journal of Animal Ecology* 73: 670–682.

Robinson R.A., Lawson B, Toms M.P., Peck K.M., Kirkwood J.K, et al. (2010) Emerging Infectious Disease Leads to Rapid Population Declines of Common British Birds. *Public Library of Science ONE* 5:8: (www.plosone.org/e12215).

Salomonsen, F. 1968 The moult migration. *Wildfowl* 19: 5-24

Sharrock, J.T.R. 1976. *The Atlas of Breeding Birds in Britain and Ireland.* British Trust for Ornithology, Tring.

Sim, I.M.W., Eaton, M.A., Setchfield, R.P., Warren, P.K. & Lindlay, P. 2008. Abundance of male Black Grouse *Tetrao tetrix* in Britain in 2005, and change since 1995-96. *Bird Study* 55: 304-313.

Sim, I.M.W., Gregory, R.D., Hancock, M.H. & Brown, A.F. 2005. Recent changes in abundance of British upland breeding birds. *Bird Study* 52: 261-276.

Siriwardena, G.M., Baillie, S.R., Crick, H.Q.P., Wilson, J.D. & Gates, S. 2000. The demography of lowland farmland birds. In Aebischer, N.J., Evans, A.D., Grice, P.V.& Vickery, J.A. (eds.) *Proceedings of the 1999 BOU Spring Conference: Ecology and Conservation of Lowland Farmland Birds*, 117-133. British Ornithologists' Union, Tring.

Siriwardena, G.M., Baillie, S.R. & Wilson, J.D. 1998. Variation in the survival rates of British farmland passerines with respect to their population trends. *Bird Study* 45: 276–292.

Siriwardena, G.M., Freeman, S. N. & Crick, H.Q.P. 2001. The decline of the Bulfinch *Pyrrhula pyrrhula* in Britain: is the mechanism known ? *Acta Ornithologica*, 36 (2).

Southern, H.N. 1970. The natural control of a population of Tawny Owls *(Strix aluco)*. *Journal of Zoology, London* 162: 197-285.

Summers-Smith, J.D. (1998) Studies of West Palearctic Birds: Tree Sparrow. *British Birds* 91: 124-138.

Sutherland, W.J. and Allport, G. 1991. The distribution and ecology of naturalised Egyptian geese alopochen *aegyptiacus* in Britain. *Bird Study* 38: 128-134.

Swann, R.L. 1988. Are all large Chaffinch flocks composed of continentals? *Ringing and Migration* 9: 1-4.

Swann, R. L. & Etheridge, B. 1996. Movements of waders to and from the Moray Firth. *Ringing and Migration* 17: 111-121.

Tapper, S.C., Potts, G.R. & Brockless, M.H. 1996. The effect of experimental reductions in predation pressure on the breeding success and population density of grey partridges *Perdix perdix*. *Journal of Applied Ecology* 33: 968-979.

Taylor, I.R. & Walton, A. 2003. Conservation of Barn Owls (*Tyto alba*) and the role of nest site provisioning in South Scotland. Thompson, D.B.A., Redpath, S.M., Fielding, A.H., Marquiss, M. & Galbrath, C.A. (eds.) *Birds of Prey in a Changing Environment. pp 417-426. The Stationery Office, Edinburgh.*

Tewnion, A. 1966. The Green Woodpecker in Clackmannanshire. *Scottish Birds* 4: 95-96.

Thiel, A.E. & Lindsay, H. 1999. Clackmannanshire Local Biodiversity Action Plan. Habitat Audit. Technical Report. Alloa: Clackmannanshire Council.

Thom, V.M. 1986. *Birds in Scotland.* T.& A.D. Poyser, Calton.

Toms, M.P. 1999. Could climate change pull the Barn Owl back from the brink? *BTO News* 223:10-11.

Toms, M., 2003. The BTO/CJ Garden *BirdWatch Book*. BTO, Thetford.

Turner, A.K. (2006) The Barn Swallow. T & A.D. Poyser, London.

Tyler, S.J. 1972. Breeding Biology of the Grey Wagtails. *Bird Study* 19: 69-80.

Tyler, S.J. & Ormerod, S.J. 1994. *The Dippers*. T. & A.D. Poyser, London.

Wernham, C.V., Toms, M.P., Marchant, J.H., Clark, J.A., Siriwardena, G.M. & Baillie, S.R. (eds.) 2002. *The Migration Atlas: movements of the birds of Britain and Ireland.* T.& A.D. Poyser, London.

Winstanley, D., Spencer, R. & Williamson, K. 1974. Where have all the Whitethroats gone? *Bird Study* 21: 1-14.

Worden, J., Crowe, O. Einarsson, O,. Gardarsson, A., McElwaine, J.G. & Rees, E.C. 2006. *Population size and breeding success of the Icelandic Whooper Swan Cygnus cygnus: results of the January 2005 International census.* Unpublished report. WWT. Slimbridge.

Yarker B. & Atkinson-Willes GL 1972. The numerical distribution of some British breeding ducks. *Wildfowl* 22: 63-70

Birds of Clackmannanshire Artists' credits

Paul Bartlett: pages 132, 133, 134, 135.

Keith Brockie: pages 45, 46, 47, 48, 52, 53, 54, 55, 56.

John Busby: pages Foreword, 28, 37, 57, 58, 59, 60, 61, 62, 63, 64, 138, 147, 149, 154, 155, 169, 179, 180, 187.

Richard Daly: pages 106, 108, 113, 114, 115, 116, 117, 118, 121, 122, 145, 146, 166, 183, 185.

William Neill: pages 65, 66, 67, 68, 69, 70, 140, 148, 150, 152, 153, 173.

Darren Rees: pages 71, 72, 73, 74, 75, 76, 77, 78, 89, 98, 99, 100, 101, 102, 103, 104, 137, 139, 141, 151, 159, 161, 165, 167, 170, 171, 172, 174, 177, 181, 182, 184, 190, 192, 193, 195 and cover.

Derek Robertson: pages 90, 91, 92, 97, 105, 112.

Jonathan Sainsbury: pages 109, 110, 111, 156, 157.

John Threlfall: pages 38, 39, 40, 41, 42, 43, 44, 49, 50, 51, 83, 84, 85, 86, 87, 88, 107, 119, 120, 142, 143, 144, 163, 164.

Ian Wallace: pages 158, 175, 176, 186.

Darren Woodhead: pages 79, 80, 81, 82, 93, 94, 95, 96, 123, 124, 125, 126, 127, 128, 129, 130, 131.

Species Index

This index lists the pages for the species accounts using the common English names.

Breeding species	Page	Breeding species	Page
Barn Owl	76	Long-eared Owl	78
Blackbird	109	Long-tailed Tit	97
Blackcap	100	Magpie	83
Blue Tit	90	Mallard	42
Bullfinch	133	Meadow Pipit	124
Buzzard	53	Merlin	55
Carrion Crow	87	Mistle Thrush	111
Chaffinch	125	Moorhen	58
Chiffchaff	98	Mute Swan	38
Coal Tit	92	Oystercatcher	60
Collared Dove	74	Peregrine	56
Common Crossbill	132	Pheasant	48
Common Gull	68	Pied / White Wagtail	122
Common Sandpiper	66	Raven	88
Coot	59	Red Grouse	45
Cuckoo	75	Red-legged Partridge	46
Curlew	65	Redshank	67
Dipper	108	Redstart	114
Dunnock	118	Reed Bunting	135
Feral Pigeon	71	Ringed Plover	61
Gadwall	40	Robin	113
Garden Warbler	101	Rook	86
Goldcrest	89	Sand Martin	94
Goldfinch	127	Sedge Warbler	104
Goosander	44	Shelduck	39
Grasshopper Warbler	103	Siskin	128
Great Crested Grebe	51	Skylark	93
Great Spotted Woodpecker	82	Snipe	63
Great Tit	91	Song Thrush	110
Green Woodpecker	81	Sparrowhawk	52
Greenfinch	126	Spotted Flycatcher	112
Grey Heron	49	Starling	107
Grey Partridge	47	Stock Dove	72
Grey Wagtail	121	Stonechat	116
Herring Gull	70	Swallow	95
House Martin	96	Swift	79
House Sparrow	119	Tawny Owl	77
Jackdaw	85	Teal	41
Jay	84	Tree Pipit	123
Kestrel	54	Tree Sparrow	120
Kingfisher	80	Treecreeper	105
Lapwing	62	Tufted Duck	43
Lesser Black-backed Gull	69	Twite	130
Lesser Redpoll	131	Water Rail	57
Linnet	129	Wheatear	117
Little Grebe	50	Whinchat	115

Breeding species	Page	Breeding species	Page
Whitethroat	102	Wren	106
Willow Warbler	99	Yellowhammer	134
Woodcock	64		
Woodpigeon	73		

Non-breeding Species (with map)

Barnacle Goose	141	Guillemot	155
Black-headed Gull	153	Hen Harrier	148
Black-tailed Godwit	152	Jack Snipe	151
Brambling	158	Long-tailed Duck	144
Cormorant	147	Pink-footed Goose	139
Dunlin	150	Pochard	143
Fieldfare	156	Red-b'd Merganser	146
Golden Plover	149	Redwing	157
Goldeneye	145	Whooper Swan	138
Great Black-backed Gull	154	Wigeon	142
Greylag Goose	140		

Other species recorded during the Atlas period

Arctic Skua	177	Quail	168
Bewick's (Tundra) Swan	160	Red Kite	170
Bar-tailed Godwit	173	Red-breasted Goose	162
Black Grouse	167	Red-necked Grebe	168
Brent Goose	162	Rock Pipit	185
Canada Goose	161	Rose-coloured Starling	184
Common Tern	180	Ruddy Duck	166
Garganey	163	Ruff	172
Glaucous Gull	178	Sandwich Tern	179
Goshawk	171	Scaup	165
Green Sandpiper	175	Short-eared Owl	181
Greenshank	176	Shoveler	164
Hooded Crow	181	Snow Bunting	186
Iceland Gull	178	Spoonbill	169
Little Egret	169	Waxwing	183
Marsh Harrier	170	Whimbrel	174
Nuthatch	184	White-fronted Goose	160
Osprey	171	Wood Warbler	182
Pintail	163		

Species only recorded between 1974 - 2002

American Wigeon	188	Golden Eagle	188
Black-throated Diver	188	Great Grey Shrike	189
Corn Bunting	189	Great Skua	189
Corncrake	188	Grey Phalarope	189
Curlew Sandpiper	189	Grey Plover	189
Dotterel	189	Kittiwake	189
Fulmar	188	Knot	189
Gannet	188	Little Ringed Plover	188

Species only recorded between 1974 - 2002 cont

Breeding species	Page	Breeding species	Page
Little Stint	189	Slavonian Grebe	188
Mediterranean Gull	189	Spotted Redshank	189
Red-throated Diver	188	Wood Sandpiper	189
Ring Ouzel	189	Yellow Wagtail	189
Shag	188		

Species recorded prior to the start of 'modern recording' in 1974

	Page		Page
Bittern	191	Nightjar	191
Desert Wheatear	192	Pallas's Sandgrouse	191
Golden Oriole	191	Pied Flycatcher	192
Hoopoe	191	Storm Petrel	191
Night Heron	191	Wryneck	191

Species only recorded during the post Atlas period (2008-2011).

	Page
Common Rosefinch	193
Reed Warbler	193
White-tailed Eagle	193

Notes